*Roland H. W

# The Seven Cities of the Apocalypse and Greco-Asian Culture

PAULIST PRESS
New York/Mahwah, N.J.

*Also by Roland H. Worth, Jr.*
*published by Paulist Press*

THE SEVEN CITIES OF THE APOCALYPSE AND ROMAN CULTURE

**Acknowledgements**
The publisher gratefully acknowledges the use of the following: material from William J. Hamilton, *Researches in Asia Minor,* Volume I. Reprinted by Georg Olms Verlag, 1984. Used with permission of the publisher. Material from Andre-Jean Festugiere, *Personal Religion among the Greeks,* (Berkeley, California: The University of California Press, 1954), © 1954 The Regents of the University of California. Used by permission of the University of California Press. Excerpts from Cicero reprinted by permission of the publishers and the Loeb Classical Library from *Cicero: On Invention, The Best Kind of Orator, Topics, Volume II,* translated by M. Hubbell, Cambridge, Mass.: Harvard University Press, 1949.

Unless otherwise noted, all scripture quotations are from the New King James version of the Bible.

*Cover design by Moe Berman*

Library of Congress Cataloging-in-Publication Data

Worth, Roland H., 1943–
    The seven cities of the apocalypse and Greco-Asian culture / Roland H. Worth, Jr.
        p.  cm.
    Includes bibliographical references and index.
    ISBN 0-8091-3877-8 (alk. paper)
    1. Seven churches.  2. Christianity and culture—Turkey—History—Early church, ca. 3–600.  I. Title.
BR185.W68   1999
228'.067–dc21                                                              99-21274
                                                                                CIP

Published by Paulist Press
997 Macarthur Boulevard
Mahwah, New Jersey 07430

www.paulistpress.com

Printed and bound in the
United States of America

# Contents

Preface     1

Introduction     5

1   Glorious Ephesus: The City, the History, the Culture     9

2   Glorious Ephesus: Artemis and Her Competitors     31

3   Monotheism in Ephesus     52

4   Rival Smyrna     69

5   Monotheism and Polytheism in Smyrna     82

6   Regal Pergamon: The City's Civic Monuments and Polytheistic Religions     106

7   Regal Pergamon: Divided Christianity and Societal Allusions in John's Mini-Epistle     123

8   Mercantile Thyatira     154

9   Invincible Sardis     169

10   Philadelphia: City of Opportunity     194

11   Undecided Laodicea     205

Notes     220

Bibliography     316

Index     365

# Preface

I never intended to use over seven hundred books, commentaries, histories, articles, and scholarly dissertations. It just worked out that way.

I was intrigued by the subject of the social, cultural, and historic background to the book of Revelation—to the facts and realities first-century Christians in Roman Asia took for granted, but which to us two thousand years later represent the "great unknown." I'm not one to disparage textual exegesis. I've spent too many years in the pulpit, preached too many sermons, and prepared too many debate notes to look with disdain upon that fundamental tool for handling the sacred text. On the other hand, I know full well that even in my own efforts to preach and teach, I make repeated passing references that are understood full well by my audience, but which someone from a different culture (or a different century!) would only grasp the general meaning of rather than all the implicit overtones.

The same is true of scripture. We can find invaluable moral, ethical, and religious lessons working solely with the exegetical tools we have available. But if we can understand the political, social, moral, and religious environment in which these individuals lived, worked, and prayed we carry our knowledge a step further and see the *additional* overtones and implications that would or could have come to mind when they read John's composition. In short, it makes us a more informed reader.

Yet there is a remarkable scarcity of books that bring together what is available. The closest we come are works on archaeology that present illustrations of biblical references as well as provide insights into how ancient society functioned. When we attempt to blend together archaeology, exegesis, history, and ancient thought we come to passing allusions in various

1

books rather than any detailed treatment. The one volume that comes the closest to accomplishing this is Sir William Ramsay's famous *The Letters to the Seven Churches of Asia*. Although it is still a valuable resource, there is no denying that it is over ninety years old and a multitude of new and then unknown data and interpretation is now available. Hence I have attempted to weave together the now available, widely varied strands of information into a form where it will be both understandable and usable by the modern reader, as well as filling a niche in the available literature.

This is the product of years of research, during which several other books have seen publication. Research is often like that: You take a little bit here, a little bit there, you blend it together, you mix it up—and then you keep adding more "ingredients" until you have enough to accomplish your purpose. The resources utilized in this project could have been dramatically increased, but I reached the point where additional work in English-language sources appeared unlikely to yield sufficient returns to justify the extra months. Perhaps a few decades down the road someone with better intellectual credentials than I would ever claim to possess will take this yet further. But, then again, I haven't quite figured out why no one has not already done so with this theme.

I would like to thank the Inter-Library Loan Department of the University of Richmond for its fabulous work in obtaining rare and difficult to obtain books and pamphlets. Although its own collection provided the foundation of books on which I built, the inter-library system provided additional publications that provided invaluable supplemental information. I never cease to be amazed by the ability of those in the Inter-Library Loan Department to satisfy so many of my intellectual research needs.

Union Theological Seminary here in Richmond deserves my deep gratitude as well. Its magnificent biblical and religious studies collection provided the material for my 1992 book *Bible Translations: A History Through Source Documents*. In the current study, it provided the vast bulk of the commentaries and explicitly religious-theme volumes utilized in this study, with the University of Richmond providing most of the strictly historical and "secular" volumes. The generosity of Union Theological in permitting non-faculty and non-students to use its library can only work to the advantage of those doing research on any biblically related theme.

—ROLAND H. WORTH, JR.

# Introduction

The purpose of this volume involves far more than biblical exegesis—it is an effort to set John's seven mini-epistles in Revelation 2 and 3 within the historical, social, and religious context of Roman society in general and Roman Asian society in particular.[1] This requires an investigation of first and second century A.D. practices and attitudes that John's readers took for granted, but with which modern readers are unfamiliar.

The need for such information should be immediately obvious to anyone middle-aged or older: America, in particular, is simply not the place it was in 1960. Societal change has been so profound and widely accepted it seems almost revolutionary if not reactionary to wish to restore the moral attitudes and preferences of an era little more than thirty years in the past. To younger people that rather recent history is found in the opinions and attitudes of their parents and is still, paradoxically, too current for the history books.

If one casts one's frame of reference further back, comprehension becomes even more difficult. True, we recognize the *facts*: such and such happened at such and such a point in time. We may even understand some of the surrounding context that set the stage for those bare-bones' realities. Yet it is extremely difficult to grasp what the people of that period felt and thought, their underlying attitudes and convictions—not just those that *we* find significant but also those that *they* found important and even vital.

No society is stagnant. At any given point one finds tendencies in more than one direction. Our efforts at simplicity easily gloss over the competing theories and claims of any given epoch. We have seen this in our own immediate American political past: When in 1992 Newt Gingrich's change-minded Republicans gained the first Republican majority in the House of Representatives in decades, only then did some become aware that there were literally millions of Americans who had lived through and perceived the 1960s, 1970s, and 1980s diametrically differently from the way they had typically been pictured in the mass media. What had been viewed by the dominant opinion-makers as acceptable and desirable change had been viewed by this *different* group as perplexing, threatening, even dangerous. Such factors were also present in the first century of the Christian era and require a fuller presentation than the casual background survey that sometimes suffices for study of the New Testament.

Such data may not be needed for the correct exegesis of the scriptural text. On the other hand, who can doubt that it is extraordinarily easy to read into the text assumptions alien to the era in which it was written? To be fair to the text, we must be aware of the practical applications of the text to our era while being alert to the distinctive and different context in which the message was originally written.

Hence the need for a volume that sets Revelation within the context of the society within which the author wrote. The value of such a study goes beyond this. *Much of the New Testament is Asian-originated or Asian-targeted by the various writers.* If ancient tradition is right, John's gospel account of Jesus' life originated in Ephesus. Peter writes to Christians in Asia and nearby provinces (1 Pt 1:1). Colossians and Ephesians were written to cities located within Roman Asia. To better understand the historical and social setting within which Asian Christians lived and died is to better grasp the background behind much of the New Testament.

To do this in the fuller sense the topic deserves requires us to wander down unexpected pathways. Some of these are explicitly religious: what were the rival religions of the day, what were their practices, and how popular were they?[2] Some are historical: what was the origin and developmental history of the cities to which John wrote? Some are political: how were the cities governed and how did the Romans govern an area so unlike their own in temperament and tradition? Others are economic: how did these people earn their livelihoods?

The list goes on and on. Whatever will help us better understand the individual cities as actual historical, living entities—*that* is the subject of this book. Although what we know will never represent the entire picture, decade by decade the body of data has grown and continues to grow.[3] An impressive body of data exists that is so large and detailed that a volume such as this is a feasible undertaking. By studying that data we will not only be better able to understand John's mini-epistles within their historical context, we will be more sympathetic and understanding of society in that day and age.

The appropriateness of relying upon apparent contemporary and historical allusions has been challenged. For one thing, it has been argued that the number and certainty of historical allusions have been overstated.[4] Whenever one makes a particular subject the center of one's analysis, it opens him or her to the danger of giving it disproportionate attention. In reality this is an argument against excessive overstatement rather than against the basic approach. The historical, social, and cultural allusions we present are not always inescapable readings of John's remarks, but they are reasonable readings and ones that would surely have occurred to many of his contemporaries. Hence the appropriateness for our emphasis upon them.

The stress on local allusions also lays one open to the accusation that John must be confusing the church in each city with the city itself.[5] It is not, however, that John confuses the two or blurs the lines of distinction, but that he recognizes that local allusions drive his points home far stronger than vaguer, more general arguments.

It has also been a matter of concern that the emphasis on such matters diverts one from the pivotal role of John's use of the Torah and the Prophets in shaping the imagery and content of his book. But this does not have to be an either-or situation. John's rhetoric *is* deeply rooted in the Old Testament, though allusions to Jesus' own teachings are not unknown. To illustrate from the latter category, it has correctly been pointed out that the warning to Sardis to be on the alert lest it fall is deeply rooted in Jesus' admonitions to spiritual watchfulness. This does not require a repudiation of the allusion to Sardis's own history, as has been argued,[6] but an acknowledgment that John's allusions can tap into multiple frames of reference.[7] By doing so John enhances the power of his argument to those to whom he is writing.

Nor were these references of such a provincial or purely local nature as to rule out their value to the other churches receiving his epistles. As Charles H. H. Scobie has effectively argued,

> We have no good reasons for doubting that the members of the different communities would be familiar with well-known characteristics of the other communities. The seven cities were situated in relatively close proximity, and travel and communication among them were easy. The fierce civic pride and the long-existing rivalry among the cities is well attested, and this is surely something which Christians would not immediately and totally shed with their conversion to the new faith.[8]

They were acquainted with these facts; we are not. By pointing attention to them, we can gain potential insights and note possible allusions that would easily have occurred to the alert reader of the first century. Doing so, we are better prepared to approach the book not only from our own standpoint, but from that of John's contemporaries as well.

# 1

## Glorious Ephesus: The City, the History, the Culture

In the late twentieth century Ephesus can be visited in comfort as one of the many historical tourist attractions of Turkey. In past centuries both visitors and those engaged in archaeological work had to endure severe conditions in order to examine this important site of Paul's work and John's ministry. Writing in 1882, Laurence Oliphant noted: "There are two ways of doing Ephesus: you may either go there and, like the Apostle, 'fight with beasts,' in the shape of donkeys and donkey boys, or you may wear yourself to death under the blazing sun, alternately scrambling over its rocks, and sinking ankle deep in the mire of its marshes."[1]

Travelers had very different reactions to the site. Looking at its physical setting a nineteenth-century archaeologist was impressed by its physical attractiveness:

> The summit of Mount Prion commands a beautiful panorama. To the south-west is seen the well-cultivated island of Samos and the mainland beyond. Westward is the open sea, bounded by an irregular coast-line made historically interesting by the site of the ancient city of Colophon, and the cave of the famous oracle of Claros. Northward the city of Ephesus with its massive ruins lies at your feet; the plain (T-shaped) is watered by four rivers, three of which have ever-changing beds, and is bounded on all sides, except westward, by mountains. In the distance is seen the picturesque Tmolus range, which carries the eye far away to the extreme distance where often sky and mountain blend.[2]

On the other hand, from the standpoint of past history versus present reality, it was also a discouraging sight. The loss of the harbor went hand-in-hand with the filled-in area becoming

9

swampy; the dispersal of the population resulted in the reversion of one of the greatest cities of Asia into a wilderness. In the 1830s Robert Walsh had these severe contrasts in mind when he wrote:

> [The present site] forms a sad and striking contrast to its former splendour. The traveller lands on a dismal swamp at the mouth of a river, choked up with sand. Beside this is an extensive jungle of low bushes, the retreat of wolves and jackals, and all the wild animals whose solitary and predatory habits lead them to those haunts, which had once been, but are no longer the habitations of men. From thence he advances up an extensive and fertile plain, through which the Cayster winds, exhibiting all the capabilities of culture and abundance, but now a rank marsh, scattered over with muddy pools, the retreat of flocks of aquatic fowls, among which are sometimes seen flights of swans, indicating the permanent character of nature still remaining unchanged, though the habits of man are altered.[3]

The city itself was ancient. In Greek legend the Amazons founded not only Ephesus[4] but also the cult of Artemis—or at least a predecessor cult that later generations regarded as synonymous with Artemis.[5] Even if there is some token historical seed in this tale, it was a minor one.[6] The formation of the city was essentially far more conventional: it was founded by Greek colonizers,[7] around 1100 B.C.[8]

During its Greek phase it went through three periods: rule by kings, rule by an oligarchy of leading citizens (aristocrats), and finally rule by those branded (at least in retrospect) as tyrants.[9] In the seventh century B.C. the Cimmerians ousted the Greeks,[10] and the city enjoyed a period of independence.[11] About the middle of the sixth century it was absorbed into the country of Lydia during the reign of King Croesus[12] and from thence to Persian control. During the Panionic Wars between the Ionians and Persia (500–494 B.C.), Ephesus remained a bystander. This allowed the city to escape destruction after the Persian triumph.[13]

After the Greek defeats of Persia in 480 and 479 B.C. the Ephesians were more optimistic about a rebellion and decided to cast their lot with Athens. During the Peloponnesian War, however, they switched allegiance to the Spartans. This period of independence ended when the Persians regained control of the metropolis.[14]

After Alexander the Great died, King Lysimachos moved the city and dramatically increased the population by compelling two other towns to move their populations to the new site.[15] Ephesus passed into the control of the Seleucids, and when Antiochus the Great was defeated in 190 B.C., it became part of the Pergamonese kingdom.[16] From the Pergamonese it passed on to Rome.[17]

When Mithridates roused Asia to revolt against Rome, Ephesus enthusiastically joined the rebellion. During his stay in the city Mithridates ordered resident Romans to be exterminated throughout the province. Appian recorded that 80,000 were killed; Plutarch almost doubled that figure to 150,000.[18] The Ephesians enthusiastically joined in the butchery. In an infamous and unprecedented violation of the right of asylum traditionally attached to the Temple of Artemis, the Ephesians invaded its sacred precincts to carry out their slaughter.[19]

With the tide shifting against the rebels the Ephesians passed a resolution rejecting Mithridates's authority. The Romans were not impressed and came down hard on the rebellious cities in general and on Ephesus in particular. In addition to huge costs involved in housing and maintaining the victorious Roman troops, a massive twenty-thousand-talent indemnity was levied upon the rebellious region. This figure increased sixfold in the following thirteen years because of interest accrued on the loans obtained to pay off the indemnity. As if this did not injure the economy enough, piracy prospered as the desperate and self-serving took advantage of the unsettled conditions.[20]

During the Roman civil wars heavy taxes were laid upon Asia to finance competing armies fighting in the region.[21] With the end of the civil wars Ephesus and other cities of Asia entered a period of sustained prosperity and economic growth.[22]

In the first centuries A.D. Ephesus was also a major population center. Most estimates cluster around a figure of approximately 200,000[23] or 250,000 residents.[24] Some go as high as 300,000,[25] 400,000,[26] and even 500,000.[27] Even a minimal estimate comes up with 51,000 residents[28]—not in the same league as the other figures but still a respectable-size town.

Hard evidence for the population is difficult to come by. The physical size of the city argues that the estimate went downward.[29] On the other hand, a surprising number of individuals can be crammed into a limited amount of space, as in the teeming cities of Asia. In addition, a population estimate would have to be factored upward to include at least the area closest to the city's walls.

A second century A.D. text referring to 40,000 citizens of the city has been used as a basis for population estimates in the 200,000-plus range. It has been argued that this is a misreading of the text.[30] Even some who embrace this denial of the traditional understanding of the inscription concede that a 200,000 figure is still sustainable.[31] However, if the reading had been valid, it would unquestionably have further enhanced the power of the argument.

Most likely, the 200–250,000 population estimate is closest to the reality. As such, it was one of the five largest cities in the empire.[32] The second-century emperor Antonius Pius (reigned 136–61) described Ephesus as "the greatest metropolis of Asia."[33]

As a "free city," Ephesus had the right of internal self-government and exemption from having Roman troops stationed in the city.[34] As an assize town, the Roman governor held regular court sessions to try significant cases that could not be handled on a lower level.[35]

During the second and third centuries the centralizing trend seemingly inherent in any major empire was already eating away at the status of free cities, limiting their rights and placing power in small, hereditary oligarchies. Both the narrative of the silversmiths' riot against Paul in Acts and the events of Revelation 1–3 (regardless of dating) occurred while local authorities still retained major vestiges of genuine free action. Yet even then they recognized that it had to be exercised discreetly lest the Romans use local excesses as an excuse to curb their powers or impose retaliatory measures.[36]

Real power lay in the city's council, over which the town clerk had much influence. At least through A.D. 160 the decisions of the council had to receive approval by the city's assembly, a procedure that increasingly became a mere formality. The fact that the town clerk insisted that the accusations against Paul should be presented to a legal meeting implies that the city's

general assembly of citizens was still capable of making decisions independent of both the council and town clerk.[37] The
most important meeting of the assembly appears to have
occurred once a month with two or more less significant meetings held at other times. The division of function and responsibility between these sessions is unknown.[38]

During the first half of the first century A.D. the governing
council appears to have continued its long tradition of annual
election by lot. The Roman preference for long-term or permanent position-holders (as in the Roman Senate) began to break
through that local tradition during the Flavian emperors. By the
time of Trajan it is possible to read of men such as P. Cornelius
Ariston, who held council membership for nineteen continuous
years, impossible under the older method of selection.[39] Theoretical independence was still honored. When the Emperor
Hadrian wished to give two men council membership as a
reward for the faithful service they had given to him, he conspicuously avoided directed appointment; rather, he *requested* that
the Ephesians grant the honor.[40]

The town clerk was elected by the council[41] and his more
proper name—emphasizing his role as public servant—was
people's clerk. Although theoretically subject to the council, he
exercised effective power far beyond the council and effectively
functioned as the top local official. Coinage from the first century shows him in this role, and one document even joins his
name with that of the year's proconsul, presenting him as if on a
par in importance (on a strictly local basis) with that Roman official.[42] This ascendancy over the council is not that odd when one
considers that as of A.D. 104 it had 450 members.[43] Its unwieldy
size required the delegation of much of its power.

A position called clerk of the council also existed, but far
less is known about this post. In the third century the two positions of people's clerk and clerk of the council were merged into
one.[44]

A central responsibility of the government was to offer sacrifice to the deities worshiped in the city, who were believed to protect the community. Just as the medieval Catholic Church had a
saint's day for every day of the year, there was a civic calendar of

gods in ancient Ephesus. One was to be honored each and every day. An Ephesian law of c. A.D. 250 spells this out in detail:

> The Prytanis (that is to say, the first magistrate of the city) ignites the flame on all the altars and offers up incense and sacred herbs; he provides, at his own expense, victims to be sacrificed to the gods on the days laid down by the law, numbering one hundred and ninety victims whose heart and thighs will be removed beforehand, and one hundred and seventy-five complete victims; the public hierophant will give him counsel and will teach him which victim is determined by law to be offered to the gods.
>
> He will have canticles sung during the sacrifices, processions, and nocturnal ceremonies where these are compulsory according to custom, and he will have prayers said for the Roman Senate, the people of Rome, and for the people of Ephesus. The Prytanis will give the appropriate honorarium to the hierophant, the sacred herald, the fluteplayer, the trumpeter, the second hierophant, and to the man who examines the sacrificed victims and to the curette of the week.[45]

In reading this, one is brought face to face with the difficulty any faithful Jew or Christian confronted if he desired to engage in any major political office. Although not all were involved in this explicit an entanglement, so pervasive was polytheism that *some* involvement of *some* type was inevitable in the very act of service to the community. The difficulty was intensified because prominent families were expected by society to exercise leadership roles, and a Christian of such a class would be especially noticeable by his absence from participation in practices and rites traditionally associated with his leadership position.

Note also the great monetary expense major civic involvement required. In this case it was especially heavy: the city did not provide the sacrifices; the officeholder did. The appropriate honorarium for so many individuals intensified the financial load yet further, since it was not a one-time affair but a daily requirement.

Economically, the city was prosperous throughout the first century. Three major trade routes came together at Ephesus and helped make this possible. One brought the products of Galatia to the city via Sardis. Through Colossae, another major trade route carried goods originating in (and beyond) the Euphrates Valley. The third routed the products of the Maeander and Lycus valleys into the city through Magnesia.[46] Although this was not the shortest route to the East and to trade partners beyond the boundaries of the empire, it was the quickest traveled and therefore more widely used.[47]

Although some have speculated that the city deteriorated economically between the visits of the apostle Paul and the writing of the book of Revelation late in the century,[48] the evidence indicates, at most, a decline rather than a catastrophe. (Of course, if one assumes an early date for John's apocalyptic writing, the economic conditions of Paul's day would have been essentially the same as those of John's.) Both before and after the first century A.D. the city was praised repeatedly as a major center of commerce for the region.

In the first century B.C. Strabo the geographer called it the "great[est] emporium of Asia."[49] Although silting in the harbor was already a problem in his day, Strabo considered that otherwise the location of the city was ideal. The "city grows daily and is the largest emporium in Asia this side of the Taurus."[50] Pliny speaks of the city as the "great luminary of Asia."[51]

In the second century Aristides spoke of the international reputation of the city as one penetrating even into the more obscure parts of the empire:

> I am of the opinion that all men, however many live from the Columns of Heracles [Straits of Gibraltar] to the banks of the River Phasis [at the extreme east of the Black Sea], know Ephesus well because of its internationality, its traffic, and the stay that one may enjoy there. They all go there as if to their own homeland and no one can deny the facts, that is that Ephesus is the general bank of Asia and the place one hurries to, to find credit. Its frontiers stretch beyond the sea and on the land, and it is able to satisfy all sorts of needs.[52]

The wealth was both manifested and produced by several economic factors. It remained the most important banking center in Asia throughout the first centuries A.D.[53] Its naval trade was both regional and long distance, to far-flung parts of the empire.[54] The products exported were varied and included the various items discussed in the chapter on Asian trade in general—for example, Asian peaches were expensive luxuries imported to distant Rome itself.[55] The establishment of a Fishing Customs Office in Ephesus during the late 50s of the first century indicates the degree of exportation of such products.[56] Oysters harvested from nearby waters were considered a delicacy for any aristocrat's table.[57] In regard to minerals, from near Ephesus came the best red lead (used in making paint) found in the entire empire.[58] These products and others from more distant regions worked together to produce the prosperity necessary for the welfare of a huge community.

In the lamentable trade in humans, the city had a long-established reputation. It had been a major regional slave market for hundreds of years before the Roman ascendancy over Asia.[59]

Based upon Cicero's open espousal of the attitude, it is generally believed that the upper levels of Roman society abhorred commercial involvement as a matter of fundamental philosophy. *True* stature had to be sought through land ownership.[60] Steven M. Baugh argues that however true that may be as a generality, there is little evidence of the large villa-based style of land ownership in Asia that would be expected—or demanded—if the local aristocracy and power structure had adopted a similar way of thinking.[61] Indeed the largest landowner was not a private individual but the temple of Artemis.[62]

Pivotal to the economic success of Ephesus was the use of its harbor, the largest one in the Aegean Sea.[63] Continual silting threatened to reduce or eliminate the usability of the harbor and thereby undermine the local economy. In Acts we read that Paul's ship stopped at Miletus rather than the larger Ephesus, and this has been read by some as an indication of how bad the silting problem had become.[64] Regardless, during the reign of Nero, the Asian proconsul Barea Soranus took a step toward remedying the problem by thoroughly dredging the harbor.[65] One of the longest surviving inscriptions from the city, 155 lines long, details the revision of tariffs for the city as codified by Nero in A.D. 62. It has been suggested, with considerable justice, that this revision was motivated by the fact that the major dredging of the harbor the previous year had once again opened the port to heavy usage.[66]

During Domitian's reign, silt was again removed by dredging.[67] A few decades later, Emperor Hadrian attempted to solve the problem by diverting the course of the River Cayster.[68] By the fourth century the harbor was turning into a swamp. With the empire in collapse, trade crippled, and the harbor a disaster, by the tenth century the city itself was completely abandoned.[69]

Today the silted-up harbor has created a new shoreline at least six miles away from the ancient city.[70] The old harbor is now a massive swamp.[71]

Although the port of Miletus could be substituted for Ephesus (as in the case of Paul above), the main beneficiary of any shipping diversion was Smyrna,[72] the bitter rival of Ephesus. When both Paul and John lived, the worst of this lay in the future. The silting was an impediment not a disaster, an inconvenience not a catastrophe.[73]

At times the silting problem was reinforced by what we today would call environmental pollution, the illegal dumping into the harbor of unwanted remnants of the various cargoes that entered the harbor. This went hand in hand with overweight cargoes that inflicted damage upon the piers. In A.D. 161 the proconsul became so outraged at these shenanigans that he ordered a fine imposed in all such future cases. The offending parties were required to appear personally before the proconsul for additional punishment. In his decree the proconsul candidly confessed that he was under heavy pressure from above to remove the abuses: "For, since our great emperor himself has shown concern for the protection of the harbour, and since he has continuously been sending dispatches on this matter, it is not right that people who ruin the harbour should be let off merely by paying a fine."[74]

What with the acknowledged dangers inherent in seafaring, it was natural to seek a divine blessing upon those involved in the trade. And since Artemis was the preeminent deity of the town, it is not surprising that her protection was sought. On the day each year when the port officially opened after its winter closing, the priests of Artemis carried her statue to the waterfront. There they dipped it into the water as a sign of her blessing upon the merchant vessels that brought prosperity to the city and as a symbol of her protection upon the vessels' sailors during the following year.[75]

To better understand the city, it would be appropriate to describe some of the physical structures and facilities that everyday citizens used. Three major thoroughfares are especially worthy of note: the Harbor Street (in its most elaborate incarnation known as the Arcadian Way), the Marble Street, and the Street of Curetes.

The Harbor Street dates all the way back to Hellenistic times; it ran the five or six hundred yards from the harbor itself to the Great Theater. Under the Emperor Arcadius (A.D. 395–408) renovations expanded it to its most elaborate form. Massive gates were located at both the harbor and theater ends of the street. The street itself was an impressive twelve yards wide, with porticoes (covered walkways) running its length on both sides. Mosaics covered the floors of these colonnades. Even game boards were carved in some places for the benefit of those citizens who had some time to spare. Behind the covered walkways were a multitude of shops for busy citizens. For safety and convenience, it was kept lit at night, as were several other major city thoroughfares.[76]

The Marble Street began at the Koressos Gate (on Mount Pion) beyond the Great Theater, where the Harbor Street intersected it. A portico was erected along the west side of the street during the reign of Nero, but it did not reach its highest level of beauty until centuries later: In the fifth century the Ephesian citizen Eutropios paid for the marbling of the road, hence its modern description. Also dating from this period of major improvements are remnants of a sewage disposal canal, complete with manhole covers. When the Marble Street reached the Celsus Library (across from the suspected brothel), it turned sharply. This transition to the Street of the Curetes was marked by a two-story gate similar to the Athenian Gate of Hadrian. In front of it stood a statue of Artemis. Dr. Ulgur Onen notes, "It was a favorite technique in the Roman urban concept to visually mark the end of a long street with a gate, so as to arrest the eye."[77]

The Street of the Curetes was also marble-paved. Along both sides of the roadway were statues of prominent citizens, with their names written on the pedestals. These were abundant and honored a wide variety of individuals who had served the community, from top political and religious figures down to prominent and respected writers, rhetoricians, and other citizens. A major problem occurred with the passage of time: where to put new statues when all the reasonably available space had been utilized? The solution was to replace some of the older images with new ones in honor of more recent civic and religious leaders. The problem of a different name being on the pedestal was solved by changing the side that faced the street, producing a clean surface on which to engrave the name of the newly honored.

Under the Street of the Curetes have been found additional remains of the city's ancient sewage system. The Temple of Hadrian and the Fountain of Hadrian are among the impressive facilities that lined the street during the second century.[78]

In describing these major thoroughfares it is easy to forget that even the Street of the Curetes was designed to make a *business* area look beautiful rather than to be an escape from the economic world. "Behind the pedestals [honoring the citizens], rows of columns supported the arches which shaded the sidewalks. Shops, stores and business offices of every description opened to these sidewalks. This street was spanned at convenient intervals by "arches of triumph" as well."[79]

Various fountains served to beautify the city. The Fountain of Pollio was erected in A.D. 93 in honor of C. Sextilius Pollio. It was decorated with statues of a reclining warrior, Ulysses, and others.[80] The Fountain of Trajan was erected in the early years of the second century. Its basin was three feet wide and thirty-six feet long. It was surrounded by a two-story colonnade on three of its sides. A more than two-story statue of Trajan honored his triumph over the Parthians.[81]

As in any self-respecting city with a Greek heritage, gymnasiums occupied places of honor in the public mind during both the Greek and Roman eras. A typical gymnasium of the era has been described this way:

> The building was in essence an open court for wrestling and similar sports and a running track. To these many refinements were gradually added, and the fully developed gymnasium of the Hellenistic and Roman age was a most elaborate structure. The central court was surrounded with colonnades, and off these opened a variety of rooms—a cloakroom where the members undressed and left their clothes, an

anointing room where they rubbed in the oil which was kept
in a neighboring store, a dusting room where they powdered
themselves, rooms for ball play and for the punch ball, a
bathing establishment with its usual suite of cool, tepid, and
hot rooms, and plunge baths, loggias, fitted with seats, and
halls, which could be used for rest and conversation or alternatively for classes: some gymnasia possessed regular lecture-
rooms, planned like miniature theaters.[82]

Like the country club or exclusive club of the twentieth century, the gymnasium also served as a convenient place for socializing with friends and arranging business deals.[83] Culture,
recreation, business—the gymnasiums were a one-stop location
for many social dealings.

Ephesus had at least four major gymnasiums.[84] The East
Gymnasium contains a number of statues of girls and women,
and for this reason it has been suspected that it was set apart for
the use of the women of the community. It dates back to the late
second century A.D.[85] The Theater Gymnasium is located to the
west of the Great Theater. It was ultimately destroyed by fire.[86]

The Vedius Gymnasium was erected in the middle of the
second century by P. Vedius Antoninus, a wealthy Ephesian. It
combines the functions of a gymnasium (from the Greek tradition) and baths (from the Roman tradition), bringing together
the two cultural strains so vital to the success of the city. Toilets
in this facility were not designed for public use but for specified
subgroupings: inscriptions indicate that several guilds had one
each for their respective members; the prosperity and prestige of
the bankers' guild can be seen in that *three* were set aside for its
members' exclusive use.[87]

The massive Harbor Gymnasium-Bath complex adjoined
the harbor itself. It contained a large, square arena with covered
running tracks on each side, a modest-size gymnasium, baths,
and a large supply of bathrooms. It was 270 yards in width and a
mammoth 650 yards long, covering the distance from the harbor
to the Great Theater. Three large windows (thirty-three by thirty-
three feet each) gave a direct view of the harbor.[88]

Since the earliest parts of the complex date to the period of
the first Olympic games held in Ephesus (circa A.D. 90), it has been
speculated that it was erected in large part to provide facilities for

the athletes that flocked to the city. Regardless of the initial incentive for its construction, it continued to be expanded during the following centuries until it reached the ultimate dimensions already noted.[89]

Another mark of a cultured city was its public baths. There were six major baths in Ephesus. They existed both as part of a gymnasium-bath complex and as independent establishments. The Baths of Scholasticia adjoined the Temple of Hadrian, on its right, and was originally erected in the second century A.D. Falling into a period of neglect and disuse, the lady Scholasticia rebuilt it in the fourth century. It remained in use at least through the eighth century, the latest date for which coins have been uncovered in the ruins.[90]

Public restrooms were common in Ephesus, and low charges were levied for their use.[91] The one located between the Scholasticia's Baths and the so-called brothel is especially well preserved.

> People sat on all four sides of the rectangular structure. A continuous flow of water ran in a sewer deep below the seats to provide flushing. A narrow canal ran inside the perimeter in which water ran continuously. It was completely public [individual stalls did not exist], where people met, talked and exchanged dinner invitations.[92]

The wealthy had the option of erecting latrines on their own premises and sometimes did so. Depending upon the location, aqueduct water carried away the waste. In other cases the accumulated waste would be removed by merchants specializing in manure.[93] Such options were beyond the means of the more-or-less middle class of the day, but the public facilities were well within their resources.[94]

Chamber pots were standard in homes. Although they might be emptied in the streets,[95] the easy availability of public facilities argues for a public bias against such a procedure. The pots could be emptied either on the various dungheaps or into containers provided at the place of business of merchants who utilized urine in their production processes.[96]

The cultural life of the city was supported by other important institutions beyond the gymnasiums and the baths. From the standpoint of size alone, the Great Theater dwarfs all of them. It could hold between twenty-four thousand and twenty-five thousand onlookers.[97] It was almost five-hundred feet long. Built on the western slope of Mount Pion, the seats were divided into three sections, each with twenty-two rows of seats. Six gates facilitated quick filling and emptying of the auditorium. The stage itself was twenty feet deep and eighty feet long. Although designed for conventional theater purposes, gladiator fights were, on occasion, held there as well.[98]

The facility was a long-established recreational site even in Paul's day. A major rebuilding program was initiated during the reigns of both Claudius (A.D. 34–41) and Trajan (A.D. 98–117).[99] These were the peaks of an ongoing project that was initiated by Claudius and was carried on for the following seventy years, until Trajan brought it to completion.[100] When the apostle Paul faced the rioters (recounted in the book of Acts), there was almost certainly scaffolding at different places in the facility, and the whole affair was undoubtedly observed by workmen who viewed it as an interesting and entertaining diversion from their own daily labor.[101]

The riot was an economic protest by the makers of idols, who saw their lucrative business in dramatic decline due to the success of Christianity in drawing disciples away from polytheism (Acts 19:26). They grafted their own interests onto civic pride in Artemis (19:27–28) and ignited a major riot (19:29) for which they had no legal basis because "the courts are open, and there are proconsuls" (19:38) to handle any legitimate grievance.[102] Perhaps they did not take this course because direct action was more emotionally satisfying and the bringing of accusations could be both time-consuming and expensive.[103] Even assuming they had a conscious intention of preferring riot to law, their disturbance may well have occurred in the month of Artemisia,[104] since both cultic and image-maker sensitivity would have been at their height during that month-long series of celebrations held in Artemis's honor.

Built during the reign of Nero (A.D. 54–68), the city's stadium was located about 70 yards from the Vedius Gymnasium. The athletic field was approximately 100 feet wide and 765 feet long, and seventy-five thousand people could sit around it. Athletic contests, chariot races, and horse races were commonly held within it. In order to conveniently hold gladiatorial contests, an adjoining circular space was prepared to the east of the stadium.[105]

Another athletic facility was the Halls of Verulanus, which measured 600 feet by 720 feet. It was named after Caius Claudius Verulanus, an imperial priest of Asia. During the reign of Hadrian the priest personally paid to have the racetrack surface paved with marble and in honor of his generosity his name is commonly attached to the complex. The most dramatic event to occur in the Halls actually occurred years prior, in A.D. 96, when Apollonius of Tyana claimed to have seen a vision there in which the emperor Domitian was killed. The story goes that this precipitated a mob overturning Domitian's statue in the imperial temple. Fortunately for the participants, the claim of Domitian's death turned out to be true.[106]

The Odeion (concert hall) was so named by the pioneer Ephesian archaeologist T. Wood. It seated at least fourteen hundred people, with some preferring an estimate as high as twenty-two hundred. The lack of any drainage system implies that some type of covering existed to shield those present from the elements. In the second century it underwent major renovations. In this cultural interpretation of the facility, one would expect it to have been "used for poetry-readings, small concerts and prize-giving ceremonies."[107]

Others prefer to call the building the Bouleuterion or Council Hall. This reading fits in well with the facility's proximity to other government buildings in the Government Agora. Even more important is the lack of rooms behind the supposed "stage wall" facing the seats, a lack that is quite surprising if it was actually used for theatrical functions.[108]

The Commercial Agora/Marketplace was located in the lower part of the city and measured about 330 yards in width and length. A portico surrounded it on all four sides, and commercial businesses of different types operated on at least three sides. In the center stood a large marble sundial.[109]

The Government Agora was located in the upper part of the city. It measured 480 feet by 168 feet, and several government structures faced into it. Porticoes marked its boundaries at both the north and south. Its existence in a separate section of the city from the Commercial Agora was justified not only due to the size and prestige of the city but as a practical means of escaping the garbage and odors that inevitably existed at the other site.[110]

One vital government building was certainly the *Prytaneion* or Town Hall. Built early in the first century A.D., civic banquets were regularly held here. More important, it was the site of the eternal flame of the goddess Hestia Boulaia. As goddess of fire and the family hearth she became, by extension, goddess of the family unit and of the broader family, the civic community. A sanctuary in her honor was maintained on the premises, and a priesthood existed to ensure that the fire never went out. Since Artemis was patron goddess of the city, her statue was also found in the Prytaneion and there was considerable overlap in personnel between those who served the two goddesses.[111]

Because of its cultural significance, the Library of Celsus made an important contribution to the city's status. Although small by comparison with its mammoth rivals in Pergamon and Alexandria, its ruins are so much more complete that they provide an outstanding example of how libraries were constructed in the days of the Roman Empire.[112] It was constructed some time in the second decade of the second century by his son to honor Tiberius Julius Celsus Polemaeanus. So respected was the father that the normal rule against burials inside the city was waived to permit him to be interred inside the library.[113] The facility could hold about ninety-five hundred scrolls,[114] perhaps four thousand in the central reading room proper (which was 55 by 36 feet in size) and the remainder in the galleries stretching above it.[115]

The final building that deserves mention is the so-called brothel, dating from the fourth century. Although the identification of the building with that purpose is open to vigorous challenge, it should not be forgotten that Ephesus was a prosperous seafarers' town. Though one may not be certain *where* the brothels were located, that they *were* present was inevitable.[116]

## Culture and Society

Having stressed the physical assets of the city, the remainder of this chapter will emphasize the more explicitly cultural and social aspects, though even here a discussion of physical remnants will again inevitably arise.

One fundamental prerequisite of quality living in any day and age is an accessible water supply. Ephesus collected water from five different streams and springs and funneled it into the city through a well-developed aqueduct system. One part of the system began at the Marnas River, four miles away. The aqueduct system carried it through the Dervend Mountains to the thousands who lived in the city. The aqueduct system provided the water necessary for the various public fountains, and the city's pipes were directly tapped into by many urban homes. The civic system was supplemented by private wells dug on behalf of city homeowners.[117]

With such a substantial population located within a rather modest physical area, it is natural to question how the city was able to accommodate such a large number. We know that other cities, such as Rome and Antioch, built what we today might call apartment buildings. Although these, in a narrow sense, have not been documented for Ephesus, a somewhat similar approach was confirmed with the discovery of apartment complexes working their way up the hillsides. Five- and six-levels high, a series of manmade terraces enabled each level to have its own entrances while making maximum use of the available space. Underground pipes provided both water and sewage lines for the various levels.

In one set of such hillside homes uncovered in the 1960s, the first two floors were used for commercial purposes, as bars, shops, or business offices of various sorts. The third level consisted of small, presumably cheap, apartments—perhaps used by the poorer operators of the facilities found on the two lower levels, among others. In contrast, the next two levels were larger, clearly luxurious facilities. Well-preserved frescoes were uncovered and marble sculptures.[118]

One regional specialist describes typical upper-class facilities in this way:

> The interior courtyard surrounded by columns on three or four sides formed the heart of each dwelling. The other rooms: sitting room, dining room, bedrooms, the jutting windows and niches for fountains, the place for the cult of

the domestic gods, the kitchens, the hot and cold baths, the toilets, heating rooms and cellars were set out around this courtyard but with adaptations for the incline. Larger houses were built on two stories linked by a stair. On the upper level were the bedrooms and private rooms....In the interior courtyard could be seen columns with Doric, Ionic or Corinthian capitals, supporting a roof around the periphery, for the center remained uncovered. In the courtyard fountains filled with marble provided freshness. The walls and floors were covered with marble or decorated with frescoes. Several layers of frescoes have been uncovered, attesting to the fashions of the times or the tastes of the owners. The painted motifs are of Eros, scenes of comedy or tragedy, Socrates, trees, plants and animals.[119]

Those of even greater wealth might own one of the substantial villas that dotted the surrounding hills. With even more elaborate facilities, these were comparable in quality to the better ones located in other parts of the empire.[120]

Important as it was to bask in temporal possessions, the community also recognized the importance of cultural and medical facilities for both personal and corporate well-being. At Pergamon, Smyrna, and Ephesus the medical craft was well organized. "At Ephesus there was a *synedrion* of medical teachers who sponsored public medical competitions each year, a kind of medical Olympics; and one of the competitions seems to have been in surgery."[121]

The status of chief doctor *(archiatros)* of Ephesus represented the highest medical status a local physician could obtain. In some cases the title was granted due to skill; in other cases it was bestowed on the physician-son of someone already holding the title.[122]

The Jewish doctor Julius was granted this select status, showing that there were no rigid barriers against Jews. During the two-day Asclepius festival the *archiatros* presided over various medical "contests." Since these were held in connection with honoring a pagan deity, *religious* activities in Asclepius's honor must have been involved as well.[123] How then was Julius able to reconcile his Judaism with the pagan accessories that went with the post? Apparently some way was found, because the Jews of the city regarded him as an acceptable member of their community, as manifested by their accepting supervision of his burial site.[124]

This has been explained by some on the grounds that such necessary pagan religious activities did not compromise one's actual, personal faith.[125] Another possibility is that, recognizing the monotheistic demands of Judaism, there were certain elements of the proceedings from which he was discreetly excused. Although it is easier to think in terms of Jewish (or Christian) compromise, in this environment, a cosmopolitan community such as Ephesus might well have found *reverse* compromise acceptable. They might yield on certain contentious points that would have excessively antagonized the minority monotheistic community, or allowed the ritual to be carried out in a way that was not explicitly pagan. Just as Paul saw no problem with eating meats sacrificed to idols *if* one's dining companions did not make an issue of it having been so sacrificed (1 Cor 10:25–33), a similar reticence might have permitted orthodox Jewish participation in certain civic roles and activities that good conscience would otherwise have denied them.

Just as the medical craft occupied a place of honor in Ephesus, so did the rhetorical studies of the period. In regard to these Ephesus and Smyrna were the two major Asian centers to which one traveled in order to pursue an advanced education.[126] Although the Sophist style of oratory did not come into its own until the second century, it already had many resident practitioners in the century of Paul.[127] Philosophical studies were popular. Heraclitus was an Ephesian who went on to wide renown in the field. Nicknamed "the Dark" because of the difficulty many had in understanding his philosophy, he stressed flux and constant change as central to interpreting reality.[128]

Ephesus was a city where there were many pleasant alternatives to serious thought, distractions that could fill so much of one's time that there was no opportunity left—perhaps even no *desire* left—to pursue matters of reasoning and the human mind. The pagan prophet Apollonius saw the multitudes idly wasting away their lives while ignoring the need for such "superior" pursuits. Philostratus records his rebuke, how he dissuaded and discouraged them from other pursuits and urged them to devote themselves to philosophy alone, to fill Ephesus with real study "rather than the idleness and arrogance he found there, for they were devoted to dancers and taken up with pantomimes, and the whole city was full of pipers, full of effeminate rascals, and full of noise."[129] He alienated his Ephesian disciples by refusing to permit such activities and branding them as completely unacceptable.[130]

The occult/magical arts provided supernatural assurance to the multitudes. These took several forms, and Asia was recognized as one of the best places to master them.

One such art was the symbolic interpretation of natural phenomena to provide advance warning of the future. One inscription on an Ephesian building tells its readers, "If the bird is flying from right to left, and settles out of sight, good luck will come. But if it lifts up its left wing, then whether it rises or settles out of sight, misfortune will result."[131]

Magical incantations[132] were a two-edged sword. From the positive standpoint, they provided both protection and an assurance that one's needs would be met. In this form they could be recited verbally or worn in the form of a protective amulet or charm. From the negative standpoint, they could be recited to inflict harm and misfortune on one's enemies. The two forms went by the generic label of *Ephesia grammata* (Ephesian letters), a phrase that shows the city's recognized status in providing them.[133]

Genuine Ephesian charms and amulets were prized possessions. People traveled immense distances to obtain them.[134] Barren and unable to conceive? Purchase one and rest content that pregnancy would come your way. Your offspring in extremely bad health, perhaps in despair of life itself? The purchase of the right amulet guaranteed a turn for the better.[135]

The trade was not merely the product of knowing conmen or restricted to the ignorant and unlearned, neither from the standpoint of purchasing the product nor creating it. Extremely learned men could become deeply involved in the craft.[136] The zeal with which some intellectuals of the day pursued the supernatural arts suggests that we have here not just superstition but also a striving to fill some inner need of the soul that was not being satisfied. Hans Dieter Betz identifies this need as one of reassurance in an era when the traditional polytheistic faiths were facing widespread skepticism,

While other people could no longer make sense of the old religions, [the magician] was able to. He knew the code words needed to communicate with the gods, the demons, and the dead. He could tap, regulate, and manipulate the invisible energies. He was a problem solver who had remedies for a thousand petty troubles plaguing mankind: everything from migraine to runny nose to bedbugs to horse races, and, of course, all the troubles of love and money. In short, it was this kind of world in which the magician served as a power and communications expert, crisis manager, miracle healer and inflicter of damages, and all-purpose therapist and agent of worried, troubled, and troublesome souls.[137]

From the political standpoint, soothsayers were in the most danger; the supposed future might not be the one officially sought by the existing powers. Punishment ranged from banishment to death.[138] Yet so intense was the desire to see into the future that the problem rose time and again and the practice could never be permanently suppressed.[139]

The Ephesians existed not just as individuals but in organized cooperative bodies as well. They existed as groups around their gymnasiums. They existed as groups in various business enterprises. They existed as groups in their various religious endeavors.

On a secular note, guilds are well attested throughout Asia.[140] Inscriptions document a wide variety in Ephesus itself. There were architects and fishermen, bankers and bakers, basketmakers and bathworkers, carpenters and cobblers, hemp-weavers and linen-weavers, silversmiths and slave dealers, wineskin-makers and wool dealers.[141] It has been conjectured that some or all of these various guilds occupied their own distinct districts within the city, as was the practice in other communities.[142]

The silversmith guild's role in the riot against Paul, recounted in Acts, reveals that group at its hostile worst. Such excesses must have been rare, for the institution maintained an overall reputation as one of the city's respected institutions, as indicated by it being the administrator for a number of trust funds. For example, one first century silversmith by the name of M. Antonius Hermeias left a fund of fifty thousand denarii for the maintenance of his tomb.[143]

Other groups provided similar services. Three surviving memorial monuments bear witness to the Jewish community acting in a similar way. In one case the inscription reads, "Cared for by the Jews," and another, "This tomb is cared for by the Jews in Ephesus."[144]

Ephesus, like many other cities throughout Asia, had associations of prominent senior citizens who banded together in what they called a *gerusia,* which might be called civic burial-site maintenance societies.[145] The prestige of individual members was magnified by the participation of others of similar status. Independently each had a degree of importance—by working together as a *collective body* the organization exercised even greater political clout than the individual members. This was magnified even further as the trust funds to maintain the grave sites grew ever larger.

The presence of differing personalities and differing local customs and expectations would surely have produced significant local variances in the actual functions and work of these bodies. The one in Hieraopolis (near Laodicea), for example, delegated grave maintenance to one of the eight subcategories of members rather than making it a function of the entire organization.[146] The gerusia in Sidyma (late second century) limited its membership to exactly one hundred men.[147]

The gerusia in Ephesus appears to have begun as the managing organization responsible for the finances of the temple of Artemis,[148] a function it later lost.[149] The donations to the group (for burial-site maintenance and other purposes) represented an ever-growing treasury that made the organization both important and, if one owed it interest on the funds it loaned out, the cause of resentment as well. By the early second century A.D. the heirs of those owing loans were in full mutiny and refused to repay what they owed. The gerusia sought and obtained intervention by Emperor Hadrian to ensure that the loans were repaid.[150]

Funds were left for additional purposes as well. In A.D. 104 Gaius Vibius Salutaris left a bequest of over forty-two hundred denarii. He left detailed instructions that annual gifts be bestowed upon hundreds of citizens and that certain religious activities be undertaken with the remaining funds. The annual financial gifts included payments to over three hundred members of the Ephesian gerusia itself.[151]

# 2

# Glorious Ephesus:
# Artemis and Her Competitors

The religious structure of ancient Ephesus can be divided into two categories: Artemis—and everybody else. Indeed, this phenomena dates back to Ephesus's early centuries.[1] This is not to say that these other groups were unimportant, but that her temple was so elaborate and imposing and the social impact of the cult so great that no rival came close. We will give precedence to studying in detail the nature of her cult, therefore, and only then pass on to the various other polytheistic movements that existed in the community. Having done that, in the next chapter we will discuss monotheism and possible textual allusions in their Revelation mini-epistle that Ephesians might find specially significant due to local conditions and local history.

## Artemis

The silversmiths who rioted against Paul bragged that "all Asia and the world worship" Artemis (Acts 19:27). In the middle of the second century (between A.D. 162 and 164), the Ephesian governing council used similar rhetoric:

> Since the goddess Artemis, leader of our city, is honored not only in her own homeland, which she has made the most illustrious of all cities through her own divine nature, but also among Greeks and also barbarians, the result is everywhere her shrines and sanctuaries have been established, and temples have been founded for her and altars dedicated to her because of the visible manifestations effected by her.[2]

Artemis in her Ephesian form was honored on coinage from more than fifty Asia Minor communities.[3] Her cult has been documented by either literary references or archaeological remains in such places as France, Spain, and Italy to the west, the Black Sea's northern coast to the north, and Phoenicia and Israel to the south.[4]

There was a very special relationship between Ephesus and the cult because of the presence of her temple in their midst, just as there was between the papacy and the city of Rome. Each affected the other and had a pervasive influence on the culture and general community attitudes. Artemis was recognized by the city as its patron goddess[5] and, in turn, regarded itself as her special protector.[6]

The earliest shrine at the temple site is suspected to have been established in the tenth century B.C.; the earliest one for which there is actual archaeological evidence dates to the seventh century B.C.[7] Cybele, the mother-goddess of Asia Minor, was worshiped in the area long before the first Greeks arrived. The Greeks, however, introduced Artemis and eventually the two were effectively fused into the image of one goddess,[8] though this did not preclude the existence of a separate cult in honor of Cybele as well. The community was sufficiently prosperous that as early as the sixth century B.C. the Artemis temple was erected completely of marble. The grander of the edifice was enhanced by Croesus. When he conquered the city in the sixth century B.C. he bestowed expensive gifts upon the temple so that both its appearance could be upgraded and its physical size expanded. Soon the site was so well established that pilgrims were traveling from distant countries to offer their sacrifices.[9]

After Xerxes successfully battled the city-states of Greece, he passed through Ephesus in 478 B.C. So great was the prestige of Artemis that he permitted his army to loot all the Greek temples in the city—except that one. What Xerxes refused to do, Herostratus accomplished. Insane and seeking an eternal reputation, in 356 B.C. he set aflame the famous temple. So massive was the damage that the local citizens pooled their resources to erect a new structure. The destruction of the temple posed an obvious theological difficulty: If Artemis truly existed, how could she permit such sacrilege? The Ephesians developed a stock response,

"Because our Goddess had gone to Pella to be present at the birth of Alexander the Great."[10]

In 334 B.C. the grown Alexander passed through the city. While there he was painted by Apelles. This showed him in a deified kind of pose with lightning bolts grasped in both hands. The image was promptly set up in the temple.[11] The populace drew the line at his offer to finance the completion of the facility in exchange for his name being inscribed upon it. They discreetly passed on the grounds that it was inappropriate for one god to give to another god.

The lack of his financial support did nothing to hinder the grandeur of the rebuilt temple. In the second century B.C. Antipater of Sidon prepared a list of the seven wonders of the world. He included the colossus of Rhodes and the pyramids in Egypt—and from Ephesus, the temple of Artemis. Herodotus described it as "a building worthy of note."[12] Greece was famous for the wealth and labor of love poured into its temples. Pausanias spoke of how Asia was even more so: "They have such temples as are not to be found in any other place. The first of these, both for its magnitude and riches, is the temple of Ephesian Diana."[13]

The widely traveled Antipater of Thessalonica praised the beauty of the temple as exceeding all but one of the ancient sites he had visited:

> I've seen Babylon's walls wide enough to take traffic.
> I've seen the statue of Zeus on the banks of the Alpheus.
> I've seen the Hanging Gardens and the Sun's Colossus.
> The enormous labour of the Pyramids towering upwards,
> The immense tomb of Maussolus, but once
> I'd set eyes on
> The temple of Artemis with the clouds almost touching
> It put all other marvels into the shade.
> Except for Olympus
> I'd say the Sun shed its light on nothing sublimer.[14]

No matter how impressive its physical facilities, no religious institution can retain the same level of enthusiasm over any prolonged period of time. The Artemis cult seems to have gone into a period of relative neglect in the second half of the second century and about A.D. 200 a large fund was raised to provide an adequate financial base to support her cultic ceremonies into the future years.[15] In A.D. 263 Gothic invaders attacked Ephesus and destroyed the temple.[16] Although this did not destroy the cult, it was a body blow to its prestige and self-image.

It was standard practice for Greek temples to face east; the temple of Artemis defied this tradition by facing west.[17] As it existed in the first century the temple was between 160 and 180 feet wide by about 360 or more feet deep.[18] It was constructed on an underlying platform of 239 by 418 feet.[19] Its spacious dimensions made it four times the size of Athens' Parthenon[20] and about two-thirds that of the later St. Peter's Basilica in Rome.[21] The platform was apparently added to escape the problem of water seepage in the marshy area where the temple was located.[22] The addition of the thick platform, however, required that the original two steps that took one to the temple entrance level had to be expanded to at least ten steps.[23] The structure was supported by a forest of over a hundred columns,[24] each six feet thick[25] and ascending fifty-five to sixty feet[26] into the air. Relief figures were carved on three dozen of the bases that supported the individual columns.[27]

Two vital parts of the temple were its main altar and its inner sanctuary. The altar was located on its own large platform to the west of the temple. A spacious ramp led up to it; the altar site itself was sixty-six by one-hundred feet. The nature of the altar and its immediate surroundings remains conjectural though it appears to have been horseshoe-shaped and was marbled on its sides.[28]

The inner sanctuary (*cella*) may well be called the holy of holies because this was the location of the sacred image of Artemis herself. The *cella* measured seventy feet by seventy feet.[29] There was a twenty foot by twenty foot altar within, and apparently behind it stood the fabled Artemis.[30] Standing fifty feet from head to toe, she perpetually stared out upon her worshipers.[31]

The structure, of course, was made out of marble, as had been the sixth-century B.C. structure that preceded it.[32] Fragments of the complex that have survived from the structure indicate the use of both gold and vivid colors to decorate the facility.[33] Although certain aspects of the temple are certainties and others reasonable probabilities, yet other aspects remain speculative. For example, was the *cella* where the Artemis statue was located open to the sky?[34] Regardless of the unsettled questions, all visitors, regardless of gender and social status, had free access to the courtyard of the temple and to the outer perimeter of the building; only the priests and priestesses were admitted into the inner sanctuary where the statue was maintained.[35]

A standard Christian attack on idolatry was rooted in the fact that idols were, by their very nature, manmade. Artemis, however, was an "image which fell down from Zeus" (or "heaven" in other translations) (Acts 19:35). This "cannot be denied," asserted a first-century town clerk of Ephesus (Acts 19:36). This allegedly heavenly origin of the image allowed her worshipers to assert that, however much the Christian critique might be applied to others, *this* object of adoration did, indeed, come "from heaven" rather than human hands.[36]

The claim of a heavenly origin of the image has been taken to indicate that it was formed out of a meteorite.[37] In turn this has been taken to mean that either *in its untouched* form it possessed a crudely female shape[38] or that it was carved *from* a meteorite. Of course there is no necessary contradiction between these, as its crude shape could very well have provided the incentive for it to be "polished" into a full image. This also does not answer the question of *how much* of the statue actually came from the meteorite. If the estimate of fifty feet is anywhere near true, then it seems inescapable that the meteorite formed only *part* of it, most likely the head, with the remainder being added to complete the statue.[39]

The significance of the shape or form of the Artemis image has been a subject of much discussion. In the West she was known as Diana and was portrayed as a slim, sleek huntress. Not so in the Asiatic East. Since the days of Jerome she has been pictured in the popular mind as an unrealistic and not quite human creature, having numerous breasts.[40] This remains a popular, probably majority, perhaps dominant, interpretation of the copies of her image that have survived.

Negatively, it is argued that the objects cannot be breasts for they lack nipples.[41] Likewise, it is contended that their location on most depictions is below the area where breasts would occur.[42] One wonders, however, how much physical exactitude should be expected, *regardless* of what the objects are.

More telling is the argument that at least one statuette depicting Cybele clearly indicates the presence of breasts beneath her clothing, yet also has objects that look like the "breasts" on Artemis. Even the male Zeus is depicted as having similar protuberances as Artemis.[43]

What substitute is there for breasts, however? Dissenters from the traditional interpretation argue that the alleged breasts are actually eggs.[44] They are a symbol/result of fertility, which Artemis stood for.[45] What *kind* of egg though? Some say bee eggs.[46] Just as in Athens the owl was the symbolic presentation of Athena, in Ephesus Artemis was represented by the bee.[47] Her priestesses were nicknamed "bees,"[48] and the city itself used the bee as a civic symbol.[49]

Others say they are *ostrich* eggs.[50] Although it is easy to dismiss this as geographic misplacement—Turkey not being associated with ostriches in the modern world—in ancient days ostriches had a far wider geographic distribution than they do today. Yet this writer's mind still rebels; the bee suggestion makes far more sense in light of the tie-in with the cult, if one is to pursue this line.

Some see other objects in nature being pictured. Charles Seltman believes they represent date clusters. The sect considered the date-palm sacred and the likely color they were painted (gilt or golden) represented the actual color of "ripening dates."[51]

Oddly enough, some see a *male* sexual allusion. Since the testicles of sacrificed bulls are known to have been attached to Artemis's statue, some believe these are pictured on the statues and mistakenly taken for breasts.[52]

Others prefer even more exotic theories. "Zodiacal signs" are found her surviving images and she was interpreted as helping create the destiny of each individual—helping in times of war and childbirth, for example. Hence some redefine the "breasts" as either planets and/or stars and interpret them as an expression of Artemis's power over destiny.[53]

Andrew E. Hill has suggested the fascinating possibility that the "breasts" actually represent a distorted memory of the "scale armor" worn by certain ancient goddesses. "This coat of mail usually consisted of a series of rounded metal plates secured in layers with leather thongs."[54] Artemis herself was connected with the legends of the supposed Amazon warriors who worshiped her in the ancient past. Because of the relationship of Artemis with fertility, the original military ornamentation became modified in the direction of what could be interpreted as breasts.[55]

*Should* the traditional interpretation be rejected?[56] That they are breasts fits well with the highly charged sexuality accompanying elements of her cultic practice—sacred prostitution. Breasts also fit in well with her image of *nurturer* of the human race in general and of mothers in particular. The effort to turn them into eggs or dates redefines them as *indirect* sexual/nurturing images rather than *direct* ones. And since Artemis is supposed to represent the goddess in idealized *human* form, a *direct* sexual/nurturing image in the forms of female breasts makes far more sense. It seems especially odd that the more sexually explicit second half of the twentieth century would attempt to *de*sexualize the imagery.

This brings us to the paradoxical sexual ideas inherent in the Artemis cult. Artemis was considered on the one hand as the incarnation of perpetual virginity, yet on the other of the sexual instinct, with motherhood and maternal concerns its highest expressions.[57]

Some attempt to reconcile her role as embodiment of sexual expression with her embodiment of being a *parthenos* (virgin) by arguing that the expression *really* carries the connotation of "unmarried" rather than "virginal."[58] On the other hand, the Greeks, for all their freewheeling sexual ways, held a high regard for purity of lineage and in the marital context wanted absolutely no doubts on the question. The concept of an idealized child-bearing goddess would more naturally go hand-in-hand with one who was chaste rather than one who was merely unmarried.

Others attempt to resolve the paradox by arguing that in at least some Greek myths virginity was restorable—to goddesses even if not to humans. Allen H. Jones draws attention to the story in Pausanias concerning the goddess Hera, who would annually bathe in a spring that restored her virginity. Jones suggests that the ritual bathing of cult statues grew out of this myth—a practice that is documented for several goddesses, including Artemis (though in this case at Corinth rather than Ephesus).[59]

Perhaps the best reconciliation is on the psychological level. To the extent that the female of the species has a "natural" role, it is that of childbearer. She is *born* virgin but her body is designed to bear children and in the normal course of things she will carry out both functions. The cult of Artemis astutely recognized that a woman's course represented *neither* childbearing *nor* virginity as a normal lifetime status; *both* occurred and both were natural and to be respected and honored.

One might go one step further and find in this recognition the basis (outside of the idolatry itself) of the most repellent aspect of the Artemis cult to its Judeo-Christian foes, that is, its ritual prostitution. In putting childbearing on a moral par with virginity, the cult expressed a recognition of the legitimacy of sexual expression in its most honorable form. But by approving ritual prostitution it seemed to endorse sexual expression at its most debased level, as a form of sexual release independent of commitment, love, and tenderness. For many, any excuse for sexual conduct is adequate and much of the appeal of ritual prostitution likely grew out of this. Yet even here there may be a theoretical undercurrent designed to elevate the practice higher than cynics tend to view it: If both virginity *and* married sexuality/childbearing are honorable and praiseworthy, is not the *transition* from one to the other a kind of "sacred act" in itself? Viewed from that perspective, one can see how a religious system that idealized virginity and marriage could yet be turned upon itself to glorify the violation of the sexual exclusiveness we find, from the Judeo-Christian perspective, inherent in a proper sexual relationship.

Strabo refers to priestesses whom he calls *parthenoi,* suggesting that at least among one group of Artemis devotees continuing virginity was obligatory.[60] Rather than the cultic prostitution being engaged in by a separate type of priestess, some interpret their title as an honorary one that continued to apply to them even when they engaged in sexual intercourse with cultic worshipers.[61] On the other hand, we read inscriptions of a later period concerning the presence of *married* priestesses,[62] indicating a different set of assumptions and presumptions. Furthermore, we know that certain male priests engaged in ritual self-castration[63]—surely about as *literal* an endorsement of sexual abstinence and virginity as one can obtain!

The male eunuchs were called *megabyxoi* and occupied the most respected position in the hierarchy of the temple. At least in the days of Strabo one had to be *non*-Greek to be admitted to the ranks.[64] The word itself is Persian (meaning "set free by God" or, less likely, "given by God"), and that also points to a non-Greek origin of the office.[65] The inclusion of such a priesthood may in part be explained by the merger of the images of Cybele and Artemis. Cybele's lover, Attis, castrated himself,[66] and the inclusion of such a priesthood would tend to cement the equivalency of the two goddesses.

The priests were not merely eunuchs; they were *self-castrated* eunuchs, the castration being performed while in a religious frenzy. Some interpret this as a giving up of their fertility to the goddess; others take it to be an attempt to *preserve* the seed, based upon the ancient belief that the generative potential originated in the head and was only transmitted by the generative organ.[67] Perhaps one is guilty of a post-pagan perspective, but one would also think that it would be viewed as a self-denial of the "ultimate" sensual pleasures, representing the greatest sacrifice—short of death itself—that a male could make.

Was there still a eunuch priesthood in the days John wrote? It has been noted that when Strabo wrote about these men late in the century before Jesus, he used the past tense, as if they no longer existed:

> [The Ephesians] used to have eunuch priests, whom they would call Megabyzoi. They were ever looking elsewhere for people worthy of such a high position and they used to be held in high honor. It was necessary for virgins to serve with them. Nowadays, some of their customary practices are preserved, and others less so.[68]

The last sentence could be construed as indicating that he was not certain how uniformly these prior customs were being maintained; he only knew that the pattern was erratic and inconsistent. Nor do we know whether the custom came back into popularity at a later date, since there had been ancient precedent for it.

The ongoing castration rites of Cybele's priests and the presence of the cult in Asia would certainly have encouraged such a reversal.

As to the women of the cult, the female *parthenoi* have already been mentioned. Plutarch compared this large group of women with the Vestal Virgins at Rome—and since we know how deadly serious the Romans held their virginity requirement we have further indication of literalness regarding the followers of Artemis. The *parthenoi* were divided into three categories: the most important was the priestess, who was engaged in actual direct cultic activities. The novice was one preparing to undertake the obligations of priestess. And a category that might be called retired priestess oversaw the instruction of the novices.[69]

Another group of male priests was called the Essenes (this group had no doctrinal or religious connection with the Jewish sect by the same name). According to Pausanias, Essenes had to live a life of sexual abstinence for a year.[70] In the religious sphere, they seem to have offered regular sacrifices on behalf of the city. In the social sphere, they arranged what we would call fellowship meals, events that the public enjoyed after the strictly religious activities of the cult were completed.[71]

The Curete priesthood also provided an important linkage to the local political power structure. Although in mainstream Greek tradition the Curettes were thought of in connection with Zeus, an Ephesian legend claimed that they played a vital role in protecting Artemis at her birth by scaring off a dangerous female deity. Since the Ephesians were also convinced that Artemis was born near their city, a Curette priesthood was a natural one to create. Unlike Artemis worship in other locales, this priesthood was unique to Ephesus. They were responsible for both banquets and sacrifices during the annual celebration of the goddess's birth.[72]

Music played an important role in the cult. In this category come the hymn writers attached to the temple.[73] A boy's choir performed in connection with religious ceremonies.[74] Drummers and flute players entertained during the quasi-sacred meals performed after services.[75]

Dancers represented another category of temple attendant. Indeed, shrines of many cults maintained a corps of dancers specializing in whatever dances were most associated with that particular religion.[76] At one of the annual Ephesian festivals for

Artemis twenty dancers were involved in the entertainment.[77] Indeed, the Artemis cult had two different types of dancers, "toe dancers" and a group that performed with weapons.[78] Dancers of the temple held their meetings in the government Prytaneion. During the first century the status of the dancers was such that their names were inscribed on the columns of the Prytaneion.[79]

All together, at least twenty-three different categories of religious and utilitarian employees/servants of the temple are documented, but little more than their bare existence is known for most.[80] On the strictly religious side, among those not already mentioned, were skilled teachers/theologians who expounded and explained the ancient myths their religion celebrated.[81] On the more utilitarian level, there were the equivalent of receptionists, a cleaning staff, and guards.[82]

Being composed of fallible human beings, it was inevitable that the cult would be faced with at least occasional scandals involving conduct that defied the standards of the prevailing paganism. The most well-known occurred during the first century and revolved around the selling of priesthoods.

It was acceptable practice in Asia Minor (and occasionally in other regions) for city officials to sell the priesthoods in various local cults.[83] The earliest documented case was at Miletus (c. 400 B.C.) and the highest known price was at the city of Cos, where during the first century B.C., one individual paid between nineteen and twenty thousand drachmas for his priestly position.[84] The priestly position bestowed not only the inherent honor and prestige connected with the priesthood of the particular cult but also a guaranteed annual income from the temple regardless of what services the individual performed or did not perform. Furthermore, having purchased a priesthood, it became the buyer's right to resell it if he could find an able and willing purchaser. The resale value was presumably based upon the prestige of the position and how many rights and privileges (especially monetary) were retained by the original holder.[85]

During Claudius's reign, Ephesian excesses regarding the purchase of priesthoods came to the boiling point. During the Asian proconsulship of Paullus Fabius Persicus the proconsul took steps to curb the blatant abuses that had developed. Priesthood holders were going so far as to borrow money, not merely against the funds that were due in the *current* year but even against those they would not receive till the *following* year. Administrative conduct at the temple had also become sloppy if not outright dishonest; slaves were even being drafted instead of using the available government-owned ones. Victors in the various contests at the annual Artemis festival were being lavishly fed and entertained—all to the financial injury of the temple.

The proconsul imposed spending limits and banned paying priests from future revenues. An unknown number were deposed from their positions. The holders of these involuntarily vacated posts were reimbursed—but at a mere 1 percent of the original purchase price. Provincial financial limitations were given as the reason, but annoyance at the behavior probably absolved any minor guilt that was felt. In taking these drastic steps the governor took pains to assert that it was his duty "to make provision for the welfare, not only for his year of office but for all time also, both of the province as a whole and the several cities." He implied that this intervention represented the kind of constructive policy the emperor himself endorsed and encouraged.[86]

A considerable income was necessary to support the large staff of priests, priestesses, and to finance the annual month-long festival in the goddess's honor, not to mention more mundane operating costs. Often it was a case of too little money chasing too many expenses. Throughout the first and second centuries A.D., staff cutbacks repeatedly occurred to narrow, if not eliminate, the financial gap. Needed repairs were also postponed in order to minimize the deficit.[87]

Funds came from a number of sources. The temple issued a large number of loans not just to Ephesians but also to parties throughout Asia.[88] One source for these funds was the temple's own accumulated resources. On the other hand, huge sums were also maintained there by citizens and people from other lands for the safety it provided. The rationale was, as Dio Chrysostom wrote, that "no one has ever yet dared to violate that place, although countless wars have occurred in the past and the city has often been captured." It was unthinkable that they would "take any of these monies when any need arises" or to "borrow them....No; on the contrary, they would sooner, I think, strip off the adornment of the goddess than touch this money."[89] That *they* would not cheat the treasury was one thing; whether this attitude also precluded lending out the funds *to others* is less certain.[90] Indeed, by lending it out this way the odds would be minimized that any *direct* temple borrowing from those trust funds would ever occur.

Gifts of money for immediate projects and the erection of facilities by a generous donor[91] provided an additional means of providing for the welfare of the cult and its adherents without actually increasing its costs. For example, a massive marble portico stretched from the gate of the city to the temple so that foul weather would not keep away those wishing to worship. It was the gift of Damianus, a wealthy philosopher.[92]

Cash bequests from the wills of wealthy individuals were so common among devotees of the various ancient deities that the Romans imposed major legal hurdles to their recognition. Legacies were permitted to be given to only a few major deities and only if a carefully specified legal procedure were followed.[93]

Of even greater ongoing importance was the bequest of substantial pieces of land, which could be used to obtain additional funds (through rental or crop sales) on an indefinite basis after the patron's death. Boundary stones indicating ownership by the temple have been located as much as twenty-five[94] and thirty miles outside the city.[95] The Artemisium—as the temple was known—appears to have owned a minimum of seventy-seven thousand acres of quality farmland in the surrounding region.[96] Non-farm resources provided an additional cash inflow. The Artemisium owned "sacred ponds" on the Cayster River, providing revenue from fish sales.[97] In light of such economic resources it is not surprising that there was an officially recognized "sacred rent office" that oversaw the leasing of the temple's various possessions.[98]

A great many slaves were owned by the Artemisium, but how they fitted into the income-producing function of the cult is uncertain. If the dominant assumption that slaves were little utilized for agricultural purposes in Asia is valid, they would not have provided most of the labor that produced the crops and hence wealth that ultimately flowed into the temple from its various properties.[99] On the other hand, it is hard to see how temple-centered activities would have been sufficient to keep them all busy. One possibility is that many were released into the custody of others to earn for the temple an annual stipend. It was common, in an urban context, to find slaves working as dependent businessmen and household servants, and rented-out temple slaves would fit quite naturally into this picture.[100]

### The Varying Roles of Artemis

Having surveyed the Artemis cult from an organizational and financial perspective, we need to return to its religious and social function in order to understand more fully its place in the society of the first century.

*Artemis was viewed as protector of women.* In non-Ephesian contexts we know that young girls and newlyweds often gave clothing to Artemis.[101] Many of these were retained by the temple as potential garments for the local statue of the goddess.[102] Clothing was also given by expectant mothers in hope of a safe birth and those suffering from various physical distresses in hope of relief.[103] Although there is no direct documentation that the custom existed in Ephesus itself, it *did* exist at other Artemis shrines and the Ephesian cult is known to have sent appropriate garments to the Artemis sect in Sardis. It is a virtual certainty that the practice existed in Ephesus as well.

*Artemis was viewed as protector of the criminally accused.* The right of asylum went back an unknown time before Alexander the Great.[104] Alexander recognized a protected area of about two hundred yards around the Artemisium, a figure very likely extended by Mithridates. Mark Antony expanded it yet further, bringing part of the city proper within the protected region.[105]

It should be noted that the right only extended to the *accused*, not to the *convicted*. As the late third-century, possibly early-fourth-century tale *Clitophon and Leucippe* puts it, the protecting power of the goddess applies "only before the court has pronounced its verdict; the goddess has never loosed a criminal from his chains or rescued a condemned felon from his deserved fate; her altars are for the unfortunate, not for the guilty."[106]

We may read into this a shade of defensiveness caused by the rampant abuse of the asylum right even in its proper, narrow form. Apollonius of Tyana expressed his annoyance at the abuse of the asylum right in an epistle he wrote to his Ephesian disciples during the first century:

You are devoted to holy ceremonies no less than to honour-ing the Emperor. In general I cannot condemn your custom of inviting and being invited to feasts; but I do condemn the people who by night and day share the home of the goddess, otherwise I should not see issuing thence thieves and rob-bers and kidnappers and every sort of sacrilegious rascal; for your temple is just a den of robbers.[107]

*The Artemisium provided social welfare functions for the needy.* Local citizens suffering through a prolonged period of hardship could always count on assistance. Likewise, travelers passing through the community, in need of immediate but temporary assistance, received what they needed.[108]

*The Artemisium provided social function opportunities for its members.* It was common for pagan temples to have the ancient equivalent of a church social hall for dining and socializing, where small groups of members would gather.[109] In addition, reli-gio-civic associations of citizens would hold their periodic festivi-ties there as well.[110] Not inappropriately for a world-renowned facility, the Artemis dining hall at Ephesus was designed to be the largest of any in the world.[111]

*The Artemisium functioned as a place of public display and pub-lic record.* The temple played a vital role in the cultural and civic interests of the community. "The temple was considered to be the proper location for the dedication of various inventions and the displaying of different kinds of works of art. It also served as the public archives for various civic inscriptions. Many inscrip-tions authorized by the city of Ephesus contain the directive to inscribe them in the temple of the goddess."[112]

From the varied functions the cult performed we can better grasp that it was a *living* institution, deeply involved in the needs and aspirations of the city where it was located. It did not define religious expression as a withdrawal from the world but as an active involvement in a wide variety of society's social needs and desires.

### Artemis's Month: The Artemisia

Every cult had its own calendar of religious events. As the dominant sect in Ephesus, Artemis occupied a special point of honor. The month of Artemisia (overlapping our March and April)[113] was named in her honor and served as the occasion of the most prolonged celebrations. A series of unrelated contests were held later in the same month. In the second century A.D., the civic assembly and governing council of Ephesus decided that the entire month should be set aside for the activities in her honor. The civic decree read:

> The people of Ephesus thought it would be appropriate for the *entire* month which has this holy name to be consecrated and dedicated to the goddess; by his decree, we have decided to establish the following cult in her honor: that the month of Artemision should be sacred throughout *all* its days and that on those days of that month, feasts and the celebration of Artemisia should take place, so that, in fact, the *whole* month should be consecrated to the goddess. The greater the honor rendered to the goddess, the surer our city is to remain ever more blessed with good fortune and glory.[114]

By doing this, the existing, originally separate, noncultic events of the month were effectively blended into the public consciousness as *part* of her festival. During the month the population of the city would temporarily swell to as high as a million people, as devotees, fun seekers, and tourists poured into the city to enjoy the many special entertainments and athletic events.[115] The hero of *Clitophon and Leucippe* describes the Mardi Gras–like conditions of the city during the month, "It was the monthly festival of Artemis, and the whole place was full of drunken roysterers; the whole night long the entire market-place was occupied by crowds of people."[116] On a more positive note, it was a socially sanctioned pairing-off time, during which would-be husbands could openly search out potential wives—and vice versa.[117]

In the major religious celebration of the month, Artemis's statue and those of twenty-nine other deities were taken from the Artemisium, carried through the town in joyous procession, and brought to the Great Theater. The massive procession that performed this task was led by civic officials, visiting dignitaries, priestesses, entertainers, and such. Proudly conscious of the honor of their task, they marched the idols through the city streets to the delight and pride of the thousands who lined the way. At the Great Theater the idols were placed upon individual pedestals so they could "enjoy" the dancing and music along with the live audience.[118]

The month included a wide variety of predominantly "secular" social, athletic, and cultural events. Athletic events allowed the physical prowess of participants to be demonstrated as well as providing entertainment for those who watched.[119] Horse races pleased and excited the crowds as well.[120]

Although such events contributed to the popular success of the Artemisia, cultural activities were even more important.[121] There were plays and dramas for the edification of the community. There were oratory and poetry contests and the public reading of decrees praising those who had served the community both locally and abroad.[122] There were dance performances[123] and music concerts[124] to lift the public spirit. Dance and music celebrations were performed not only at the Great Theater but even in the Artemis temple itself.[125]

These activities were supplemented by animal sacrifices, religious processions, and private banquets.[126] Whatever appealed to a person could be found somewhere during the Artemisia.

Although the month-long festival was the longest one in Artemis's honor, her birthday festival also deserves attention. This was held on the sixth day of the month Thargelion, which overlapped our May and June. The routine called for a religious procession of specially chosen clerics and lay believers to begin at the Magnesian Gate. After obtaining the various sacred images from her temple, the procession proceeded to the theater for ceremonies in Artemis's honor. At some point it became customary to transport the images in a cart, though this may have been an innovation that was not instituted until after Hadrian's reign. After everything was completed the leaders of the celebration left in procession through the Coressian Gate.[127]

Ceremonies were also held outside the city on Mount Solmissus. Strabo recounts: "A general festival is held there annually; and by a certain custom the youths vie for honor particularly in the splendour of their banquets there. At that time also a special college of the Curetes holds symposiums there and performs certain mystic sacrifices."[128]

The nature of these mystic rituals is unknown. A first century A.D. inscription refers to a respected woman "who was a priestess of Artemis in a holy manner and carried out worthily both the mysteries and the sacrifices."[129] A second inscription of the same period uses the same words to describe a different priestess.[130] One second century priestess describes herself as "having performed the mysteries."[131] At some point the Artemis cult went through one of those periods of decline found in all religions, for we find a third-century priestess describing herself as "having *revived* all the mysteries of the goddess and [having] restored them to the ancient custom."[132] Because these and other references are so brief, we are left uninformed as to the rites expected both in honor of her birth and upon other occasions.

## Other Goddesses

Various other goddesses were worshiped in Ephesus, such as Aphrodite,[133] Athena,[134] and Demeter.[135] Athena is mainly known through references to her Ephesian sanctuary.[136] At least as late as the third century A.D. there was a great deal of local enthusiasm for the cult.[137] The Phrygian Great-Mother had her body of local worshipers as well.[138]

The priests and priestesses in charge of the worship of Hestia fulfilled an officially recognized government function. The "eternal fire" of Hestia that they maintained was considered vital to maintaining the well-being of the city and its people.[139]

The Greek settlers who took Artemis with them into their Asian colonies identified her with the existing native mother-goddess Cybele.[140] The merger of the two was never total; although much Cybele *imagery* was used to modify that of the western-style Artemis, Cybele worshipers continued to maintain her as a separate cult. In Ephesus her temple was about a half-mile from that of Artemis.[141]

## Other Gods of the City

The healing god Asclepius had his worshipers in Ephesus.[142] Likewise the Phrygian god Zeus Sabazios was worshiped within the community.[143] Apollo was honored under a variety of names, such as Klarian Apollo and Apollo Patrois.[144]

When Mark Antony entered the city, decorations of thyrus wands and ivy were abundant as part of the traditional decorations for the Dionysia, held annually in the honor of Dionysus.[145]

This annual festival was an extremely popular one and included events in the Great Theater.[146] In addition to the successful public cult, evidence exists of at least one private in-home cult created in his honor.[147]

Dionysus had a large number of followers in the city.[148] If John wrote his gospel in Ephesus, it would have been natural for converts to compare the positive water-into-wine miracle of Jesus at the marriage feast of Cana with the negative and destructive use of wine in the Dionysus cult that was so popular in their community.[149]

*Egyptian Deities*

A sixth century B.C. bronze statue portraying an Egyptian priest was discovered in one of the wealthier homes of Roman-era Ephesus. This would suggest that the owner was a devotee of an Egyptian deity, perhaps even from that country himself. The discrepancy between the age of the statue and the age of where it was found suggests that the statue was among those antiquities plundered from Egyptian grave sites.[150] The presence of the cults of Isis and Serapis in Ephesus probably dates back to the days of Cleopatra's sojourn in the city with her lover, Mark Anthony.[151]

Ptolemy I had invented the Serapis religion in an effort to blend the polytheism of Egypt and the Greeks into a harmonious whole. The Egyptians themselves soon turned against it, but among both Greek and Romans it enjoyed a continuing popularity. Indeed, during the days of the Roman Empire virtually all major cities in the eastern part of the empire included a Serapis cult among its established sects. Commonly the Egyptian female deity Isis was either worshiped in the same facility or in her own shrine.[152]

The Ephesian temple of Serapis—or the Serapeion—was located near the western gate into the Commercial Agora.[153] It was a second-century-A.D. addition to the city.[154] In front of the temple lay a spacious courtyard (240 by 353 feet), surrounded on three sides by porticoes that were almost eight yards wide. On the southern side of the courtyard, facing the entrance, lay the temple itself. It was ninety-three feet wide and its eight frontal Corinthian columns soared fifty feet into the air.[155] So large were the doors leading into the *cella* where worship was performed that they were mounted on wheels to facilitate opening and closing.[156] Beneath the paving stones on the floor of the temple were conduits that provided water to several places within the structure.[157]

In the State Agora the foundations of a small temple have been located that some identify as dedicated to an Egyptian deity, quite possibly Isis. It was constructed in the closing half of the first century B.C. and alterations were made at least as late as A.D. 200. An Amon-Re image is one indication of the use of the facility in connection with an Egyptian cult. A nearby font usable for sacred ablutions has also been located, which would tie in well with the known practice of the Isis movement.[158]

As with other polytheistic groups, it was quite possible for an additional deity to be worshiped at the temple site as well. In this case an altar was erected to Isis within the Artemis temple during the Hellenistic period, prior to the Roman takeover of the region.[159]

### The Emperor Cult

A strong link between the Artemis cult and emperor worship goes back to 29 B.C. in Ephesus. In that year part of her temple was set aside as the *Augusteum,* to be used for the worship of Roma and "the divine Julius."[160] An altar was installed[161] along with a statue of Augustus three times his actual height.[162] This move not only exhibited Ephesian loyalty to Rome but it also bore witness to the compatibility and friendship of the Artemis cult to the imperial system. Even so, the continued presence of the Augusteum did not prevent the Romans from seriously considering revoking the Artemisium's sanctuary rights after a long period of reported abuses. It required powerful lobbying of the Roman Senate to preserve the traditional refuge right.[163]

Ephesus was not able to gain permission to erect its first official imperial temple until late in the first century. During the second-century reign of Hadrian it was granted permission to erect a second one. In the third century Caracalla granted yet a third, more or less: the Ephesians could erect a temple in honor of his *brother,* while he granted to the Artemisium the right to be recognized as the temple in his own honor.[164] Due to massive resentment against the excesses of Caracalla, Ephesus later lost the right to have a temple in his honor,[165] thereby reducing the cult temples to two.[166]

In Acts 19:35 *(KJV)* Ephesus is called the *neokoros* of

Artemis. Rendered by expressions such as "temple-keeper" or "temple guardian," it appears to have originally meant "temple-sweeper."[167] With its stress upon service, it came to become a title of honor and was applied to both individuals and groups to mark their dedication to serving a particular religious movement.[168] So widespread was this usage that Josephus goes so far as to call Israel the "temple-keeper of God," using the term *neokoros*.[169]

The term was also used to apply to the imperial cult. After the (temporary) addition of the Caracalla temple, we find an Ephesian inscription that refers to the city as the "greatest and most highly esteemed metropolis of Asia and temple-warden *(neokoros)* of Artemis and three times temple-warden *(neokoros)* of the emperors."[170] Later writers sometimes padded the figures by lumping in the Augusteum with the separate temples and claiming that the city was "*four* times temple-warden."[171]

Whether the late-first-century temple should be attributed to the reign of Vespasian or Domitian is a subject of considerable controversy. Its traditional name implies that it was either constructed (or begun) while Vespasian ruled.[172] Others take the view that it was originally a *Domitian* temple but that, soured by his bitter record of excesses, it was rededicated to his far more respectable predecessor.[173]

This temple contained a "four times life-size" statue of Domitian.[174] Or at least that is the most common identification given since parts were uncovered in 1930.[175] This identification has been challenged on the ground that the face is more like that of Titus, his younger brother. On the other hand, even a defender of the reidentification concedes that the image is different from those normally found in Roman works and reflects a distinctive provincial interpretation of Titus's appearance.[176] Yet if it varies that substantially from the "real" appearance of Titus, one would seem open to the counter-challenge that the provincial interpretation actually represents a reworking of Domitian's appearance. Regardless of which approach is correct, it was clearly designed to awe the observer and to contribute to the visible prestige of the imperial cult in Asia.

# 3

## Monotheism in Ephesus

### Judaism

Surprisingly little is known about the Jewish community in this largest metropolis of Asia. Josephus refers to Augustus's decree protecting its Sabbath observance rights and related matters.[1] He also refers to the resistance of the Ephesians to recognizing the rights the empire had guaranteed to them.[2] According to Irenaeus, Theodotion—who was responsible for a translation of the Torah and prophets into Greek—was considered an Ephesian.[3] After the Bar-Kochba revolt was crushed in Palestine in the second century, a large number of Jews took refuge in the city.[4]

Among those who made his new home in the metropolis was Trypho,[5] who engaged in a major religious disputation with the Christian Justin when he passed through the community.[6] The ancient church historian Eusebius calls Trypho "the most distinguished among the Hebrews of the day."[7] Whether this is literally true or not, Trypho's presentation of Judaism was certainly a very able and skilled one. F. F. Bruce points to the high level on which the debate took place: "Possibly it has been edited for publication, but even so it remains a most illuminating and attractive account of the way in which cultured Jews and Christians could debate the points at issue between them. There is a good deal of hard hitting on either side, but the debate is conducted with great courtesy."[8]

The fact that they were still in vigorous disagreement did not cause the two disputants to part in bitterness and anger. At the closing of the "Dialogue with Trypho" we read,

> Then Trypho, after a little delay, said, "You see that it was not intentionally that we came to discuss these points. And I confess that I have been particularly pleased with the confer-

ence; and I think that these are of quite the same opinion as myself. For we have found more than we expected, and more than it was possible to have expected. And if we could do this more frequently, we should be much helped in the searching of the Scriptures themselves. But since," he said, "you are on the eve of departure, and expect daily to set sail, do not hesitate to remember us as friends when you are gone."...After this they left me, wishing me safety in my voyage, and from every misfortune.[9]

Whether it was the coincidence of personalities involved or whether the civilized discourse reflects a greater willingness among Ephesian (in contrast to Smyranean) Jews to prefer intellectual to physical confrontation we do not know. Just as Jewish rabble-rousers were able to encourage the legalized "lynching" (burning) of Polycarp in Smyrna, later claimants to the name Christian would similarly disgrace their faith in the reverse direction by physical violence. Here in Ephesus a much different attitude prevails.

Inscriptional evidence about the Jewish community is surprisingly scant for such a huge city. One inscription briefly refers to the presence of a synagogue,[10] though its actual location is unknown.[11] Certain Jewish sounding names have been found in inscriptions from the first centuries A.D. Some are connected with references making the Jewish connection explicit—such as a second-century epitaph for a priest. Most, however, provide insufficient information to determine whether the individuals are traditional Jews, Jewish-Christians, or even apostate Jews who had fallen into paganism.[12]

A few additional physical remains have survived. The Library of Celsus (second century A.D.) had a menorah cut into its steps.[13] In the so-called Cemetery of the Seven Sleepers, Roman-era remains include "several terra-cotta lamps displaying the menorah, and a unique glass showing the menorah flanked by the *shofar* and *lulab*."[14]

## Christianity

As a major port city of Asia, at least some returning pilgrims from the Jewish Feast of Pentecost (Acts 2) surely passed through the community, if they were not already residents of the city. On the other hand, there is no indication of an already existing church in the city when Paul visited it on his second missionary journey. His leaving behind such dedicated Christians as Aquila and Priscilla (Acts 18:19) would surely have resulted in a congregation being formed: if they had no hesitation in bringing the significance of the resurrected Christ to a capable Jewish advocate of John the Baptist (Acts 18:24–28), one is safe to assume they would have been at least equally vigorous in discussing Jesus with less learned orthodox Jews.

Did this probable congregation continue to exist at the time of Paul's return? When Paul returns on the third missionary journey, the two go unmentioned and have presumably moved on. A church, as such, goes unmentioned. This does not necessarily exclude the existence of a church, however. Although Priscilla and Aquila are only mentioned in Acts 18 in a worship connection in regard to the synagogue—where they found Apollo—their own Christian "heresy" (from the orthodox Jewish standpoint) would certainly have required them to *also* meet in a distinctively *Christian* assembly on the first day (rather than seventh day) of the week as was customary in other places (Acts 20:7; 1 Cor 16:1–4). However small their numbers may have been, it surely was a *church*.

Not many years passed between the two visits to Ephesus—perhaps as few as about five. One would expect even a *small* congregation to have survived that length of time. Perhaps because of space considerations the author of Luke-Acts passes this by, as he does so much else in his work. Be that as it may, what Paul finds in Ephesus is described not as a "church," but rather as "some disciples" (Acts 19:1) and they are identified quite clearly as followers not of Jesus but of John the Baptist (19:2–7). After being forced out of the synagogue due to local opposition, Paul "continued for two years, so that all who dwelt in Asia heard the word of the Lord Jesus, both Jews and Greeks" (19:10). This has led to the reasonable speculation that many, perhaps all, of the seven churches of Asia were formed during this period.[15]

Two incidents concerning Paul's life during this period deserve comment (others will be discussed as historical allusions later in the chapter). First of all, we know that due to Jewish

resistance in the synagogue, "he departed from them and withdrew the disciples, reasoning daily in the school of Tyrannus"
(Acts 19:9). In the western text of the Greek New Testament
there is a gloss as to the exact hours he worked there, "from the
fifth hour till the tenth," that is, from 11 in the morning to 4 in
the afternoon.[16]

Although the western text is generally looked down upon in
regard to such glosses, this addition certainly fits the cultural traditions of the period, a midday siesta being quite common.[17]
Hence F. F. Bruce comments that "more people would normally
be asleep in Ephesus at 1 P.M. than 1 A.M."[18]

There would have been at least two good reasons for select-
ing unorthodox hours such as these. One would be cost. Assuming Paul had to pay for the facility, these hours would have been
unpopular and any charge extremely modest. And, if the place
was being provided free, it would have imposed a minimum
financial loss upon the owner. A second reason these hours
would have been natural ones to choose was that individuals
could have come at that time whose workday obligations would
have kept them busy the remainder of the day. It maximized the
number who could hear Paul's teaching. In light of such factors
the western gloss, even if considered noncanonical, certainly represents reasonable speculation as to Paul's teaching hours.

A second characteristic of this period was the scar that it left
on Paul's memory: In 2 Corinthians, Paul refers to the "trouble
which came to us in Asia: that we were burdened beyond measure, above strength, so that we despaired even of life. Yes, we had
the sentence of death in ourselves, that we should not trust in ourselves but in God who raises the dead" (1:8–9). In the previous
epistle to the same city this traumatic experience may have been
in mind when he says, "In the manner of men, I have fought with
beasts ["wild animals," *NRSV*] at Ephesus" (1 Cor 15:32).

It is easy to take this in a very literal sense, rather than as a
vivid description of the ferocity of his foes:[19] "His words seem to
imply that Paul had in mind a certain definite and unique event;
that he was, in act, actually condemned while in Ephesus to a
combat with wild beasts in the arena."[20]

Yet this tempting reconstruction has several serious difficulties. We know that Paul had friends even among the pagan reli-

gious leadership of the city and that they worked to keep harm from coming to him (Acts 19:31). Likewise, the political power structure as embodied in the town clerk refused to tolerate a riot against him but demanded that any accusations be handled in a proper legal way (Acts 19:37–38). Since Paul was there several years, it is always possible that their sentiments turned against him or were effectively neutralized by the degree of civic hostility toward him, but *if* it did so we are left uninformed as to how it was accomplished. Furthermore, if the civic officials insisted that he be treated legally, how could he have *legally* been thrown to the animals in the Ephesian stadium? He was a Roman citizen, and the only way to inflict capital punishment on him was to strip him of his citizenship, a legal right that he still possessed at a later date when he appealed Palestinian charges against him all the way to Caesar.[21] Finally, the stadium conflict with the animals is allegedly explicitly mentioned in 2 Corinthians and alluded to in 1 Corinthians. Why then, when Paul presents a lengthy description of his sufferings in 2 Corinthians 11, is it totally omitted?[22]

Perhaps a decade after his departure from Ephesus something happened to alienate the bulk of Asian Christians—which would include those at Ephesus. Paul alludes to this in 2 Timothy 1:15–18,

> This you know, that *all those in Asia have turned away from me,* among whom are Phygelus and Hermogenes. The Lord grant mercy to the household of Onesiphorus, for he often refreshed me, and was not ashamed of my chain; but when he arrived in Rome, he sought me out very diligently and found me. The Lord grant to him that he may find mercy from the Lord in that Day—and you know very well how many ways he ministered to me at Ephesus.

This can be read in one of two ways: (1) back in Asia itself, Paul was being rejected[23] or (2) the Asian community *where he wrote from* (almost certainly overwhelmingly non-Christian) was rejecting him. If the latter were the case, the text would more likely have read "all those *from* Asia have turned away from me" rather than "all those *in* Asia" have done so. One might attempt to salvage this basic approach by arguing that those *non-*Christian friends and colleagues he had once enjoyed back in

Asia had now turned against him. Yet if the rejection were limited to them would we not expect some more explicit allusion to their non-believing status? The same difficulties arise if we take the text to be referring to *Christian* Asians resident where Paul was writing from.[24]

It is commonly assumed that Paul was imprisoned twice, the second leading to his execution by Nero. Some interpret the Asian rejection of Paul as referring to his first trial;[25] others to the second.[26] The inherent logic of the situation would seem to have magnified the psychological pressures upon those who stood faithful to Paul—to stand by him once was dangerous; to do so yet a second time would open oneself to much increased imperial skepticism as to one's own motives, intentions, and loyalties.

Wherever and whatever the cause of the disaffection, the Ephesian Alexander has sometimes been singled out as the key villain. In 1 Timothy 1:19–20 Paul says that Alexander had left behind "faith and a good conscience," had shipwrecked his faith, and that Paul had delivered him "to Satan" so that he might "learn not to blaspheme." By the time of Paul's second epistle the situation was even worse:

> Alexander the coppersmith *did me much harm.* May the Lord repay him according to his works. You also must beware of him for he has greatly resisted our words. At my first defense no one stood with me, but all forsook me. May it not be charged against them. But the Lord stood with me and strengthened me, so that the message might be preached fully through me, and that all the Gentiles might hear. And I was delivered out of the mouth of the lion. (2 Tm 4:14–17)

Paul's words could indicate that the pressure and danger had simply become so great that his would-be witnesses had deserted him. But the mention of Alexander in the previous sentences could also indicate that it was because of Alexander's actions and opposition that they had felt forced to retreat from Paul's side. Alexander has been read as retaliating for the church discipline imposed upon him by Paul.[27] Some have suspected that Alexander had become an informer against Paul in Asia[28] and may even have traveled all the way to Rome to testify against him.[29] Of course this is speculation, although reasonable speculation. Its fundamental assumption is that "Alexander" and "Alexander the coppersmith" in the two pastoral epistles are one and the same.[30]

Whatever temporary split there may have been between Paul and the Asian Christians, it was not one that tore them away from orthodoxy as defined by both Paul and John. In 2 Corinthians 11:13–15, Paul had warned of those who were "false apostles, deceitful workers, transforming themselves into apostles of Christ." John tells that such individuals had come to Ephesus—and been rejected by the brothers and sisters in that city's church (Rv 2:2). Likewise, John urged caution, not credulity, in examining the credentials of those claiming to be prophets (1 Jn 4:1). Merely claiming to be a Christian teacher counted for nothing if the claimant did not "abide in the doctrine of Christ" (2 Jn 9).

Yet there was always inherent in any group of human beings the danger that self-interest or enticing nonapostolic doctrine could entice disciples away from the apostolic preaching and practice. Indeed, Paul warned them that even from among the elders "men will rise up, speaking perverse things, to draw away the disciples after themselves" (Acts 20:28–30). As of John's Revelation that had not yet occurred. Nor does Paul, in his remarks speaking of his own rejection, imply or state that this had (at least not yet) caused a drift in the religious and moral thinking of the Ephesian Christians.

Though John finds them in his mini-epistle as quite orthodox and firm defenders of the faith, there were some *faith in practice* problems that *did* bother the congregation. Although they had rejected the false apostles (2:2) and worked diligently for Christ's cause (2:3), "nevertheless I have this against you, that you have left your first love. Remember therefore from where you have fallen; repent and do the first works, or else I will come to you quickly and remove your lampstand from its place—unless you repent" (2:4–5).

This weakened love has been interpreted in two different ways.[31] Some take it to be the love of Christ, which had somehow become less important to them through the passage of time.[32] However, John had just stressed not only their exposure of false apostles (2:2) but also their continued diligence in serving the Lord (2:3).[33] This suggests that their problem lay not in divinely orientated love but in a different area of "love in its outward and social manifestations."[34] Indeed, as has been pointed out, the very passion for fully serving Christ and demanding full ortho-doxy can work to choke out the desirable attitudes believers are supposed to have toward each other. *Having* truth becomes a substitute for *living* truth—a recurring problem in following cen-turies. Indeed, since the apostolic tradition insists upon both,"it is only a *perversion* of orthodoxy that results in hardness" and mistreatment toward fellow believers.[35]

When we pass to the second century A.D., some have found an individual mentioned in the New Testament moving into prominence in the Ephesian church. Paul wrote his letter to Philemon in order to encourage that slave owner to accept with-out vindictiveness the return of his runaway servant Onesimus. Since there was a bishop in Ephesus in the early second century (c. A.D. 107–17) by the name of Onesimus, it has been speculated that Onesimus was freed and moved to Ephesus where he even-tually became a bishop. Certainly Onesimus was a resident of Asia, for in writing the Colossians, Paul refers to "Onesimus, a faithful and beloved brother, who is one of you" (Col 4:9). Since he is explicitly referred to as a Colossian, one is tempted to dis-miss the second-century bishop as a different individual who happened to have the same name. To make the two the same requires the not-impossible assumption that the runaway Ones-imus was a very young man, and that he was well along in years when he finally became a bishop in Ephesus.

About the same time as Onesimus (whoever he was) began his episcopate in Ephesus, Ignatius passed through the city on his way to martyrdom. From the epistle Ignatius wrote to Eph-esus we can observe some of the significant changes that had occurred in the life of the church since Paul's day.

In Paul's day we read of there being "elders of the church" at Ephesus (Acts 20:17), in the plural rather than singular. Fur-thermore "bishop," in the epistle to Titus, is a synonymous term with "elder" (1:5, 7). Church officers are not referred to in any of John's mini-epistles in Revelation 2 and 3. Some have insisted that the "angel" of each church refers to the leader of each con-gregation and that this proves the existence of the "monarchical episcopate" in which one individual served as the exclusive bishop. Assuming an early date (c. Nero) for Revelation, we would have a severe problem explaining the existence of a structure so conspicuously different—especially in the case of Ephesus—from that Paul left behind. If we accept a late date for Revelation (that is, Domitian), the propriety of such an organizational departure from the Pauline past must still be explained. Furthermore, when Ignatius visited the city the presbyters/elders were *still* authority figures, though the focus of power had clearly shifted to the bishop. How then could John, only a decade or little more earlier, have intended to convey a one-man rule over the Ephesian (and other) churches?

By the time of Ignatius's visit during the first decade of the second century[36] the bishop had become the dominant power and the presbyters/elders were expected to play a supporting role. Yet the relationship was to be one, not of who had the most or superior authority, but of thoroughgoing cooperation.

> Wherefore it is fitting that ye should run together in accordance with the will of your bishop, which thing also ye do. For your justly renowned presbytery, worthy of God, is fitted as exactly to the bishop as the strings are to the harp. Therefore in your concord and harmonious love, Jesus Christ is sung. And do ye, man by man, become a choir, that being harmonious in love, and take up the song of God in unison, ye may with one voice sing to the Father through Jesus Christ, so that He may both hear you, and perceive by your works that ye are indeed the members of His Son. It is profitable, therefore, that you should live in an unblameable unity, that thus ye may always enjoy communion with God.[37]

The presbyters are also described as retaining some element of authority as well: "so that ye obey the bishop and the presbytery with an undivided mind, breaking one and the same bread."[38] Is this merely a courtesy toward the presbyters, who have no real independent authority, or is the function of the bishop inoperable without the concurrence and approval of the elders? If the latter, then the bishop has still not broken free of the earlier equality among elders. He is still to gain a full superiority of position (rather than merely title) that would allow him to set the agenda for the presbyters and exercise effective veto power over the presbytery. Which represents the actual situation in Ephesus at this time, we do not know.

It is of interest, however, that the authority of the bishop is linked with the presbyters rather than with the apostles. The idea of the bishop in some type of apostolic succession role plays no part at all in Ignatius's argument. Although apostolic succession provided an effective rationalization for the bishop's authority at a later date, reliance on such reasoning appears to have come after the development of the office as superior rather than as rationale for its elevation.

In our stress on the organizational aspect of early second-century Ephesian Christianity, it is easy to overlook other information Ignatius's epistle provides about the congregation. We discover that its members had a modest problem with "false doctrine." They did not permit anyone "to sow" such doctrine among them. Instead, they refused to listen lest they be deceived by it.[39]

Some apparently had a tendency to be a bit lackadaisical in their church attendance: "Take heed, then, often to come together to give thanks to God and show forth His praise. For when we assemble frequently in the same place, the powers of Satan are destroyed and the destruction at which he aims is prevented by the unity of your faith."[40] Whatever minor problems existed the group continued to be "renowned throughout the world."[41]

As we pass even further a more pervasive influence on what by now was clearly an emerging Catholicism can be found in (or blamed upon) the Ephesian heritage. Sherman E. Johnson, for example, argues that "since Mary is so prominent in the Christian tradition of Ephesus, it takes little imagination to see that with the coming of the new faith she came to replace Artemis in the love of the people."[42] Since there is no trace of the quasi-supernatural veneration of Mary in the New Testament, this is clearly a development of a later age. There was no better place for this to develop than in Ephesus, with its pride in the mighty Artemis, purging her of the associated immoralities, stressing the kindness and human loving aspects traditionally attributed to her, and blending it with the natural respect due to the mother of the Lord—but in the process transforming Mary into something far above and beyond anything claimed for her in the apostolic age.

### Possible Historical and Societal Allusions in John's Mini-Epistle Text of the Epistle

"...To the angel of the church of Ephesus write, 'These things say He who holds the seven stars in His right hand, who walks in the midst of the seven golden lampstands: "I know your works, your labor, your patience, and that you cannot bear those who are evil. And you have tested those who say they are apostles and are not, and have found them liars; and you have persevered and have patience, and have labored for My name's sake and have not become weary. Nevertheless I have this against you, that you have left your first love. Remember therefore from where you have fallen; repent and do the first works, or else I will come to you quickly and remove your lampstand from its place—unless you repent. But this you have, that you hate the deeds of the Nicolaitans, which I also hate. He who has an ear, let him hear what the Spirit says to the churches. To him who overcomes I will give to eat from the tree of life, which is in the midst of the Paradise of God."'" (Rv 2:1–7)

*The Lack of Love and Local Ephesian Attitudes*

In our earlier discussion we expressed the judgment that when John rebukes them for "hav[ing] left your first love" (2:4) he refers to their passion for the Lord—it had become sterile, rote practice rather than showing the enthusiasm that marked their early days as Christians. True, they were still *doing* the right thing but it had become an end in itself rather than an expression of love for their Lord.

Most commentators prefer to have the reference apply either exclusively or in addition to a diminishment of love in the relationship of Ephesian Christians with each other. Martin Kiddle argues that in doing this, they had allowed prevalent antisocial tendencies to grip and undermine their own discipleship.

They had lapsed into a fault which the ordinary life of a city of Asia was subject to an extraordinary degree. Ephesus itself was a city where trade guilds, clubs, and the home all suffered from the diseases of fractitiousness and rancour. The pagan philosopher Apollonius of Tyana, speaking to the citizens of Ephesus not long after John addressed the Christian Church, found the same need to stress the importance of a spirit of amity.[43]

If John's reference is to the relationship of the Christians to each other—and even to outsiders—this makes a great deal of sense. Our external environment shapes our attitudes and expectations; when that environment is destructive and dominated by anti-Christian forces it is extremely easy for Christians to live down to their environment. This is true even, as in Ephesus, when perceptive pagans recognized that the social atmosphere was destructive of virtue and goodwill.

### The Threat to Be Moved Out of Their Place Unless They Repent

Jesus warns the Christians in Revelation 2:5, "Remember therefore from where you have fallen; repent and do the first works, or else I will come to you quickly and remove your lampstand from its place—unless you repent."

David Chilton sees here two possible historical and local allusions that would easily have come to the mind of the first-century Ephesians.[44] Ephesus itself was continually threatened with being "removed...from its place." The ongoing nightmare of the city was that the River Cayster would so fill the harbor with silt that it would ultimately be unusable. This would transform the prosperous seaport into an impoverished inland city separated from the sea by a marsh.

Furthermore, just as the Christians had manifested "works," "labor," and "patience" in spiritual matters (2:2), their city had manifested similar virtues in keeping the harbor usable. Yet by the middle of the first century the silt problem had become a major problem once again. In a secular sense the community might be said to need to "repent and do the first works" (2:5), that is, act as vigorously against this problem of silting as they had done in the past, instead of allowing it to continue on and on until it became disastrous.

*The Tree of Life*

In encouraging the Ephesians to right their difficulties John reassured them, "To him who overcomes I will give to eat from the tree of life, which is in the midst of the Paradise of God" (2:7). The reference to the "tree of life" would have struck a responsive chord in those rooted in the Bible, among those versed in non-biblical Jewish literature, and among pagans as well.

Writing for an audience well grounded in the Old Testament—for any other of Revelation's heavy reliance on Old Testament imagery would have been of little value—we can safely assume that the primary root of any parallel phrase found in both the Bible and the contemporary world lay in the biblical text itself. The idea of the tree of life—or of *a* tree of life—represents an allusion found a number of times in the scriptures prior to John.

The primary allusion is certainly to the initial use of the term in the Garden of Eden. There "the tree of life" is defined as one whose fruit would enable one to "live forever" (Gn 3:22). Since God did not prohibit partaking of this tree (unlike the tree of the knowledge of good and evil), the idea is surely that by *continuing* to partake one could "live forever." If a one-time partaking were sufficient to gain eternal life, then it was a mere accident of chronology that they had not already eaten of the tree prior to their sin, thereby protecting themselves against the death that was the ultimate punishment for their transgression.

In the book of Proverbs, the usage shifts from living eternally to living abundantly; the point shifts from chronological life to qualitative life. We read of wisdom, "She is a tree of life to those who take hold of her, and happy are all who retain her" (3:18). The lifestyle of the follower of God is also pictured in such terms, "The fruit of the righteous is a tree of life, and he who wins souls is wise" (11:30). A tree of life carries with it the ideas of happiness and joy as well; "Hope deferred makes the heart sick, but when the desire comes, it is a tree of life" (13:12). It has the connotation of constructive beneficialness in Proverbs 15:4, "A wholesome tongue is a tree of life, but perverseness in it breaks the spirit."

In noncanonical Jewish speculative literature we also find the tree of life presented as the reward for the righteous. In the *Testament of Dan* (5:11–13) the earthly triumph of God is pictured, in which "Eden" will exist in the form of a purified new Jerusalem reigned over by the Messiah.

> And he will set free the prisoners of Beliar (the souls, that is, of the saints); and he will turn the hearts of the disobedient back to the Lord again; and he will give to them that call on him eternal peace. And *the saints will rest in Eden,* and in the new Jerusalem will the righteous rejoice, and it will be to the glory of God for ever. And no longer will Jerusalem lie in ruins, nor Israel endure captivity; for the Lord will be in the midst of it, living together with men, and the Holy One of Israel will reign over them in humility and poverty. And he who has faith in him will reign in truth in the heavens.[45]

We would naturally expect in such an Eden the tree of life found in the biblical prototype of the concept. In the triumph pictured in the *Testament of Levi* (18:9–14), the Divine triumph is explicitly pictured in terms of such access.

> And in his priesthood the Gentiles will increase in knowledge on the earth, and be enlightened through the grace of the Lord; but Israel will be weakened through ignorance, and plunged into darkness by sorrow. In his priesthood will all sin come to an end, and the lawless cease to do evil; and the righteous will rest in him. And he will open the gates of Paradise, and destroy the power of the sword that threatened Adam. *And he will give the saints the right to eat from the tree of life,* and the spirit of holiness will be on them. And Beliar will be bound by him, and he will give power to his children to tread the evil spirits underfoot. And the Lord will rejoice over his children, and take pleasure in those who are dear to him for ever. Then will Abraham and Isaac and Jacob shout in exultation, and I will be glad, and all the saints will be clothed with joy.

In 1 Enoch 24:3–25:7 there is a lengthy description of the triumphant human race once again being granted access to the tree of life once freely available to Adam and Eve.

And the seventh mountain was in the midst of these, and it excelled them in height, resembling the seat of a throne: and fragrant trees encircled the throne. And amongst them was a tree such as I had never yet smelt, neither was any amongst them nor were others like it: it had a fragrance beyond all fragrance, and its leaves and blooms and wood wither not for ever: and its fruit is beautiful, and its fruit resembles the date of a palm.

Then I said: "How beautiful is this tree and fragrant, and its leaves are fair, and its blooms very delightful in appearance." Then answered Michael, one of the holy and honoured angels who was with me, and was their leader. And he said unto me: "Enoch, why dost thou ask me regarding the fragrance of the tree, and why dost thou wish to learn the truth?"

Then I answered him saying: "I wish to know about everything but especially about this tree." And he answered saying: "This high mountain which thou hast seen, whose summit is the throne of God, is His throne, where the Holy Great One, the Lord of Glory, the Eternal King, will sit, when He shall come down to visit the earth with goodness. And as for this fragrant tree no mortal is permitted to touch it *till the great judgment,* when He shall take vengeance on all and bring (everything) to its consummation forever. It shall then *be given to the righteous and holy.* Its fruit shall be for *food to the elect:* it shall be transplanted to the holy place, to the temple of the Lord, the Eternal King.

> Then shall they rejoice with joy and be glad.
> And into the holy place shall they enter;
> And its fragrance shall be in their bones,
> And they shall live a long life on earth,
> Such as the fathers lived:
> And in their days shall no sorrow or plague
> Or torment or calamity touch them."

Then blessed I the God of Glory, the Eternal King, who hath prepared such things for the righteous, and hath created them and promised to give to them.[46]

Although we must rank the biblical precedent as dominant in determining John's use of the tree of life imagery, that in no way means that this is the only reason he utilized it. Although John is certainly not interested in promoting the pagan rivals to Christianity, the tree of life allusion was one that would conjure up positive images in their minds, independent of any biblical associations. Those living in a pagan society—whether of Jewish or Gentile ancestry—would be aware of these parallels no matter how hostile they were to polytheism.

William M. Ramsay sums up the importance of the tree symbolism to Asian Greek and the underlying Greek heritage in general:

> The tree was as significant a symbol of life-giving Divine power to the Asian Greeks as to the Jews, though in a different way. Trees had been worshipped as the home of the Divine nature and power from time immemorial, and were still so worshipped, in Asia Minor as in the ancient world generally. On some sacred tree the prosperity and safety of a family or tribe or city was often believed to depend. When the sacred olive-tree on the Acropolis of Athens put forth a new shoot after the city had been burned by the Persians, the people knew that the safety of the State was assured.
>
> The belief was widely entertained that the life of a man was connected with some tree, and returned into that tree when he died. The tree which grew on a grave was often thought to be penetrated with the spirit and life of the buried man; and an old Athenian law punished with death any one that had cut a holm-oak growing in a sepulchral ground.[47]

Sacred trees and groves were common to ancient cults in Asia Minor,[48] not only in unorganized settings but at certain cult sanctuaries and temples as well.[49] These places continued to be resorted to at least into the sixth century A.D.[50]

Artemis and tree worship were closely connected in Greece,[51] and the goddess had many sacred groves throughout the Greek world.[52] Tree imagery was intimately related to Artemis in Asia as well. The original Artemis shrine in Ephesus appears to have been in the open air beneath an oak tree. In following centuries, the shrine remained at the same spot, and it appears that the original connection between Artemis and the sacred tree beneath which she was worshiped was never forgotten.[53]

One indication of this is the fact that in Ephesus there was a wood dedicated to Artemis[54] in which her priests offered their sacrifices and enjoyed their feasts in her honor.[55] Another indication is that the date palm was sacred to Artemis[56] and occurs commonly on the coinage of the city from about 400 B.C. to around A.D. 250. It is used as a symbol of the city, in connection with Artemis, and in other mythological settings as well.[57]

# 4

# Rival Smyrna

## The City Itself

Describing his 1864 visit, Henry J. van Lennep spoke of the damage the passage of time had done to the city's greatest visible landmark:

> After a ride of an hour and a quarter we reached the ruins of Sardis, mostly situated on the left of the road. The citadel, rendered so famous by the history of ages preceding the Roman conquest, was built upon a high and steep hill; earthquakes, and the action of the weather upon the soil, which contain no rocks, have gradually torn it down; only a small piece of wall yet stands erect upon the edge of the precipice to tell of its former power, and even that may suddenly disappear.[1]

The ruins of the stadium and the theater and once-important buildings were still visible.[2] In spite of the decay of the physical remnants of the community, the location remained visually impressive. Just a few decades after van Lennep, another visitor to the site wrote that "as seen from the bay in front, [it] is still one of the loveliest sights in the Levant."[3] Indeed, the beauty of the city itself was one of the proverbial claims of the city in the first centuries A.D.[4]

The satirist Lucian (middle second century A.D.) indicates that the city was renowned both for its physical beauty and the beauty of its women. In one dialogue a speaker recognizes not only a particular woman's astounding beauty, but also deduces from it that she must be from Smyrna, "for when she passed, one of the spectators, looking at his neighbour, said, 'Such are Smyrna's beauties!' And it would not be surprising that the most beautiful of Ionic cities should produce the most beautiful woman. And it seemed to me that the speaker must have been a Smyrnaian, so proud was he about her."[5]

Strabo the geographer speaks of the beauty of all sections of the city when he writes, "And now [Smyrna] is the fairest city on earth, having a fortified part on the hill, but its greater part in the plain beside the harbor and the temple of the Mother-Goddess, and the Gymnasium."[6]

Smyrnaian coinage of the period of both Alexander Severus (A.D. 222–35) and the even earlier Caracallus (A.D. 211–17) bears the proud claim, "First of Asia...in beauty and size."[7] A public inscription of the early-third-century period likewise asserts that Smyrna is "the First [City] of Asia in beauty and size, and the most brilliant,...and the ornament of Ionia."[8]

The city's climate reinforced the location's physical attractiveness, at least for a good part of each year. In the late 1800s, Major General Sir Charles Wilson described the climate as comfortable half of the year but given to extremes during the other half:

> The spring and autumn are temperate and delightful; the winter, though snow lies only on the mountain tops, is comparatively cold, and a damp, chilly wind that springs up suddenly, blows down from the mountains; the summer heat is intense, the shade temperature being frequently 100 degrees F in the day, and 92 degrees at night, but it is tempered by a sea breeze, the Imbat, which blows nearly every day throughout the summer months.[9]

Although the sea breezes could dilute the intensity of the worst heat, nothing could remove the horror when an earthquake hit the city—a danger throughout the region. A major quake inflicted serious damage to the city during the reign of Claudius (A.D. 41–54).[10] An even worse catastrophe occurred late in the following century: in one three-year period one massive quake was followed by several additional ones. The famous orator Aelius Aristides moved Emperor Marcus Aurelius to tears by his vivid description of how the "city had been blotted out by earthquakes and chasms that opened in the ground."[11] So moved was the emperor that he generously assisted in the reconstruction of the city. So devastating had been the damage that Philostratus called the rebuilding program nothing less than the "[re]founding" of the city."[12]

The city was located about thirty-five travel miles north of Ephesus,[13] a two-day journey,[14] and sixty-eight miles south of Pergamon.[15] In the first and second centuries of the Christian Era it enjoyed a sizable population. Estimates cluster around the figures of 100,000,[16] 200,000,[17]—with some estimates going as high as 250,000[18] and even 400,000.[19] Any of these translate into the city being a major population center for the province.

In favor of a larger rather than smaller population estimate is the repeated claim of the city's coinage that it was "first" in Asia both in size and beauty. Even assuming considerable exaggeration, this would still argue for the city being among the most populous cities of the province, since any more blatant misrepresentation would have run the danger of making it a laughing-stock, with attendant humiliation of civic pride—as close to a "mortal sin" as possible in civic affairs of the province. Outsiders recognized it as one of the two cities of the province that made no efforts to limit its growth or expansion.[20]

Like all ancient cities, regional agricultural products flowed into the town and, when their quality was unusually good, became export items for the sea trade. The Roman agricultural author Varro cites the Smyrna region as providing an excellent example of high productivity due to unusually fertile soil: "There are many trees which bear two crops a year, such as the vine on the coast near Smyrna, and the apple in the district of Consentia."[21] Philadelphia, Sardis, Smyrna, and Ephesus were all recognized as major wine producers. The vintage of the Ephesus region was considered the most inferior of the four and that of Smyrna as being not only good but outstanding.[22]

The visitor to the city was bound to pay special attention to several of the physical and natural structures central to the city's social and economic functioning. At the heart of the list goes the seaport. Pliny refers to the ongoing battle for economic and social preeminence between Smyrna and "Ephesus, the other great luminary of Asia"[23]—a competition our chapter title refers to. The major trade route that wound its way eastward and inland provided it with such an abundance of exports[24] that it made the city the main rival of Ephesus in its sea trade. It did not finally achieve dominance until after the early centuries A.D. with which we are primarily concerned.[25]

Unlike Ephesus's harbor—which ultimately became unusable due to silting—Smryna's facilities were merely compromised rather than destroyed. Smyrna was blessed with two harbors. The smaller one was nearest the city; it was nearly enclosed and ultimately became unusable due to silting. This loss did not hinder the use of the larger, outer harbor, and thus trade continued[26] even into the twentieth century. Writing in 1871, Ellen Clare Miller could still call Smyrna "the great port of Asia Minor."[27] Thirty-two years later another traveler to the region referred to its "fine harbor," which continued to provide anchorage for shipping.[28] Perhaps the ultimate indignity for Ephesus was that until the twentieth century, most visitors to Ephesus had to reach there by the port of her old rival, Smyrna.[29]

Several other important "secular" sites within Smyrna deserve attention. Overlooking the Gulf if Izmir, the theater was located on the northwest hillside of Mount Pago and could accommodate some twenty thousand onlookers.[30] After the serious quake during the reign of Claudius and the even worse ones in A.D. 178–80, the theater was among the civic buildings requiring major rebuilding.[31] The walls survived until the 1630s, when they were salvaged by local residents for other construction projects.[32]

The city's stadium was located on the west of Mount Pago.[33] It was built, in part, on a curving substructure, which supported those seats that could not be accommodated on the hillside section of the facility.[34] By the 1800s most of the visible ruins had been removed and the remainder virtually destroyed in the latter part of the century. Writing in 1895, one seasoned local traveler recalled, "The substructures that existed a few years ago have been destroyed to make room for a Turkish house, and it is now only possible to distinguish the general plan."[35]

Not all sites known to have existed can be located. There were several race courses both in and near the city (according to literary sources), but their location and physical attributes are now unknown.[36]

No city exists without a government of some sort. What has survived of the government agora in Smyrna appears to owe its form to the reconstruction carried out after the mammoth quake of A.D. 178.[37] It includes statues of Demeter, Poseidon (Neptune), and Artemis.[38]

The residential areas spread between the harbor and the acropolis on Mount Pago to the south.[39] Aqueducts brought water to the city; parts of the system still survive.[40] Strabo praised the physical layout of the city, "The division into streets is exceptionally good, in straight lines as far as possible; and the streets are paved with stone." On only one point does he fault the city fathers: for not providing "underground drainage" when they paved the streets. Because of this oversight "filth covers the surface, and particularly during rains, when the cast-off filth is discharged upon the streets."[41] Based upon twentieth-century experience in that geographic area, heavy rains would have intensified this sewage pollution problem in low-lying areas next to the city.[42] The lack of adequate drainage would also have produced localized flooding in those areas.[43]

The first-century city had a long history, in which it took considerable pride. Although it would be appropriate to survey the history at this point, it would be somewhat redundant since certain of the apparent local allusions rely heavily on that heritage. Thus it would be better to present those matters in that context, in the following section.

## Historical and Social Allusions
### Text of the Epistle

"And to the angel of the church in Smyrna write, 'These things says the First and the Last, who was dead, and came to life: "I know your works, tribulation, and poverty (but you are rich); and I know the blasphemy of those who say they are Jews and are not, but are a synagogue of Satan. Do not fear any of those things which you are about to suffer. Indeed, the devil is about to throw some of you into prison, that you may be tested, and you will have tribulation ten days. Be faithful until death, and I will give you the crown of life. He who has an ear, let him hear what the Spirit says to the churches. He who overcomes shall not be hurt by the second death.'" (Rv 2:8–11)

Of five possible allusions (two of which are considered together) we find four that are either neutral or complimentary and only one which is hostile. The two considered together erect a parallel between Christ and the city's history and the remaining three concern parallels between the encouragement of Christians to be faithful (Rv 2:10) and attitudes and practices found in the Smyrna community.

*The Myth of Civic Permanence: Dead and Came to Life/First and Last*

Jesus describes himself as "the First and the Last, who was dead and came to life." The first reference presents Jesus' eternal existence (cf. Rv 1:8; 1:18); the second refers to his triumph over death through the resurrection. In a secular and civic sense this provides both a parallel and a contrast with Smyrna. Smyrna was a city that, in a very real sense, had perished and then been restored to life. This carries with it a contrast to Jesus' abiding nature (first and last) in that the city lacked true permanency. Charles C. Whiting observes, "This letter begins by holding up to the Christians in that city One who can claim greater antiquity and longer life. However old Smyrna was, it certainly was not the First and however long it lasts it certainly will not be the Last. This is what Christ claimed to be."[44]

Although there was at least one nearby settlement at a much earlier date, the site of Smyrna itself was colonized in the eleventh century B.C. by Greek settlers. The original city was located on the northern side of the bluff the town faced. That community was destroyed around 600 B.C. by King Alyattes of Lydia. Some writers speak in terms of the city no longer existing, while the more cautious speak in terms of the *practical* destruction of the city; that is, it was plunged downward from the status of being a major town to that of being occupied by a relative handful of villagers with, perhaps, additional remnants remaining in other nearby villages.[45] Ancient writers themselves spoke in terms indicating an absolute destruction, however much this may have marginally overstated the situation.[46] Any passing allusion by John would be far more likely to this commonly held assumption than to literal exactitude. Furthermore, since there is a profound difference between a mere village and a truly Greek city, Smyrna's city status had certainly died and been reborn.[47]

Responsible for this rebirth was no less a major historical personage than Alexander the Great, in 334 B.C. Pausanias tells the story this way (since he refers to the Smyrnaians accepting a new city site this itself would seem to imply that descendants of the original inhabitants continued to live in the vicinity):

> Alexander founded the modern city from a vision he had in his sleep: he was hunting on Mount Pagos, and on the way home from his hunt they say he came on the sanctuary of the Vengeances, with the spring in front of the sanctuary and a plane tree growing over the water. While he was asleep under the plane tree the Vengeances appeared to him and commanded him to build a city there and bring the people of Smyrna to it, turning them out of the earlier city. So the Smyrnaians sent ambassadors to ask at Klaros what their position was, and the god answered with this prophecy:
>
> > "You shall live three and four times happy
> > At Pagos, across the sacred Meles."
> > So they moved willingly.[48]

Some see in the reference to "first" and "last" a reference to the never-ending competition between Smyrna, Ephesus, and Pergamon for recognition as "first of Asia." William Barclay finds a quiet rebuke to their bountiful civic pride in this description of the Messiah: "In comparison with His glory all earthly distinctions are worthless."[49] "Beside the glory of Christ all human titles are of no importance and all human claims become ridiculous."[50]

There is an obvious difficulty is determining what "last" refers to in this context. If Jesus is *first* in the debated Pergamon-Ephesian-Symrnaian sense of "primary" or "of most importance," in what sense would Jesus be regarded as *last*? Monotheism in both its Christian and Judaic expressions was looked down upon as contemptible, in the "last" place vis-à-vis religious acceptability. Paradoxically, Jesus was actually "first" (in power, prestige, position, authority, and so on) while the world regarded his religion as being in "last" place in the religious universe. This seems to be a little too much reaching for parallelism, however. Any intended parallel would be more likely to refer to the more obvious similarities discussed in the earlier part of this section.

*Civic Moderation: Ten Days of Suffering*

The remainder of the apparent or possible local allusions come from the words of encouragement found in Revelation 2:10: "Do not fear any of those things which you are about to suffer. Indeed, the devil is about to throw some of you into prison, that you may be tested, and you will have tribulation ten days. Be faithful until death, and I will give you the crown of life."

Some attempt to make "ten days" a reference to the idea of completeness rather than to an actual period of time. Other references to "ten" (commandments, plagues, and so on) are introduced either in support of this attitude or simply as precedent for the numerical reference.[51] Others see in it a psychological predisposition—to round numbers[52] or as an allegedly natural symbol for being entire and complete.[53] Others see the importance as lying in the fact that boundaries or limitations have been set to how long it will last.[54]

Most simply take it to mean a short period of time.[55] Various Old Testament texts are introduced to prove this meaning,[56] but a careful reading can make one wonder whether the idea is really *intended* by those passages or whether it is *assumed* and the texts introduced because they *might* have such an idea in mind. When one turns to the Revelation text one is on stronger ground, for the very use of the term *days* (rather than *years* or a longer period of time) is most conducive to a shorter rather than a prolonged period of time being under consideration.[57] In spite of these indications of brevity, some dissenters believe it could refer to "a moderate space of time"[58] or even "a prolonged but not unlimited period."[59] Some even speak in terms of years.[60]

Gerhard A. Krodel stresses that imprisonment was never on a long-term basis under Roman law. Imprisonment was for one of three purposes: (1) to enforce obedience to the magistrate's decisions; (2) to detain until trial; or (3) to detain after trial under execution.[61] This is typical of those who mention the purpose of confinement in the first century: it was designed for a relatively short period of time rather than permanency. At this point we have a problem: John is writing Revelation 2:10 to encourage his readers to stand up to the stress and pressure certain of them will face. *But how can a short-term confinement be reassuring when that is all it would*

*be anyway–short term? Furthermore, if the confinement is almost
inevitably going to lead to a legal judgment against the Christian and
then, after a period of further confinement, to death, where are the words of
encouragement?* In light of John's intent and the fact that prisons
were designed to be mere waystations to governmental wrath, one
seems pressed to conclude that John's reference to prisons means
that the typical punishment for a Christian would be prison alone—
not execution. In keeping with this is the fact that by the time of
Polycarp there were only twelve martyrs in the city, and that modest
number was reached by including the victims from Philadelphia.

What we see then in the short duration of imprisonment—and
apparent imprisonment alone—is a reference to Smyrna as a moderate, self-contained city, capable of accepting unofficial synagogue
or pagan cultic oppression but generally hesitant to back such
actions with official civic endorsement. This is not only in keeping
with the imprisonment-only scenario of John but also with the later
reputation of the community. Writing around A.D. 230, Philostratus
wrote that the city had a well-established reputation for caution in
its public policies and decisions. Smyrna, he wrote, "more than any
other city sacrificed to the sophistic Muses." The youth of the surrounding region, Greece, and even Egypt, flocked there for an education in the best "Greek rhetoric." Philostratus proceeds from the
presence of this large foreign contingent to argue the beneficial
results on the community: "A city which is much frequented by foreigners, especially if they are lovers of learning, will be prudent and
moderate in its councils, and prudent and moderate in its citizen
assemblies because it will be on guard against being convicted of
wrongdoing in the presence of so many eminent persons."[62]

## Civic Loyalty: Faithful to Death

The kind of absolute loyalty that is expected of Christians in
Revelation 2:10 ("faithful until death") represented the kind of
steadfast support and allegiance Smyrna had demonstrated in
regard to Rome. Cicero describes the community as "our most
trusty and long-standing allies,"[63] a statement that has also been
translated "our most faithful and most ancient ally."[64]

As J. Massyngberde Ford well sums up, Smyrna "is bidden
to show the same loyalty on the spiritual level as she did on the

political."[65] And, as Ramsay well expresses it, "It cannot be a mere accident that the only one of the Seven Churches, with which the epithet faithful is associated in the letters, is the Church of that city which had established its historic claim to the epithet in *three centuries of loyalty,* the city which had been faithful to Rome in danger and difficulty."[66]

Whether Rome's enemy was Mithridates, Carthage, or the Seleucid kings, Smyrna stood at her side. Even when the tide seemed to turn against Rome, Smyrna refused to trim its sails to the changing political and military winds. The most vivid example is found in the early first century B.C., when Mithridates inflicted a major defeat on the Roman army. Not only was the army licking the severe wounds of its defeat, its soldiers were literally in need of whatever could be provided them—even clothes. When a Smyrnaian assembly heard of the disaster and the affliction, its members literally shipped off their own clothing to meet the need.[67] When Rome was in political control of the region, she remembered the sacrifice and the abiding loyalty: Smyrna was granted the status of free [self-governing] city.[68] Christ appeals to the Smyrnaian Christians to be as steadfast in loyalty—in bad times as well as good—as their community had been in the dangerous days before Rome's triumph was assured.[69]

*Secular and Religious Recognition: The Crown of Life*

John assured his readers that if they were "faithful until death" that Christ "will give you the crown of life" (Rv 2:10) Students of the biblical text have interpreted this as parallel to "the festive crown of victory" in athletic contests[70] or a "royal crown of triumph."[71] Both fit in well with the actual biblical texts,[72] and in either case the usage fits well with contemporary ancient practice. However, there are additional "crowns" in the pagan experience that could easily have come to the mind of the original readers and one—because of its special Smyrnaian usage—would have been inescapable.

## THE CROWN OF ATHLETIC VICTORY

Although regal crowns were not numerous, athletic ones were common.[73] Smyrna's athletic games were known throughout the province.[74] The games were liberally financed by the municipal government.[75] The imperial cult also conducted periodic games there in honor of the emperors.[76] It has been reasonably speculated that these imperial games represented potentially serious "flash points" for the local Christians.[77] After all, it was at this point that polytheism most intimately interlocked with imperial power, a combination that could be dangerous when combined against the believing community. Winners at the imperial and other games were given a garland to wear as a crown of recognition for their success.[78] Although a natural allusion for John, one wonders whether it is sufficiently unique to Smyrna for this to have been in the author's mind: so many communities held periodic games that some additional comment would seem to be required for this to be a specific local reference.

### ARTISTIC ALLUSION TO HOW DIVINE APPROVAL WAS PICTURED

One writer who prefers an athletic basis for John's crown reference suggests as an alternative that John alludes to the ancient method of showing "a crown of light surrounding the head" to indicate "divine beings" or "blessed mortals."[79] Such "halos" were retained in post-pagan art with a similar intent. The more generalized an allusion one seeks, the more this is appealing; the more one expects a Smyrnan-specific allusion, the less likely it seems.

### PAGAN CULTIC RITES CONNECTED WITH WEARING A CROWN

The explicitly religious use of crowns—in actual practice, commonly a garland of flowers—was widespread in the ancient world, as well as their use when the "religiousification" of a "secular" occasion was sought. As Ramsay, an authoritative student of ancient customs, has written:

> Crowns were worn chiefly in the worship of the gods. The worshipper was expected to have on his head a garland of the flowers or foliage sacred to the god whose rites he was performing. The guests at an entertainment were often regarded as worshippers of Bacchus and wore the sacred

ivy: frequently, also, the entertainment was a feast connect-
ing with the ritual of some other deity, and the crown varied
accordingly.[80]

Cybele's special stature in Smyrna makes the allusion especially appropriate, because such garlands were worn in her cultic
rites.[81] Pagan priests were known to wear honorary crowns in connection with certain of their rites, such as sacrifice.[82] In the Mysteries of Dionysus the presiding priest allegedly wore a crown.[83]
Indeed, a symbolic crowning was part of the initiation into at least
some cults.[84] If a cultic allusion is intended by John, it would seem
to be broader than a Smyrnaian-specific one. The point would be
that while the polytheistic sects could offer only a crown of flowers, Jesus could offer a crown of life. They could only offer a crown
in this life; Jesus offered a very real crown in the next.

### A POLITICAL-SOCIAL HONOR INVOLVING PUBLIC SERVICE

The position of "crown-wearer" was unique to the province
of Asia and certain nearby islands. To hold the position required
wealth, since it involved performing both explicitly municipal
duties and priestly sacrifices on behalf of the community.
Although only one crown-wearer served at a time, one could be
reappointed or occupy other important civic positions simultaneously.[85] The position "was open to women: a certain Koskonia Myr-
tos held it in Smyrna in 83 A.D.; another woman, Korre, at some
time in the Roman period. Herakleides, the eminent sophist, was
Crown-Wearer about the end of the second century A.D."[86]

### A POLITICAL-SOCIAL HONOR BESTOWED POSTHUMOUSLY BY THE CITY

Several inscriptions have survived at Smyrna with the
names of individuals being honored by the community.
Although done in other cities as well, the practice appears to
have been more common in Smyrna than in many other places. It
appears that this public avowal was bestowed upon an individual's death, which would tie in well with the crown of life the
Christian would receive upon his or her death.[87] The community
could only give an *engraved* crown of honor, while the Lord could

give the crown of *life,* of survival of death and post-earthly reward.

### A GEOGRAPHIC ALLUSION TO
### THE "CROWN" OF BUILDINGS IN SMYRNA

The remaining two suggestions offer more explicit tie-ins with the city of Smyrna itself. The acropolis at the top of the city's hill contained expensive and impressive public buildings. They constituted a "crown" for the city in keeping with its pride and self-esteem.[88] This constitutes the most explicit tie-in between John's allusion and the city of Smyrna itself. If, however, John intends to invoke *multiple* allusions—specific and nonspecific—it is quite credible that he has more than one of these in mind, with the less geographically specific ones intended for those located in more distant towns and less knowledgeable about local peculiarities.

# 5

# Monotheism and Polytheism
# in Smyrna

## The Synagogue

The resident Jewish community received a major infusion after the fall of Jerusalem, as various Jews sought a safe haven outside their homeland.[1] The synagogue of the city is of special interest to us for two reasons: (1) the possibility that women may have played leadership roles far greater than those generally assigned to them in first- and second-century Judaism; and (2) the real meaning of the pungent denunciation of the "synagogue of Satan" (Rv 2:9) that existed in the city.

A marble plaque probably dating to the second century A.D. provides a fascinating reference to a prominent woman in the local Jewish community:

> Rufina, a Jewess, head of the synagogue, built this tomb for her freed slaves and the slaves raised in her house. No one else has the right to bury anyone [here]. If someone should dare to do, he or she will pay 1500 denars to the sacred treasury and 1000 denars to the Jewish people. A copy of this inscription has been placed in the [public] archives.[2]

"Head of the synagogue" renders into English the Greek *archisynagogos*. Taken literally, this would indicate the formal recognition of Rufina as leader of the Smyrnaian synagogue. Since this violates the norm for synagogues in the ancient world, several approaches have been taken to move this description into conformity with the dominant practice.

For example, it could have been a courtesy title, bestowed either because of her marriage to the leader of the synagogue or because of the respect others had for her. In other words, it could refer to a de facto rather than a de jure status. Bernadette Brooten reasons that "her Roman name and her wealth could indicate that she was a member of a leading family of Smyrna."[3] If this is correct, a general yielding to her suggestions and requests would have been common, if not automatic. She would have had to work *not* to be accepted as a dominant creator of the synagogue consensus. Of course, there is a thin line between de facto and de jure, unofficial and official leadership; superiority of prestige can easily lead to superiority of position—as apparently occurred in the evolution of bishops out of the rank of presbyters. Another possibility is that the title refers to her being recognized as the chief *woman* rather than the chief *person* within the synagogue.[4]

Even assuming that Rufina's description represents an official title does not resolve the question of the *propriety* of her holding such a leadership position, either from the New Testament or Old Testament standpoint. Indeed, one could reasonably conjecture that such a blatant departure from what was generally considered to be the teaching of the Torah and prophets might represent a *partial* explanation for the severity of the local condemnation of the Jewish community as a "synagogue of Satan." It was bad enough that they rejected Jesus; here they were adding insult to injury by flying in the face of a "universal" Jewish practice.

The question of female synagogue leadership ties in with the broader question of the public role of women in civic affairs in Asia. Just as Rufina is given a title that, in a male, would normally prove an active leadership role in the synagogue, there are numerous inscriptions giving "secular" or "non-Jewish" leadership titles to women as well. These cases also raise the question of to what degree these are honorary designations and to what degree they represent actual, personal position-holding and authority.[5]

Regardless of the interpretation we put on the data, there is clearly a regional trait of *some kind* involved, because "the prominence of women is not uniform across the whole of Asia Minor. The phenomenon is most noticeable on the West Coast, especially in Caria and Ionia, less noticeable on the Southern Coast, very infrequent in the north of Asia Minor (Bithynia and Pontus) and seems not to occur at all in the regions of Galatia and Cappadocia."[6]

Inscriptional evidence provides limited additional insight into the members of the Smyrna synagogue besides Rufina:

There are only two other Jewish inscriptions from Smyrna which mention office holders. CII 739 is a donative inscription made by one Irenopoios, who was an elder and father of the tribe, and the son of an elder; CII 740 is a further donative inscription, probably from the same synagogue. Another inscription not included in the CII names a Roman citizen, Lucius Lollius Justus, who was a scribe of the Jewish community in Smyrna. Further inscriptions from Smyrna include a magical amulet, and a 45–line inscription from the time of Hadrian (117–138), listing donations to the city, one line of which refers to former Judeans who had donated 10,000 drachmas.

Of the titles in these inscriptions, elder and scribe are fairly common elsewhere, and father of the tribe seems to be analogous to father of the synagogue. That both father and son bear the title elder in CII 739 could mean that in Smyrna titles could pass from father to son, whether automatically or not is another question.[7]

Four basic answers have been given to the question of the identification of the "synagogue of Satan" in Smyrna (Rv 2:9) and the "synagogue of Satan" in Philadelphia (Rv 3:9).

## 1. SOME TAKE IT MORE OR LESS LITERALLY

The most literal interpretation is that these individuals were actually and consciously worshiping Satan. Although, through the ages there have been scattered groups who have actually done so, this represents such a fundamental rejection of everything "Jewish" that one would expect something a shade more restrained, something that participants could at least rationalize away with a bit less embarrassment.

Just a step removed from this first view is the opinion that they were not worshiping Satan personally but were members of a hybrid Jewish-pagan cult.[8] This would fit in well with John's usage. If a place of idolatrous worship could be rebuked as "Satan's throne" (Rv 2:13), a Jewish group that combined superficial Judaism with polytheistic worship would surely be worthy of the description "synagogue of Satan."[9] Their internal, theoretical rationale for the worship of such opposites would likely be something along the line "that different peoples really worshiped the same god under different names, and that names and cults could therefore be united."[10]

Yet we have a very serious problem: certainly in the second century we know that the opposition of *orthodox* Judaism resulted in the execution of Polycarp, and we know nothing of any persecution stirred up by a Judeo-pagan sect. Unless we are to hypothesize that it had disappeared by this later date, this seems odd indeed. Furthermore, John's rebuke is aimed at those "who say they are Jews and are not" (Rv 2:9; cf. the identical expression in 3:9), which would most naturally fit the Jewish community at large rather than some (presumably small) fringe movement. In addition, if the postulated sect was hostile to Christianity, how could it have avoided vigorously attacking mainstream, orthodox/synagogue Judaism in the city as well? This would make inexplicable the great popularity of the city as a new home among Jews fleeing Palestine and the ravages that accompanied the destruction of the Temple in A.D. 70.

### 2. ANOTHER POSSIBILITY IS THAT THE SYNAGOGUE WAS SATANIC IN EITHER DESTRUCTIVE CONDUCT OR UNINTENDED DESTRUCTIVE RESULT

Assuming Christianity to be the divinely prophesied and intended replacement for Judaism, to oppose Christianity and to persecute it would be nothing short of furthering the destructive goals of Satan. Since the antagonism at Smyrna appears to have been especially intense, there would be a natural tendency to make explicit an accusation that might not ordinarily have been expressed in so blunt a form. If, in their efforts to crush Christianity, they had acted in a particularly unscrupulous manner, by casting aside even elementary restraint in their effort to crush the movement, the condemnation would have been even more deeply felt—and resented.

Presumably sentiments along this line underlie the remarks of those who interpret the phrase in light of the pain and suffering the church was undergoing. For example, G. Campbell Morgan suggests that the poverty found among the Smyrnaian Christians (Rv 2:9) grew out off "libelous statements" from synagogue zealots "as to their [Christian] character, their purpose, and their modes of life. The stories told had aroused the pagan population, and in all likelihood, there had followed the confiscation of their goods which had reduced them to the point of actual want."[11] Whether through discreetly encouraged mob action or through the instigation of legal action against a despised quasi-legal/illegal sect makes little difference. When passions go deep enough and victory must be obtained at any cost, character assassination and libel is the order of the day. If this is seen all too often in controversies between Christians, why should it seem odd if synagogues in certain cities encouraged similar excess in their controversies with believers in Christ?[12] Of course their real goal was not the impoverishment of their enemies per se, but the crushing of their movement.[13]

Others see the designation arising not out of evil intent but evil result. The synagogue had inadvertently become an object of Satanic temptation to the Christians: The Jewish religion was legally protected while Christianity "was an illegal and proscribed religion." Weaker Christians solved the problem by signing onto the synagogue roll while privately worshiping as Christians, just as centuries later certain Spanish Jews joined the Catholic Church while continuing to carry out their Jewish practices in private.[14] This assumes that Christianity at this stage was formally proscribed. It also overlooks the intense anti-Christian activism in Smyrna, which virtually requires a consciously intended rebuke of the synagogue's policies rather than a criticism of its unintended results.

3. OTHERS TAKE IT AS A CHRISTOCENTRIC DESCRIPTION OF THE JEWS
AT LARGE (AT LEAST IN SMYRNA) FOR THEIR REFUSAL TO ACCEPT
JESUS AS MESSIAH AND SON OF GOD

Paul had stressed that *true* Jewishness lay not in one's ancestry but in personal loyalty to God, "For he is not a Jew who is one outwardly, nor is that circumcision which is outward in the flesh; but he is a Jew who is one inwardly, and circumcision is that of the heart, in the spirit, and not in the letter; whose praise is not from men but from God" (Rom 2:28–29). In a similar vein, John the Baptist had vigorously rebuked those of his day who were confident that their ancestry alone guaranteed acceptability to God (Mt 3:9).

Such concepts built upon the foundation already laid by the Old Testament. With all its emphasis on the outward, it never ceased to plead for inward spirituality as well. It even used circumcision terminology to make the point, "Therefore circumcise the foreskin of your heart, and be stiff-necked no longer" ["...do not be stubborn any longer" *NRSV*] (Dt 10:16). To love God fully was the result of having a circumcised heart (Dt 30:6). In their rebellion Jeremiah rebuked the people as being "uncircumcised in the heart" (Jer 9:26). No wonder then that Paul could write of Christians, that "we are the circumcision who worship God in the Spirit, rejoice in Christ Jesus, and have no confidence in the flesh" (Phil 3:3).

Here, in the mini-epistle to Smyrna, John rebukes those "who say they are Jews and are not" and *immediately* shifts to a description of them as "a synagogue of Satan" (Rv 2:9). If John—as he clearly seems to be doing—is denying the status of *true* Jews to ethnic Jews, then his immediately following rejection of them as "a synagogue of Satan" would indicate that he is also denying that they are recognized by God as a true synagogue.

It is important to recognize that neither John nor the author of any other New Testament book provides such a blanket indictment of all first-century Jews upon all occasions. However much the clinging to Judaism after Christianity had come to be viewed as rejection of God's true purpose for humankind, the harshest rhetoric is reserved for only a few cases. This, in turn, argues that it was the *degree* of active hostility that produced the rebuke rather than a desire to be derogatory toward Jews in general—which would be transparently absurd since those utilizing such rhetoric in the New Testament are normally ethnic Jews themselves.

### 4. A FOURTH APPROACH MAKES THE TEXT REFER TO A BODY OF CHRISTIAN HERETICS

The reference has been applied to "rival Christian groups" in general[15] and to "false Judaizers," in particular, Christian heretics who would turn the church into a mere sect of Judaism.[16]

There is only one New Testament passage that might point in this direction. In James 2:1–4 we read that a rich person and a poor person might "come into your assembly" and—

improperly—be treated in very different ways. The word "assembly" renders "synagogue" and is the only application of the term to a meeting of Christians. Hence it would be a major departure from customary usage to apply the term to a group of unorthodox Christians.

Furthermore, the periodic opposition of synagogues in various cities is repeatedly referred to in the New Testament. If the synagogues in Smyrna and Philadelphia were especially pronounced in their animosity, labeling them "synagogue(s) of Satan" would be a natural result. There are enemies and there are enemies—and it is common to apply more vigorous denunciation to the more hostile ones. In the second century the hostility in Smyrna was so intense that it led to the martyrdom of Polycarp. It is also worthy to note that the "Martyrdom of Polycarp"[17] lumps together the victims of Smyrna and Philadelphia, as if these two communities were still objects of unusually intense Jewish opposition.

Adela Y. Collins reminds us that in the case of Smyrna the text proceeds directly from the "synagogue of Satan" (2:9) to the danger of persecution for their religious faith (2:10): "No matter how strong the tension between an allegedly Judaizing Christian group and the group loyal to John the prophet [the author of Revelation], it is unlikely that members of one Christian party would accuse members of another Christian subgroup before local or Roman authorities. The former would be too vulnerable themselves to take such a step."[18]

## The Church

We have no record in the New Testament of the founding of the congregation. It was quite likely the result of the great burst of proselytizing that occurred throughout Asia during Paul's two-year stay in Ephesus (Acts 19:10).

When it comes to the social and economic status of the membership, we know that they functioned under adverse circumstances. We read that they endured "blasphemy" (Rv 2:9). This can be read either in a strict religious sense of vigorous and vicious rejection of the claims of Jesus, or as character assassination aimed at the believers themselves.[19] As if this were not tragic enough they also endured "tribulation and poverty." Economic boycott or exclusion,[20] theft[21] through rioting[22] or other means, the destruction produced by vandalism—such fruit of the lying tongue can impoverish a despised minority community in any day and age.

Not to be overlooked is that most may well have been from the lower part of the economic totem pole to begin with: they may have been relatively rather than absolutely poor, even before their suffering.[23] A small amount of adversity would inflict immense harm on those whose margin of survival was minimal to begin with.

Had the legal process yet been utilized against the Smyrnaian Christians at the time John composed his mini-epistle? That they endured "tribulation" is directly stated by the text (2:9), but such could even more easily be inflicted by non-legal or extra-legal means rather than through the use or abuse of the judicial process. The explicitly legal persecution is presented as in the near future: "Do not fear any of those things which you are *about* to suffer. Indeed, the devil is about to throw some of you into prison, that you may be tested, and you will have tribulation ten days. Be faithful unto death, and I will give you the crown of life" (Rv 2:10).

Since individuals were kept in jail not as an end in itself but as detention prior to release or punishment (execution, banishment, and so on) it is easy to read the text as a euphemism for the severer consequences that normally followed imprisonment, especially when John adds the reference to being "faithful unto death."[24] Yet Acts indicates that an outraged community was quite capable of convincing the city magistrates to beat individuals and throw them in jail—with the magistrates, when emotions had cooled down, discreetly trying to let them out of prison without even an apology (Acts 16:20–23, 35–40). This was not how imprisonment was supposed to function, but it indicates what could happen when the hostility level was high. In deciding whether exposure to death was in John's mind, we can consider the significance of the *number* of Christians John anticipates will suffer.

If we accept the validity of using "*some* of you"—a translator's gloss used to complete the meaning of the Greek text when rendered into English, a gloss utilized by virtually all versions—then the persecution would affect a minority within the church, a limited number. We are in the unusual situation of being able to introduce second-century evidence that—assuming it is accurate—verifies our minimalist interpretation of the text. Although the rhetoric of the "Martyrdom of Polycarp" (especially chapters 2–4) easily leads one to think in terms of massive persecution and executions, yet when one reaches chapter 19 of the account one discovers that one is actually speaking of very few Christians being executed: "This, then, is the account of the blessed Polycarp, who, being the twelfth that was martyred in Smyrna (reckoning those also of Philadelphia), yet occupies a place of his own in the memory of all men."

Note that in the century since Christianity had arrived only twelve believers had died for their faith in Smyrna and Philadelphia combined. This raises some very serious problems with the traditional maximization of first-century persecution. Having gone through periods of repression by both Nero and Domitian, it still required this mid-second-century burst of oppression to raise the two-city total of martyrs to a modest twelve! Furthermore, it is commonly asserted that Revelation was written because of—or in anticipation of, or both—a massive persecution in Asia. Yet a minimum of fifty-plus years after it was written (much more, if we accept an early date for the composition of the book), we find the death toll finally reaching twelve—and that only because fatalities in two cities are combined and because the most recent deaths, contemporaneous with Polycarp, are also included. Where is the bloodbath that is taken for granted by the traditional reading of the Revelation text and early church history?[24]

Even so, martyrdom could and did occur—with all the pain, suffering, and humiliation of those so mistreated. A detailed examination of the mid-second-century fate of Bishop Polycarp of Smyrna provides an example of what could be involved when public sentiment swung so vehemently against Christians that public authorities felt compelled to act.

Certain local Christians were tortured and then burned to death (chap. 2).[26] Others who were condemned to death were first "stretched out upon beds full of spikes and subjected to various other kinds of torments" and then consigned to "the wild beasts" to be killed (chap. 2). Some had approached the danger foolishly, voluntarily surrendering themselves for trial and death.

Quintus of Phrygia is singled out as an object lesson of the folly of doing so: after convincing "some others" to join him, the specter of death was so terrifying that he apostatized (chap. 4).

Blood and backsliding were not sufficient for the crowd, and they screamed out for the body of the leader: "Away with the atheists; let Polycarp be sought out!" (chap. 3). At first Polycarp was unwilling to leave the city but was finally convinced of the prudence of doing so. He wandered from one rural hiding place to another until a tortured slave finally betrayed his hiding place. A mounted posse brought the slave with them in order to be sure they went to the right place. They caught up with the bishop on a Friday evening and found him in a small building from which he could have easily escaped. Convinced by an earlier "vision" (chap. 5) that he was ordained to face death, he voluntarily surrendered instead of fleeing. He even ordered a meal to be served to the arresting officers. After he was granted the privilege of an hour or two to pray before being hauled away, some began to feel guilty about the treatment of "so godly and venerable an old man" (chap. 7).

Presumably because of his age and his captors' guilty misgivings about treating him harshly, he was permitted to ride a donkey through the night hours back to Smyrna. He was met by an *irenarch* (roughly equivalent to chief of police) by the name of Herod. Herod summoned him to join him in his chariot and urged him to change his mind: "What harm is there in saying, Lord Caesar, and in sacrificing, with the other ceremonies observed on such occasions, and so make sure of safety?" At first Polycarp maintained his silence and then firmly refused to take the suggestion. The irenarch and his father (who was also with him) spoke bitter words against Polycarp and physically threw him out of the chariot, causing him to injure his leg. In spite of the pain the bishop "went eagerly forward with all haste, and was conducted to the stadium, where the tumult was so great, that there was no possibility of being heard" (chap. 8).

The resident proconsul respected Polycarp's age and pleaded with him to relent.[27] "Swear by the fortune of Caesar; repent, and say, Away with the atheists." Those last four words were acceptable to Polycarp, and he faced the crowds and cried out, "Away with the atheists" (although with a different meaning). Urged by the proconsul to say the rest, he firmly refused: "Eighty and six years have

I served Him, and He never did me injury: how then can I blaspheme my king and my Saviour?" (chap. 9).

The proconsul again urged him to "swear by the fortune of Caesar." Polycarp gently rebuked him for acting as if he did not know that "I am a Christian. And if you wish to learn what the doctrines of Christianity are, appoint me a day, and thou shalt hear them." With the angry and boisterous crowd present, the proconsul had little room for maneuver and postponement. "Persuade the people," he challenged. Polycarp responded that it would be proper to describe his faith in detail to the proconsul since government is ordained by God. "But as for these [in the crowd] I do not deem them worthy of receiving any account from me" (chap. 10).

The proconsul then threatened him with death by beasts or by fire—neither of which fazed the bishop (chap. 11). Rather than being beaten down by his confrontation with power, the longer it went, the more confidence was exhibited by the accused. Finally the astonished proconsul

> sent his herald to proclaim in the midst of the stadium thrice, "Polycarp has confessed that he is a Christian." This proclamation having been made by the herald, the whole multitude both of the heathen and Jews, who dwelt at Smyrna, cried out with uncontrollable fury, and in a loud voice, "This is the teacher of Asia, the father of the Christians, and the overthrower of our gods, he who has been teaching many not to sacrifice or to worship the gods."
>
> Speaking thus, they cried out, and besought Philip the Asiarch to let loose a lion upon Polycarp. But Philip answered that it was not lawful for him to do so, seeing the shows of wild beasts were already finished. Then it seemed good to them to cry out with one consent, that Polycarp should be burned alive. (chap. 12)

This they proceeded to do.[28] Though the most intemperate enemies of Smyrnaian Christianity had triumphed, their success was not sufficient to blot out the good reputation Polycarp had among both Christians and among "the heathen themselves" (chap. 19). If anything, the mob-inspired death of a respected senior citizen could only be looked upon, in quieter moments, as a sad commentary on social excesses.

Stepping back several decades to when Polycarp was a much younger man and in the earlier years of his bishopric, we can discover the attitudes and opinions of this much-respected leader of the Smyrnaian church through a letter he wrote to the Philippians.[29]

Although Polycarp occupied the position of bishop that did not mean, at this point in early history, that he exercised episcopal authority over other congregations or other bishops in different communities. When he writes to the Philippians he does so with the respect due from an interested and concerned outsider. Indeed, he did not insert himself into the local situation by some theoretical right to do so, but rather because they had requested his advice, "These things, brethren, I write to you concerning righteousness, not because I take anything upon myself, but because ye have invited me to do so" (chap. 3). The implication seems to be that, bishop or not, he lacked the authority to do so unless they requested assistance. Nor does he write upon his own independent authority but in conjunction with "the presbyters" (introduction).

Polycarp deals only briefly with various doctrinal errors, "For whoever does not confess that Jesus Christ has come in the flesh, is antichrist; and whosoever does not confess the testimony of the cross, is of the devil; and whoever perverts the oracles of the Lord to his own lusts, and says that there is neither a resurrection nor a judgment, he is the first-born of Satan" (chap. 7). He is especially concerned with practical, daily Christian living and remaining faithful (chaps. 4–5, 10, 12), even though certain believers were clearly suffering persecution (chap. 9).

Polycarp stresses the external standard of biblical revelation both by his repeated allusion to and quotation from it and by even clearer implicit and explicit assertions of its authority. "Knowing, then, that God is not mocked, we ought to walk worthy of His commandment and glory" (chap. 5). "Whoever perverts the oracles of the Lord" to satisfy his own desires and fancies is explicitly condemned as "the first-born of Satan" (chap. 7). He expected his readers to be knowledgeable in the scriptures as well. "For I trust that ye are well versed in the

Sacred Scriptures, and that nothing is hid from you; but to me this privilege is not yet granted" (chap. 12). This admission of a personal shortcoming is a bit odd in light of the many texts Polycarp alludes to in his epistle. Perhaps we should seek a psychological explanation for the incongruity: the paradox might be explained if Polycarp was near the beginning of his episcopate and still felt a certain insecurity because of the responsibility that went with his position.

The stress on the authority of scripture is personally applicable: Polycarp holds himself answerable to master the text though he had "not yet" accomplished that goal. This personal applicability indicates that he regarded the position of bishop as in subordination to the written word. He does not deal with what would happen if the apparent requirements of the sacred text conflicted with the doctrine, practice, or interpretation of the bishop. Perhaps at this stage it was considered inconceivable, though Paul's warning to the elders in Ephesus in Acts 20 put Asian Christians on notice that such a situation could indeed occur.

In the case of such a collision what would occur? Would institutional loyalty to one's superior require the membership to submit? Was the bishop's very continuation in office conditional upon his loyalty to that text as understood by those over whom he served? When there was disagreement, which had the final say: authority based in consensus, or authority based in the bishop-leader? Polycarp seems to recognize that there are situations when the church leader must yield to others who lack official position: "Be all of you subject to one another" (chap. 10), though he does not spell out the circumstances and means by which this laudable principle could be implemented. When personal authority of the bishop is considered, Polycarp only asserts it as being exercised in conjunction and agreement with other church leaders, "Wherefore, it is needful to abstain from these things [sinful attitudes and acts], being subject to the presbyters and deacons,[30] as unto God and Christ" (chap. 5). If he has a superior or overruling authority, he does not assert it.

Another valuable source for the Smyrnaian church in the early decades of the second century is the writings of Ignatius, who was on his way to Rome to be martyred. He wrote epistles to both the church at large and Polycarp in particular, and in both he reveals a picture of what Smyrnaian Christianity was like at that time.[31] Unlike Polycarp, Ignatius repeatedly emphasizes in his epistles the definitive authority of the bishop. Authority was implicitly shifted from the consensus of the church or even the presbytery to the personal position of the bishop. In doing so he made a critical contribution to the episcopacy as a self-perpetuating institution answerable to no external local authority. In the short term, this changed little or nothing. But with the passage of time this became the precedent for more explicit claims and the development of scriptural interpretations to justify them.[32]

Ignatius's epistle to Smyrna provides insight into what he believed to be the problems and needs of his time. In the epistle Ignatius is highly concerned with the doctrinal threat posed by those attempting to "dehumanize" Jesus at the point of the crucifixion. He stresses that Jesus suffered on the cross "that we might be saved." This was a very real, personal suffering. They were wrong who asserted "as certain unbelievers maintain, that He only *seemed* to suffer, as they themselves only seem to be [Christians]" (chap. 1). He introduces incidents from after the resurrection to establish his thesis (chap. 3). He urges the Smyrnaians to "pray to God for them, if by any means they may be brought to repentance, which, however, will be very difficult" (chap. 4). He argues that their attitude had resulted in barrenness so far as the humanitarian aspects of true Christianity: "They have no regard for love; no care for the widow, or the orphan, or the oppressed; of the bond, or of the free; of the hungry, or of the thirsty" (chap. 6).

The biblical writings are authoritative. He refers to those who refuse to be persuaded by "the law of Moses, nor the Gospel even to this day, nor the sufferings we have individually endured" (chap. 5). "It is fitting, therefore, that ye should keep aloof from such persons, and not to speak of them either in private or in public, but to give heed to the prophets, and above all, to the Gospel, in which the passion [of Christ] has been revealed to us and the resurrection has been fully proved" (chap. 7).

Ignatius concludes his lengthy rebuke of these Gnostic-type heretics with the plea, "But avoid all divisions, as the beginning of evils" (chap. 7). He then immediately stresses the essentialness of accepting the local bishop's authority (chaps. 8 and 9). The reasoning seems to be—as in the case of his epistle to Philadelphia—*avoid division by being faithful to the bishop.*

To present his case for the authority of the episcopate, Ignatius demands:

> Let no man do anything connected with the Church without the bishop. Let that be deemed a proper Eucharist, which is [administered] either by the bishop, or by one to whom he has entrusted it. Wherever the bishop shall appear, there let the multitude [of the people] also be; even as wherever Jesus Christ is, there is the Catholic Church. It is not lawful without the bishop either to baptize or to celebrate a love-feast; but whatever he shall approve of, that is also pleasing to God, so that everything that is one may be secure and valid. (chap. 8)

> It is well to reverence both God and the bishop. He who honours the bishop has been honoured by God: he who does anything without the knowledge of the bishop, does [in reality] serve the devil. (chap. 9)[33]

The fact that scripture commands believers to partake of the Eucharist (Lord's Supper) is inadequate to establish the propriety and legitimacy of one's observance; *that* requires the presence of the bishop. The fact that one is wholeheartedly and sincerely attempting to obey Jesus' command to be baptized is inadequate to establish the propriety and legitimacy of one's conversion act; *that,* once again, requires the presence of the bishop. The legitimacy of fundamental, biblically ordained actions requires an *additional* factor: the physical presence of the bishop. *The question of legitimacy is shifted from the scriptural basis of practice to the participation of the proper church official.* This elevation of leadership authority lays the groundwork for defining orthodoxy in terms of institutional loyalty and, by doing so, prepares the way for the dramatic expansion of a bishop's rights and privileges. This easily evolves into proving orthodoxy by institutional loyalty rather than by the power of argument based upon the scriptural text. A declining literacy rate in the following centuries reinforced this tendency.

Ignatius wrote to three of the seven churches John corre-

sponded with. In writing to both the Ephesians and the Philadel-
phians, Ignatius strongly asserts the rights of the local bishop,
but in neither case does he spell out his assertions as bluntly as in
writing to Smyrna. Unanswerable is the question of whether this
indicates that the supremacy of the bishop was more strongly
opposed in Smyrna—hence the forcefulness of the demand—or
whether it was most accepted in that city—thereby encouraging
Ignatius to assert the doctrine in the most forceful manner.

Likewise, one's judgment on this matter determines one's
conclusion as to which of the communities accepted the
bishop/presbytery distinction the most. Respect is certainly
expressed toward the Smyrnaian presbytery, "I salute your most
worthy bishop, and your very venerable presbytery, and your
deacons, my fellow-servants, and all of you individually, as well,
as generally, in the name of Jesus Christ" (chap. 12). Polycarp's
own disinclination to be acknowledged as superior to the presbytery—as exhibited in his epistle to the Philippians—would seem to
argue that Ignatius's forcefulness is in the hope of encouraging
Polycarp to claim and exercise actual superiority.

Yet even Ignatius is not willing to dismiss the authority of
the presbytery. He wishes the bishop to rule supreme but not
without others to occupy an inferior position of authority, "See
that ye all follow the bishop, even as Jesus Christ does the Father,
and the presbytery as ye would the apostles; and reverence the
deacons, as being the institution of God" (chap. 7).[34] The bishop
is not paralleled with the apostles (as one would expect if the
concept of apostolic succession were being advocated) but with
Christ. Yet this seems to imply an even *higher* expression of
authority: just as Jesus had unquestionable authority to say and
demand whatever he wished of the apostles, does Ignatius not
imply that the bishop occupies a comparable role of ultimate
authority? Even if we infer too much from Ignatius's parallelism,
there seems no way to avoid the conclusion that he viewed the
episcopacy as inherently and vastly superior to the presbytery.

In spite of such assertions even Ignatius is unwilling to permit too arbitrary an exercise of the bishop's power. "It is fitting,
O Polycarp, most blessed in God, to assemble a very solemn
council, and to elect one whom you greatly love, and know to be
a man of activity, who may be designated the messenger of God;

and to bestow on him this honour that he may go into Syria, and glorify our ever active love to the praise of Christ [before the Christians in Antioch]" (chap. 7). If Polycarp could unilaterally select the individual then a "council" was hardly needed in which others (the presbyters, certainly; perhaps the deacons; maybe even certain of the members at large) could have their say. Here we seem to be dealing with a *consensus* selection rather than an empty *ratifying* formality of a council that feels it has no other alternative. The authority of an Ignatius-style bishop is to be great, but there are still to be clear limits—of discretion if not of authority in an absolute sense.

### Polytheistic Movements Found in Smyrna

The temples found in the community were both numerous and physically impressive. The ancient Philostratus refers to "the marvelous temples in that city."[35] Apollo had his own shrine[36] and that in honor of Zeus was especially popular.[37] A relatively late addition to local deities—at least so far as having an official temple—was Asclepius and his healing cult. In the second century A.D. Pausanias spoke of how "the Asklepieion by the sea at Smyrna came from Pergamon in our own time.[38]

A substantial number of inscriptions have survived speaking of individuals named Dionysos, which would suggest that the god was extremely popular in the city.[39] Athletic competitions—games— were annually held in his honor.[40] In his local incarnation he was worshiped under the fuller name of Breseus Dionysos.[41] The addition of Breseus refers to the fact that *this* Dionysos was a bearded— that is, adult—version of the deity, in contrast to the youthful one more commonly worshiped in other areas.[42] Local coinage from A.D. 89–96 depicts the younger Dionysos hugging his mother with the older, bearded Dionysos standing behind them.[43]

As early as the seventh century B.C. a beautiful temple was erected in Athena's honor. Among its decorations were a number of lions' heads. These were selected not just as an artistic touch but because the lion was the traditional symbol of the city.[44]

In his own unique niche was Homer. Smyrna insisted that he had been born there. A pre-133 B.C. statue of him was erected at Pergamon with a poetic inscription poking fun at the claims of

Smyrna and others that claimed they were the birthplace of that great Greek poet.[45] Reverence transformed Homer both here and in other places into an object of worship, and in Smyrna a temple was dedicated to him as well.[46] Strabo calls it "the Homereion, a rectangular colonnade, containing a shrine of Homeros and an image. For these [Smyrnaians] lay an especially strong claim to the poet."[47] Smyrnaians asserted it time and time again in their various writings,[48] to the point that they clearly believed it themselves—whether they could convince others to honor their claims or not.

Although Pergamon was the most important site of emperor worship in the province, Smyrna can be fairly regarded as the second most significant site.[49] When emperor worship in Asia became officially acceptable to the Romans in 29 B.C., it was still linked with the worship of divine Roma itself. In A.D. 23 the towns of the province jointly urged that a second imperial temple be constructed. This would be dedicated not only to the emperor but also to his mother—and to the Roman Senate as well, thereby satisfying both power centers of the empire. Although Tiberius granted the request, the cities of Asia were unable to agree on which of them would provide the site for the new center of worship. After three years of this regional controversy, Asia passed the question to the Roman Senate to decide. Eleven Asian cities sent delegations to plead their respective cases.

Pergamon was eliminated from competition because it already had a temple. Miletus already had its major cult of Apollo, and Ephesus a renowned edifice honoring Artemis. It was felt that the prestige of these two cults was so great that they would tend to obscure the priority that Rome would naturally wish to be given to the imperial cult.

Smyrna and Sardis were considered the two most important alternatives remaining. Opinion shifted in favor of Smyrna because of its long and friendly relationship with Rome, both political and religious. Indeed, the locals had erected a temple in honor of Roma as far back as 195 B.C.[50] In the early second century A.D. Hadrian authorized the building of additional temples—in his honor, of course—in both Pergamon and Smyrna.[51]

## Cybele

The Cybele cult began in the Phrygia (in Asia Minor) and had spread to Greece by the beginning of the fourth century B.C., after which it spread both southward into Egypt and eastward into Italy.[52] As the third century B.C. ended, Rome was very uneasy due to the war pressures of the day and the uncertainty of Rome's military future.[53] Since Rome had already secured major successes in the ongoing Punic Wars, it has been suggested that additional factors must also have been involved in the decision to introduce the cult into the capital itself.[54] To accomplish this, a diplomatic mission traveled to Pergamon. King Attalus escorted them into Phrygia and, "putting into their hands a sacred stone, which the inhabitants said was the mother of the gods, bid them convey it to Rome."[55] When this was done in 204 B.C., the result was that Cybele was the first Eastern originated cult to be openly and officially accepted at Rome itself.[56]

Cybele (sometimes spelled Kybele) was known by a number of titles, such as Phyrygian Mother[57] (because of where the movement came into existence), Mother of the Mountain,[58] and Great Mother.[59] As one moved further west she was known as Meter and those who worshiped her in Latin called her Mater Magna.[60] In its Asian usage, the full name bestowed on the goddess typically incorporated that of the local community where she was worshiped.[61]

She was popular throughout Asia,[62] though her popularity, relatively speaking, began to decline with the reign of Augustus.[63] Ephesus was a major worship site for the goddess.[64] Her temple in Sardis was a branch of the one in Ephesus—at least according to an inscription found in the Ephesian temple.[65] There were sanctuaries for her in Pergamon and Smyrna as well.[66] In Smyrna she was honored as the special patron of the community[67] and her temple was called the Metroon.[68]

Two ancient tributes to the goddess provide an idea of the enthusiasm in her worship. In a hymn from the second or third century A.D. we find these words of praise:

> Rightly Thou art called the Mother of the Gods
> Because by Thy loyalty
> Thou hast conquered the power of the Gods.

Verily Thou art also the Mother
Of the peoples and the Gods,
Without Thee nothing can thrive nor be;
Thou art powerful, of the Gods Thou art
The queen and also the goddess.[69]

In A.D. 363 Emperor Julian penned these words of adulation for the goddess while enroute to battle the Persians:

> Who is then the Mother of the Gods? She is the source of the intellectual and creative gods, who, in their turn guide the visible gods: she is both the mother and the spouse of mighty Zeus; she came into being next to and together with the great creator; she is in control of every form of life, and the cause of all generation; she easily brings to perfection all things that are made; without pain she brings to birth, and with the father's aid creates all things that are; she is the motherless maiden, enthroned at the side of Zeus, and in very truth is the Mother of all the Gods. For having received into herself the causes of all the gods, both intelligible and supra-mundane, she became the source of the intellectual gods.[70]

This lavish praise is bestowed upon a deity of rather unpleasant heritage. Originally Cybele was a hermaphrodite. The gods removed the male element, turning her into a female deity. She was so moved to jealousy by her lover, Attis, that she drove him insane and he died after self-castration but was restored to life.[71] In light of the double castration that is central to the myth, it is not surprising that her priests were eunuchs. This was self-performed, often during the frantic ritual emotional outbursts that accompanied the annual festival in her honor.[72]

This festival began on March 15 of every year. The most detailed account that has survived comes from Rome, but is probably very similar to the rituals followed in Phrygia and the nearby regions.[73] The contemporary descriptive phrase for certain of these days has survived. On March 15, the "entry of the reed," there was a recalling of how Attis had been abandoned along the Gallus River. On the "entry of the tree" (March 22), a pine tree was cut and Attis's image attached. Both were then placed in the goddess's temple and a period of mourning for Attis's death began, which continued through the following day.

A pine tree was necessary because the legendary Attis had died beneath one. On March 24 self-flagellation was practiced during dancing. At the height of the emotional build-up, those opting for self-castration would perform the act. "The day of rejoicing" followed, during which the priest would assure all that Attis had survived. There would then be ceremonial anointing and entertainment for the group. March 26 was a "day of rest" and on March 27 the goddess's statue was taken to the river, washed, and then returned in joy to her edifice.[74]

Cybele, of course, was worshiped throughout the year. One characteristic of all pagan worship of the day was the use of instrumental music. The ancient writer Censorinus wrote of the rationale:

> If it [music] were not welcome to the immortal gods, theater spectacles would not have been instituted to conciliate the gods, the horn-player would not be used in all sacrifices in sacred temples, nor would triumphal parades be conducted with the horn or bass-horn player in honor of Mars, with the cithara for Apollo, with the pipes for the Muses.[75]

The preferred instrument(s) naturally varied from sect to sect. In the case of Cybele, her musicians "played pipes made with reeds like oboes or bagpipes," while a rattle was the instrument of choice for musicians of Isis and the cithra for those of Apollo.[76]

In addition groups called *ballatores* were attached to major Cybele centers to provide dance entertainment.[77] One did not, however, have to go to the temple to cross paths with such performances and performers. Corps of dancers often toured the countryside. They utilized ecstatic

> mad dancing that produced a great impression on observers and was also easily and often seen, since its practitioners wandered about in public in search of an audience. To the sound of rattles, tambours, and shrill pipes, with their heads tipped back or rolling wildly on their shoulders, accompanied by their own howls and yells, they whirled about and worked themselves into a state of frenzy. Then they held out the begging bowl.[78]

## Isis and Sarapis

Isis and Sarapis are commonly linked in modern discussions and deserve to be, yet in actual practice the ancient world found it quite feasible to *de*link them. Isis and Sarapis could be—and were—worshiped separately, for example, in separate temples within the same sacred complex. Yet in other situations—usually in smaller communities—the two cults shared the same site. An individual might be either a worshiper or cultic cleric of Isis, Sarapis, or both.[79] At least this is true of male clerics; women clerics appear to have been strictly functionaries of Isis.[80] Although both men and women were numerous in the service of the two gods, Isis found more favor with women than other goddesses.[81] The female proportion of the devotees of Isis seems to have varied considerably from place to place, however.[82] Even so, one ancient record presents Isis as proclaiming, "I am the one called the Deity by women."[83]

In the early cult Osiris played the role of Isis's husband. Beginning with Ptolemy I, there was a conscious effort to push Sarapis (also spelled Serapis) into his place. This was an intentional politico-religious policy of Ptolemy. He was convinced that a deity blending Hellenistic traits of Asclepius and Zeus with an Egyptian deity would work to unify the Greeks and Egyptians who resided within his kingdom.[84]

The choice of Isis was a wise one. She was the most popular Egyptian goddess[85] and her worship survived at least a half-century after the destruction of her most important temple and the closing of all her other temples by imperial order in A.D. 384.[86] Her pairing with a Hellenistic-type god created a polytheistic duo that was popular far beyond Egypt's own borders. This included, of course, Asia. Nearly all the major cities at or near that province's coast are known to have had cults devoted to either Sarapis, Isis, or both.[87] So well known was the cultic site at Ephesus that Lucius referred to Isis as "Thou who art worshiped in the shrine at Ephesus."[88] Records reveal that at the shrine in Smyrna, geese were considered sacred and wandered around the premises untouched by the citizenry.[89]

A number of factors interlocked to maximize the appeal of the Isis cult. It minimized social differences and the cleavages easily imposed by varying ethnic background.[90] In an age when sexual promiscuity was often taken for granted, devotees were expected to abstain from all such indulgences.[91] Not only did faithfulness guarantee a pleasing afterlife, it secured considerable blessings in the here and now.[92] From the standpoint of late twentieth century feminism, the goddess can even be viewed as something of a pioneer for women's rights. One often-quoted prayer to the goddess includes the confident assertion, "You have made the power of women equal to that of men."[93]

Isis was acknowledged to possess vast healing talents. Diodorus argued that the commonness of her divine healing had created a reputation for her throughout the then-known world.

> For standing above the sick in their sleep she gives aid for their diseases and works remarkable cures upon such as submit themselves to her; and many who have been despaired of by their physicians because of the difficult nature of their malady are restored to health by her, while numbers who have altogether lost the use of their eyes or of some other part of the body, whenever they turn for help to this goddess are restored to their previous condition.[94]

She also exercised her powers over hostile forces. She possessed the power to save from war, death in prison, and drowning at sea. Of the last we find one ancient writing, "When men may be destroyed and their ships wrecked and sunk, / All are saved if they pray that You be present to help."[95] Traditionally Fate itself held in thrall even the gods. As Herodotus wrote, "Fate cannot be escaped, not even by a god."[96] In the early second century A.D. Isis's claims increased to the point where she now had the power to change the decisions of Fate itself.[97]

Although playing an inferior role relative to Isis in the period of the Roman Empire, Sarapis still possessed great power. He was considered capable of healing both miraculously and by assisting natural means. Because of this healing role his shrines often had the equivalent of hospitals, as in the case of Asclepius.[98] By the third century A.D. his claimed power over Fate was as explicit as that of Isis.[99] When death finally came, one faced Sarapis as judge.[100]

An important social aspect of the movement can be seen in

the cultic meals of the adherents. Looking at what is known of them in the Sarapis element of the movement,[101] we discover that these collective meals were held, verbally at least, on behalf of the deity. The deity himself was assumed to be actually present. There would have been some type of modest sacrifice to the god and then the partaking of the joint meal.[102]

The seating capacity of a cultic meeting room was usually limited, typically accommodating ten guests or fewer.[103] Hence it is clear that these religious or quasi-religious occasions were not designed as a major social bonding mechanism (as in twentieth-century potluck suppers and such), but functioned on a much more limited group-bonding basis. Although these group meals were held in temples open to the public, they were customarily for intra-sect convenience only. A certain member—in a minority of cases, a woman—would extend the invitation to several other members to dine together at a meeting room in the temple. Paul's reference to a Christian being seen eating in an idol's temple (1 Cor 8:10) presumably refers to an exception to this generality, when an occasional outsider was permitted to attend.[104]

# 6

## Regal Pergamon: The City's Civic Monuments and Polytheistic Religions

During the days of the Persian Empire, one of their viceroys was in charge of Pergamon. Xenophon's famous army passed through during its outward bound stage. Lysimachus utilized the military skills he had exercised under Alexander the Great during his lifetime to gain control of the western part of Asia Minor. Pergamon enters the picture because he located his treasury there, nine thousand talents. Philetaerus successfully revolted against King Lysimachus in 282 B.C. and created the kingdom of Pergamon.

Since Philetaerus was a eunuch and physically unable to sire a son for the throne, he adopted Eumenes, who took over upon his adopted father's death. His successors ruled under the designation of Eumenes or Attalus for the following century and a half. It was a prosperous period for the city, and it accumulated fame as a major center of Hellenistic culture. Although a gradually expansionist power for its first sixty years, the new kingdom was slowly pushed back to the point where its very existence was in danger. Roman intervention saved the day and allowed the kingdom to enlarge to its maximum size.

In 133 B.C. Attalus III died and left his entire kingdom to his western benefactors. He probably had several motives for this action, but from the standpoint of political reality it was unquestionably a prudent maneuver since the kingdom's long-term survival required at least the tacit support of the Romans. Although greeting the gift with caution, the Romans saw in it an action in their own self-interest as well and moved to incorporate the kingdom. They renamed it Asia and acknowledged Pergamon as its capital.[1] Due to its inferior economic position compared to Smyrna and Ephesus, de facto supremacy gradually shifted away from Pergamon. Apparently, after the time period we are primarily interested in (the first and second centuries A.D.), the Romans took the step of making Ephesus the capital.[2]

Whatever political and military advantages allegiance with Rome could give, there was no protection against the vagaries of nature, which respect no regime. In A.D. 166 a major outbreak of plague spread through the community, inflicting many deaths.[3] During the reign of Valerius I (A.D. 253–60) a mammoth earthquake inflicted so much damage that the city never regained its previous prestige.[4]

Along with the advantages of adherence to Rome came disadvantages such as abuse from an ill-tempered ruler. Nero's love for all things Greek is well known. The down side to this was his desire to *possess* Greek sculpture and art as well, even if it had to be obtained by unscrupulous means. Although Tacitus indicates that the great fire of A.D. 64 provided Nero with the excuse for his art expropriation policy, it had begun at an earlier date when Barea Soranus was proconsul over Asia.[5] Both Delphi and Olympia were stripped of many of their artworks to satisfy this imperial appetite. Not only did Greece fall victim but also Hellenized Asia. Rioting in Pergamon did nothing to stop the implementation of the despised policy; art treasures were forcibly removed to Rome. The Roman proconsul so conspicuously *avoided* crushing the resistance that his enemies used it as evidence that he had actually *encouraged* the anti-exportation violence. Although the evidence was weak, the Senate sentenced him to death.[6]

Such local outbreaks were produced by external power attempting to implement a hated policy. Domestically, the community had a reputation for stability and social consensus. Livy (who died in A.D. 17) described Pergamon as a city where "one brother wore the name of king, but all brothers ruled."[7]

Geographically the town was located forty-five miles northward of Smyrna and eighty-five miles away from its most dangerous political rival, Ephesus. Its biggest lack was that of a port. One had to travel fifteen miles to the town of Elaia, which had access to the sea.[8]

Yet the city enjoyed its distinct benefits. Although Asia as a whole was preoccupied with growing (and importing) sufficient foodstuffs to feed its own population, Pergamon was well-blessed with fruitful corn-growing land in nearby areas.[9] The community enjoyed an ample supply of water brought in from a distance. The supply system represented an outstanding technological feat for its day. It began 375 meters above sea level, had to cross two separate valleys (with an intervening high point) and slowly rise to Pergamon itself, the highest point of which was almost as high as the water source itself—335 meters above sea level.[10]

Visitors could hardly avoid being awed by the physical appearance of the town itself:

> This magnificent city of Greco-Roman civilization was built on four rising terraces. The first terrace (the theatre terraces) leaning against a supporting wall has the Agora on the right, the Temple of Caracalla on the left, and in the middle the largest theatre in the world with 80 rows of seats. On the second terrace, and above the theatre, stands the great Altar of Zeus. From there one can reach the third terrace where stand the Temples of Athena and Polias. On the fourth terrace is the Temple of Trajan. Thus the city of Pergamum consists of four terraces each rising above the other, and presenting with the harmonious arrangements of its buildings, one of the most beautiful historical panoramas in the world.[11]

Guy Pentreath commented in a similar vein after his own visits to the site, "No architect could be presented with a more convenient natural site on which to create an architectural sensation."[12]

We can gain an insight into the practical side of urban life in Pergamon through its civil ordinances. A Roman-era partial copy was uncovered in 1901. Representing an estimated 40 percent of the complete inscription, it lays out the police-type functions of the *astynomoi* (lesser magistrates of the town).[13]

Road obstructions not authorized by the government could be ordered removed. If the removal was not carried out, the offender could be fined. Minor rural roads in the surrounding territory had to be a minimum of twelve feet in width and major thoroughfares thirty feet. Upkeep of the roads was the responsibility of the immediate and nearby owners of property the roads serviced.[14]

The actual construction of these roads and their upkeep was probably assumed by the city in return for a specified cash payment. This is supported by the fact that the city-owned slaves had the responsibility for street paving. Furthermore "the magnificent and uniform paving which we see today in the principal streets of excavated cities" such as Pergamon would not have been possible if such matters were subject to the variable finances and desires of individual landowners.[15]

Medieval and Elizabethan property owners might feel no responsibility for wastes they dumped outside their properties, but the Pergamonese government was not so tolerant. If a lower-ranking official could not convince the perpetrator to clean up his mess, then the *astynomoi* could be summoned. They had the authority to have it done on their own initiative, bill the owner for the cost, and tack on a fine for his obstinacy.[16]

Since houses in the confines of an urban setting normally either shared adjoining walls or joined each other going up the sides of the hills, careful regulations covered the responsibility of the owners when various types of problems arose.[17] Private cisterns were inspected annually.[18] The law included regulations as to the type of drainage required for public restrooms.[19] Public fountains could not be used to wash cooking utensils or clothing. Animals were forbidden to use them as well. The right of what we today would call "citizen's arrest" was bestowed upon any individual witnessing a violation of the legal use of public fountains. The citizen was rewarded with half of the resulting, very large fine.[20]

Several of the city's major physical facilities deserve special attention. High on the list of important sites are the city's three theaters. The eighty-row mountainside facility was originally constructed in the third century B.C. Major innovations were added by the Romans.[21] It could hold between ten thousand and fifteen thousand people.[22] Regardless of the exact number, the view has been called "truly breathtaking"[23] and "a unique view, a view possessed by no [other] Greek theater."[24]

Located outside Pergamon's ancient boundaries were two additional theaters, far outshining the ancient original one in seating capacity though not in physical grandeur. One held thirty thousand individuals and the other an even more impressive fifty thousand.[25]

After Emperor Caracalla traveled to the Pergamonese Asclepeion seeking healing, the grateful emperor provided the city with a number of buildings and the massive fifty-thousand capacity amphitheater.[26] It was one of only seven in the entire Roman East specifically constructed for gladiatorial fights and related "entertainments."[27]

Another site clearly intended for athletic events has often been called a stadium. John H. Humphrey wonders whether this may have actually been a hippodrome for chariot races. The typical running track in a stadium was between 10 and 33 meters wide, while the Pergamonese facility is about 58 meters. In length it measures some 280 meters, while athletic facilities were usually 70 meters or shorter. The oddity of the unexpected dimensions combined with the "extraordinary Romanization of Pergamon" inclines Humphrey to the belief that its actual purpose was chariot racing.[28]

Preeminent among all ancient libraries was that of Alexandria. Its closest rival was that of Pergamon.[29] It was a well-decorated facility. Halfway across the northern wall stood a large image of Athena.[30] Statues of Homer and others have also been found in the ruins of the library.[31] Based on an estimate of the number of holes in the wall (which would have held individual scrolls), the main reading room would have had the capacity for somewhere between 12,500 and 17,000 manuscripts.[32] Since the total capacity of the library was believed in the ancient world to have been as high as 200,000 scrolls,[33] this would suggest that many works (presumably lesser used ones) were stored in a separate but related facility and brought into the reading room as needed.

During Julius Caesar's invasion of Egypt, the Alexandrian library suffered major damage from fire. Cleopatra found a way to deal with this problem; she convinced her lover, Antony, to give her the library at Pergamon.[34] How much of this scheme was actually carried out is unknown but one can readily imagine Pergamonese patriots obstructing it as much as they could.

Egyptian and Pergamonese literary pride clashed at an even earlier date, with important implications for the written word. The story told in the ancient world was that the library of Pergamon had grown so large that its Alexandrian competitor felt embarrassed by the competition. Since scrolls were written on papyri from Egypt, Ptolemy banned any further exports, thereby crippling the growth of the Pergamonese facility.

The kingdom of Pergamon ordered that animal skins be utilized as a replacement. The popularization of this writing material[35] created a new product for local export. Ultimately the word *parchment* evolves from a reference to this Pergamonese "paper." Since the new Asian product resulted in a much thicker writing surface, scrolls became thicker and bulkier. This, in turn, encouraged locals to popularize the codex (book) form of the written manuscript.[36]

In the modern western tradition, athletic and educational centers represent two essentially contradictory types of facility: one is for brawn, and one is for intellect. The gymnasiums of the Greek world defied this modern division. Intellectuals such as Socrates and Plato both held their famous lectures in the gymnasiums of their day.[37] Walking in that tradition, the gymnasiums of Asia Minor provided a convenient setting for both athletic activity and the cultivating of intellectual pursuits.

Pergamon boasted the most spacious gymnasium ever constructed in the Greek world: it measured 490 feet by 650 feet.[38] Spread over three ascending terraces, the three levels appear to have functioned as separate facilities based upon age. The lowest was reserved for male adolescents and the highest for young men. Although dating back to the days when Pergamon enjoyed its role as an independent kingdom, it continued serving the intellectual-athletic interests of its citizenry throughout the period of Roman rule. The Romans appear to have made most of their changes and adaptations in the upper facility rather than in the other sections.[39] Among the gymnasium's assets were a 195–meter running track and a thousand-seat theater.[40]

There were at least four additional gymnasiums in the city. If one divides the mammoth complex we have discussed based upon age, one can push the total number of gymnasiums to a minimum of seven.[41]

These varied public facilities served a large urban population. Estimates cluster around the figures of 120,000,[42] 160,000,[43] and 200,000 residents.[44] A few argue for an in intermediate figure[45] or one dramatically lower than any of these.[46]

## Polytheism in Pergamon

The four most important cults in the city were those of the male deities Zeus, Dionysus, and Asclepius, and the female deity Athena.[47] Asclepius will be given in-depth treatment later in this chapter, not just because of his local importance but also because the movement's world-renowned healing center was located in Pergamon.

Zeus Soter (Jupiter Savior) was recognized as king of the gods as well as their father. The ecumenical nature of polytheistic deities can be seen in the fact that the chief priest of Zeus Soter doubled as leading priest of the cult of the divine Augustus.[48] Zeus inspired the monumental altar sometimes considered the throne of Satan (see the discussion in that context).

Although the imperial cult might be regarded as the most politically important one in the city, that of Athena enjoyed as much public respect and the city's most impressive cultic setting. As Emil G. Kraeling writes, "On the most prominent spot and visible from afar stood the temple of Athena, the patron goddess of the city. Its priestesses were highly respected, and memorial inscriptions to some of them stress the fact that they had conducted their office in a manner worthy of the goddess and of their native land."[49]

The temple was separated from the city's hillside theater by a colonnade. A narrow staircase joined the two facilities.[50] In popular folklore, those who walked this corridor were certain to have their wishes granted.[51]

Creature comfort was important in the design of the facility and, presumably, of other urban Pergamonese temples as well. "The spacious stoas [porticoes or colonnades], which allowed ample shelter against heat and cold, together with the shady courtyard supplied a great need for public places where people could walk, sit, chat, observe and do business."[52] The temple, like many others, preserved title to an unknown amount of land outside the city. These properties served to produce revenue. Furthermore, the temples claimed the right to invoke religious (not secular) sanctions against those involved in disputes concerning the properties.[53]

Each individual pagan temple had a prescribed ritual to be

performed by worshipers intending to enter its precincts. That required by the Athena temple in Pergamon has survived, though from the pre-Roman period.

> These are the rules of purification for entry into the temple of the goddess, whether for citizens or others: they must abstain from their own wife or husband for that particular day, and from the wife or husband of another for two days, and must perform the ceremonial ablutions. Similarly they must abstain for two days from contact with a dead body or a woman in childbirth. After a funeral ceremony they must receive ritual aspersion and entry through the gate where the holy water vessels stand, and they shall be purified the same day.[54]

Dionysus was the official god of the rulers of Pergamon in its days of independence. The kings claimed to be both Dionysus's successor as rulers of the kingdom and his earthly, contemporary embodiment.[55] The sect retained its popularity in the Roman era as well.[56] Since the god's symbol was the bull,[57] it was natural that the members of the religious society in charge of administering the rites of the group were called *bukoli* (ox-herds or cattlemen).[58] They are often referred to in surviving inscriptions.[59] The *silens* (dancers) of Dionysus provided entertainment in the theaters of the city.[60]

Just as the temple of Athena can most conveniently be located in relation to the mountainside theater, so can the temple of Dionysus. "Supporting [the theater] from below was a series of retaining walls topped by a stoa and processional way, leading up to a temple of Dionysos."[61] This small temple was built during the second century B.C.. During the reign of Caracalla (A.D. 211–17) it burned down and the emperor financed its rebuilding and renovation.[62] Caracalla had been especially sympathetic toward Pergamon and upon the completion of the temple was worshiped there as the "new Dionysus."[63]

The Red Hall of Pergamon was almost certainly a place where one or more Egyptian gods was worshiped,

> This is a large architectural complex built of red brick, but once faced with marble. The central building is a basilica (about 200 x 80 feet [60 x 25m]) with a nave, two aisles, and

an aspe, and it is flanked by two circular buildings (about 50 feet [18 m] in diameter), and there are courtyards to the west of them.

In front of the whole, to the west, is a large courtyard, beneath which the Selinus River flows in two vaulted canals. Found in the complex are fragments of colossal double statues (each carved on one side as an atlantes or male figure and on the other side as a caryatid or female figure), with Egyptian-type coiffures.[64]

With the auxiliary buildings and surrounding court, one is speaking of a complex about 328 feet wide and 656 feet long.[65] The central worship facility towered over 75 feet from foundation to roof. A hollow in the marble at the entrance may well have contained the ancient equivalent of holy water—assuming an Egyptian cult site, probably water brought from the mother of life, the Nile.[66] It was constructed in the second century A.D., probably during the reign of Hadrian,[67] and bears witness to the growing popularity of Egyptian religions during that century.[68]

The complex is commonly considered to have been a combined worship site for at least Isis, Sarapis, and Harpocrates.[69] Some have attempted to limit it to being a Sarapeum, an identification that has been challenged on the grounds of over-specificity[70] and the nature of the finds at the site.[71] Hence it seems most likely that the main hall itself functioned as the cult center of Sarapis or Isis, while the "lesser" gods of their homeland were reverenced in the remainder of the complex.[72]

Long before Rome gained possession of Asia, the region had a long tradition of king worship.[73] It has been speculated that regal claims to deityship represented a practical means for conquerors to assert effective superiority over local religious and political institutions while not overtly replacing the existing structures.[74]

Although Smyrna's dedication to the imperial cult goes back further chronologically, Pergamon was the officially recognized center for the movement.[75]

It was the first Asian city to build a temple in honor of an emperor, Augustus. Centuries later came one in honor of Trajan and, last of all, a third in honor of Severus.[76]

Trajan's early-second-century temple was the most impressive cultic site erected in his honor in all of Asia.[77] It was located not just on the acropolis of the city but at its highest point. The site measured at least 190 feet by 223 feet, with the temple itself occupying about one-third of the area.[78] The original construction was enhanced by the addition of six pillars on the front and nine on each of the other sides.[79] Since Emperor Hadrian had both authorized and heavily financed the construction, it was not inappropriate that after his death he also was worshiped at the temple.[80] At an unknown date it was destroyed by an earthquake.[81]

One auxiliary to the emperor cult was that of the imperial choir. One such chorus existed at Pergamon and provided music during the worship. In addition to these public activities it had its own private rituals, limited to the membership of the choir.[82] In the early second century A.D., it had thirty-six members, thirty-two of whom possessed the cherished Roman citizenship. The fee to join was extremely high. This not only made it seven times more expensive than any other known civic/religious group in the city but also guaranteed the elite status of the membership. Once in the choral society, membership could be passed on to the next generation at a dramatically reduced figure.[83]

Holding the presidency of the choir boosted not only the individual's pride and prestige but also resulted in dramatically increased financial expenditures. As a contemporary record (c. A.D. 110) records, "The president will also provide the singers with garlands on the monthly celebration of Augustus' birthday and on the birthday of the other Emperors, and on the [days of the] Mysteries garlands for their meeting hall and for the members and their sons each day, as well as pastry, incense and lamps [for the rites] to the Emperor...."[84]

Organizations of singers existed for other deities as well. At Pergamon, for example, we find a boys' choir at the Asclepeion.[85] The elite economic status of the imperial choral society was unusual. Most were composed of professional or semi-professional singers who found in it a means of earning or supplementing their livelihood. Because of the costs involved in maintaining a choir, some groups simultaneously worked for more than one organization. For example "hymn-singers" (Greek, *hymnodos*) in Ephesus served both Artemis and the city government. Likewise, in

Smyrna, the *hymnodos* served the imperial cult and found singing employment elsewhere as well. In Rome the *hymnodos'* service of the imperial cult was combined with service to Sarapis.[86]

These are far from exhausting the complete list of deities honored and revered in the community. Demeter was worshiped in a sanctuary site located on the northern slope of the acropolis. It was built in the second century B.C.[87] The temple to Hera was located near the mountainside theater. An idol of Zeus was found among the ruins of the structure.[88]

As discussed in an earlier chapter, Cybele worship was introduced to Rome through Pergamon. Although not one of the city's leading sects in the early centuries A.D., it is of importance because the earliest surviving account of its central mystery—or mystic rite—is from Pergamon. Dated A.D. 105, fuller accounts occur only from a much later date, when the theology had evolved into an apparent intended analogy to Christian baptism.[89]

### Asclepius and His Asklepieion

The most important center of Asclepius worship in the Roman age was at Epidaurus in the Peloponese Islands. The second most important was found at the Asklepieion outside Pergamon.[90] What these and most other worship sites had in common were non-urban settings. Plutarch had observed this, "Why is the sanctuary of Asklepios outside of the city? Was it because they reckoned it a more wholesome kind of living outside the city? For the Greeks have placed the edifices belonging to Asklepios for the most part on high places where the air is pure and clear."[91]

Considerable controversy has raged over whether Asclepius was originally considered a deity or was a respected folk hero whose veneration ultimately transformed him into a supernatural being.[92] Either way, by the centuries of which we speak he had clearly crossed the line into deityship. He was normally pictured as a kind and caring deity, seeking the welfare of those who sought his counsel.[93]

In the fourth century B.C., Archias, a well-to-do citizen of Pergamon, was seriously injured while hunting. Since his stay at the Epidaurus shrine resulted in his being cured, he decided to finance the establishment of a similar facility in his hometown.[94]

Thereafter many thousands of individuals—famous and obscure, rich and of limited means—came to seek the healing they could not find elsewhere. It was not until the second century A.D., however, that the Asklepieion reached its height of popular respect.[95] Local pride was reflected in the use of one of the facility's buildings on the coinage of the city.[96]

Among its famous visitors was the pagan prophet Apollonius. He was "pleased with the temple of Asclepius" when he visited it. He even "gave hints to the supplicants of the god, what to do in order to obtain favorable dreams" that would reveal the best healing regimen for them.[97]

Locals who moved on to fame and fortune remembered this important hometown institution. Earinus, a slave whose home was Pergamon, rose to the position of cupbearer to Domitian. To show his reverence and respect, he sent his mirror and locks of his hair to the Asclepius complex.[98]

Not everyone recalled the institution with such respect. Emperor Caracalla came in A.D. 215 seeking a cure. Emperor or not, he left unhealed.[99]

The Asklepieion measured some 361 feet by 427 feet.[100] A narrow "holy road" carried the searcher for healing 820 meters from the city itself to the shrine. The section nearest the site, at least, had large colonnades on both sides of the road.[101]

The complex included a number of facilities not related to its central healing purposes. Among these were a small library[102] and a theater that could seat thirty-five hundred individuals.[103] Four temples on the site antedate the Roman era: naturally there was one to Asclepius. But there was also one each for the goddess Hygieia, for Apollo, and for Telesphoros.[104] In A.D. 150 a wealthy consul erected a new temple in honor of Asclepius.[105] It was dedicated to Zeus as well.[106]

The healing process began with obtaining the guidance of Asclepius as to the recuperative procedure to follow. A section of sleeping rooms was set apart for new arrivals, where they sought the dreams that would reveal how they would be healed.[107] Before this, certain preliminary rituals had to be performed, and it was expected that if one's inquiries *were* answered by dreams that an appropriate thankfulness would be manifested toward the deity.

The sanctuaries of Asclepius had on their walls carved

announcements spelling out in detail the procedures to be gone through by the health-seeking pilgrims. The inscription from Pergamon is missing the beginning and some other fragments. on. Even so, this presumably first-century version of an earlier set of inscriptions provides invaluable light on what was expected of a devotee at the Pergamonese healing shrine.[108] First came offerings to Zeus and to Artemis and to Earth itself.

> Having done this, let him preliminarily offer up a suckling pig on the altar to Asclepius, and lay on the table of sacrifices the right leg and entrails. Let him then contribute three obols to the treasury.
>
> In the evening, let him offer three nine-braided cakes, two of them in the outer hearth to Luck and Remembrance, the third in the sleeping-room to Themis. Let him be ritually clean in the aforementioned respects, and from sexual intercourse, and goat's meat and cheese and [...] [come in after abstaining] on the third day.
>
> Let him who sleeps there take the wreath off and lay it on the bed. If anyone wants to submit inquiries concerning one single matter several times, let him offer up preliminarily a pig. But if he wants to ask about another matter, let him preliminarily offer up another pig according to the regulations.
>
> For the smaller sleeping-room, the entrant shall be similarly clean ritually. Let him make offerings to Zeus Apotropaios ["who wards off"] of a nine-braided striped cake, and to Zeus Meilichios ["the merciful"] a nine-braided striped cake, and to Artemis Prothyraia and Artemis [...] and to Earth, to each a nine-braided cake. Let him contribute three obols to the treasury.
>
> All persons offering cult to the god, as they follow the priest and [...], shall take part in the offering procession with a cake soaked in honey, oil, and incense. In the evening, let all those who have made the preliminary sacrifice [...] to the sleeping-room, and all those who have taken part in the offering procession offer up three nine-braided striped cakes, one each to Themis, to Luck, and to Remembrance.
>
> They shall provide the god with good securities for the healing instructions [received by dreams during the nights in the sleeping-rooms]—whatever he may do to them—to render their accounts within a year [...] thank-victims for cure,

not less than a year old. They shall contribute the thank-offerings for a cure to Asclepius' treasury, a sixth of a Phocacean stater to Apollo and a sixth of a Phocaean stater to Asclepius, when they are restored to health, and whatever else the god may require.

Claudius Glycon, the priest for ritual, set this up.[109]

The advice obtained could easily result in the following of a physical regimen to produce health improvement. Indeed, it is suspected that this was the main method by which Asclepius produced physical improvement among his pilgrims. It has been described as "a mixture of a spa, a health farm and Lourdes."[110] Indeed the apparent high proportion of natural cures has led one scholar to suggest that, "Asklepios was perhaps more a patron of the medical centre than a wonder-working god."[111] Since a cure by the dominant natural means required a lengthy stay (unavailable and unaffordable to most of society) one cynic has described the second century A.D. facility as "a kind of health resort" limited to "members of the wealthy leisure class."[112] Unlike certain other of Asclepius's shrine sites, surgery was not an option.[113]

The best self-documented account by a visitor to Pergamon is from the hand of Aelius Aristides, who came there only after a year-long stay in Smyrna. His account reveals in detail the extreme physical discomfort suffered by many visitors and how the Asclepius-ordained mild physical challenges helped even the despairing to summon their own healing resources. Of his condition at the time of his decision to proceed to Pergamon he writes:

> When I had been brought back from Italy, having collected in my body many ailments of every sort as a result of the continued hardships and storms which I had had to endure while traveling through Thrace and Macedonia (and I was already ill when I started out), the doctors were at a loss: not only could they think of nothing to help me, but they were not even able to recognize what was wrong with me to begin with. The most painful and distressing part of it was that I could not breathe; only with the greatest difficulty at times and with a dread that I might not succeed was I able to draw breath, and then only heavily and barely enough. My throat was constantly choked up; shivers ran through the sinews of my body; I needed more covers than I could stand. And

there were countless other things wrong with me. They thought I should try the hot baths; they might make my condition better, or else I might find the atmosphere more supportable. It was already wintertime, and the baths were not far from the city.

That was when the Savior first began to give me revelations. He ordered me to walk barefoot, and I cried out in my dream as if I were wide awake and the vision had been carried out: "Great is Asclepius! the order has been fulfilled!" That was what I dreamed I cried out while walking forward. After this came the god's invitation and my departure from Smyrna to Pergamum to my good fortune.[114]

A multi-pronged approach to healing was utilized. This carried an implicit recognition that an individual played a pivotal role in healing and that it was not a matter of relying on the deity alone,

> Data recorded in literature and in many inscriptions that have been found clearly indicate that the more practical therapeutics of the temple made use of external applications of lotions and ointments, exercise, baths followed by friction and other manipulation, diet, and often a general hygienic regimen.
>
> Asklepios has been called the father of health gymnastics. It is stated that at Pergamon the xyster, or rough brush, was invented for rubbing after the bath (Martial, xiv. 51). Religious healing practice raised two important hygienic measures, cleansing the body and moderation in eating and drinking, to divine commands.
>
> In addition to the above measures, there are many suggestions in the methods associated with incubation closely simulating what remedies, presumably made from herbs and roots were combined in administration with incantations and magic formulas.[115]

Hence the curative regimen could include everything from relatively passive cold baths, mud baths, and massage to moderate activity (walking), to vigorous activity (riding), with a wide variety of internal and external medications to further stimulate physical progress.[116] The public at large recognized that the god would typically command such exercise and moderate self-denial. In the words of Marcus Aurelius, "We commonly say: Asclepius prescribed to someone horseback riding, or cold baths, or going barefoot."[117]

It was quite in the Greek tradition that intellectual stimulation was a respected part of the curative routine for a goodly number of pilgrims. The physician Galen wrote,

> Asclepius ordered not a few to write odes as well as to compose comical mimes and certain songs (for the motions of their passions, having become more vehement, had made the temperature of the body warmer than it should be); and for others, these not a few either, he ordered hunting and horseback riding and exercising in arms; for he desired to awake the passion of these men because it was weak.[118]

Direct, miraculous intervention was also claimed for the god.[119] Among the inscriptions found at the site is one from Julius Meidias, who had previously suffered from some type of bleeding "under the biceps." A woman named Eveteria spoke of her own divine healing, of how "her eyes [had been] cured."[120]

Some of the claimed miraculous healings sound odd to the modern ear because they involved not just one miraculous healing but double miracles: one disease is replaced with another, and the *second* disease is then removed. We read of one "wealthy man" who traveled to Pergamon from Thrace as the result of a dream. After he arrived at the Asklepieion another "dream appeared to him, the god prescribing that he should drink every day of the drug produced from the vipers and should anoint the body from the outside. The disease after a few days turned into leprosy; and this disease, in turn, was cured by the drugs which the god commanded."[121]

Around A.D. 100 Teucer the Cyzicenean sought relief from the epilepsy that made his life difficult. Seeking a cure, one ancient authority writes,

> he came to Pergamum to Asclepius, asking for liberation from the disease. The god appearing to him holds converse with him and asks if he wants to exchange his present disease against another one. And he said he surely did not want that but would rather get some relief from the evil. But if at all, he wished that the future might not be worse than the

present. When the god had said it would be easier and this would cure him more plainly than anything else, he [Teucer] consents to the disease, and a quartan fever attacks him, and thereafter he is free from epilepsy.[122]

So far we have been considering the *healing* aspects of the Asclepius cult. In doing so it is easy to overlook the explicitly *religious* aspects lying behind it. As in other cults one finds regular sacrifices (some of which are referred to above) as well as hymn singing in the god's honor.[123]

The greatest cult festival was the Asklepieia. This included offerings of respect not only to Asclepius himself but to other gods as well, especially those connected with healing. A bull was offered and its four parts presented at the altars of Asclepius, Zeus, Dionysus, and Athena. One by one, songs of praise were offered to each deity. Other gods might not receive a physical sacrifice yet be counted worthy of a verbal one. For example, Telesphoros received such honors because of his stature in the region.[124]

# 7

# Regal Pergamon:
# Divided Christianity and
# Societal Allusions in John's Mini-Epistle

## Text of the Epistle

"And to the angel of the church in Pergamos write, 'These things says he who has the sharp two-edged sword: "I know your works, and where you dwell, where Satan's throne is. And you hold fast to my name, and did not deny my faith even in the *says* in which Antipas was my faithful martyr, who was killed among you, where Satan dwells. But I have a few things against you, because you have there those who hold the doctrine of Balaam, who taught Balak to put a stumbling block before the children of Israel, to eat things sacrificed to idols, and to commit sexual immorality. Thus you also have those who hold the doctrine of the Nicolaitans, which thing I hate. Repent, or else I will come to you quickly and will fight against them with the sword of my mouth. He who has an ear, let him hear what the Spirit says to the churches. To him who overcomes I will give some of the hidden manna to eat. And I will give him a white stone, and on the stone a new name written which no one knows except him who receives it."'" (Rv 2:12–17)

Little is known of the Jewish community in Pergamon. It has been reasonably speculated that Pergamon's status as capital of the province resulted in an intensity of opposition to monotheism that was not found elsewhere. Even a broadminded proconsul, inclined to let the locals run things as much as they could, would be inclined to take a more zealous role in his own capital. This natural inclination would be intensified by the importance of the emperor cult in the community and the need of the proconsul to uphold the respect and prestige of the emperor.

If such factors created difficulties for Christianity, one would anticipate similar difficulties for Judaism as well. Although inhibited by legal protections from direct oppression, under such conditions there would be the tendency to yield the minimum amount required. Again, it was not unknown to bend the rules slightly *against* Judaism: During the proconsulship of Flaccus (62–61 B.C.) the local community is among those explicitly referred to as being prohibited from sending the temple tax to Jerusalem.[1] Certainly any implicit or explicit limitation on Jewish rights would be most strictly applied in Pergamon due to its being the official capital of the province.

As to Christianity, it is uncertain how the congregation came to be formed. Paul's multi-year stay in Ephesus provides a convenient chronological event that could easily have led to its creation. On the other hand, Paul's Asian labor could merely have reinforced a gospel labor that had been underway for years.

John's mini-epistle stresses that the congregation had upheld its faith with its blood: "You hold fast to my name, and did not deny my faith even in the days in which Antipas was my faithful martyr, who was killed among you, where Satan dwells" (Rv 2:13). The reference to not "deny(ing)" his faith has been taken as an indication of official prosecution[2] rather than mob violence, quite possibly with "enforcement of emperor worship" in the community.[3] Whether Antipas[4] fell afoul of emperor worship zealots or the zealots of other cults or simply had the misfortune to be known by inquisitorial enemies of the faith, prosecution was unusually easy. Because Pergamon was the capital, the proconsul would have to spend a goodly amount of his term in that city. Hence while in other cities the case might drag on for many months, until the proconsul arrived, an allegation in Pergamon would be examined far more quickly. Since the proconsul was the only individual authorized to order the death penalty, this put Christians in Pergamon at special risk.[5] Of course it simultaneously *lowered* the risk for Christians in other communities.

John does not assert that the Pergamonese congregation was in any immediate danger, though one could argue that there is an ominous tone to his rhetoric; if it happened before there would certainly be the additional psychological foreboding that history could repeat itself. At least so far as John's explicit teaching, the congregation's gravest short-term danger was that of internal heresy. He labels the two groups Balaamites (Rv 2:14) and Nicolaitans (Rv 2:15). In Ephesus the Nicolaitans had been a danger successfully resisted (Rv 2:6). Here their seductive efforts were reinforced by the Balaamites, and John is clearly uncertain whether, unencouraged, the congregation will have the collective zeal and passion to repel the assault on its moral integrity. Indeed, the presence of such a dual internal threat is mentioned in none of the other epistles.

The relationship of the two groups to each other has been much discussed. There are three basic approaches. The conclusion most often adopted is that two different heretical groups are under discussion.

A closer reading[6] could lead one to conclude that there is one heretical *group* (the Nicolaitans) and one heretical *movement* (that named after Balaam) that has not yet risen to the level of an internal dissident body. In the text itself we read of how certain people "hold the doctrine of the Nicolaitans" (2:15), as if they are members of a recognizable group. In contrast, we do not read of the *followers* of Balaam but of those who "hold the *doctrine* of Balaam" (2:14), as if what joins them together is a common error rather than loyalty to an erroneous group as well.

A large number of commentators[7] have argued that the Balaamites and Nicolaitans actually are one group, though two different labels are applied to it. Two basic arguments support this thesis. First of all, they hold to the same doctrine. The closest to textual proof of this is found in Revelation 2:15, "Thus you also have those who hold the doctrine of the Nicolaitans, which thing I hate." (But does not the word "also" most naturally imply that *two* groups are under consideration?[8]) Shared doctrine leads Gerhard A. Krodel to identify the groups as one.[9] In a similar vein M. Eugene Boring writes, "Since these are described in identical terms, they are probably all designations of the same group or movement."[10]

This does not necessarily follow. The "also" in verse 15 seems to argue powerfully against this. Furthermore, in the narrow compass of such a short epistle, the very lack of space would likely rule out any discussion of the differences. (Even the similarities are sketched out in a minimum number of words.) Modern experience shows the danger of uniting movements that have dramatic differences. Methodists and Baptists have much in common, but who but the most unlearned would allow the similarities to lead to the conclusion that they are two names for the same movement? The critic of infant baptism obviously dissents from the practice of both the Methodists and Presbyterians on this matter. But would the critic jump to the conclusion that they are alternate names for the same group? When information is extremely limited and we discover two *apparently* separate groups, we should be extremely reluctant to conclude that the names apply to the same body of people.

The other means of proving this thesis that there was only one Balaamite-Nicolaitan movement is to resort to name meanings. William Barclay argues the case this way:

> The name *Nicolaus,* the founder of the Nicolaitans, could be derived from two Greek words, *nikan, to conquer,* and *laos, the people. Balaam* can be derived from two Hebrew words, *bela,* to *conquer,* and *ha'am, the people.* The two names, then, are the same and both can describe an evil teacher, who has won victory over the people and subjugated them to poisonous heresy.[11]

The speculativeness of the argument is obvious: there is an obvious important difference between *could, can,* and *is* (the former referring to possibilities and the last to certainty). If the epithet "Balaam" is selected because of what the historical Balaam had done to undermine Israel and the existence of parallel actions in the spiritual Israel of the church, then the *meaning* of the name Balaam had no significant role to play in the choice of the name. It was because of what he had done—rather than what his name meant—that the word is applied to the first-century movement. These factors also argue against finding in the meaning of the terms an indication that the movement represented an early form of clericalism in the region.[12]

We know nothing certain of the origin of either the Balaamite or Nicolaitan movements. As early as Irenaeus, however, there was a tradition that the group had been created by "Nicolas, a proselyte from Antioch" (Acts 6:5) who was one of the seven "deacons" chosen in Jerusalem in the earliest years of the church to minister to that congregation's physically destitute. At *that* point all seven are described as "full of the Holy Spirit and wisdom" (Acts 6:3), and it must be assumed that any heretical drift occurred at a later date. It is hard not to suspect, however, that the verbal similarity between the name of the deacon and the heretical movement in Asia led to the identification rather than any actual historical tradition. On the other hand, church leaders *can* go bad (as Paul pointedly stressed to the elders of Ephesus in Asia, Acts 20:28–31) and this conceivably could be such a case.

Be that as it may, at least the teaching of the two groups can be reconstituted in its two central assertions from how John describes the Balaamites willingness to "eat things sacrificed to idols and to commit sexual immorality" (Rv 2:14). These teachings were "also" advocated by the Nicolaitans (2:15). Both of these teachings deserve careful consideration.

### *"Eating Things Sacrificed to Idols"*

Since Paul had spoken of occasions when it was *right* to partake of such sacrifices (1 Cor 8–10), some have speculated that John is attacking Pauline doctrine.[13] Although a verbal contradiction can easily be erected, it is hard to believe that a *real* adversarial position is being taken by John against Paul. Paul's missionary work among the Gentiles had created bitterness among Jewish traditionalists in the church. They had been angered because he did not make the Gentiles be circumcised (Acts 15:1), but this was only the tip of the iceberg: their underlying demand went far beyond this, that Gentiles must "keep the law of Moses" in its entirety (Acts 15:5), thereby transforming the church into a sect of Judaism.

The issue was brought before all the apostles in Acts 15 and a consensus was reached, which was summed up in a short epistle (Acts 15:23–29). They explicitly repudiated the Jewish traditionalists for "unsettling your souls, saying, 'You must be circumcised and keep the law'—to whom we gave no commandment" (verse 24). They unanimously agreed (verse 25) that Paul's policy was acceptable to them (verses 25–27). With the approval and endorsement of the Holy Spirit (verse 28) they had determined to hold their conduct demands on the Gentiles to the minimum (verse 28), which they summed up in four prohibitions, "That you abstain from things offered to idols, from blood, from things strangled, and from sexual immorality [from fornication, *NRSV*]. If you keep yourselves from these you do well" (verse 29). *Acts presents this as a victory for Paul: how then are we to assume that Paul blatantly departed from this unanimous decision in his later epistle to Corinth?* We would seem to be on far sounder ground in assuming that any difference comes from Paul dealing either with aspects of the question that the few words of the general prohibition did not cover or with situations not intended to be covered by the apostolic decision in Acts 15.

We must remember that the question of how this principle applied was an inevitable one: the tokens of paganism were anywhere and everywhere, pervasive throughout the society. One literally could not exist in most of the Roman world without rubbing shoulders with it.[14] Gentiles who once had casually partaken of the token gestures of paganism had to decide how the prohibition affected actions that once had not even given them pause.

In helping the Gentiles deal with these matters, Paul deals with three questions in 1 Corinthians: Is it right to eat such meats in the equivalent of a pagan religious social hall, with pagan friends at all, and is it right to partake when one is told the idol-dedicated source of the meat? The apostolic decree from Jerusalem *could* prohibit all of these but was it intended to do so? Paul clearly believes the answer is a very conditional no.

Paul treats with the most publicly visible act first: eating in one of the social facilities that adjoined most pagan worship facilities and which we have already discussed in relation to at least two pagan deities.[15] Paul insists that there is nothing wrong if two conditions are met. First, one must truly recognize that idols represent nothing real (1 Cor 8:4–6); if one has divided sentiments or is unsure, it would be wrong. Second, if one recognizes that this will cause *other* Christians one knows to eat such things and undermine *their* faith, then one is to abstain (1 Cor 8:9). Note that permission is given, but a very limited permission.

Indeed, even that seems virtually removed when Paul challenges, "If anyone sees you who have knowledge eating in an idol's temple, will not the conscience of him who is weak be embolden to eat those things offered to idols? And because of your knowledge shall the weak brother perish, for whom Christ died. But when you thus sin against the brethren, and wound their weak conscience, you sin against Christ. Therefore if food makes my brother stumble, I will never again eat meat, lest I make my brother stumble" (1 Cor 8:10–13). It is almost as if Paul is saying: in the abstract there is nothing wrong with it, but in the real world you are not likely to run into a situation where you can safely exercise your liberty.

The matter of eating in the privacy of a friend's or associate's home does not expose one to public scrutiny, and Paul's admonition does not mention the danger of being seen by a spiritually weak brother who would be encouraged to violate his conscience. In such a private gathering it becomes a matter of one's host's conscience: if the host makes a point that the meat has been offered to idols, one must explicitly decline to partake (10:23–29)[16]—again, a very careful limitation on any liberty that is granted.

Finally, if one pushed the apostolic consensus far enough one would have starved, because meats for sale in the marketplace of any pagan city was commonly "offered" in some vague, mechanical sense to the pagan deities before it was sold. Paul's principle is simple: Don't ask; just buy it (10:25). All this can be summed up this way: Consider food as offered to an idol *only* if you are explicitly told it is. Don't go looking for a fight, but if its source is pointed out to you, avoid partaking. In short, Paul is not engaged in some random dismissal of the need to abstain from food offered to idols but is concerned with how one *implements* that principle—that generalization—in an overwhelmingly pagan society.

Of course this in no way denies that Paul's teaching would represent a useful pretext to "justify" abandoning *all* inhibitions on the subject. But his careful limitations clearly indicate that such would have represented an abuse of his doctrine.

### *"Commit[ting] Sexual Immorality"*

Committing sexual immorality was the second form of behavior that set apart the Balaamite and Nicolaitan movements from apostolically approved Christianity. In the previous case we have Pauline teaching that could—with only modest difficulty—be used to justify defying the preexisting apostolic consensus on moral behavior. When we turn to sexual immorality in its various forms,[17] one has no specific text to distort, but one *does* have principles that could be twisted. Paul's doctrine of grace could be twisted to justify living however one wished (Rom 6:1-2). Paul's stress on Christian liberty could likewise be melded into a theory permitting the abandonment of Christian restraint. Paul himself recognized the danger, for he warned that "you, brethren, have been called to liberty; only do not use liberty as an opportunity for the flesh, but through love serve one another" (Gal 5:13).

Whether distortions of Pauline teaching were utilized at all we do not know—certainly Paul knew that some existed and was appalled (cf. Rom 3:8). They could just as easily have pleaded some type of direct divine revelation. Indeed, Balaam claimed to be a prophet, and we might even have in the adoption of his name as an epithet a hint that the reprobates also made such claims. Such would be very useful, for it would free the advocates from the need to justify their teaching on Pauline (or Johannine) precedents: after all, weren't they inspired too?

These distortions of Christianity had one great appeal: they made life more comfortable in a pagan society. They allowed one to live at greater peace with the existing religio-political structure while maintaining at least verbal allegiance to Christianity. And, of course, one was freed from those pesky prohibitions on moral behavior that might inhibit personal pleasure.

John has not given up hope on the Pergamonese congregation, but he recognizes the power of the internal threat—and wants to be sure that the brethren neither surrender nor despair. They could not control what the Roman government might do to them, but they certainly *did* have some control over what the congregation was like, both in its practice and ideals.

Having examined the internal tensions within the congregation, let us broaden our horizon and examine the possible societal allusions that John uses in urging them to preserve their moral orthodoxy.

## Societal Allusions in the Epistle

### *"Satan's Throne" (Revelation 2:13)*

Whether commentators seek deeply for societal references or not, this phrase brings out in virtually all interpreters the desire to find a specific local allusion. There are at least three major interpretations and two less often adopted ones. There are so many that commentators easily make "Satan's throne" a dual allusion or even a triple one.[18]

THE POLITICAL EXPLANATION

This comes in two variants: the strictly *political* (Pergamon being the capital of the province) and the *politico-religious* (the natural importance of the imperial cult in such a setting.

In its most limited form the strictly political explanation refers to the fact that Pergamon was the capital.[19] Implicit in this is the belief that Roman power was either inherently Satanic, was being used in a Satanic manner, or was being used by Satan to accomplish his goals. Usually the exact reasoning behind the identification is not spelled out. An exception is Austin Farrer, who grounds the identification in the fact that Satan was, effectively, "the god of the Romans," and Pergamon was the capital of that empire's Asian province.[20]

Adela Yarbo Collins finds the Satanic allusion grounded in the rhetoric of the book itself. "In chapter 13...Satan is said to have given his authority to the Roman empire. So by Satan's throne the Roman seat of government is probably meant."[21] In yet another sense the capital could be considered Satanic because the Roman courts in Pergamon were being used by Satan to inflict anti-Christian persecution.[22]

Although a proconsul did not actually sit on a throne, the usage was in accord with that part of the world. A supporter of the political interpretation argues that "the Persian satraps of old were sometimes described as occupying thrones, and an Oriental writer could well view a Roman governor in the same light."[23]

The political and the religious interlock in the imperial cult. Since by monotheistic definition, the worship of a human is of its essence Satanic, it is easy to find in the imperial cult John's frame of reference. Some simply find his rationale in the *fact* of the imperial cult.[24] This leaves unanswered why *this* city should receive the label when so many others, with official or unofficial imperial worship sites, were not so branded.

For others, the identification has been grounded in several

different contributing factors. Pergamon was the first city in Asia to have the cult.[25] Others cite the archaeological remnants referring to Pergamonese adoration of the emperor as a god.[26] It was one of its major centers,[27] not just because of the presence of one of the few imperially recognized temples[28] but also because of the inherent importance that would occur in any city that combined such a function with that of being a provincial capital. Furthermore, if, as normally believed, emperor worship was a "spiritual" export of Asia, Pergamon was under a multiple condemnation beyond those already considered: in pre-Roman days her kings had been routinely considered living gods.[29] She had pioneered the concept.

### THE RELIGIOUS EXPLANATION

This explanation has at least three varieties (a fourth, if one includes the imperial cult, discussed above). The magnificent Zeus altar is an obvious frame of reference, followed by the importance of the Asclepius cult to the community, not to mention the presence of a wide variety of other pagan cults. A twist on this final approach is to make the reference be to a special zeal for polytheism in Pergamon.

**1. Zeus and his altar.** The altar complex was already three hundred years old by the time John wrote[30] and had required the talents of at least forty sculptors.[31] By boasting of the triumphs of the gods as a means of celebrating their own military triumphs, Pergamonese civic bravado and religious piety were merged together in the great altar and the battle frieze that faced it.[32] The battle motif of the frieze serves to glorify the gods but also to elevate the stature of the Attalids, whose battlefield victories had manifested valor and successes they considered worthy of the gods themselves. Although only one ancient writer actually refers to it,[33] a comparison of the remains to then-contemporary and later sculpture directly exhibits its wide-ranging influence.[34]

Howard F. Vos describes the edifice this way:

> The rectangular foundations of the altar were 125 by 115 feet. The altar rested on a great horseshoe-shaped plinth, 30 feet high. The arms of the horseshoe flanked twenty-eight 50–foot steps which approached the altar on the western

side. These steps led through an Ionic colonnade into a square court where the altar proper stood.

The three outer sides of the monument were sculptured with scenes of struggle between gods and giants (the former defeating the latter in a struggle symbolic of the conflict between civilization and barbarism) and scenes representing the defeat of the Gauls by King Eumenes. The famous frieze was eight feet high and was placed eight feet above the base of the podium. Another frieze ran around the three inner sides of the altar court on the upper level. This sculpture depicted events from the life of the legendary hero Telephus, son of Hercules, traditional founder of the city. Only the Parthenon frieze exceeds in length that of the altar of Zeus at Pergamum, which was about four hundred feet long.[35]

It is more common to find the identification of Satan's throne with the altar[36] than to find a discussion of the reasons *for* the identification. Those who take the time, however, do make effective arguments. First of all, the imagery "of an altar as a throne is known from very early times"[37] and, would be consistent with what is known of ancient ways of thinking.

The *visual* argument derives from its physical setting. Built on a hill towering eight hundred feet above the city, it might well have been pictured as a throne from which the false worship of Zeus seduced humankind. Not only its location above the city and above all other altars, but its physical design suggested a similar idea: "With its flanking columns on three sides, it *looked* like a huge throne."[38]

The *theological* argument derives from Zeus's importance in Greek mythology as father and king of gods. Although *any* god represented an antithesis to Yahweh (and thus a Satanic parallel), Zeus's leadership role in pagan myth made him arguably the most *explicit* challenger to the true deity. And of all the altars erected in his honor one would be hard pressed to find one grander than this one, located in his asserted birthplace.[39] Hence the epithet would be especially telling and appropriate because of this traditional Zeus-Pergamonese linkage.

The *epithet* argument derives from the fact that Zeus claimed the title Savior,[40] a claim that would have been especially annoying to Christians. The *frieze* argument derives from the

repeated use of snakes and snake-like imagery on the frieze surrounding the altar.[41] The biblical linkage of snake imagery with
Satan and Satanic seduction goes all the way back to the first
chapters of the book of Genesis.

These approaches can be supplemented by additional argumentation not found in the literature surveyed for this book. For
example, the large number of gods that are depicted on the
altar's frieze (at least seventy, plus giants)[42] could easily be presented as a compelling embodiment of polytheism's multiple-
deity claims. In addition, the grandeur of the frieze is so great
that *some* kind of reaction is virtually demanded, even by the
strictest monotheist.[43]

Some have explicitly argued against the identification. For
one thing, in the remainder of Revelation it is not traditional
Greek religion (manifested in such cults as Zeus) that is pictured
as the enemy but Rome in its religious and political hostility to
Christianity.[44] Furthermore, by the first century A.D. few took the
god myths seriously "and it would have been a waste of the powder and shot of Christian invective to attack them."[45] This particular critic identifies the Satanic throne as the imperial cult.[46] By
the same logic, however, how could this be, since it is unlikely
that the imperial cult itself was taken very seriously as a religious
phenomena? (Its significance as a token of political loyalty to
Rome is something else again.).

Perhaps the best argument against the identification can be
found in that the same verse brings out the fact that Christians in
the city had been persecuted:

> Since [the expression] stands in some kind of connection
> with the persecution of the church there, it can hardly refer
> to some mere show-place of the city, such as the temple of
> Aesculapius or of Zeus, but must be some institution con-
> nected with the politico-religious world-power of Rome,
> whether as the seat of proconsular administration or the
> centre of the organization of the worship of the Emperor by
> the priests of the temple "of Augustus and Rome" which was
> at Pergamos.[47]

**2. Asclepius cult.**[48] Four arguments suggest this identification. First, the traditional *symbol* for Asclepius was the serpent.[49] In

the fully Hellenized form of the cult he was pictured as an idealized human being; the staff he held, bearing the serpent, was traditionally associated with his name. In Asia, though, the serpent motif itself retained its dominance.[50]

Second, *Savior* was a *term* commonly applied to the god.[51] Third, throne imagery is associated with him. The Greek traveler Pausanias speaks of the god as "sitting on a throne with a staff in his hand, and his other hand upon the head of a serpent."[52]

Fourth, the Pergamon complex is said to have been the dominant or most important one in Asia, and the most popular.[53] Some challenge this last point,[54] an argument reinforced by the fact that the Asclepius cult does not seem to have reached its greatest heights of popularity until the late first century.[55] We would naturally expect John's criticism to have been aimed at a cult not only of great reputation but of *long-standing* great reputation. Such arguments are effectively neutralized if we accept the claim that although Asclepius was worshiped in other places as well, he was regarded as a uniquely *Pergamonese* deity who happened to be worshiped elsewhere.[56] Although religious theologies evolve over a period of time, it would seem unusually arrogant for Pergamon to assert such a credo if the idea of the god's healing center had to be imported from elsewhere. To assert credibly a uniquely Pergamonese identity one would normally expect the worship to have been important there at least as long as in other communities.

Donald Guthrie cautions that since the Asclepeion "was a shrine of healing...it is difficult to think that it would call forth the description of Satan's seat."[57] William Barclay reasons similarly when he argues that "the Christians would regard the place where men went to be healed—and often were—with pity rather than with indignation."[58] With the substitution of "ambivalence" for "pity," I am inclined to agree. If healing is an honorable and desirable goal, the Christian would surely have felt happiness for the recuperation but disappointment at it being attributed to a false god. Hence ambivalence would be a far more likely attitude than the kind of passionate hostility implied by John's expression "Satan's seat." The only situation in which this reasoning would seem to be assailable was if there were some particular and distinctive offensiveness of the Asclepius cult not found in the case of its rivals—and such a characteristic is unknown.

**3. The degree of polytheism and its acceptance.** The pagan cults, as a collective group, could be considered Satan's throne, and with differing degrees of clarity several writers seem to think in such terms.[59] For example, one writer finds the expression a reference to the "multiplicity of forms of paganism";[60] in a similar vein, another finds in the phrase an "allusion to the rampant paganism of Pergamum."[61] Another decides that the "deeply entrenched pagan worship" was what "justified the apocalyptist's phrase."[62] The biggest problem with this approach is that since similar cults could be found in any major town (not to mention smaller ones), this would hardly qualify the city as especially deserving John's epithet. One way of dealing with this problem is to stress that the shrines of not one but of several of the gods were more prominent than those found in other communities.[63]

Others find in a peculiar local enthusiasm for idolatry the derivation of John's condemnation. Church writers in the sixth century (Andreas) and in the tenth (Arethas) attribute John's condemnation to the city "being idolatrous beyond the rest of Asia."[64] A twentieth-century writer, though without documentation, observes that "some say there were more idols in this city than in all Asia combined."[65] From John's day or before, concrete evidence is lacking.[66] Indeed, one wonders *how* one judges relative enthusiasm: one may be able to gather whether enthusiasm is present or not, but singling out one place or group as superior in this regard would seem to be hopelessly subjective.

Along the same line, some see a religious creativity and vibrancy lacking elsewhere. One writer seems to have such a concept in mind when he speaks of the city "as a brilliant center of pagan religion" in a number of different forms, "including Caesar worship."[67]

*Visually* idolatry could be said to dominate the city. J. P. W. Sweet, who does not accept the interpretive approach we are examining, concedes that even in the late twentieth century "the temples of the Acropolis can still be seen from miles away, dominating the town."[68] One could speak of it being ruled by its false religion, and from that it is but a step to the throne imagery that goes with ruling power.

G. R. Beasley-Murray notes the possibility that "the hill itself, *with its temples*" might be under consideration. He points to how the mountain of God in Ezekiel 28:14, 16, is transformed in apocryphal literature into the *throne* of God (*Enoch* 25:3). In a similar way the hill of Pergamon, with its hilltop of false gods, might be translated into the throne of anti-God or Satan.[69]

### THE MORAL EXPLANATION

One might argue that the community was not merely idolatrous but unusually and pervasively immoral, even for an idolatrous city.

The problem with this approach is proving it. No ancient citations are introduced to prove that those of the first (or near) centuries regarded Pergamon as unusually corrupt. Nor does the reasoning used to back up the assertion seem particularly compelling. Andrew Tait roots the "Satan's throne" allusion to the presence of so many pagan cults[70] and then describes some of the moral excesses these groups engaged in.[71] The problem with this is that those *same* cults existed in other cities as well, and the *same* excesses grew out of them there as well. What made Pergamon so different as to deserve John's searing condemnation?

Joseph A. Seiss sees the paganism as part of a much bigger problem: "great wealth, luxury, and boasted learning" teamed with "corrupting heathenism" and a pronounced hostility to Christianity above that of other cities. "We know something of the style of life which characterized Pompeii; and Pergamos was even more corrupt."[72] But, again, on the basis of what reasoning or ancient perception do we regard the decay as exceeding that of other ancient communities?

John T. Hinds argues that "the place was so peculiarly filled with wickedness that it was represented as being the very location of Satan's throne." He promptly concedes, "Just what particular form of wickedness led to this designation is not known."[73] True— and since accusations of peculiarly deep moral depravity (at least in comparison with other Asian cities) are not explicitly or implicitly made by John, it would seem best to hesitate before embracing this interpretive option.

## THE PSYCHOLOGICAL EXPLANATION

This explanation hinges on the visual impact the city had in its physical surroundings. Some have approached the subject from the standpoint of the hillside theater, in particular, creating a chair/throne appearance. Peter Wood argues that the order of churches addressed in chapters 2 and 3 are a natural reflection of the order in which John's messenger would deliver the epistle to the individual congregations. Having delivered it earlier to Smyrna, the messenger would then have approached Pergamon

> from the south. Seen from a distance, the familiar description of Pergamum as a "conical hill" is at once realized to be inadequate. The great theater rises above the Temple of Dionysos for about one hundred and seventy feet, with eighty rows of seats. Unusually steep, and built into the side of the hill, it creates the impression of a vast arm-chair...tottering, as it still does, like a giant throne above the plain.[74]

Others approach the matter from the standpoint of the entire physical setting being majestic and regal. A nineteenth-century visitor notes that "especially from the plain toward the southwest...it stands out distinctly against the sky and seems to exult itself above all the hills."[75] A scholar writing in the 1960s states: "Of all the cities in this region, the situation of Pergamum is unquestionably the most impressive. The first view of the hill on approaching from the south is not easily forgotten. Smyrna on Mt. Pagus is superbly placed, but for sheer power and majesty the citadel of Pergamum is unrivaled. A royal city indeed."[76] Note how the regal terms *power, majesty,* and *royal* come spontaneously to the author's mind.

It is not surprising to find the entire setting presented in throne-like terms. William M. Ramsay found the presence and power of the imperial cult the main reason for John's "remarkable expression."[77] The supplemental explanation he provides roots the throne description in the regal image provided both by the history of the city and, even more so, by its location and physical appearance:

Pergamum had for centuries been the royal city, first of the Attalid kings, and afterwards the viceroy or Proconsul who represented the Emperor in the Province. History marked it out as the royal city, and not less clearly has nature done so. No city of the whole of Asia Minor—so far as I have seen, and there are few of importance which I have not seen— possesses the same imposing and dominating aspect. It is the one city of the land which forced from me the exclamation, "A royal city!" I came to it after seeing the others, and that was the impression which it produced.

There is something unique and overpowering in its effect, planted as it were on its magnificent hill, standing out boldly in the level plain, and dominating the valley and the mountains on the south. Other cities of the land have splendid hills which made them into powerful fortresses in ancient time; but in them the hill is as a rule the acropolis, and the city lies beneath and around or before it. But here the hill was the city proper, and the great buildings, chiefly Roman, which lie below the city, were external ornaments, lending additional beauty and stateliness to it.[78]

At a different point in his narrative, Ramsay grapples with the psychological factors that create this regal, royal surmise:

Beyond all other sites in Asia Minor it gives the traveller the impression of a royal city, the home of authority: the rocky hill on which it stands so huge, and dominates the broad plain of the Caicus so proudly and boldly....It is difficult to analyze such impressions, and to define the various causes whose combination produces them; but the relation of the vast hill to the great plain is certainly the chief cause. It would be impossible for any stronghold, however large and bold, to produce such an impression, if it stood in a small valley like those of Ephesus and Smyrna, or if the valley and the city were dominated by the still greater mass of the enclosing mountains. The rock rules over and as it were plants a foot upon a great valley; and its summit looks over the southern mountains which bound the valley, until the distant lofty peaks south of the Gulf of Smyrna, and especially the beautiful twin peaks now called the Two Brothers, close in the outlook. Far beneath lies the sea, quite fifteen miles away, and beyond it the foreign soil of Lesbos: the view of other lands, the presence of hostile powers, the need of constant care and watchfulness, all the duties of kingship are forced on the attention of him who sits enthroned on that huge rock.

There is here nothing to suggest evanescence, mutability, and uncertainty, as at Sardis or Ephesus; the inevitable impression is of permanence, strength, sure authority and great size. Something of the personal and subjective element must be mixed up with such impressions; but in none of the Seven Cities does the impression seem more universal and unavoidable than in Pergamum.[79]

In light of such reactions to the site, would not the idea of Satan's throne represent a natural combination of the physical setting with theological condemnation?

### Christ's "Sword" (Revelation 2:16)

Jesus warns the Christians in the city, "Repent, or else I will come to you quickly and will fight against them with the sword of my mouth" (Rv 2:16). Although a political allusion is only one of the tempting choices in determining the identity of Satan's throne (see above), this verse's "sword" reference is an inescapable allusion to the imperial power as expressed through its Asiatic proconsul. The Greek word for "sword" found here "is not the oriental scimitar or the ordinary cutting sword employed by many nations, especially the Greeks, but a two-edged, sharp-pointed weapon used by the Romans....In Roman estimation the sword was the symbol of highest official authority possessed by the proconsul of the province, and included the power of life and death."[80]

This was especially relevant because Pergamon was the provincial capital:[81] the proconsul who ruled from there had the power of life and death over those before his court.[82] In an earlier chapter we discussed the issue of whether the capital had been shifted to Ephesus by the time John wrote and decided that it was most unlikely. If the status had already shifted to Ephesus or, more likely, *begun* to shift due to the moving of select governmental functions, the political allusion of the "sword" would have been germane.[83] In fact, even if the process had been completed, the city's past historic character as the center of regal and then proconsular judgment would justify its inclusion.

The *spiritual* point is that while the Romans claimed the

power of life and death, it was Jesus who really possessed it. Jesus had the power to bring to justice heretics, just as the proconsul had the power to bring to justice rebels against legitimate order. This was especially significant in light of the problem of Balaamites in the congregation; Balaam had died by the physical sword (Nm 31:8).[84] Jesus was quite willing to inflict the spiritual equivalent upon Balaam's spiritual descendants.

### *"Hidden Manna to Eat" (Revelation 2:17)*

Revelation 2:17 contains the three final phases that may be partly rooted in then-contemporary societal allusions, "He who has an ear, let him hear what the Spirit says to the churches. To him who overcomes I will give some of the *hidden manna* to eat. And I will give him a *white stone,* and on the stone a new name written which no one knows except him who receives it."

The one of the three with the least likely social allusion is the reference to "hidden manna." In a strictly Christian context, this has been interpreted as a reference to the Lord's Supper,[85] with Jesus being the bread of life (Jn 6:31–35). Since partaking of that supper on an ongoing basis was a "given" within the Christian community (cf. Acts 20:7 and its mention in 1 Cor 16:2, where a weekly service was engaged in), it is hard to see how they could be promised a reward they were already receiving. Although the later application of the description to communion is understandable and appropriate, a direct reference is very unlikely.

The bread/Jesus equation in John 6 can be developed apart from communion as well. By so doing, Revelation 2:17 has been taken as a reference to receiving Jesus himself as the reward for faithfulness.[86] Although not impossible, Jesus is the *speaker* here. We would not normally expect him to be the gift as well.

The future aspect of the reference is more understandable when one remembers that Jesus described eternal rewards in terms of a meal or banquet (Mt 8:11–12; 22:2–13). John's usage could well reflect that idiom.[87] In the context of Revelation itself, the phrase has been interpreted as equivalent to "the marriage supper of the Lamb" mentioned in 19:9.[88]

We should remember that in one sense the manna was hidden *even in the biblical sources.* The only sample of it preserved

(Ex 16:33–34) was in the ark in the Holy of Holies. Only the high priest was permitted therein, and that only once a year (Heb 9:4–7). It was permanently hidden from most of the population. One could argue that John builds upon this fact, and that instead of only the high priest seeing the manna as part of his reward for doing his priestly duty, all Christians would not only see but also partake of manna as their reward for doing their duty to God.

The theme of an explicitly Messianic banquet is developed far more in apocryphal than biblical sources, and an allusion to those sources has been suggested.[89] A borderline text (accepted as canonical by the Catholic Church) is 2 Maccabees 2:4–8, where Jeremiah hides the ark (with its incense) in a cave. It was to remain there "until God gathers his people together again and shows them mercy." The *Apocalypse of Baruch* (sometimes called *2 Baruch*) at first walks in that same tradition and has it placed in a hiding place underground (6:7–10). Later, however, it is placed in heaven until the days of the Messiah (29:2–7). "And it will come to pass at that self-same time that the treasury of manna will again descend from on high, and they will eat of it in those years [of the Messiah's reign], because these are they who have come to the consummation of time" (29:8).

In the apocryphal remarks we might have a Jewish allusion perhaps, though John's thought could have equally well grown out of the biblical reasoning we have examined. Can we find a more explicitly pagan or Gentile one? Frankly, no. At the most, we are often left with an interesting conjecture that falls short of the needed clarity.

Gerhard A. Krodel attempts to find a "double entendre" with emperor worship. "Those who worship before Satan's throne, refusing to offer granules of manna, frankincense, to him in the censer on his altar, to them Christ will 'give some of the hidden manna,' heavenly frankincense, when they begin to reign with him as kings and priests unto God."[90] What Krodel does not attempt is to explain why manna and frankincense should be accepted by us as meaningful parallels. John W. Court, however, informs us of such a rationale: "'Manna' in pagan Greek and Latin (Galen of Pergamum and Pliny, *Natural History*) indicated a crumb of incense used to prove loyalty to [the] Emperor."[91]

## The "White Stone" (Revelation 2:17)

If we had to search out a pagan parallelism to the promise of manna, when we turn to the promise of a white stone we are faced with the opposite problem, choosing among several possible societal allusions. Although the text calls it a *psephos*–"a smooth stone, a pebble, worn smooth as by water, or polished"[92]–much of the discussion on the matter assumes that it is a *tessera* that is being described. As William Ramsay notes, "There is no English word which gives an adequate rendering, for the thing is not used among us, and therefore we have no name for it. It was a little cube or rectangular block of stone, ivory, or other substance, with words or symbols engraved on one or more faces. Such *tesserae* were used for a great variety of purposes."[93] Three broad categories of explanation have been given for John's reference.

### DIRECT ALLUSION TO ACTUAL PRACTICE

In this approach John is referring to one or more contemporary practices found in or known to his world.

**1. Legal allusion to acquittal.**[94] Even those with minimal knowledge of ancient customs are likely to know that in ancient trials in the Greek world jurors voted by dropping white (acquittal) or black (conviction) stones dropped into an urn. An obvious difference is that in Revelation the individual himself receives the stone.[95] Further, the implied jury in Revelation would almost certainly be Jesus himself–a one-man jury–while the custom of casting stones grew out of the need to have a convenient vote-counting mechanism to handle large juries.

**2. Athletic allusion: proof or reward for victory.** Hans Lilje argues this interpretation from the general pattern of authenticating victories: "The custom was that the *agonothetes,* the man who was in charge of the games, distributed to the winners, as a sign of victory, smooth white stones or pebbles on which their names were incised (white is the color of victory); when they went home with these 'white stones,' everyone could see that they were winners in the contests."[96] John Albert Bengel cautions that the new name and the stone it is engraved upon are described in the text as if *the reward itself* rather than as representing something else,[97] which would be the case in the athletic allusion and virtually any other interpretation imaginable. Although true, that does nothing to explain why it would be a reward in itself. Rather than constituting a reason to avoid searching for what it is intended to imply (Bengel's point), it still leaves us searching for a more complete explanation.

Some find a more specific allusion to the practice concerning gladiators rather than athletic victors in general. A cube of stone or ivory, with the athlete's name engraved upon it, was "given to successful gladiators."[98] This was bestowed at the end of one's career, so the idea was to provide public recognition of the gladiator's successes and accomplishments.[99] However, Revelation's allusion to also receiving a new name was not part of this procedure.[100]

On the other hand, it has been argued the ceremonial *tessera* that he was given *did* have more than just his name on it, that it also contained the letters *sp* (possibly standing for the Latin *spectatus*)[101] The word indicated that an individual was not only valorous but of proved value that no reasonable individual could doubt. Perhaps in a very loose sense this might be constituted as a new name or recognitionary title. However, if, as argued, this was a standard practice, then the same contraction was upon each, which is clearly contradictory to John's point ("a new name written which no one knows except him who receives it"). The question is further complicated by the question of identifying just what the *sp* was supposed to stand for.[102]

**3. Admission ticket scenario.** James M. Efird contends that such objects were sometimes "used as the ticket for admission into a certain society, group, or other association." Working from this belief he considers the white stone as carrying "that same connotation, admission to God's new age freed from the hardships of persecution."[103] Robert M. Mounce notes that in the ancient world small *tesserae* of stone, metal and wood were used for several purposes and deduces that "here it would serve as a token for admission to the heavenly banquet."[104] In a much more down-to-earth fashion, others have speculated that John's white stone is equivalent to admission emblems used by Christians in their own private feasts and festivities.[105]

Colin J. Hemer considers the strongest ground for an admission ticket interpretation to be a detailed inscription that has survived from second-century Pergamon. It recounts in detail, membership requirements and fees for a local association. In light of such strict and detailed rules, he deems it probable that they would issue some such indication of group membership.[106] Citing the German commentator Heinrich Kraft as authority, Charles H. Giblin contends that the verses refers to a regal invitation engraved "on a small stone" and notes that this "reflects a custom known from Asia Minor."[107]

**4. Priestly allusion: The ornamentation of a Jewish high priest.** Three ornamental attachments of the high priest have been suggested as the possible basis of John's "stone" reference. *The first is to the Urim and Thummin.*[108] Donald D. Guthrie argues that these "bore a name they were not allowed to disclose,"[109] a contention for which he does not provide biblical documentation. Marcus L. Loane also assumes (without argumentation of textual proof) the existence of some kind of writing on these stones. Since only the high priest had access to them, the name would be uniquely known to him,[110] as in John's promise concerning the white stone.

The nature of the Urim and Thummin has generated much speculation. We know that they were small enough to be worn in the high priest's breastplate (Lv 8:8). The two carried with them the symbolism of the importance of the high priest's work, for they were to be worn "over Aaron's heart when he goes in before the Lord" (Ex 28:30). They could be "consult[ed]" (Ezr 2:63; Nh 7:65, in both of which only "a priest" is referred to as utilizing them rather than specifically the high priest). In a similar vein, in Numbers 27:21 we read that the high priest Elezar "shall inquire by the judgment of the Urim; at his word they shall go out and at his word they shall come in, both he and all the children of Israel with him, all the congregation." Here the answer is seemingly the equivalent of a yes or no, suggesting the idea that they may have been cast as lots to decide the matter. (The references in Ezra 2:63 and Nehemiah 7:65 also concern questions that could be answered yes or no.) Whether they were somehow means of divine communication above and beyond this rudimentary level need not concern us in this context. What *is* of importance is that there is no evidence that they had any kind of name written upon them. Possibly of greater importance, there is no evidence in the Revelation text of the stone being used for communication purposes in either sense. Furthermore, although Christians are described in the New Testament as priests (1 Pt 2:5, 9), only Jesus is described as high priest (Heb 6:20; 7:26–8:1). If the white stone was intended to carry a high-priestly symbolism, then one would expect Revelation to describe Jesus *receiving* the white stone rather than giving it to others.

*The second stone reference is to two onyx stones worn by the high priest.* According to Exodus 28:9–12, the high priest wore two such objects, with the names of six tribes on each. David Chilton, who suggests this explanation, concedes that onyx was the wrong color (black). (One might also note that two stones are twice as many as John mentions.) Bdellium, however, was white, and that is mentioned both as the color of manna (Num 11:7) and in connection with onyx in Genesis 2:12. Chilton suggests that John is mentally combining these images and comes up with a white/bdellium stone as a result.[111] Perhaps, but a more concise and less indirect source would be inherently preferable to one that maximizes conjectural linkages that operated on a subconscious basis in the original author.

*A third possible reference is to the valuable stones worn on the breastplate of the high priest.*[112] W. Boyd Carpenter points out that if this is the underlying reason for the selection of a stone as a reward, that it ties in extremely well with the manna that John had just mentioned: Both are "wilderness and Jewish illustrations. Against it, however, must be set the fact that the word here rendered 'stone' is never so applied, a different word being used both in the LXX [Greek Old Testament] and in this book to denote a precious stone."[113] In addition, when one examines the description in Exodus 28:15–21, one find that each stone was to bear the name of one of the twelve tribes of Israel (verse 21). John's "stone" was individual rather than tribal, was a "new" name, and was a unique one unknown to others. On all these points it differs from the Exodus precedent. The greater the *number* of divergences, the less likely that it is being used.

Although there is a symbolic aspect to the preceding category of allusions, here the symbolic element becomes dominant. It does not merely build upon existing practice but assumes John is seeking a kind of spiritual parallel and that it is so dominant that the historical core of the reference is minimized.

**1. Symbolic of loyalty and allegiance.** In Rome, prominent and wealthy families had clients. In a derogatory sense we might call them hangers on. In a more generous sense we might call them non-family semi-dependents. The plebeians gave special honor, attendance at, and support to their superior and their superior provided a daily dole. It has been argued that the wealthy family provided clients with a *tessera,* which would indicate that they had the right to partake of the family's largesse of food and/or money. Hence it could be used symbolically of the patron/client relationship and the loyalty and allegiance/reward system that was at its heart.[114]

Colin J. Hemer cautions that he himself has never found any ancient documentation for the alleged practice by wealthy benefactors. He argues that the most explicit surviving description of the practice (Juvenal, *Sat.* 1.95–134) is far more consistent with the benefactor being personally acquainted with all his clients, thereby making the use of such tokens unnecessary.[115]

**2. Symbolic of providing what was needed.** A *tessera* could be provided as a welfare measure by a local government. In Rome the government issued a *tessera frumentaria,* which was exchanged for corn by the local poor.[116] Like the modern welfare system, these were issued on an ongoing basis. When a distribution of cash was desired, a *tessera nummaria* would be issued.[117] On an individual basis, wealthy citizens of Asian cities often provided a *tessera* to needy citizens so that they might be provided a food allotment.[118]

**3. Symbolic of imperishability.** Buildings collapse with age. Empires divide and vanish. On the individual level, each of us dies and is buried. Very few things seem to last forever—at least in comparison. A stone is certainly one of them: they are here today and they'll be here tomorrow regardless of what else vanishes. The stone image can also be combined with the idea of something precious and valuable and by the addition of the color allusion; "white" has the connotation of purity as well. Hence some find in a stone's "permanence" the symbolic root for John's implicit use of the stone for a permanent, eternal reward.[119]

### EXPLANATIONS ROOTED IN POPULAR SUPERSTITIONS

The earlier explanations are ones that are rooted in actual practices which might well be regarded with positive attitudes by later generations. Here we enter into the area of superstitions, with all the negative overtones that carries for the modern world. Indeed, the avowal of such a root explanation carries with it an extremely negative connotation of the spiritual perceptiveness of early Christians in general and certainly John in particular.

**1. Magical amulets.** In one form or another this approach has been "widely favoured by recent commentators."[120] "Although they could often serve to introduce desirable qualities such as love, wealth, power, or victory, amulets were usually used to cure medical complaints (both injuries or illnesses) and to thwart the demonic influences often held responsible for disease."[121] These were popular among both pagan Gentiles as well as Jews.[122] Hence, in spite of its superstitious roots, there was widespread societal acceptance in both the monotheistic and polytheistic traditions.

The identity is more often assumed than argued:[123] Why would John so blatantly seem to violate the theological demands of his own faith to make his point? Certainly he *could* have, but if he did, what was the rationale for it? We can usually see his apparent use of other societal allusions as religiously neutral or deduce how pagan attitudes or customs could be sufficiently germane to be used by him. How so in this case, where a rationale seems more than usually required?

There are further difficulties as well. An amulet carried a magical formula, not a person's name, as John's "stone" does.[124]

A clear conceptual difference is that magical amulets were to obtain *future* good fortune, while the stone promised by John is given as the reward for *past* faithful service. The superstitious sought out the amulet for personal protection. John's stone was not sought out; it was provided on the initiative of the giver rather than the receiver. Taken together, these present major difficulties to the amulet interpretation of John's text.

**2. Myth of precious stones that fell with the manna in the wilderness.** Rabbinic stories tell of precious stones falling in the wilderness along with the manna.[125] Whether such tales date back to the first century is unknown. It is a transparently improbable story: God was far from happy with his people at the time he sent them the manna. The *last* action attributable to God, in that context, would be to reward them with precious jewels. If the people had had a forty-year accumulation of precious jewels available when they reached the promised land, they wouldn't have needed to conquer it—they could simply have bought it! Conceptually there are important differences as well. Whatever happened in the wilderness went hand in hand with ongoing punishment; in John's allusion the stone is a reward for good behavior. In the wilderness tale, the "stones" continue to be given for years; in John's narrative it is a one-time affair. Likewise, the story has the individual receiving many such objects; in John's version only one is received.[126] In the rabbinic gloss, the "stones" were obviously for use in this life; John's "stone" is given when one enters the next life. Hence the current author is hard pressed to find here an explanation for John's usage.

*5. The "New Name" Written on the Stone (Revelation 2:17)*

POSSIBLE JUDEO-CHRISTIAN BASES FOR THE ALLUSION

These come in three forms but none of them excludes the possibility that John *also* had in mind an allusion to history or polytheistic religious practice.

**1. A new name for God.** In light of the apparent uniqueness of the new name—a different one provided for each individual—it is hard to see how God preferring one specific new name would create a meaningful parallel. To fit Revelation 2:17, it seems one would have to conjecture that God would adopt as many new names as there will be triumphant believers.[127] Possible, but one would prefer more specific evidence.

Sir William Ramsay thought he found such evidence in the inherent requirements of any new name that would be bestowed. He concedes that the new name is one

> given to the victorious Christian [and] marks his entrance on a new and higher stage of existence; he has become a new person. Yet this alone would make an inadequate and unsatisfying explanation. *We miss the element of authority and power, which is imperatively demanded to suit the case of Pergamum.* To furnish this element the New Name must be the name of God.[128]

Could not the "element of authority and power" Ramsay considered needed be conveyed not by the name being that of God but by the fact that the ultimate power in the universe—the Lord Jehovah—bestows the name? What additional "element of authority and power" would be needed?

**2. A new name for Jesus.**[129] W. J. Limmer Sheppard argues that the new name "is not the name of the person receiving the stone; it is something better; it is the 'new name' of God in Christ, a higher revelation of Him than has ever been communicated here, designated as 'mine own new name' in Chapter 3:12."[130] In 3:12, however, the name is written *on* the believer while in 2:17 it is written on a stone and *given* to the believer. The idea of reward is inherent in both texts, so John may be intending parallel ideas, but that is far from using 3:12 to establish the identity of the name in the earlier text.

In Revelation 19:12 we read of the exalted Christ, "His eyes were like a flame of fire, and on his head were many crowns. He had a name written that no one knew except himself." Gerhard A. Krodel speculates that this name of Christ may be the one that the Christian is promised.[131] On the other hand, can such a widely given name be one that "no one knew" (2:17)?

**3. A new name for the individual believer.** The giving of an individual new name (though not a secret one) certainly found Old Testament precedent. Abram became Abraham (Gn 17:5);

Sarai became Sarah (Gn 17:15); Jacob became Israel (Gn 32:28). But even here this was the exception, not the rule. Is there anything in the New Testament era that might form a more immediate precedent for John's reference?

Some find it, at least in part, in "the already established custom of taking a new name at baptism."[132] Hugh Martin is clearly tempted by this approach but stops short of embracing it: "There is evidence that such a custom became established at a very early date and is perhaps referred to here."[133] Oddly enough, out of the apparently huge number of first-century Gentile converts, we read of no such custom at all, which would certainly suggest a backreading into the first century of a later custom. The only exception is Saul's conversion on the road to Damascus, and God changing his name to Paul. Martin is fair enough to point out that both New Testament usage and later custom also provide evidence against the practice: "The list of first generation Christians in Romans 16:3–16 shows that it was not then felt necessary to change names with heathen associations. Most of the names in a list of eighty-seven bishops in north Africa in A.D. 256 are ordinary pagan names, many of them incorporating names of gods. Clearly the practice of giving Christian names was not universal."[134] In light of the silence of the New Testament on the subject, a better judgment would be that, with a very few exceptions (and all except Paul's *are* speculative), the custom did not exist. And if the custom did not exist, then John could not be alluding to it.

### POSSIBLE PAGAN BASES FOR THE ALLUSION

**1. A religious basis in pagan name changes and secret names of God.** Just as followers of Jesus, at some point, began to adopt the practice of name change at baptism, it has been speculated that pagans had an analogous custom: adopting a second name when they entered the service of a specific deity. William Ramsay was inclined to interpret an obscure reference in Aelius Aristides's *Hymn to Asklepios* to indicate this practice.[135] Colin J. Hemer is extremely tempted by this approach but ultimately rejects it as too conjectural both as to the meaning of Aristides's text and other sources that may hint at the practice.[136]

Another possible precedent was the custom of polytheistic

religions to have a special name for their god. This was revealed only to adherents and was never shared with outsiders.[137] Although we could have a societal basis here if the "new name" of John refers to a new name of God (rather than the individual), the *rationale* behind being given the name is clearly alien to Johannine monotheism: by knowing the name one had control or power over the god.[138] By knowing the true, hidden name one entered into a kind of balance of power with the deity; although one remained a subject of that divinity, one now could invoke its power to guarantee the temporal results one sought and the supernatural being was obligated to exercise its powers toward that goal.

**2. A social basis in name changes as a sign of gratitude.** L. van Hartinsveld, without documenting specific cases, contends that "it is a common Oriental ideal that upon entering a new situation a person should have a new name."[139]

J. Massyngberde Ford speaks of serious illness, in particular, as motivating the name change: "A change of name was often given in the case of serious illness. If the patient survived, the new name bore a reference to life or to some Old Testament saint whose life was especially long. A new name, therefore, denoted a new person: it was often theophoric, i.e., compounded with a name of God."[140] But how ancient is this custom? Ford does not speculate on the matter. William Ramsay refers to it as an "old" practice but only describes the way it was practiced among nineteenth-century Jews in Palestine.[141]

**3. A historical allusion in Emperor Augustus taking that name upon himself.** The most likely pagan societal allusion in John's mind (if one was intended at all) can be found in the granting of a new name to the empire's first emperor. In 27 B.C. Octavius came to power in Rome. So profoundly important was the occasion in the history of the nation that the Senate set out to choose a new name for its leader. It turned to the old sacred term *augusta* and decreed him to be "Augustus." The selection was not only ego-building for its recipient, but it also seemed justly appropriate. After all he

> had been the saviour of Rome, and...already the popular belief had begun to regard [him] as an incarnation of the divine

nature in human form, sent down to earth to end the period of war and introduce the age of peace. This sacred, divine name marked out the man to whom it was applied as one apart from the world, standing on a higher level, possessor of superhuman power in virtue of this new name and transmitting that power through the name to his descendants.[142]

Although all of this would obviously not be true of the triumphant Christian being rewarded in Revelation 2:17, yet the idea of receiving an honored name—a uniquely *new* name as well—is inherent in John's text. Just as the triumphant Augustus had been renamed, the triumphant Christian would enter into the eternal kingdom with a new identity.

This scenario is of special relevance to Pergamon since it was the center of provincial emperor worship. The new name given to that worshiped human deity was given by a merely worldly institution—important as the Roman Senate was. The Christian's new name would be given not by his or her fellows but by the true God. Indeed, the new name would be given for *not* worshiping the renamed military hero turned emperor and god, whom Pergamon zealously worshiped.

# 8

# Mercantile Thyatira

According to Strabo, Thyatira was originally a Macedonian colony. It functioned as a garrison post to protect the road that ran between Pergamon and Sardis. It also functioned as a buffer to protect Pergamon from its enemies. Geographically, the city was in a very exposed position. The ground it was erected upon had only a modest elevation, in contrast to the more easily defended communities built upon hills or mountains. In large part because of its exposed position, it never rose to recognition as a major civic power in its own right. It was important, not for its own sake, but as a staging ground for any assault upon Pergamon. The city was a pawn in any power struggle aimed at Pergamon, and the citizens recognized the fact all too well.

Thyatira served as the headquarters of Antiochus III prior to the battle of Magnesia. The Romans won that battle, and Thyatira was added to the kingdom of Pergamon. After an interim of about half a century it passed into Roman control as part of the inherited Pergamonese kingdom.[1] While Claudius reigned, the city was granted permission to mint its own coinage.[2] Perhaps as a sign of growing prosperity, the number of surviving coins increased greatly in the second century and reached a peak in the third.[3]

Assuming that Thyatira did not erect and maintain milestones outside the area of its own jurisdiction, its boundaries stretched at least ten miles along the road leading to Sardis and six miles on the one leading to Pergamon.[4] Its population was only about twenty-five thousand,[5] in marked contrast to such massive metropolises as Ephesus and Pergamon.

Contrary to the Greek Asiatic norm, there is no evidence of "tribal" divisions of the population of the city.[6] Combined with the abundance of inscriptions mentioning guilds, this has naturally lead to the conclusion that government was effectively organized by guild rather than on the usual tribal basis.[7] As a city walking in the Greek heritage, it had the amenities one expected in a community with such a background, such as three gymnasiums.[8]

Regardless of whether city government was exercised through the guilds, they occupied a central role in the life of the city due to their number and large membership. Some have gone so far as to suggest that Thyatira "possessed more trade guilds than any other Asian city."[9] Whether this is literally true or not, it certainly had a large number. Coins and written records refer to wool-workers, weavers, tailors, linen-makers, leather-workers, and shoemakers. There were also potters, blacksmiths, and bronzesmiths. There were bakers, dyers, and slave merchants:[10] all the varied types of trades one would find in a large urbanized community.

It should be remembered, however, that guilds had a *mixed* membership. Although sometimes viewed as analogous to modern unions, which are composed of "laborers," guilds were composed of all members of a craft: owners, freedmen "employees,"and even slaves. They could be citizens of the city or foreigners resident in the community.[11] Although there was no legal requirements that one be a guild-member,[12] it was natural that one would want to be. The guild consisted of individuals one was bonded with by trade and occupation; it was composed of individuals with similar interests and concerns.[13] It provided opportunities for an active social life within the confines of a group most likely to share one's own priorities.[14] Of course, it was the social aspects that would most compromise a Christian's convictions; the guilds were normally up to their necks in idolatry, even as part of their guild rituals,[15] and open condoners and practitioners of sexual immorality at their guild social functions.[16] Yet to have a social life in a guild-heavy community like Thyatira, how was one to avoid membership and participation? If one were too actively isolated from the group, one risked the kind of economic retaliatory action that any organized group can inflict upon a nonconforming outsider.

One constructive option would have been *Jewish* guilds. Certainly such guilds existed in Egypt during the reign of Trajan[17] and are datable to the second or third century in the Asian city of Hierapolis.[18] It is quite possible that such organizations existed in other Asian communities in the first century,[19] especially in those with heavy guild membership and a substantial number of Jewish residents. To the extent that Jews were willing to tolerate the presence of Christians (at least those who were ethnically Jewish), Christians possessed at least a partial safe harbor from the more blatant contamination found in the pagan variety of such organizations. On the other hand, Jewish guilds were no more immune to pagan contamination than the Christian church in Thyatira (cf. the discussion of Jezebel below). One might or might not be freed from a varying degree of the pagan religious practices and temptations to sexual immorality. If the guild was highly monotheistic, one ran the danger of exclusion upon the basis of one's heretical Christian faith. As in the modern world, there were not always easy or comfortable solutions for living by biblical ethics in an unbelieving world.

To be officially recognized as a guild, the association had to obtain a license from the Roman government. Since there were a multitude of such associations, not only in Thyatira but throughout the empire, and since the records specifically allude to the official recognition of only a few, this raises the problem of how strenuously the law was applied.[20] It could be that they tolerated a de facto rather than de jure status for such institutions because their open-ended membership virtually assured that Roman loyalists would be represented in sufficient number to prevent the guilds from being converted into bases of anti-Roman rebellion.

In at least some of the craft guilds of Thyatira, the presidency was held on a hereditary basis.[21] Statues were erected in honor of respected guild leaders, complete with appropriate flowery inscriptions. This was especially the case when the individual also served well in some significant public office. One example that has survived concerns the slave merchants' guild. It complimented its leader because he had "acted scrupulously" during the term he served in the civil office known as the *agoranomos* [market director]. In addition, "he has presented largess to the city from his own resources, in a most generous way, during the festival of the *Augustii* [the emperors]."[22]

The *agoranomos* appears to have played a pivotal role in maintaining equitable relations between employers and the various groups found in Thyatira and other cities. In the second century B.C. the people of the city of Paros, through the governing council,

praised the local agoranomos because "in respect to those who
work for wages and those who hire them, he saw to it that neither
should be treated unjustly; according to the laws he compelled the
former not to break their agreements but to go to their work, and
the latter to pay their workers without litigation."[23] Presumably the
*agoranomos* continued to play a similar role in the first centuries
A.D. in Thyatira, since inscriptions have been found in the post
holder's honor not only from the slave merchants' guild but also
from the shoemakers, dyers, and bakers.[24] As W. H. Buckler
observes, "Such expensive compliments imply that to be on good
terms with him was distinctly to their interest."[25]

### Religions in the City

Although Thyatira was a religious city (anything else would
have been profoundly noticeable in the ancient world), it was the
center of no major regional or international sect.[26] Artemis was
worshiped at Thyatira,[27] as was Cybele.[28] The Sambathe had her
Sambatheion near the city, which had a well-known oracle movement.[29] This was a "Jewish-pagan mixed cult."[30] It is uncertain
whether the membership consisted of Jews who had forsaken
monotheism or Gentiles attempting to find a halfway house
between Judaism and traditional polytheism.[31] The Jewish element in this cult has been vigorously challenged, as we will see in
our more detailed examination of the Sabazios cult when we
study Sardis.

When we turn to the male gods, the most important,
because he was patron deity of the city, was Tyrimnos[32]—or, to
give him his full title, Helios Tryimnaios Pythios Apollo.[33] He was
traditionally pictured "as riding forth on his charger with a bat-
tle-ax over his shoulder. This hero was merged with Apollo and
subsequently appears on coins as a standing rather than a
mounted figure, but still carrying an axe. He was a 'propolis'
god, having his temple outside the city walls."[34] Regular games
were held in his honor.[35]

In light of the god's civic status, it is not surprising that the
trade guilds of Thyatira explicitly recognized this Apollo as their
divine patron and protector.[36] Some have argued that, due to his

popularity in that community, there is conscious use of Apollo imagery in the horsemen imagery of Revelation 6.[37]

Just as Tyrimnos and Apollo tended to be merged into one, a lesser version of the same phenomenon occurred in regard to the emperor: the emperor was viewed as the son of Apollo and therefore Apollo worship became simultaneously an act of emperor worship.[38] The imperial cult also made substantial encroachments upon the worship of Tyrimnos. His long-established festival of Tyrimnea was broadened to include the emperor by adding the imperial title Sebasta. Whether sacrifices were offered to the emperor apparently varied from one festival to another. "At Thyatira in one case [that is known] the sacrifices were made only to the god, that is Tyrimnus, but in another the prayers and sacrifices were offered to the god and the lord emperors."[39]

Little is known of Judaism or Christianity in this Asian city. Although Christianity may have arisen independently of her action, it is highly tempting to connect its introduction into the city with the conversion of Lydia by Paul in Philippi (Acts 16:13–15, 40).[40] She is described as one "who worshiped God" (Acts 16:14), which suggests a proselyte to Judaism, otherwise we would simply expect her to be called a Jew. The presence of a husband is not mentioned.[41] She urges Paul to "come to my house and stay," and the implication is that he did so (Acts 16:15). (Note the "my house" rather than "our house" or similar phraseology.) It was a considerable household she presided over, since we read of "brethren" and how "they" (not he or she) "encouraged" Paul and Silas before they left the city (16:40).

She was a merchant, lodged in Philippi as "a seller of purple" ["purple cloth," *NRSV*] (16:14).[42] Although she could have been there as an independent sales merchant, Emil G. Kraeling's speculation that she was there as an agent for a Thyatarian guild is also possible. Her being female might indicate she was its specialist in women's export clothing.[43] Since the Roman government exercised a monopoly on purple beginning in Nero's reign (if not earlier), her business inevitably required a connection with the imperial regime. Without government approval her business could not exist.[44]

John's mini-epistle singles out only one local fault: toleration for a woman he calls Jezebel (2:20). The condemnation is not that all or even most of the members were following her practice; the condemnation is that they permitted her to go unopposed. But *why* would this situation exist? Perhaps the reason is found in her claim to be "a prophetess" (2:20); she may have been presenting her doctrine as divine revelation. Divine revelation it wasn't, but divine retribution on both her and her followers was guaranteed (2:22–23).

Thyatira played no significant role in the regional or universal church in the following centuries. What impact it did have was probably negative: According to Epiphanius of Cyprus (fourth century) the Thyatarian church had embraced Montanism a century earlier. It has been reasonably speculated that the high Montanist evaluation of Revelation played a key role in increasing skepticism of the book in other regions.[45]

### Societal Allusions
### Text of the Epistle

"And to the angel of the church in Thyatira write, 'These things says the Son of God, who has eyes like a flame of fire, and the feet like fine brass; "I know your works, love, service, faith, and your patience; and as for your works, the last are more than the first. Nevertheless I have a few things against you, because you allow that woman Jezebel, who calls herself a prophetess, to reach and beguile my servants to commit sexual immorality and to eat things sacrificed to idols. And I gave her time to repent of her sexual immorality, and she did not repent. Indeed I will cast her into a sickbed, and those who commit adultery with her into great tribulation, unless they repent of their deeds. And I will kill her children with death. And all the churches shall know that I am He who searches the minds and hearts. And I will give to each one of you according to your works. But to you I say, and to the rest in Thyatira, as many as do not have this doctrine, and who have not known the depths of Satan, as they call them, I will put on you no other burden. But hold fast what you have till I come. And he who overcomes, and keeps my works until the end, to him I will give power over the nations—'He shall rule them with a rod of iron; as the potter's vessels shall be broken to pieces'—as I also have received from my Father; and I will give him the morning star. He who has an ear, let him hear what the Spirit says to the churches."'" (Rv 2:18–29)

*Geographical Allusion to Laodicea's Military Weaknesses*

The faithful Thyatarian Christian is promised, "He who overcomes and keeps my works until the end, to him I will give power over the nations—'He shall rule them with a rod of iron; as the potter's vessels shall be broken to pieces'—as I also have received from my Father" (Rv 2:26–27).

In Daniel 2, God's kingdom starts as a "stone" that breaks apart a statue and grows into a world-covering kingdom. Jesus tells the apostles that they will sit on twelve thrones, judging Israel (Mt 19:28), and Paul says "saints [Christians] will judge the world" (1 Cor 6:2). Whatever is intended by these passages, John's description is clearly in accord with such imagery.

The "rod of iron" (Rv 2:27), writes Leon Morris, is "presumably a staff tipped with iron." The reason is that

> the verb rendered "rule" (2:27) literally means "shepherd." We usually think of the shepherd in terms of kindness and tender care. But the shepherd was an autocrat. His power over his flock was absolute, and it is this aspect of the shepherd's life that is in view. Shepherding with an iron rod might denote no more than strength or firmness were it not linked with breaking to pieces like clay vessels (cf. Ps 2:9; Jer 51:20).[46]

We may well have here a geographical contrast with the city's transparent military weakness. As J. Massyngberde Ford comments,

> The reward is significant in the light of Thyatira's position as the weakest of the seven cities. One notes that a certain irresistible power is promised to the weakest city of the seven, for with Thyatira's disadvantageous position we may contrast the high acropolis of Sardis, the huge hill of Pergamum, the mountain walls of Ephesus, the castled hill of Smyrna (each with their harbors), the long sloping hillside of Philadelphia which rises above the plain, and the plateau of Laodicea with its long walls.[47]

We could have, in the conquest rhetoric, a coinage allusion

as well: Tyrimnos is portrayed on the city's coins as a horseman going forth to conquer.[48] What Jesus promises is the certainty of the conquest, not to all Thyatirans but to those who are of Christ in that community. The "rod of iron" is to be used in a punitive manner, such as the breaking of "potter's vessels" (2:27). Tyrimnos was also "often associated with punishment."[49]

### Allusions to the City's Patron Deity, Tyrimnos

The only time in the book of Revelation that the explicit phrase "Son of God" is used is in 2:18, though it is implied in other places (such as 2:27 and 3:5). Tyrimnos was considered a son of Zeus, and this word could have been chosen to make the point that Jesus represented the true son of God while Tyrimnos represented only an imitation.[50] A blow at emperor worship could also be intended, since the emperor was looked upon as Apollo incarnated,[51] as a son of God in his own right. Again, the emphasis would be on reality versus polytheistic imitation.

### Allusions to the City's Brass Industry

In Revelation 2:18 Jesus is described as having "eyes like a flame of fire, and his feet are like fine brass." The bronzesmiths appeared to have enjoyed special prestige in the city: one coin from Thyatira shows a goddess waiting to receive a helmet that the bronzesmith is finishing. The reference in 2:18 to "fine brass" was used, some have suggested, due to the importance of this guild in the city.[52]

Some go even further. E. M. Blaiklock notes that the word translated "fine brass" ["burnished bronze," *NRSV*] in 1:15 and 2:18 is " 'chalcolibanos' [and is] found nowhere else in Greek." From this he concludes that "it may have been a Thyatiran trade name, caught up for local colour by the writer on Patmos."[53]

Others note that the city produced high-quality bronze. Crafted into top-grade weaponry, its various bronze products could be treated and polished to a gold-like shine.[54] The eyes "like a flame of fire" (v. 18) fits well with the accompanying reference to "fine brass," because the effective use of fire was vital to the crafting of such products.[55]

Others think a specific bronze statue in the town is in the author's mind.[56] The point would then be: You look (perhaps daily) at an idol that looks like this; in Jesus the Risen you have the reality. Others seem to assume the comparison intended here is with the popular image of Apollo.[57] Others suggest a contrast is intended with "the statues of the Emperors,"[58] presumably since emperors were pictured as Apollo-like.

### Societal Allusions in Describing "Jezebel" (Revelation 2:20–24)

In dealing with Jezebel there are three relevant questions that need to be answered: her identity, the character of the moral evil she encouraged, and the nature of the punishment her followers were threatened with. In regard to all three there are possible societal allusions. None is overly strong, but taken together they represent a stronger argument than when analyzed separately.

WHO IS "JEZEBEL"?[59]

Jezebel's claim to authority was at least partially based upon her claim to be a "prophetess" (2:20). Presumably this is how they got to know "the depths of Satan, as they call them" (2:24); that is, through the revelations she provided. Whether these were explicitly labeled as such by her[60] or whether this is John's way of mocking her claims to being a channel of divine revelation, the point would be much the same: she was claiming to lead them into the realm of a supernatural reality that unguided mortals could not hope to reach.

From her claims and her reception, it is clear that she occupied a major role in the church, either on a de facto or de jure basis. Some make her authority overt and open: "It is likely that this woman was accepted on the grounds of her charismatic gifts as leader of the community."[61] The well-known New Testament bias against explicit female leadership in the churches would surely have excluded such a role. Even if this had been ignored and Thyatira were following a dissenting pattern, one would expect a clear-cut condemnation of her abuse of the position of leader (in furthering heresy) rather than an attack on her alleged prophetic role only.

Others prefer the scenario that she was wife of the dominant leader of the congregation. A minority of manuscripts have the reading "your woman Jezebel," which carries with it the connotation of "your wife."[62] This requires the assumption that the "wife" is that of the "angel" being written to, and that the "angel" is the leader of the church. This provides several difficulties. The *entire* congregation is being rebuked rather than just the leader. The image may be of the *church* (personified) as "married" to the woman. This is, of course, assuming that the textual reading is valid, and the actual evidence for it has not convinced textual experts to insert it into the text.

A third approach is that she was a converted pagan priestess. It has been speculated that she may have served as a priestess-oracle at the Sambatheion, located near the city.[63] The converted priestess scenario[64] then provides a local societal allusion as well as a tie-in with both her prophetic claims and possibly being the wife of a church leader. Indeed, based upon the Old Testament use of the image—it is unknown in the New Testament outside the present passage—one would anticipate an outsider converted to the faith. The original Jezebel was a foreigner (non-Israelite) who married into the royal family of Israel (1 Kgs 16:31). Her husband was a weakling (cf. 21:6–7), and she was able to exercise regal authority either independently (19:1–3) or under the guise of her husband issuing her order (21:8–10). She furthered cultural and religious subversion by encouraging his people to join her in her idolatry (16:31–33). Hence it would not be surprising if she had married into the church and, rather than leaving her idolatry behind, had returned to it independently, and through a weak husband furthered her spiritual subversion of the church. This is conjectural, but it would certainly explain the choice of the epithet in this case and the lack of its use in other situations (the Nicolaitans and the Balaamites) where similar moral and spiritual drift was afoot.[65]

The possible social allusion arises from the conjectured economic status of both women. The Old Testament match of Jezebel and Ahab was made to cement the commercial ties between Tyre and Ahab's Samaria. The successful trade link brought prosperity to Samaria but also encouraged the importation of pagan deities from Tyre. The parallel with Thyatira is thought to be that Jezebel encouraged religious and moral compromises within local guilds as a means of protecting the economic interests and prosperity of Christian businessmen.[66] Just as Samaria without its pagan trade partner would have been grievously weakened, the believing businessman of Thyatira would have had his markets and product sources gravely narrowed, if not eliminated, if his religion caused him to be on the outs with those in the same trade.

### THE NATURE OF THE IMMORALITY JEZEBEL CONDONED

Figuratively, joining in worship of pagan deities was branded in Exodus as "play[ing] the harlot with their gods" (Ex 34:15). Hosea rebukes a much later generation because "you have played the harlot against your God" by worshiping such alien deities and indicates that they thought they were going to benefit financially by doing so (Hos 9:1). There would certainly be a parallel if the speculation that Christians were being tempted to drift into the forms of polytheism to keep their fellow guildsmen happy is sound.

Furthermore, in the Old Testament, Israel was counted as God's wife (Is 54:5; Jer 3:20). Similarly, spiritual Israel, the church, is counted as the bride of Christ (Eph 5:23–28), a point that Paul seems to apply not only to the church collectively but simultaneously to individual Christians (2 Cor 11:1–3). Hence if the church—or an individual member—wanders off into the apostasy of semi- or overt paganism, it could be described by an alarmed observer as spiritual adultery, as in the current passage.[67]

In the ancient world spiritual adultery easily became the sanction for literal adultery, as in the sacred prostitution of the Artemis cult. The various groups also tended to remove the absolute prohibitions against such practices found in both Judaism and Christianity, thereby permitting extramarital affairs and prostitution in an even broader area.[68] Either approach would be in keeping with the literal and metaphorical use of the expression. Again, if guild groups are the target—as is often believed[69]— the lack of Judeo-Christian "inhibitions" provided abundant opportunity for lasciviousness and quite possibly overt adultery.

Can we tell which form of adultery was uppermost in John's mind? Commentators seem to have a predilection for the spiritual/religious interpretation. To establish this, both Old Testament texts[70] and New Testament verses[71] that are written of literal sexual misconduct are cited as examples of the former. Hugh Martin argues against a literal reading, "It is difficult to believe that actual immorality was practiced and defended within the church membership."[72] On the other hand, typical American church members of the 1950s would have found it unimaginable that only forty years later some church leaders would defend divorce for any and all reasons, heterosexuals living together without marriage, and the solemnization of homosexual liaisons. Whether one approves or denounces such changes, they are a matter of objective fact. Why should it seem odd that at least some early Christians also drifted from their once stern "moralism"?

Some turn to the most relevant book of all—John's own "Revelation"—to see how he used the term. Several passages (Rv 17:2; 18:3, 9) are introduced to prove a religious compromise interpretation.[73] However, is the intention of the passages to rebuke *idolatry* or the political, social, and moral compromises rulers and the business class made in order to maintain their wealth and position? Even if one includes narrow religious compromise in this list, one has still expanded it into a substantially different approach than the traditional idolatry one. Furthermore, literal idolatry is distinguished from sexual immorality in Revelation 21:8 and 22:15; in Revelation 9:21 it is distinguished from their "sorceries." Hence John's usage is compatible with either approach—quite possible because he intends *both* approaches or, at least, intends not to exclude either approach. He writes rhetoric to apply to both situations rather than to just one. He seems to have in mind any and all types of moral and religious compromise that a Christian might be tempted to, out of whatever motive.

Just as it is wrong to limit the sin John condemns to idolatry, it is equally wrong to limit it to sexual transgression, especially if one attempts to single out one particular type.[74] Likewise, to make the "adultery"/"sexual immorality" equivalent merely to being tempted by accepting Jezebel's teaching[75] begs the question of what her teaching was.

### THE IDENTIFICATION OF THE "BED" OF HER PUNISHMENT

The term translated "bed" in Revelation 2:22 is broad enough to refer to more than one situation, depending upon the intent of the author.[76]

*It can refer to a sickbed* (and is so rendered by the *NKJV* and *RSV*).

*It can refer to a deathbed,* the logical culmination of the thoughts of a sickbed and a nonrecovering patient. We have two images of those joined to her: adults and children. The idea of adultery requires an adult, while the idea of blindly following her teaching fits best with the image of a child. In both cases we have the idea of being joined to Jezebel in her heresy.[77] The punishment threatened on both fits in with the sickbed interpretation. The "great tribulation" (2:22) threatened upon her adulterous partners would include the pain and anguish coming from their disease or affliction and carry the danger of death. In the other identification of her disciples as "children" (v. 23) the death theme is made explicit. They are warned of "death"; the use of the word "kill" in this context would also most naturally suggest physical death. The "bed" could be the deathbed of those who followed her. However, only Jezebel is *explicitly* threatened with being cast into the "bed," while tribulation and death are aimed at her disciples.[78] Since the image of adultery requires that those threatened with tribulation also shared her "bed," it would hardly need to be made explicit in their case. If children and adulterers are two images for the same group, it would not need to be made explicit in their case either, since the idea has already been introduced by implication.

*It can refer to the social use of a bed/couch used in dining.* Individuals slept on a bed/couch at night and sat on it to dine or to feast. If what are targeted are the abuses that flowed from uninhibited guild meetings in the community, we here rejoin the theme of social allusions. Hugh Martin sees a pun between sickbeds (couches) and ones used for reveling. The reference becomes one to "couches at [guild] banquets. Jezebel and her 'children'...will find themselves not on couches of pagan revelry but on couches of illness, and it will be a deadly sickness if they do not repent."[79]

*The combined use of all three terms of reference.* All three of these could well be interlocked by a shared element: sexually transmitted diseases. Gained on the "bed" of pleasure, they fester on the "sick bed," and, if one is truly unfortunate, bear ultimate physical fruit on the "deathbed." Although some varieties of these various ailments are of more recent derivation, it seems safe to assume that fatal varieties were also known in the ancient world and that John may have such a sowing/reaping scenario partly in mind.

## Joining the Biblical, Apocryphal, and Mythological: The "Morning Star" (Revelation 2:28)

When we examine the ancestry of this image, we find roots in all three sources. It was one, then, that all could grasp as representative of obtaining power and rule. It crossed the boundaries of both religion and culture.

*Biblical roots.* Just as ruling (Rv 2:27) is joined with receiving "the morning star" (v. 28), star imagery is combined with Christ as king as well. The wise men were guided by a star and they came to worship a newborn king. Likewise "a star shall come out of Jacob" is immediately joined to the promise that "a scepter shall rise out of Israel" (Nm 24:17). Zacharias spoke of the Messiah in implicitly regal terms (as one who would "save [us] from our enemies and from the hand of all who hate us" (Lk 1:71). In Revelation 22:16 Jesus describes himself as "the root and the offspring of David, the bright morning star." If it seems not excessive to read into the David reference a regal allusion, then once again the ideas of imperial Messianic rule and a star are brought together. It would be most natural, then, for the triumph of Christians also to join together these two allusions. There was also Old Testament precedent for the resurrected to be pictured as "shin[ing] like the brightness of the firmament" and "like the stars forever" (Dn 12:3).

*Apocryphal roots.* A star allusion is found in 1 Enoch 104:2: "Be hopeful; for aforetime ye were put to shame through ill and affliction; but now ye shall shine as the lights of heaven, ye shall shine and ye shall be seen, and the portals of heaven shall be opened to you." Likewise in 2 Esdras 7:97 we read that "their sixth joy will be the revelation that they are to shine like stars, never to fade or die, with faces radiant as the sun."

*Mythological roots.* This general pagan belief in the morning star (Venus) as symbolic of control and domination[80] was especially relevant to the Romans,

Venus was the mother of Aeneas, who fled burning Troy and landed in Italy. She was the grandmother of Julius, the son of Aeneas. Thus Venus is the matriarch of the renowned Roman patrician family from which Julius Caesar and Caesar Augustus descended. Venus was the national goddess of the Romans, and was named "Victrix"–female conqueror.[81]

Because Venus "was the symbol of victory and sovereignty...Roman generals owned their loyalty to Venus by erecting temples in her honour (e.g., Sulla, Pompey, Caesar), and Caesar's legions carried her sign on their standards."[82]

A secondary mythological contrast may be with Ishtar. That goddess was represented by the evening star. She embodied the idea of death.[83] In contrast, Jesus offers them the morning star, which suggests, rebirth, renewal, a new beginning. Though the Venus image is probably the dominant mythological idea in John's mind (to the extent that he had conscious awareness of the pagan parallel), the Ishtar cult imagery would make the point even more vivid to his readers.

# 9

# Invincible Sardis

Sardis has the distinction of being the only one of the seven churches with a good claim to have been mentioned in the Old Testament. In Obadiah, verse 20, we read, "And the captives of this host of the children of Israel shall possess the land of the Canaan- ites as far as Zarepath. The *captives of Jerusalem who are in Sepharad* shall possess the cities of the South." There is a consensus among scholars that this refers to the city of Sardis[1] and indicates— depending upon when one dates Obadiah—the presence of an ongoing Jewish community at least as far back as the fifth[2] or sixth century B.C.[3] Such a site for Jewish expatriates is certainly surpris- ing since deportees were generally sent into the Tigris-Euphrates valley, and we would normally expect this "Sepharad" to be within that area.[4] This is, however, an objection equally hostile to other proposed identifications such as Spain[5] or near Benghazi in North Africa.[6] If the identification is sound, as generally assumed, these Jews were presumably in Sardis after they or their parents were originally taken into Mesopotamia. They could have been there as mercenaries for the conqueror or on other grounds that made sense at the time but were unknown to later generations.

Sardis may date as far back as 1200 B.C. and was certainly one of the oldest communities of Asia Minor.[7] The independent kingdom of Lydia came into existence late in the seventh century under Gyges, the first king of the Mermnad dynasty. Perhaps the kingdom's greatest legacy to the world was its invention of gov- ernment coinage.[8] Even after the Persian takeover, Sardis minted coins for the entire western part of the Persian Empire.[9]

In 561 B.C. the legendary Croesus mounted the throne. His name became a synonym for wealth beyond human comprehen- sion. The reputation of his nation for wealth establishes the like- lihood of a foundation of truthfulness beneath the legendary accretions: even in the century before him it was called "Golden Sardis."[10] Credibility is further enhanced by the discovery of a site for melting gold within the city that is dated approximately simultaneous with his reign.[11]

After being on the throne for not much more than a decade, Croesus debated the dangerous option of challenging the power of King Cyrus of Persia. The oracle at Delphi sent back what sounded like an encouraging message, "If you cross the River Halys you will destroy a great empire." He did—but it turned out to be his own.

In 547 B.C. he crossed the Halys and devastated Cappadocia. Cyrus and his Persian foe came together in a battle in which the losses on both sides were immense but with no clear-cut winner. Cyrus refused to re-engage in battle, so the following day Croesus withdrew back within his own territorial borders. At this point he made a decisive blunder: he assumed that since Cyrus's forces had endured a major mauling, they would withdraw until the following year. With this reasonable prospect in mind, he instructed his allies whose forces had not been at the battle to wait until the following spring to join him. The allies that had been present at the battle, he ordered home with similar instructions.

At this point Cyrus gambled and committed his remaining forces. Based upon their earlier performance, Croesus's forces would have made a good showing against the Persians, but having dispersed them all over the kingdom, Croesus denuded himself of most of his military capability. In October of 547 B.C., Croesus found himself facing the huge Persian army—not at a safe distance within the security of his and his allies' massive forces but with only local forces arrayed against the Persians outside the walls of his own capital.

The Lydians had a well-deserved reputation for luxurious living, but no one gainsaid the effectiveness of their cavalry. In this case, though, they were simply too few to overcome their opponents and the Lydian combatants had to cease operations, retreat within their own walls, and prepare to outwait the Persian siege.[12]

Unfortunately for the defenders, the siege army found a way into the supposedly impregnable fortress in September of 546. The Persians promptly moved the vast royal treasury into their own boundaries.[13] Sardis's importance was recognized by making it the capital of the local Persian province.[14] Ties were further cemented by erecting the "Royal Road" from the Persian capital of Susa to Sardis.[15] This was later extended all the way to Ephesus.[16]

In 499 B.C. Greek invaders not only attacked the city but burned the shrine to Cybele. Cybele was considered such an important goddess, and the act of degradation so particularly defiling, that it set off a retaliatory war by Persia against Greece.[17]

In 401 B.C. Sardis was the launching pad of an effort by the younger brother of Artaxerxes II to overthrow him. Xenophon's famous *March Up Country* (or *Anabasis*) took the legendary Ten Thousand through the city. In 334 B.C. Sardis chose not to oppose the march of Alexander's army. After his death it was part of Antgonus's mini-empire, from which it passed to Lysimachus and then to the Seleucid Empire in 270 B.C.[18] In the following century, Sardis was absorbed into the Pergamonese kingdom and passed, as part of that kingdom, into Roman control a half century later.[19]

As with the rest of Roman Asia, the city experienced periods both of economic decline and of economic growth and prosperity that continued throughout the first centuries A.D.[20] Emperor Hadrian visited in both A.D. 123–24 and A.D. 128. In 214–15, Emperor Caracalla is known to have visited the Asian cities of Pergamon, Smyrna, and Thyatira. It is possible that during this Asian stay he also visited Sardis and Philadelphia.[21]

The hilltop of the city offered only a limited amount of room so only the Acropolis was erected there. The residential section of the city lay eight hundred feet below at the foot of the steep mountain on which Sardis was located. Only one path led up the hill, and it was steep and winding, maximizing the difficulty any enemy would face in attempting to conquer the community.[22] Erosion has destroyed perhaps as much as two-thirds of the original summit of Mount Tmolus, on which Sardis was located, leaving a very modest remnant for the modern visitor to behold.[23]

Sardis was a substantial city. As far back as the days of Croesus it had supported a local population of almost 50,000.[24] Including the immediately adjoining urban area, by the first centuries A.D. this had expanded to at least 60,000.[25] The most common estimate is in the area of 100,000[26] and some go as high as 120,000.[27]

The community had a diverse economic foundation to support its prosperity. The Pactolus continued to carry its valuable supply of gold. Silver could be found both on Mount Tmolus and at hot springs just south of the city. Tmolus also contributed antimony to use in cosmetics making or as an ingredient in medicine. It produced arsenic, used in producing pigments. Quarries for marble began a mere four kilometers from the city. Large additional supplies of these various substances—as well as other commercially valuable ones—could easily be obtained within a convenient one-day to two-day journey of the city.[28]

Wood was abundantly available for construction and any other desired purpose: oak, cedar, and pine all grew in abundance even into the nineteenth century.[29] "Agricultural products useful in industry were also abundant; the most common of these is kermes-oak, which produces a valuable red dye. The bark of pomegranates could have been used for medicine and tanning. The region north of the Hermus is covered with vaolonia oak, whose acorn is a source of tannic acid, a product essential for the tanning of leather."[30]

Local industries (located in both Sardis and nearby smaller communities economically and politically connected with it) manufactured their products for both the nearby region and for export to other cities and areas of the empire. Jane C. Waldbaum has written of this export trade:

> One town near Sardis...is known to have specialized in producing nails, another bed frames, and a third building materials, while Sardis herself was famous for the production of iron-cutting tools—knives, rasps, swords and engraving tools (all of which presuppose the working of hardened steel to suit their special functions).
>
> The peak of the Sardian iron industry came in late Roman times (3rd–4th centuries A.D.) when Sardis was the seat of an imperial weapons and shield factory of *fabrica*....Since the factory at Sardis was one of only three such establishments in Asia Minor, it must have represented a substantial undertaking.[31]

Commerce and trade might bring fame to a city in the ancient world; they certainly increased its wealth. On the other hand, even the most prosperous city must eat, and it was vital to have a nearby source of agricultural supplies because long-distance transportation was not only expensive but in times of scarcity could not be counted on. In this regard the city was blessed, for it enjoyed basic agricultural self-sufficiency.[32] Wheat and barley grew in abundance, as did a wide variety of vegetables. Being in a mountainous area, the valleys produced good supplies of apples and other fruits. Olives grew in great abundance, and their oil was used both for lighting and for the manufacture of soap.[33]

Sardis enjoyed the physical possessions that went with a prosperous Asian community of its day.[34] It had a gymnasium that occupied five-and-a-half acres. Most of the facility seems to have been completed by around A.D. 150, though substantial improvements continued to be added in the following decades.[35]

A third-century-B.C. theater continued in use under the Romans, who renovated the structure. It could seat twenty thousand people.[36] We read of troops being prepared for battle in 215 B.C. at the hippodrome/race track. This appears to have been a simple affair rather than the more traditional imposing edifice since no remains have been located.[37]

About A.D. 50 Claudius financed the erection of an aqueduct as an imperial gift to the community. The aqueduct carried water from Tmolus into the city, where it was distributed, presumably by means of storage tanks within the city, to many of the public and commercial facilities. Well-to-do homeowners also were linked into this public water system.[38] An inscription has survived listing those who obtained water from the aqueduct.[39]

The aqueduct basically utilized a preexisting system of distribution at its city end. Water pipes and a drainage system had been installed simultaneously with the major rebuilding that occurred after the massive A.D. 17 earthquake.[40]

In light of the readily available water, it is not surprising that fountains were common in the community, including one located outside of the synagogue. In the temple of Artemis a steady stream of moving water was used to enhance the physical appearance of the facility. The gymnasium complex with its accompanying baths had a large swimming pool as well as flush toilets.[41]

Having spoken of the city's virtues, it is useful to remember that all its heritage and all its wealth did not eradicate the imputation of moral laxity that pagan thought attached to the city. According to Herodotus, the women of Sardis were extraordinarily generous with their sexual favors—for money. Indeed, he sees this as part of their historical legacy.

> It [the tomb of King Alyattes] was raised by the joint labour of the trades-men, handicraftsmen, and courtesans of Sardis, and had at the top five stone pillars, which remained to my day, with inscriptions cut on them, showing how much of the work was done by each class of workpeople. It appeared on measurement that the portion of the courtesans was the largest. The daughters of the common people in Lydia, one and all, pursue this traffic, wishing to collect money for their portions. They continue the practice till they marry; and are wont to contract themselves in marriage.[42]

They never did fully live down this reputation. In the second or third century A.D., Athenaeus summed up some of the long-standing accusations against the city.

> The Lydians came to such a pitch of wantonness that they were the first to sterilize women as Zanthus the Lydian records or whoever it was that wrote the histories attributed to him....In the second book of the Lydiaka Xanthus says that Adramytes, the king of Lydia, was the first to sterilize women, and use them instead of male eunuchs.
> Clearchus, in the fourth book of his *Lives,* says that on account of their luxuriousness the Lydians planned parks and made them like gardens and so kept in the shade. For they thought it more dainty not to have the sun's rays touch them at all. They went so much further in their arrogance that they collected the wives and daughters of other men into the place which, because of their behavior, they called in irony the Place of Purity and had intercourse with them.[43]

Although theoretically written of the past, the repetition of such ancient accusations at such a late date suggests that the city's typical lifestyle was still viewed as consistent with those past amoral lapses.

## Polytheism in Sardis

Before passing to a more detailed study of two deities in particular, we should stress that Sardis shared in common with all other cities a wide variety of religious options. Among the male gods were Apollo,[44] Heracles,[45] Hermes,[46] and Zeus.[47] Dionysus was worshiped in the city from at least 350 B.C. until paganism vanished.[48]

Female deities were also numerous. These included Athena[49] and Aphrodite.[50] Kore worship is known from at least as far back as the days of Augustus. In Rome, Lucius Verus (between A.D. 161 and 169) dedicated an altar to Sardis's Kore. About the same time the Chrysanthina festival was introduced in her honor in Sardis itself.[51]

The imperial cult was, of course, represented. In light of the large assistance provided by Tiberius to help rebuild the earthquake-stricken city, it is reasonable to believe that the cult enjoyed both numerical and emotional support from a large proportion of the citizenry.[52] By the early third century there were three imperial temples *(neocrates)* in the city. They are pictured on city coins of A.D. 218.[53]

## Artemis

Dating back to 300 B.C. in its original form,[54] this was the most important temple in the city, not just because of its physical impressiveness but also because Artemis[55] had the most important individual cult in the city.[56] It was also the largest and stood up well against the Artemis shrine in Ephesus, measuring 160 by 300 feet.[57] The building itself has been described this way:

> Most of its 65–foot Ionic columns (once 78 in all) are unfluted. Some of the columns rest on rough pedestals; no doubt these were intended to be carved like those of Ephesus. The temple had twenty columns on each of the long sides and eight columns at each of the ends. The cella or main cult chamber on the east end was divided by two rows of six columns. At the west end was the treasure chamber. The capitals show a variety of form; some of the columns have richly decorated bases.

Beneath the cella were discovered the foundations of the temple built by Croesus in the sixth century B.C.[58]

Normally, Greek temples placed the entrance on the eastern side and the statue of the god traditionally faced toward the east. In this temple, the normal pattern was reversed (for unknown reasons) and the entrance faces to the *west*.[59]

The temple suffered major damage in the earthquake that rocked the city in A.D. 17. It never again measured up to its earlier glory.[60] Decades were required for substantial progress to be made at all. In fact, one of the bases prepared for the new pillars carries the inscription "the first column to rise again" and is dated from the time of Trajan's reign.[61]

In addition to the part of the facility used for other purposes, it was divided into two cellas for worship: one contained a colossal image of Artemis and the other a mammoth one of Zeus Polieus.[62] After the damage inflicted by the A.D. 17 earthquake, at least that of Artemis had to be replaced.[63] Whatever the nature of the Zeus replacement, his worship continued there unabated.[64] Throughout these centuries, the goddess Kore continued to be worshiped within the temple as well.[65] And if Artemis was not to be the sole deity worshiped in the facility, certainly there was no way one could exclude the emperor. Although emperor statues may have been introduced as early as Tiberius,[66] they were definitely included by about A.D. 150.[67]

Two difficult questions remain to be answered: the first is the relationship of the Ephesian Artemis with that of the Sardisian.[68] Is the latter to be regarded as merely a theological offshoot of Artemis or is her form in Sardis so dramatically different that we must regard her as a distinct cult, though similarly named?

Unquestionably there was an underlying tension between the two movements. The most infamous explosion was during the fourth century B.C. when the Ephesians sent gifts to the temple in Sardis and were greeted with violence.[69] To calm the storm, forty-five residents of Sardis were executed for their role in the upheaval.[70]

Another difficult question to answer is the degree to which Cybele was worshiped as a deity *independent* of her amalgamation into the image of Artemis. In favor of the amalgamation may be the fact that the Artemis temple was constructed on the site previously occupied by a Cybele shrine.[71] At least so far as Sardis, however, it has been argued that a fourth-century-B.C. relief bears witness to the continued reverence of her as a separate deity. In this relief we find Artemis in the classical pose, holding a deer, while Cybele grasps a lion in her arms.[72] Although the two images, in an identical pose, could be intended to show the *equivalency* between the two—what the goddess was, respectively, to the Greeks and to the Asians—it seems more likely that it bears witness to the community's continued respect for both goddesses as separate individuals. Of course, once one admits *equivalency,* the passage of time could well accomplish the effective merger of the two into one in the public mind. Hence we could well be dealing with a matter of *when* rather than *whether* the unification took place.

### Sabazios

Although the Sabazios cult was found as far away as the Rhineland, Belgium, and Switzerland, its greatest concentration was in the Asia Minor regions of Lydia and Phrygia.[73] In addition to its presence in Thyatira (mentioned in the preceding chapter) it was also present in at least Pergamon, Sardis, Philadelphia, and Laodicea.[74]

According to the specific community where the cult was found, there was a tendency for an additional god to be blended with Sabazios in regard to his characteristics and functions. In Pergamon and possibly at Sardis as well, the traditional link was with Zeus, and he was known as Zeus Sabazios.[75] The physical depiction of Sabazios comes in two forms. In one he quite naturally resembles Jupiter or Zeus.[76]

The dominant motif portrays him as a deity exhibiting typical regional god imagery.

> The normal type of representation of Sabazios portrays him as a deity of Asia Minor. The god is in Phrygian dress and bearded. Frequently the hand is raised in the so-called *benedicto latina,* and at times holds a staff or pine-cone. He is often pictured with animal figures and various symbols and cult-objects,

as, e.g., in the bronze relief in Copenhagen, where he is standing. He often rests his feet on a ram's head, and he is sometimes thought to have been originally a ram-god.[77]

The odds are high that Sabazios was originally one of the
fertility deities. Ultimately he became recognized as a special
protector of country people. Perhaps the protector image
explains his popularity among slaves as well.[78]

Certain Gentile thinkers equated Sabazios with the God of
Israel. Valerius Maximus asserts that anti-Jewish actions undertaken in Rome in 139 B.C. were provoked by the Jewish effort "to
infect Roman customs with the cult of Jupiter Sabazios."[79] In
Greek the polytheistic deity was called "Lord Sabazios," while to
the Jews their God was the "lord of the Sabbath."[80]

Such verbal similarities and pagan speculation has convinced a number of scholars[81] that Asia Minor Jews were especially attracted to and involved in this cultic movement. Several
lines of argument would seem to minimize any substantial Jewish
involvement though that does not rule out Gentiles patterning
the terminology and practice in what they regarded as a "Jewish"
direction.

First of all, there is no proof that Plutarch's explanation
reflected the Jewish understanding of the subject. All historians
have the desire to understand, to explain. The "oddity" of Jewish
monotheism cried out for an explanation, and it was quite natural for pagan writers to speculate on the most reasonable explanation (from their standpoint) for this strange phenomenon.
This does not necessarily mean that the community being
described accepted such a theory or that it was adapted from any
conscious claim being made.[82]

Second, there is a powerful argument from silence that can
be garnered from a major Christian foe of Jewish theology.
"There is no indication in the writings of the late-second century
bishop of Sardis, Melio, that the Jews there are syncretized or
apostate to any degree. Since his sermon is an attack upon the
Jews, we might expect him to mention such aberrations, if they
were obvious....If there had been 'Sabbath/Sabazios' speculation
among Sardis Jews, Melito would likely have noticed it."[83]

Furthermore, the surviving data directly describing the

Sabazios cult and its activities seem distinctly non-Jewish. The primary classical description (found in Demosthenes, *De. Cor.*, 259f.) "refers to nighttime libations and lustrations and daytime processions," religious forms clearly *non*-Jewish in nature."[84]

As mentioned in the previous chapter, a Jewish cult for those compromised by idolatry is only one option: equally viable is a Gentile cult adopting the Jewish God while maintaining a greater or lesser degree of loyalty to polytheism. Although the above data cast grave doubt on Sabazios being a *Judeo*-pagan cult, it is fully consistent with it being a pagan-Jewish cult.

## Judaism in Sardis

If the correlation between Sepharad and Sardis is correct, then a Jewish colony of some type existed there in the days of the prophet Obadiah. By the time of the first century, rights of the collective Jewish community were well established. As an ethnic minority that was officially recognized as a distinct community *(politeuma)*, it possessed a recognized set of self-governing rights. These rights were not unlimited but did set the boundaries within which the group could work together and carry out mutual interests. These self-governing rights could be exercised without prior government approval, for they fell within that body of rights and privileges already granted the community.[85] This included the right to operate their own internal judicial system over the group's membership.[86] This system operated in Ephesus and an unknown number of other Asian communities as well.[87]

The existence and exercise of these rights did not go unchallenged. In 49 B.C. the Jews of the city felt that their rights were being wrongfully challenged by the city government and appealed to the Roman governor. The governor came down foursquare on their side of the controversy. Although challenges to the rights and privileges of the Jewish community continued to be mounted in various other Asian cities such as Ephesus,[88] from then on the Sardis government was especially respectful of that minority's legal rights.[89]

Individual Jews were admitted to important local positions, and they were understandably proud of their civic recognition.

Inscriptions found inside the local synagogue itself speak of such cases, "Nine synagogue donors are identified as city councilors *(bouleutai);* two other men are identified as record-keeping functionaries in the Roman provincial administration *(boethoi taboulariou);* another was a former procurator *(apo epitroponu);* yet another is referred to as a count *(comes).*"[90] A. Thomas Kraabel observes that this stands in contrast to inscriptional evidence often found in synagogues, "Elsewhere, for example at Rome, the texts may emphasize one's status within the Jewish community; the Sardis inscriptions stress rather the status of Jews outside the Jewish community, in the city and its government, and even beyond."[91]

The large size and central location of the synagogue bear witness to the importance of the Jewish people in the affairs of the city.[92] Andrew R. Seager describes the physical setting this way:

> The Synagogue enjoys one of the more prominent sites in the city, at what seems to have been the civic center of the Roman and Early Byzantine periods. It is not a freestanding building, but part of the monumental Roman bath and gymnasium complex....It occupies the southeast part of the complex, flanked by the palaestra of the gymnasium and a row of shops along the colonnaded Main Avenue, the principal thoroughfare of the city. Another colonnaded street runs along the front of the Synagogue, to the east, joining the Main Avenue at what seems to have been a public plaza or forum, at least from the late fifth century onward....The upper walls and roof of the Synagogue would have been clearly visible rising above the shops and road colonnades, and citizens walking past would have been able to look directly inside, when the doors were open, through the entire length of both rooms.[93]

This synagogue is the largest one uncovered in the Roman Empire;[94] the main hall would seat almost one thousand individuals.[95] The gymnasium complex, of which the synagogue is only a part, was constructed during the rebuilding program after the disastrous earthquake in 17 A.D.[96] It took decades to erect it all. The western parts were essentially completed by about A.D. 150 and the eastern sections in the following century.[97]

At what point the synagogue took up residence in the building is uncertain—which raises the question of the location of the facility utilized in the days of John. It has been speculated that the synagogue site may have reverted to a civil function for a prolonged period. In this scenario, it likely returned to its Jewish religious use about A.D. 270 (unquestionably about A.D. 320 at the latest) and continued in the service of the Jewish community until the city was abandoned in A.D. 616.[98]

Why was the synagogue permitted such a publicly visible location, with all the implied social acceptance that went with it? This could argue for a surprising open-mindedness toward the Jewish community in a world that was commonly anti-Semitic. Alternatively, it could argue for the collective accomplishments of its members being recognized as playing such an important role in the success of the town that the group deserved de facto recognition in spite of its theological "eccentricity" (monotheism).

Far less likely is the recent conjecture that the synagogue was engaged in major social service to the community at large and was being rewarded for this service. The evidence is extremely conjectural at best. Indeed, the interpretation seems the projection into the ancient world of the modern redefinition of religion as primarily welfare/benevolence rather than reconciliation with the supernatural.[99]

How "orthodox" was Judaism in Sardis? On the one hand, there are none of the criticisms ("synagogue of Satan") found in some of the mini-epistles that might suggest either a role in persecuting Christians or departures from traditional Judaism. On the other hand, certain archaeological data has led to speculation in the opposite direction. An apparent cooking area has been located near the synagogue. In it, remains of such prohibited animals as pigs and horses have been found. This has led some to question how strictly the Torah dietary laws were observed among Sardis Jews.[100] There is no necessary connection between the synagogue and the cooking area remains, however, and the latter could just as easily have been connected with the Gentile population.

## Christianity in Sardis

How the congregation came to be founded we do not know, though a connection with the burst of missionary activity in Asia during Paul's multi-year stay in Ephesus is a quite natural conjecture. At the time of John's mini-epistle the congregation appears to have enjoyed a reputation of accomplishment and success—of being truly "alive" (3:1) John's own evaluation is that they were actually "dead" (3:1) though capable of being revived (3:3).

Neither false teaching in general nor a specific false teacher in particular is presented as their problem. Sexual immorality is not presented as their difficulty. (There is the slightest inferential hint of such, though. See the discussion of "white garments" below.) Persecution is not presented as their problem.

Hence the internal and external stimuli that could have encouraged their decline go unmentioned, as if nonexistent or insignificant. In light of this scarcity of data, perhaps Sardis serves as an illustration of one of those congregations that suddenly goes into a spiritual tailspin *for no apparent reason.* As a historian I do not like that approach. Yet such situations occur today, and it would not be all that surprising to find such having occurred among the Asian churches of the first century as well.

## Historical and Societal Allusions
### Text of the Epistle

"And to the angel of the church in Sardis write, 'These things says he who has the seven Spirits of God and the seven stars: "I know your works, that you have a name that you are alive, but you are dead. Be watchful, and strengthen the things which remain, that are ready to die, for I have not found your works perfect before God. Remember therefore how you have received and heard; hold fast and repent. Therefore if you will not watch, I will come upon you as a thief, and you will not know what hour I will come upon you. You have a few names even in Sardis who have not defiled their garments; and they shall walk with me in white, for they are worthy. He who overcomes shall be clothed in white garments, and I will not blot out his name from the book of life; but I will confess his name before my Father and before his angels. He who has an ear, let him hear what the Spirit says to the churches.""" (Rv 3:1-6)

## Surprised like a "Thief" Surprises (3:3)

### THE EARTHQUAKE EXPLANATION

No one can predict the coming of an earthquake. Even in our own highly technological age, predictions are in terms of probabilities and specified months—or longer periods of time. Earthquakes come unannounced and without warning, just as the "thief" does. All one can do is to be as prepared as humanly possible for that unknowable day and hour.

Since Sardis was a victim of several earthquakes during the first century, the earthquake explanation fits in well with the known historical information from the period.[101] In twelve years Sardis was struck by four earthquakes: after the killer quake of A.D. 17, milder ones followed in A.D. 20 (apparently),[102] A.D. 24,[103] and A.D. 29.[104]

The embodiment of the earthquake danger can be found in the first of this series in A.D. 17. A large hunk of rock and gravel was torn from the Acropolis's hillside and plunged downward, where it covered both a temple and part of the city. The people never bothered to dig it out; they simply built on top of it.[105] But the damage was far broader than in this relatively small section; it was so widespread that almost the entire city had to be rebuilt.[106] As George M. A. Hanfmann, the foremost expert on the archaeological work done at Sardis in the second half of the twentieth century, refers to it: "The cataclysmic earthquake of A.D. 17 made very nearly a *tabula rosa* out of the city."[107]

The relief the emperor gave took two forms: a direct grant and relief from certain taxes for a period of five years. Although the size of the grant is mentioned only in regard to Sardis, the implication in Tacitus seems to be that other stricken cities were also generously assisted.[108] In A.D. 22-23 a special coin was minted in Rome honoring Tiberius for this generosity. This coincided not only with the scheduled end of the five-year tax suspension but, presumably, also celebrated the successful completion of most of the rebuilding.[109]

Since Sardis "was almost entirely leveled [and] the force of the earthquake had even changed landscape forms,"[110] it is likely that this five year period only saw the completion of the first stage of a rebuilding process that took far longer. Hence the rebuilding would, proportionately, have been on the scale of that required in Rome after the great fire of A.D. 64.[111] Even the weaker later quakes created the need for additional rebuilding. Strabo wrote, "Recently it has lost many of its buildings through earthquakes."[112]

First had to come the easily overlooked but inescapable pre-requisite for rebuilding: leveling of structurally unsafe properties and the clearing away of tons of debris.[113] Both drainage and water supply (due to their obvious public safety and welfare connection) would have been high on the list of priorities. It happens that the name of the architect in charge of the aqueduct rebuilding project has been preserved, one Tiberius Claudius Apollophanes. Born in Greece, he enjoyed Roman citizenship and successfully carried the aqueduct project to completion.[114]

In order to minimize the danger from future quakes the foundations were set deeper than ever. The building ultimately utilized as the city's synagogue had foundations at least fifteen feet—perhaps even much deeper since the archaeologists stopped digging before they came to the bottom.[115] In other places the foundations were extended thirty feet below ground level[116] and walls were also built much thicker than previously.[117] Although these might seem reasonable measures, twentieth-century engineers do not believe that they would have been very helpful in future quakes.[118]

Long abandoned suburbs to the west of the city were reinhabited. Into this area flowed urban amenities such as new public baths.[119]

Yet all these precautions, all this rebuilding, all this expansion, could not stop the future quakes that would spring upon the city like a "thief." Certainly the abiding earthquake danger could have motivated John's choice of descriptions.

### MILITARY EXPLANATIONS FROM SARDIS'S HISTORY

Twice in Sardis's history the city fell to surprise assaults that came like the sudden attack of a thief.[120] In an additional case the city *launched* such an assault. Today successful assaults do not seem very startling because the erosion of twenty centuries has dramatically worn down the plateau the enemy had to seize. In its prime, though, Sardis was impressive and almost unconquerable:

> Like the other hills of the region, this site forms a small elongated plateau with steep sides and is connected by a narrow ridge with the northern foothills of the Tmolus. In fact, the hill on which Sardis perched had almost perpendicular sides except on the south. Even this approach is none too easy, and the city is virtually impregnable.[121]

The first seizure was by Cyrus in his war against Croesus in 549 B.C. In Xenophon's *Cyropaedia* we find an account of how an unexpected night strike was substituted for an apparently intended frontal assault:

> When daylight came, Cyrus led his army on against Sardis. And as soon as he came up to the walls of the city, he set up his engines as if intending to assault it and made ready his scaling ladders. But though he did this, in the course of the following night he sent some Chaldaeans and Persians to climb up what was considered the most precipitous side of the Sardian citadel. The way was shown them by a Persian who had been the slave of one of the guards of the acropolis and had discovered a way down to the river and up again by the same route.[122]

Herodotus provides a slightly different account, diverging both in regard to there having been an unsuccessful earlier assault and in regard to the safety of the path used to ascend the hillside:

> On the fourteenth day of the siege Cyrus bade some horsemen ride about his lines, and make proclamation to the whole army that he would give a reward to the man who should first mount the wall. After this he made an assault, but without success. His troops retired, but a certain [man], Hyroeades by name, resolved to approach the citadel and attempt it at a place where no guards were ever set. On this side the rock was so precipitous, and the citadel (as it

seemed) so impregnable, that no fear was entertained of its being carried in this place....

It is on that side of the city which faces Mount Tmolus, Hyroeades, however, having the day before observed a Lydian soldier descend the rock after a helmet that had rolled down from the top, and having seen him pick it up and carry it back, thought over what he had witnessed, and formed his plan. He climbed the rock himself, and other Persians followed in his track, until a large number had mounted to the top. Thus was Sardis taken, and given up entirely to pillage.[123]

It is interesting that in both versions it is a *Persian* who finds the solution: in one case an ex-slave and in the other an officer in the Persian army. In other words, *internal* betrayal was not the cause for the fall. It was arrogance—the confidence that one had an unassailable fortress that even the strongest enemy could never conquer. The arrogance element is brought out almost explicitly in a few sentences we have omitted above. These refer to how an earlier king had promised that the city would be "impregnable" (Herodotus's word) if a lion were carried around the defenses. The king readily assented and "in consequence [they] carried it round the rest of the fortress where the citadel seemed open to attack, [but] he scorned to take it round this side, which he looked on as a sheer precipice, and therefore absolutely secure."

We must move forward over three hundred years into the reign of the Syrian leader, Antiochus the Great, to discover the "impregnable" fortress falling yet again due to an attack at its most "invulnerable" point. Although Antiochus's forces had already laid siege a year, the city remained no closer to capture. The besieging army, according to Polybius, had come "to despair of taking it by storm and to believe that the one hope of getting it was by starving it out."[124] Lagoras the Cretan was well aware that the seemingly strongest point of an enemy's defenses could sometimes be turned against him, so he began a systematic study of the defenses to see if this might be another such case.

Having observed that a portion of the wall was unguarded, near a place called the Saw, which unites the citadel and city, he conceived the hope and idea of performing this exploit [of capturing the town]. The place was extremely precipitous: and there was a deep gully below, into which dead bodies from the city, and the offal of horses and beasts of burden that died, were accustomed to be thrown; and in this place therefore there was always a great number of vultures and other birds collected. Having observed, then, that when these creatures were gorged, they always sat undisturbed upon the cliffs and the wall, he concluded that the wall must necessarily be left unguarded and deserted for the larger part of the day. Accordingly, under cover of night, he went to the spot and carefully examined the possibilities of approaching it and setting ladders; and finding that this was possible at one particular rock, he communicated the facts to the king.[125]

The king accepted this plan as one worth attempting. To assure that the defenders would not detect the strategy, an attack was simultaneously staged on a different part of the wall. A Sardisian force emerged to do battle. After covertly mounting the wall itself, Lagoras's raiding party seized one gate and was quickly reinforced. The Sardisians rushed back into the city as soon as they received word, but this retreat was turned into a disaster as the Syrian forces seized the gate before it was closed. This created a second penetration point into the city, and enemy soldiers proceeded to pour in through both of the seized gates. Defense quickly became untenable, and all of the city (except for the citadel itself) fell into the hands of Antiochus.[126] The possibility of a Sardisian victory was totally destroyed.

The situation was somewhat reversed during the Peloponnesian War. On one occasion troops, apparently provided at least partially by Sardis, had used an expected night attack at a unexpected location to produce a military victory. Thucydides recounts the incident this way:

Some private citizens of Samos who wanted to overthrow the government supported their complaint. Whereupon the Athenians, sailing to Samos with forty ships, established a democracy, and taking as hostage fifty boys and fifty men whom they deposited at Lemnos, they returned leaving a garrison. But certain of the Samians who had quitted the

island and fled to the mainland entered into an alliance with
the principal oligarchs who remained in the city, and with
*Pissuthnes the son of Hystaspes, then governor of Sardis, and col-
lecting troops* to the number of 700 they *crossed over by night* to
Samos. First of all they attacked the victorious populace, and
got most of them into their power; then they stole away the
hostages from Lemnos, and finally revolted from Athens.[127]

As both the victim and inflictor of sudden, unexpected
attacks, John's "thief" imagery echoed elements from the city's
own history. His implicit challenge is, Are you Sardisians wise
enough to avoid the spiritual equivalent happening yet again?

*"White Garments" (3:5) and the Multi-Allusion of Unsoiled Garments*

The promise that "he who overcomes shall be clothed in
white garments" ["robes," *NRSV*] (3:5) is the reward for "hav[ing]
not defiled their garments; and they shall walk with me in white,
*for they are worthy"* (3:4). Hence white garb is appropriate, for
they have conquered their own baser elements, including that of
sexual philandering.[128]

Some have speculated that the allusion is based upon the
practice of wearing white to be baptized[129] or receiving a white
garment afterward to symbolize the forgiveness secured.[130] However, there is not the least New Testament foundation that this
practice dates from the first century.

On the other hand, a sign of membership in the Palestinian
sect of Essenes (a "reward" for membership, so to speak) was the
wearing of white clothing as a symbol for the purity the members
sought.[131] How much was known of the sect in Roman Asia is
unknown, and the utilizing of such a geographically and religiously "distant" allusion is highly improbable.

Others think the garments refer to the resurrection of the
body of believers.[132] Although such *might* be a possible deduction
from certain texts, Revelation itself argues against it. There
those *already* under the heavenly altar are pictured as wearing "a
white robe" (6:11). The wearing of such garments are pictured in
a scene of triumph and joy (7:11). Those wearing white are
specifically identified as doing so not because they have new
heavenly bodies but because they have successfully passed
through "the great tribulation" and because they had been

redeemed by the "blood of the Lamb" (verse 14). In 19:8 the new clothing (though not labeled explicitly as white) is specifically identified as "the righteous acts of the saints."

Four possible social allusions have been suggested to either explain John's use of the symbolism or to provide evidence of how his contemporaries might have understood it.

### WHITE GARMENTS AS THE PROPER GARB FOR WORSHIP

White garments for religious ceremonies were standard attire among the Romans.[133] Interestingly, it was in Asia Minor itself that an inscription was uncovered "which announced that soiled garments disqualified the worshiper and dishonored the god."[134] One worshiped, so one wore clean clothes. It was as simple as that.[135] Presumably, to approach the gods in stained or dirty clothes was an act of grave disrespect to the honor and importance of the deity. This has been a common attitude in society. Indeed, in our own culture, it has been only since the 1960s that casual attire has become so pervasive that its use in religious worship has become socially acceptable.

### CLEAN "WHITE" GARMENTS IN THE GYMNASIUM

Terence Kelshaw suggests that the allusion might grow out of the temptation to compromise their faith while wearing the white garments of the local gymnasium. This massive facility was part educational center, part athletic center, part public baths. It had its own pagan chapel. As noted earlier, the local synagogue was also located within its boundaries. It was a place where congeniality would be at the maximum and divisive topics carefully avoided, a place where Christians could easily be tempted to put their faith on the back burner. As Kelshaw reconstructs the problem,

> Members would pursue their chosen occupation in the gymnasium, and at some point make their way to the baths, calling in at the changing rooms where soiled garments were divested before entering the hot baths. Conversation took place there, and, as everywhere in the gymnasium, no special claims would be made for any one particular religious viewpoint. From the hot baths members moved to an oval cold-water pool, set in a lovely covered garden where the gossip continued and friendships were reaffirmed. When

the cold bath was completed a member was clothed in a white garment, a comfortable loose-fitting cover in which to stroll the gardens and forge new friendships. In this atmosphere one did not rock the boat with trifling matters like rejecting the ritual or speaking out for Jesus Christ.[136]

Although such a scenario is certainly not impossible in light of the lack of spiritual strength for which the congregation is criticized, the rebuke seems to imply a general lack of spirituality rather than a lapse produced by some specific situation (such as use of the gymnasium). This approach puts a negative spin on the subject of white garments: it involves a repudiation of the Lord, while in John's text the white garment is a reward for faithfulness to that same Lord. Although John could intend to *contrast* earthly and heavenly garments, a gymnasium allusion could also carry a positive connotation: Just as one received the white garment of the gymnasium after cleansing oneself of dirt and grime, one received the heavenly white garment after cleansing oneself of the weaknesses and sins of the present life.

### AN ECONOMIC ALLUSION RELATED TO THE WOOL TRADE

Sardis claimed to have invented the first successful method for dyeing wool.[137] Whether this claim was mythical or based in reality, there is no question that Sardis was a major Asian producer of woolen clothing.[138] So, even without any other social allusions, local citizens would have been more concerned with such matters of outward appearance than residents of cities where such production was minimal or nonexistent.

### TRADITIONAL GARB FOR FESTIVE OCCASIONS

White togas were the accepted Roman attire not just for religious festivals but for military triumphs (victory parades) and holidays in general.[139] For most citizens of Rome, the heavy, white toga was worn only upon special occasions rather than daily. But when holidays came around, white togas were worn by one and all, so much so that the city was called *canida urbs,* "the city in white."[140] We have here a case of cultural diffusion. What

began in Rome as appropriate attire at a military triumph
became attire for any time of celebration.[141]

Those who never had been to Rome could still read the
ideal in such places as the works of Juvenal:

> What! had he seen, in his triumphant car,
> Amid the dusty Cirque, conspicuously far,
> The Praetor perched aloft, superbly drest
> In Jove's proud tunic with a trailing vest
> Of Tyrian tapestry, and o'er him spread
> A crown too bulky for a human head;...
> And now the Imperial Eagle, raised on high,
> With golden beak, the mark of majesty.
> Trumpets before, and on the left and right
> *A cavalcade of nobles, all in white.*[142]

The idea of wearing white garments as appropriate attire
for a time of happiness and celebration would have posed no difficulty for the Jews. Centuries before, one of their ancient wise
men had written, "Go, eat your bread with joy, and drink your
wine with a merry heart; for God has already accepted your
works. *Let your garments always be white,* and let your head lack no
oil" (Eccl 9:8). Even the most observant Jew would find no inherent *religious* obstacle to the practice that Roman influence had
spread throughout the civilized world.

*Possible Heightened Local Preoccupation with "Death" (3:1–2)*

John rebukes the congregation as having "a name that you
are alive, but you are dead" (3:1). Alan Johnson sees in this reference an alleged "special preoccupation" with death that gripped
the city.[143] As evidence of this he cited "the impressive necropolis, or cemetery of 'a thousand hills' (modern Bin Tepe), so
named because of the hundreds of burial mounds, visible on the
skyline some seven miles from Sardis."[144]

Peter Wood argues an even more exact geographical reference: John speaks from the standpoint of what one would behold
at the local Artemesion.

> Further to the east rises the great hill of the Acropolis, centre
> to the life of ancient Sardis. On the opposite side of the
> Artemision, beyond the river and to the west, rises a range of

hills. The nearest of these are honeycombed with passages and tombs. Here is the Necropolis, "city of the dead."...The writer uses the unusual position of the city with its two hills roughly east and west, to speak of the Christians there. The church, called to be the agency of life, is fast becoming a Necropolis.[145]

Unlike many of the possible local or social illustrations found in the mini-epistles, this one requires a surprising further limiting of the description to *one apparently specific location* within the community for the illustration to "work" rhetorically. Since it is not one that quickly leaps to the mind of the modern informed reader, one wonders whether it is specific enough to have jumped to the consciousness of the first-century reader either. And if it wouldn't have, was it likely to have been the reason he chose this particular illustration?

*Blotting Out Names as a Political and Religious Custom (3:5)*

In the combination of two positive rewards ("white garments" and "confess[ing] [the disciples'] name before my Father and before his angels," comes a *negative* reward, "I will not blot out his name from the book of life" (3:5).

This is a well-established scriptural allusion. Sin had always been punishable by having one's name blotted out: God directly asserted it (Ex 32:33) and Moses took the danger for granted (Ex 32:32). Paul names several hard workers "whose names are in the book of life" (Phil 4:3). John returns to the terminology in Revelation 20, where he warns that "anyone not found written in the book of life [will be] cast into the lake of fire" (v. 15). On the other hand, "only those who are written in the Lamb's book of life" are permitted to enter the heavenly Jerusalem (Rv 21:27).

The concept was common in the secular world as well. It was not unknown, for example, for an atrocious offender to have his name *literally* blotted out or erased from the list of citizenry.[146] In Athens, for example, it was normal practice to remove from the list of citizens anyone about to be executed for a crime.[147]

Colin J. Hemer finds a possible Jewish frame of reference. A relatively early Jewish curse upon Christians was "May the Nazarenes and the Minim suddenly perish, and may they be blotted out of the book of life and not enrolled along with the righteous."[148]

Based upon the literature by and about Apollonius, he reasons that the city was well known for its vehement fractionalism. Add to this the clear importance of the Jewish community to the city and the basis was clearly present for them to utilize Gentile law against those who refused to walk in the customary rites and practices of Judaism. "At the least they could delete their names from the synagogue register when the Christian's precarious entitlement to safety lay in acceptance there."[149]

This is a quite reasonable reconstruction, but John gives not the slightest hint of any such opposition, much less a pronounced and vigorous one of the type Hemer assumes. Hence we give a low priority to this possibility having been in the writer's mind.[150] Even so, such a situation *could* easily have developed, and if it did, the Sardisian Christians who reread John's mini-epistle would likely contrast *their* treatment of being blotted out of the synagogue's register with the solemn pledge of Jesus that they would never be blotted out of *his* list of the faithful.

# 10

## Philadelphia: City of Opportunity

Philadelphia was founded by either Eumenes II or his brother Attalus II. The latter was called Philadelphus because of his obvious affection and loyalty toward his older brother. Regardless of which of the two actually founded the town, Attalus II's nickname passed into usage as the name of the community.[1] The second century A.D. population was a minimum of ten thousand and quite likely much larger.[2] City government was organized on a tribal basis, and the local guilds were officially recognized as tribes, leading to the probability that the guild associations actually ran the city.[3]

The emperor owned large estates nearby, and the income from these, of course, flowed directly to him rather than into local coffers.[4] Leather and textile businesses provided much income for the city.[5] The abundant grape crops from the area just to the northeast[6] produced a fine vintage that enhanced the city's reputation.[7] Nearby hot springs attracted many visitors who came seeking relief for their medical problems.[8]

Due to the enthusiasm with which both Greek culture in general and the various Greek cults in particular were embraced, Philadelphia was known as a "little Athens."[9] Among the various gods whose images were depicted on local coinage but whose actual temples have not yet been uncovered are Zeus, Aphrodite, Dionysus, and Helios.[10]

Because of the importance of the wine crop and its acknowledged quality, it comes as no surprise to find that Dionysus was the most important deity in the community.[11] The imperial cult was, of course, honored,[12] but in Philadelphia that honor was even easier to give since the worship of both the imperial cult and Dionysus tended to be blended together into joint worship.[13]

In its publicly acceptable side, the cult was connected with yearly celebrations of the grape harvest and of the spring crops. The combination of wine and the free interaction between men and women during these festivals offered convenient pretexts for sexual immorality. The public exposure of such incidents horrified many Romans and, upon occasion, led to the repression of the cult in parts of the empire.[14] During the worship of Dionysus, the god was believed to take possession of certain worshipers, thereby giving sanction to whatever they did, including acts of sexual excess that would normally have been rejected.[15] Although males played a significant role in cultic activities, the various historical references seem to imply that the bulk of the adherents were women.[16] Assuming a degree of sexual repression substantially greater than that of males of the day, one might explain the attraction in the theological sanction it could give to sexual conduct that would otherwise be forbidden them.

When we speak of occupations that Dionysus's cult especially appealed to, acting would be high on the list. Traveling theater guilds often constituted themselves into religious bodies worshiping the god. This provided extra protection against official and popular harassment.[17]

Did the cult have its special secrets, available only to the initiated? A villa at Pompeii includes several frescoes portraying what appear to many to be Dionysian mysteries. The interpretation of them, though, has been vigorously disputed, and some deny that there is a Dionysian tie-in at all.[18]

Whatever elements the Dionysus sect appealed to, they came primarily from the irrational or nonrational side of the participants. Perhaps the sect appealed to the anarchist repressed deeply in the soul of most individuals. Joscelyn Godwin argues for our premise—though not necessarily our conclusion—when she writes:

> Modern scholars, devotees by profession of Apollo, tend to blame the excesses of Dionysus' cult on wine, opium, ivy- or toadstool-eating, or on some primitive state of mystic participation which, thankfully, it is impossible for them to recapture. But all their efforts to understand him are vain, for he is innately hostile to rational thought.[19]

One must understand his emotional rather than his intellectual appeal.[20]

This god appealed to the "dark" side of human nature, which seeks relief from the pressures of existence through an intentional rejection of normal restraints. Drunkenness replaced sober rite; the lack of control that resulted substituted for the orderliness expected in daily routine. His worship permitted a religiously sanctioned unleashing of the forces of chaos that would, in all other contexts, be kept under strict control.[21] Hence, his image as half-goat and half-man, since he crosses the line from full humanity into a halfway state between human and beast and acts with the lack of restraint one would expect of such a hybrid. Vases depict him with satyrs, acting lasciviously and giving free rein to their desires.[22]

Dionysus represents to the modern mind the embodiment of the sexual archaistic element in pagan religion. Yet, there were polytheists who recognized that such constituted an inadequate lifestyle. In Philadelphia, for example, there survives the rules of a religious association that met in the home of a person named Dionysius and worshiped twelve pagan deities. We find within these rules a vigorous demand for sexual loyalty among married couples:

> A man [is not to take] another woman in addition to his own wife, either a free woman or a slave who has a husband, nor is he to corrupt either a child [boy] or a virgin, nor is he to counsel another [to do so]; but if he should witness anyone [doing this], he must not hide it or keep silent about it. Woman and man [alike], whoever does any of the things above written, let them not enter this house. For the gods who dwell here are mighty and watch over these things and will not hold back [punishment] from those who transgress [their] commandments.
>
> A free woman is to be pure and is not to know bed or intercourse with any other man except her own [husband]. If she does know it, she shall not be pure [as before], but is defiled and full of corruption within her family and is unworthy to worship this god for whom these rites were established, or to offer sacrifices....If anyone does any of these things with which the commandments here copied

have to do, terrible curses from the gods will come upon those who disregard them.[23]

## Monotheism in Philadelphia

Little is known of the Jewish community in Philadelphia. An intense anti-Christian sentiment seems the most likely reason for John applying to them the rebuke of being a "synagogue of Satan" (Rv 3:9)—see the discussion of the identical phrase in the chapters on Smyrna—and of being imitation Jews (3:9).

When we turn to the church, we have no hard data by which to determine the date of its founding or the circumstances surrounding it. The congregation is described as faithful and yet, paradoxically, having "little power" (3:8), suggesting that its future was in doubt. The Christians were promised that God would make their Jewish foes "come and worship before your feet" (3:9). This could refer to their conversion[24] but the fact that the "worship" is located as being done "before your feet" suggests that the element of "Christian vindication, not Jewish conversion"[25] is the point John wishes to stress. This could be produced by conversion, but it could equally well be produced by some local situation involving church-synagogue conflict that ultimately turned out in the church's favor. If an end-of-time interpretation is preferred, then the reference might well be Christ's triumph over *all* his earthly foes and their conceding his victory and that of His followers;[26] in that case the point would be an acknowledgment that the Christians were in the right and carries no overtone of conversion at all.

The letter of Ignatius to Philadelphia provides insight into local church conditions in the early decades of the second century.[27] Judaizing teachers who wished to bind the Old Testament customs and practices upon Gentiles were a special concern to him (chap. 6). The Old Testament is to be respected, but the New Testament is far superior. "For the beloved prophets announced Him, but the Gospel is the perfection of immortality" (chap. 9). Ignatius feared that division might occur in Philadelphia due to this false doctrine but expressed satisfaction that as of the time he wrote division was absent (chap. 3).

In Philadelphia "there is one bishop, along with the presbytery and deacons" (chap. 4). The presbytery, though, still has some type of respected authority, for we read that, "I flee to the Gospel as to the flesh of Jesus and to the apostles as to the presbytery of the church" (chap. 5). Indeed, Ignatius upholds the principle of the authority of the presbytery as a means of avoiding division, "For when I was among you, I cried, I spoke with a loud voice: Give heed to the bishop, and to the presbytery and deacons. Now, some suspected me of having spoken thus, as knowing beforehand the division caused by some among you. But He is my witness, for whose sake I am in bonds, that I got no intelligence from any man" (chap. 7).

Yet having asserted this *collective* authority, Ignatius immediately shifts to a distinctly *episcopal* authority as superior to that of others: "But the Spirit proclaimed these words: *Do nothing without the bishop;* keep your bodies as the temples of God; love unity; avoid divisions; be the followers of Jesus Christ, even as He is of His Father" (chap. 7). Furthermore, the "Lord grants forgiveness" to those guilty of divisiveness only if they repent and return "to communion with the bishop" (chap. 8). The possibility that the bishop himself could become apostate and that yielding to his authority in such cases would be yielding to heresy are totally alien concepts to him.

Although Ignatius upholds the gospel as authoritative, his formula for avoiding potential division is not loyalty to the preserved text but institutional loyalty to the bishop. He may well be doing this because the bishop in Philadelphia happens to be fully obeying the will of God: "For he is in harmony with the commandments [of God], even as the harp is with its strings" (chap. 1). Even so, this embracing of a dual standard of orthodoxy (loyalty to divine revelation and loyalty to bishop) holds in embryo the potential for the acceptance of any and all changes church leadership might embrace as true and proper.

### Societal and Historical Allusions
### Text of the Epistle

"And to the angel of the church in Philadelphia write, 'These things says He who is holy, He who is true, "He who has the key of David, He who opens and no one shuts, and shuts and no one opens": I know your works. See, I have set before you an open door, and no one can shut it; for you have a little strength, have kept My word, and have not denied My name. Indeed I will make those of the synagogue of Satan, who say they are Jews and are not, but lie—indeed I will make them come and worship before your feet, and to know that I have loved you. Because you have kept my command to persevere, I also will keep you from the hour of trial which shall come upon the whole world, to test those who dwell on the earth. Behold, I come quickly! Hold fast what you have, that no one may take your crown. He who overcomes, I will make him a pillar in the temple of My God, and he shall go out no more. And I will write on him the name of My God and the same of the city of My God, the New Jerusalem, which comes down out of heaven from My God, And I will write on him My new name. He who has an ear, let him hear what the Spirit says to the churches.'" (Rv 3:7–13)

*The "Open Door" that "No One Can Shut" (3:8)*[28]

A door is used as the means to get from one place to another; an open door is one in which the potential barrier to getting there has been removed. In a negative sense a door is a means to avoid a dangerous situation. Though the word *door* is not used by Paul in this connection, the idea may be found in his promise that Christians will always have the means available to escape temptation if they truly seek it (1 Cor 10:13). In the current context, a few verses later Jesus warns of the "hour of trial" to come "upon the whole world" (Rv 3:10) and how he would provide a way (a door?) out of it. On the other hand, this is presented by the writer as divine *protection* rather than a divine *way of escape,* though both could be ways of describing the same phenomenon.

In the New Testament the *explicit* uses of the term are in a positive sense of accomplishing a concrete good rather than avoiding an undesirable evil. Here the door imagery implies the removal of hindrances or the providing of clear opportunities to accomplish a desired goal. In Revelation 3:20 we read of "open[ing] the door" so Christ can come in and dine with that person. In Revelation 4:1 John sees "a door standing open in heaven," through which John entered the heavenly precincts. In

Acts 14:27 we read that God "had opened the door of faith to the Gentiles." In John 10:7–9 Jesus describes himself as "the door" through which one enters the true sheepfold. All of these are positive images, indicating or implying that concrete good will come through using the door.

Interestingly, Paul uses the image of a door twice in regard to his preaching ministry in Asian cities: "For a great and effective door has opened to me" (of Ephesus, 1 Cor 16:8–9), and "a door was opened to me by the Lord" (of Troas, 2 Cor 2:12). In an epistle to yet a third Asian city, Colossae, he asks for their prayers that "God would open to us a door for the word" so that it might spread where he was imprisoned (Col 4:3–4). Hence it would be quite in keeping with Pauline and Johannine usages to take the reference to be *open doors to spread the gospel of Christ.*[29] Either opportunities already existed or through divine providence opportunities would be opened to them to spread their faith in a hostile region.

In a *cultural sense* this was the important role Philadelphia itself had provided in regard to the surrounding region. The city was created as a base for what we might call secular evangelism, as a platform for spreading Greek civilization into the nearby areas.[30] In the first century it remained a door to the east: the imperial post road that began in Rome ran through Troas, Pergamon, Sardis, and then Philadelphia[31] before proceeding east through the very center of Phrygia.[32] Just as Philadelphia consciously and intentionally proceeded to "civilize" the region, Philadelphian Christianity would now proceed to "convert" it. The parallel would be immediately obvious to any Philadelphian citizen with the least knowledge of the city's past.

*Possible Double Allusions to the Ongoing Earthquake Danger*

To live in Philadelphia was to live in the constant danger of earthquakes, over which one had absolutely no power or influence. In A.D. 17 a mammoth quake rolled through western Asia, devastating such cities as Philadelphia and Sardis. Writing just a few years later, Strabo noted that the community was plagued afterward with seemingly endless minor quakes: "In Philadelphia...not even the walls are safe, but in a sense are shaken and caused to crack every day. And the inhabitants are continually attentive to the disturbances in the earth and plan all structures with a view to their occurrence."[33]

So common were these quakes that Strabo was amazed that the city was not abandoned:

> Philadelphia [is] ever subject to earthquakes. Incessantly the walls of the houses are cracked, different parts of the city being thus affected at different times. For this reason but few people live in the city, and most of them spend their lives as farmers in the country, since they have a fertile soil. Yet one may be surprised at the few, that they are so fond of the place where their dwellings are so insecure; and one might marvel still more at those who founded the city.[34]

In other words, the A.D. 17 quake was simply a vehement expression of a permanent problem faced by the city. Indeed, another huge quake inflicted additional massive damage soon thereafter, in A.D. 23.[35]

This ongoing earthquake danger may be reflected in two references in John's mini-epistle. When the local congregation is referred to as having but "little strength" and therefore needing the evangelistic "door" of opportunities to be opened for it (3:9), we have a description that would aptly fit the community itself. Especially after the major earthquake of A.D. 17, local confidence was severely shaken. Yet the door was open to its successful rebuilding *in spite of* its apparent—and quite real—"little strength" at the time.[36] What the city had accomplished temporally, the church would accomplish spiritually.

When Jesus speaks of the future rewards local Christians will receive, one of them is that of *stability and permanence,* and this is presented in two different ways, one after the other: "He who overcomes, [1] I will make him a pillar in the temple of my God, and [2] he shall go out no more" (3:12). The residents of Philadelphia had *relative* stability—till the next earthquake caused them to "go out" of their homes and even flee the city to protect their lives.[37] On a spiritual level, such a danger would never be faced by those who followed the Lord of the Philadelphia Christians. They would never leave; they would remain in one spot, as stable as a pillar.

*A New Name (3:12)*

As part of their reward for faithfulness, Jesus promises the Philadelphia Christians that they will be like "a pillar in the temple of my God" and that "I will write on him the name of my God and the name of the city of my God, the new Jerusalem, which comes down out of heaven from my God. And I will write on him my new name" (3:12). In short, indications of divine approval will be manifest and clear; neither the recipient nor the observer can be in any doubt.

Old Testament precedents have been sought in the attire of the high priest[38] and the blessing the entire people received from the Lord.[39] In the New Testament we read that the apostolic epistles were written in individual's hearts (2 Cor 3:2-3).

The secular/historical context that would come to the mind of the Philadelphian recipients related to their own relatively recent civic history. In gratitude for Tiberius's assistance in rebuilding the city after its near-destruction in A.D. 17, the city adopted the name Neocaesarea. It reverted to Philadelphia when Nero gained the throne.[40] In contrast to such fickleness, the names the faithful receive will be as if carved in stone; that is, they are going to be there *always* and never change.

A partial name change occurred during Vespasian's reign (A.D. 70-79) when the city gave itself the name Flavia. In this case, though, the name remained an acceptable alternative to the usual designation Philadelphia, at least into the third century A.D.[41]

A broader social allusion may be intended in their receiving the name of the new Jerusalem. This implies Paul's idea that the Christian belongs to the heavenly Jerusalem (Gal 4:26; cf. Heb 12:22). Unlike the modern world, which usually thinks of loyalties as *national*, ancients—especially in Asia—defined loyalties as primarily local and civic and only secondarily as due to the wider province or empire. Just as an individual proudly wore the name of Ephesian or Pergamonese or Philadelphian, the triumphant believer would proudly "wear" the name of the heavenly Jerusalem and of God and of his Christ. On a spiritual level that was the center of their loyalty, not any earthly power.

*Pillars with Names Written on Them (3:12)*

Jesus promises the local Christians that they will be rewarded by becoming "a pillar in the temple of my God, and he shall go out no more." Upon them will be written his own new name, that of God, and that of the new Jerusalem" (2:13).

There is only the vaguest biblical precedent for this image of individuals as pillars in God's temple. Solomon erected two "pillars before the temple, one on the right hand and the other on the left." Since they were "before" the temple, they must have been outside it, rather than inside as in the Johannine promise. In the case of Solomon's temple, there were no names on the pillars, but there were names *given* to them: "He called the name of the one on the right hand Jachin, and the name of the one on the left Boaz" (2 Chr 3:15–17, esp. 17; cf. 1 Kgs 7:21).

In 1 Maccabees 14:25–26 we find the Jewish people debating how to honor the work of liberation performed on the nation's behalf by Simon and his sons. "So they made an inscription on bronze tablets which they *affixed to pillars on Mount Zion.*" The lengthy inscription (1 Mc 14:27–49) was "set up in a conspicuous place in the precincts of the temple" (1 Mc 14:49, *NAB*).

The Gentile allusion that is most commonly made, finds in the text a Christian parallel to the imperial cult. L. van Hartinsveld, for example, writes:

> This is an allusion to a bust that the high priest of the imperial temple commissioned for himself. Carved into it were his name, his father's name and city, and the year of his administration. The high priest was in office for one year. His successor, after his year of service, also placed a memorial column in the temple. In the end there were so many that the sculptured images of the less popular figures were removed. They had to go.[42]

In contrast, the triumphant Christian would never be removed from God's heavenly temple. Even if one assumes that *all* imperial high priests followed this custom, that would still be a small minority of all who worshiped at the imperial altar. In vivid contrast, all who worshiped at *Yahweh's* altar would receive this recognition.

Colin J. Hemer warns, however, "I find no evidence that this precise custom existed, and the terms in which it is repeated by successive commentators are necessarily excluded as anachronistic by the fact that Philadelphia did not receive the neocorate until about A.D. 213."[43] He concedes that it was a logical custom and could have existed,[44] which is considerably short of the certainty with which commentators introduce the alleged custom.

Hemer concedes that "the cutting of inscriptions on columns was a common practice."[45] Hence we would be on sounder ground if we abandon a strictly imperial priesthood context and seek the explanation in the broader societal custom of putting identification names on the pedestals of statues/busts in general.[46] Likewise, one might seek an explanation in inscriptions on walls or religious sites in general.[47]

If one goes further afield than Asia, one may discover a *Jewish* precedent for literal, inscripted support columns of a religious facility. Examples from synagogues of the third and fourth century in Galilee exhibit this phenomenon; the names are those of those who helped finance the construction.[48] An example comes from Capernaum, where the excavated synagogue was discovered to contain two pillars with inscriptions. One was in Greek and the other in Aramaic. They were very short and simple. The Greek inscription read, "Herod, the son of Makimos, and his descendants."[49]

In addition to these factors, the pillar image may have been selected because of Philadelphia's earthquake danger. In a community where even the stability of the earth is an ongoing and changeable situation, a pillar is a clear allusion to the stable permanence everyone desired.[50]

## *11*

# Undecided Laodicea

Antiochus II built the city and named it after his wife Laodice. Since he divorced her in 240 B.C., that dates the founding of the city (designed to replace an earlier village) at an unknown number of years prior to that separation.[1] It was incorporated into the kingdom of Pergamon about 188 B.C.[2] and became part of the Asia that Rome "inherited" sixty some years later.

The city initially resisted Mithridates during his war against Rome. The citizenry, however, rebelled during the resulting siege and delivered its leader over to him. When the Romans triumphed, the city sent a delegation to Rome that successfully convinced the Senate to overlook the repudiation by the citizenry and to consider only the pro-Roman evidence of the siege. By this means the community escaped punitive policy that could easily have been inflicted upon it.[3]

The community was designed as part of the effort to "civilize" (that is, Hellenize) the region. If Philadelphia could be viewed as an example of the policy's success, Laodicea was an example of its failure. As Charles C. Whiting observes, "Its mission was to be a centre for the spread of Greek civilization and language in barbarian Phrygia but in this it failed so completely that Phrygia was the least Hellenized part of the province though the reason of its failure, when Philadelphia its neighbor succeeded in the same work, we do not know."[4]

Laodicea was located on a small hill between two streams that fed into the nearby Lycus River.[5] Mountains so high that snow stays on them most of the year can be seen in almost every direction.[6] Although not one of the more physically impressive sites among the seven church-cities, Laodicea can still leave an occasional visitor with an unexpected appreciation of its contextual beauty. Writing of a pre-World War I visit, Walter A. Hawley

205

happened to find himself at the ruins at a moment when atmosphere, weather, and perhaps even personal sentiment made him recognize this.

> Parts of the hills were covered with cropped, bunchy grass; parts were ploughed and sown with grain; all was strewn with bits of chiselled stone, presenting a scene of utter desolation. Yet traces of grandeur linger in the forsaken ruins.
>
> In the evening of this day of our first visit they were serenely imposing as the setting sun drove their lengthening shadows over the broken ground, and touched their tops and the encircling mountains with tints of golden red. I watched them until their colour turned again to grey, then climbed among the highest seats of the smaller theatre, whence I could see, over the roofs of the low houses of Genjeli, the fires of Yuruks glowing in the valley of the Lycus, and beyond it the crystal cascades of Hierapolis reflecting the fading light.[7]

Unlike many other communities in which the walled area contained only the acropolis, at Laodicea it contained the entire city.[8] This formed a square, approximately one mile on each side.[9] Each corner represented a compass point[10] and three roads penetrated the walls into the city.[11] In the southwest wall was the Ephesian Gate,[12] which opened to Ephesus, a hundred miles away.[13] In the northern corner was the city's acropolis as well as the entrance for the road from Hierapolis.[14] The aqueduct penetrated the southwest wall.[15] Emperors come and go and need to receive various honors from a community to verify its loyalty. So it is not surprising that during Domitian's reign, the city renamed one of its gates in his honor.[16]

Although the population of the city is not known, it was larger than nearby Colossae.[17] Strabo indicates, however, that it underwent a major population surge, "Though formerly small, it grew large in our time and in that of our fathers, even though it had been damaged by the siege of Mithradates Eupator."[18] In the same period the city's economy began to blossom, as the cloth and woolen industries began to flourish.[19]

The peak of local prosperity was not reached until the closing decades of the second century A.D.[20] If one were to list the wealthiest cities of Asia during either of the first two centuries, however, Laodicea would certainly have made the list.[21] Banking played an important role, and Cicero refers to his intention to cash a bill of exchange when he arrived there.[22]

Even so, its flocks of sheep laid the foundation for its well being; the major farm product of the area was wool. William M. Ramsay points out that this, of its very nature, required that a high percentage of agricultural land be diverted from crop production into pasture. This held down the amount available for the growth of local agricultural products and made both the city and the nearby area more dependent upon external sources for their food supply.[23]

The presence of a large-scale sheep business would have been of value to Laodicea under virtually any set of circumstances. Local enterprise enabled the city to achieve large-scale prosperity by effectively building upon this resource; Laodicea developed extensive industries that produced a wide variety of garments for the export trade. These ranged from mass-produced garments for the populace at large[24] to quality attire for the well-to-do.[25] The best local wool was soft and glossy black and often went into garments for the upper classes.[26]

Various local businesses produced cloaks, upper garments, and undergarments of various types and quality. The cheaper cloaks were called Laodicia and held around the neck by the equivalent of a safety pin. Certain high quality garments/tunics were called *trimita* and became such a prominent export of the city that by the fourth century certain documents refer to the city itself as Trimitaria.[27] Combined, they brought the city what Strabo rightly described as a "splendid revenue."[28]

Readily available water provided for the vast flocks and agriculture. As an early-twentieth-century traveler to the city wrote:

> The agricultural produce of the district, which was watered by five rivers, had a high reputation. The town itself was washed by the Asopus and the Caprousa. Nearby flowed the Lycus, which below Colossis disappeared underground to reappear on the surface about a mile further on; and in addition there was the river known today as the Tchoruk Sou, which comes down from Cadmus. A mile from the walls of Laodicea the waters of the earlier rivers joined the

Maeander. Many small streams plashed around the town....[It is] a city watered by so many streams."[29]

Asia was subdivided into smaller governing regions. Hierapolis, Laodicea, and Colossae were all in the same *conventus,* and Laodicea served as its capital.[30] Internally, the population was divided into an unknown number of tribes, including the Laodicis, Aollonis, Athenais, Sebaste, Attalis, and Ias.[31] Representatives of each of the recognized tribes served together as the governing body of the community.[32] The local Jews may have constituted a tribe as well, but, if so, their collective rights would almost certainly have been terminated with the crushing of the Jewish Revolt in Palestine in A.D. 70.[33]

On the hill of the city were located the city's two theaters.[34] One pointed in a western direction and the other northward.[35] The larger dated back to Greek days, while the smaller was added after the incorporation of Asia into the Roman domain.[36] Visiting the site in the early 1950s, Freya Stark commented, "Of the two theatres one is shuffled away by earthquakes, but the western [one] keeps the grass-grown rows of its seats intact."[37]

Located close to the city stadium's eastern end (see below) is a large Roman-era facility that has been called both a gymnasium[38] and a bath.[39] It appears to have been built during Emperor Hadrian's reign, and inscriptions at the site commemorate the emperor's visit to the community in A.D. 129.[40]

Located about one hundred yards from the stadium are the ruins of a small building with the remains of five or six tiers of seats. Although there is no supporting evidence, it has been speculated that this was a municipal council meeting facility.[41]

A true stadium was rounded at only one end, while the Laodicean facility is rounded at both and seats run all around the facility.[42] It is better to describe it as an amphitheatrical stadium, since it could be used for either purpose.[43] The size of the facility also argues for the need of a modified terminology. The normal stadium for foot races and other athletic contests was under 200 yards long.[44] Its actual length has been calculated anywhere from a minimum of some 900 feet,[45] to 1,000 feet[46] to over 1,100 feet.[47] By any of these estimates, Laodicea's facility was the longest "stadium" in all of Asia Minor.[48]

It was built or converted during the reign of Vespasian.[49] One Nicostratus financed the work, according to a surviving inscription "at his own cost." His son—who bore the same name—financed the remaining alterations and improvements.[50] The inscription says one of them had "been priest of the city and has consecrated the amphitheater stadium in white marble."[51]

In addition to athletic contests, this was the site of gladiator fights.[52] The imperial cult was among the sponsors of such combats in Laodicea.[53] Gladiatorial performances are known to have been staged in the city at least as far back as 50 B.C., for Cicero refers to them at that time.[54] A tomb inscription for gladiators has survived from the city. Although this could have been erected for those who died in training, the greater likelihood is that it identifies the grave site of those who perished in actual public contests.[55]

One cost-saving feature utilized in the construction of the amphitheatrical stadium was that of taking advantage of the city's natural geography. William J. Hamilton, an on-site investigator in the mid-1830s, observed that

> the stadium, which is in a good state of preservation, is near the southern extremity of the city. The seats, almost perfect, are arranged along two sides of a narrow valley, which appears to have been taken advantage of for this purpose, and to have been closed up at both ends. Towards the west are considerable remains of a subterranean passage, by which horses and chariots were admitted into the arena, with a long inscription over the entrance. Near the east end are the ruins of a massive pile of building, the plan of which can be distinctly traced, the walls still standing to a considerable height.[56]

The remains of one final construction project of ancient Laodicea deserve attention before we discuss the religious aspects of the city's culture: the water-supply system that provided water for the city. The potability of the city's water will be important when we discuss John's references to local society. Once again we turn to William J. Hamilton, who described the remains as they existed in the mid-1830s.

> Amongst other interesting objects are the remains of an aqueduct, commencing near the summit of a low hill to the south,

whence it is carried on arches of small square stones to the edge of the hill. Here also the water must have been much charged with calcareous matter, as several of the arches are covered with a thick incrustation. From this hill the aqueduct crossed a valley before it reached the town, but, instead of being carried over it on lofty arches, as was the usual practice of the Romans, the water was conveyed down the hill in stone barrel-pipes; some of these also are much incrusted, and some completely choked up. It traversed the plain in pipes of the same kind; and I was enabled to trace them the whole way quite up to its former level in the town....

The aqueduct on the hill appears to have been overthrown by an earthquake, as the remaining arches lean bodily on one side, without much being broken. At the spot where it reaches the town is a high conical wall picturesquely covered with incrustations and water-pipes of red clay, some of which are completely choked up; the remains of what appeared to have been another water-tower were not far distant.[57]

The water had a high lime content, as can be determined today by an examination of the surviving sections of the pipeline.[58] Since there was a real danger of this lime building up and blocking the water flow, some of the blocks containing pipes had an additional hole carved in the top. If there was no water in the system at that point, all one had to do was to backtrack to the first one that *did* have water in order to find the blockage.[59] George E. Bean, a specialist in the history of Turkey, dates the surviving sections as from the second century A.D., if not later.[60] On the other hand, the need for a steady supply of water argues that a similar system may have predated it, though that does not tell us whether it tapped into the same water resources or when the city outgrew its more immediate water supplies.[61]

### Polytheism in Laodicea

Because of its tie-in with a local intellectual, this would be an appropriate place to discuss the forms that hymn writing could take in the worship of the gods. These hymns could come in either of two forms. In the third century, Menander of Laodicea wrote an extended essay on the proper method of composing a non-sung, prose hymn to the gods. The prose composition could stress any of a number of aspects of these deities: how they came to be named, their nature, their birth, how they could reward or punish, and so on.[62]

Rhyming hymns (the more traditional meaning of the term) were common in the worship of the deities. Sometimes the words were carved in the temple walls,[63] as at the Zeus temple in Pergamon.[64] This, of course, implies congregational participation. In some religious movements it was considered proper for shouted interjections to be thrown in by enthusiastic participants. The Asclepius cult at Pergamon is an example.[65]

As in all other cities, the deities of Laodicea were numerous. On the distaff side were goddesses such as Hera and Athena.[66] Work by archaeologists from Quebec has uncovered an apparent late-second-century Isis sanctuary.[67] It is not surprising to discover that her cohort, Sarapis, was also worshiped in the city.[68]

Rome itself was personified and worshiped in Laodicea, as in so many other places, along with the cult of the emperors, but Laodicea carried this a step further: it treated Laodice as a personification of the city as well. A priest was appointed to encourage her worship among the populace at large.[69]

Mithras, Dionysus, and Helios were among the male gods revered.[70] The popularity of Apollo is indicated, ironically, by evidence preserved at the Apollo shrine at Claros: repeatedly Laodicea sent requests there for Apollo's judgment on various matters.[71] From Claros also comes no fewer than twenty-five different inscriptions referring to "prophets" of the god who came from Laodicea.[72]

Two cults stood out as more important than all the others. The first was that of Zeus.[73] So important was he that he was worshiped under the twin names of Zeus Aseis and Zeus Laodicenus.[74] Although it is known that a white pavement lay at the entrance of his temple, its location, size, and layout are otherwise undocumented.[75] The long-established Zeus festival was dramatically modified about A.D. 150: henceforth this was a combined Zeus-imperial cult feast. At the same time, the imperial cult was introduced at the Zeus cult site in the city.[76]

The second deity competing for recognition as the most important[77] was Men, the regional moon god—or, more completely,

Men Karou or the Carian Men. He was very popular not only in Laodicea and nearby Asia but also in the adjoining provinces that one day would become Turkey.[78] Although his temple was located twelve[79] or thirteen[80] miles outside of the city, inferential evidence argues that its important medical facility was not located at the temple but within Laodicea.[81] The names of prominent physicians attached to the school appear on coins issued by the city.[82] The founder of the facility was Zeuxis Philalethes. Coming after him were such figures as Demosthenes, who not only was renowned for his knowledge concerning human eyesight, but was so respected that his writings continued to be available in translation into the Middle Ages.[83]

The earliest datable reference to Men comes from 40 B.C., but his greatest popularity was during the first three centuries A.D., after which the religion seems to have undergone a rapid decline.[84] Of the seven church-cities of Asia, monuments of various types dedicated to him are found in Sardis, Smyrna, and Pergamon.[85] In addition, coins with his image have been discovered in both Sardis and Laodicea.[86]

He is normally depicted wearing typical regional attire: "Phrygian cap, trousers, boots, and cloak, and with a crescent moon at his shoulders."[87] (Regardless of local differences, the presence of a large crescent was a unifying factor and was accepted as the standard symbol of the deity.[88]) Usually he is represented as standing; less often he is depicted resting, sitting, or riding.[89] As to animal accompaniments, a bull or a cock is common.[90]

In western Asia Minor the worship of Men usually involved only small cultic centers or private altars. Further east, the cult tended to have city-sponsored religious cults as well. The best example of this was Pisidian Antioch, which not only recognized Men as the city's patron god but was also the largest center of the movement.[91]

### Monotheism in Laodicea

A colony of Jews took root here in the first century B.C.[92] In 62 B.C. the proconsul Flaccus prohibited the export of the temple tax to Jerusalem, and this restriction affected Laodicea as well as other Asian cities.[93] It is said that Flaccus seized 22.5 pounds of gold. This would equal approximately fifteen thousand silver drachmas. Since the temple tax was two silver drachmas per adult male freeman in that era, that argues for a substantial Jewish community—seventy-five hundred adult males, plus spouses and children.[94] Since the Jews were unlikely to represent more than a small fraction of the total population, that in turn argues for a good-sized urban population.

Just as John speaks censorious word of the *Christian* population, rabbis spoke similarly stern rebukes of the wealth and luxuriousness of the *Jewish* community. Indeed, this entire section of Phrygia was apparently considered by the rabbis to be afflicted with a similar problem.[95]

Nothing is known of the founding of the congregation though, as in so many other cases, it is reasonable to suppose that the congregation grew out of missionary work or contacts initiated during Paul's two year stay in Ephesus (Acts 19:10). Certainly it was in existence by the time Paul wrote to the Colossians, for he refers to the group in that epistle (Col 2:1; 4:13–16). It has been argued that the two most probable residences for the Philemon Paul addresses in the epistle of that name was either at Colossae or at Laodicea.[96] There is some evidence that at least for a while in the second century the church met not in the city itself but at a location a little over half a mile outside it.[97]

Other than John's mini-epistle, the most tantalizing reference to the congregation is found in Colossians 4:16, "Now when this epistle is read among you, see that it is read also in the church of the Laodiceans, and that you likewise read the epistle from Laodicea." What was this odd epistle, which has—at least on first glance—not survived? (Somewhere between the second and fourth centuries, a pseudo-Laodicean epistle was compiled from various Pauline texts.[98])

A careful reading of the Colossian allusion requires only that the epistle copy was to be transmitted *from* Laodicea and not that Paul himself *was* its author. But assuming, as is commonly done, that he was the author, two basic options are open: to give up hope of ever recovering the text and conclude that the epistle has been lost,[99] or to speculate that it is· one of the surviving Pauline or other New Testament epistles. Ephesians is the most often suggested, and those embracing this approach outnumber those believing the epistle to have disappeared.[100] Hebrews[101] and Philemon[102] are less often cited alternatives.

If one seeks out a non-Pauline authorship, the problem of how an apostolic epistle could ever be lost is completely removed. It also offers a fertile field for inventive reconstructions. Epaphras[103] and Luke[104] have been mentioned in this context.

Finally, there is the possibility that the epistle came *from* the Laodicean church rather than being sent to it. This was a view common in the post-biblical, medieval, and Reformation-era church.[105] A variant of this would be that it was a Pauline epistle written while in Laodicea and, for that reason, it would be unlikely to be remembered under that city's name.[106]

### Historical and Social Allusions
### Text of the Epistle

"And to the angel of the church of the Laodiceans write, 'These things says the Amen, the Faithful and True Witness, the Beginning of the creation of God: "I know your works, that you are neither cold nor hot. I could wish you were cold or hot. So then, because you are lukewarm, and neither cold nor hot, I will spew you out of my mouth. Because you say, 'I am rich, have become wealthy, and have need of nothing'— and do not know that you are wretched, miserable, poor, blind, and naked—I counsel you to buy from me gold refined in the fire, that you may be rich; and white garments, that you may be clothed, that the shame of your nakedness may not be revealed; and anoint your eyes with eye salve, that you may see. As many as I love, I rebuke and chasten. Therefore be zealous and repent. Behold, I stand at the door and knock. If anyone hears my voice and opens the door, I will come in to him and dine with him, and he with me. To him who overcomes I will grant to sit with me on my throne, as I also overcame and sat down with my Father on his throne. He who has an ear, let him hear what the Spirit says to the churches."'" (Rv 3:14–22)

*Local Roots of John's Lukewarm Allusion (3:14–15)*

Jesus rebukes the congregation with the warning, "I know your works, that you are neither cold nor hot. I could wish you

were cold or hot. So then, because you are lukewarm, and neither cold nor hot, I will spew you out of my mouth" (3:15–16).
This is commonly taken as a reference to the local water supply.
But *why* was the water lukewarm?

The broadest way to answer this question is to argue that
regardless of the specific source, *all* water found in the area
tended to be lukewarm. In the mid-1800s Sir John Fellows wrote
that he had observed that "the waters, which rise in copious
streams from several deep springs among the ruins, are also to
be found in small rivulets for twenty miles around; they are
tepid, and to appearance perfectly pure."[107]

A more specific explanation is given by those who believe
that the city tapped hot springs for its water.[108] This carries the
implication that the water *cooled* to lukewarmness by the time it
reached the city. Edwin M. Yamauchi argues that the calcareous
deposits found in the piping system leading into the city indicate
the water originated in such springs.[109] Another scholar observes
that though the hot springs explanation is very probable, it really
doesn't matter much: "Even if it was originally cold, the heat of
the sun no doubt warmed it until it was flat and unpalatable."[110]

Sometimes it is assumed or directly claimed that hot springs
at Hierapolis were the source of Laodicea's water. For example,
L. Selles writes: "There were hotsprings in Hierapolis. The water
of these springs had become lukewarm by the time it reached
Laodicea."[111] Hierapolis, however, is to the north of the city while
the water system approaches Laodicea from the south.[112]

Others find a *geographical* base for the condemnation by
pointing to the hot/lukewarm phenomenon that occurred at
Hierapolis itself. Wilfrid J. Harrington, for example, writes:
"Water from the hot springs of Hierapolis, by that time become
lukewarm, flowed over the cliff opposite Laodicea; the sulphurous water was nauseating. It seems that these factors lie
behind and give further weight to these striking verses."[113]

Hence all three allusions (hot/lukewarm/cold) might be
found in the same place and very close together: *hot* as the water
left the springs, *lukewarm* as it went over the cliff, and *cool* as it
passed on beyond the bottom of the cliff. The whitish residue
left by the sulphurous water was visible not only at Laodicea but

from distances several times further away.[114] Hence one commentator refers to it as the "visual aid the Lord used."[115]

A better way to make this concept work is by introducing a second nearby city, Colossae, and making the root of John's allusion a contrast between the water supplies of the two communities. Jack Finegan develops this approach when he writes that we see here "a play on words, contrasting what *may* have been the tepid water of the aqueduct at Laodicea with the *possibly* fresher and colder water at Colossae and with the very hot water of the cascades at Hierapolis" (emphasis added).[116] One certainty (Hierapolis's hot water) and two possibilities make for interesting argumentation but leave the case short of conclusiveness. Especially in regard to Colossae, the assumption-based nature of the argument tends to be overlooked.

A three-way comparison shifts the meaning of the text away from the mediocre interpretation of Laodicean Christianity. In the traditional approach Laodicea's sin was lack of full commitment to the Lord. In contrast, a three-city approach downgrades even further the value of that church's faith: Hot water in Hierapolis served a useful purpose, cold water at Colossae served a useful purpose, but lukewarm water is completely useless.[117] Their sin then becomes not half-commitment but *no* commitment.

### A Reference to Local Pharmaceuticals (3:18)

The local church was rebuked as spiritually shortsighted when Jesus urged them to "anoint your eyes with eye salve, that you may see" (3:18).

Sir William M. Ramsay argued, apparently presenting for the first time a local tie-in with this reference, that the earthly equivalent of the eye-salve Jesus refers to was "Phrygian powder." This "was used by ancient physicians to cure weakness of the eyes, and we may probably infer that the powder was made in Laodicea and that the physicians of Laodicea were skilled as oculists."[118] This eye salve/Phrygian powder correlation is a popular one with subsequent writers.[119] The available evidence is consistent with that approach, though it does not reach the level of an unescapable inference. C. J. Hemer notes that two ancient writers (including the great physician Galen) discuss the supplies coming from Phrygia "in contexts where Laodicea in particular is probably in view."[120]

Just what *was* this Phrygian powder? Sir William Ramsay suspected that it was some type of ointment made from bronze.[121] E. M. Blaiklock speculated: "It is a fair guess that it was the dried mud of the thermal springs. Emulsified, and heavily impregnated with mineral oils and chemicals, such mud would dry into a fine grey powder, which would conveniently mix with pure water to form a kaolin poultice, an effective remedy for inflammation."[122]

Although the regional reference to eye salve is the best one because it would have been obvious to the readers who received the mini-epistle, the large segment of John's audience that was Jewish might well have also thought in terms of the presence of such ointments in Palestine as well. In a geographically Palestinian context much is known of healing eye ointments. The Balsamodendon epobalsamum tree was utilized for its bark, its seeds, and its oil (that is, "plant juice")—all of which were used in ancient healing medications. The last was also recognized as a reliable eye ointment. The technical name for this "oil" was opobalsamum and was considered what we today would call a wonder drug.[123]

Ointment sticks (originally called *collyrium*) were rubbed upon the eyes or other parts of the body for healing purposes. "As time went on, the term 'collyrium' came to designate all eye disease remedies, prescriptions being given [by physicians] also for the production of liquid collyria and collyria resembling fish scales, but the prescriptions for ointment sticks were still predominant."[124] The Talmud speaks of the propriety of using collyrium even on the sabbath, with the proviso that the ointment be mixed before the sabbath began.[125]

Hence the early Christians would have been well aware that eye problems often had an available remedy. Just as they went to trusted physicians to obtain balm for their physically distressed eyes, they were to go to Jesus to obtain the spiritual "eye salve" that would eliminate the difficulties in their spiritual view.

### The Clothes-Buying Allusion (3:18)

Jesus pictures the need for the local church to set itself aright under the imagery of spending its money for new clothes, "I counsel you to buy from me...white garments, that you may be clothed, that the shame of your nakedness may not be revealed" (3:18). The moral point is that they might live a life of moral purity,[126] symbolized by the pure white garments they wear.

On a natural plane, it would be extremely difficult to find a more appropriate allusion in a city so dependent upon the clothing trade.[127] Qualitatively, none could exceed the product of the city. Its wool and wool products were among the highest quality found anywhere in the empire.[128]

A second allusion may be intended in the "white garments" they were to buy. This was in marked contrast to the black wool used so commonly in their own clothes production.[129] What they most needed was *not* what was most characteristic of the local situation. Just as the congregation did not have the right spiritual temperature and did not use the right eye salve so they could see, likewise the right type of spiritual "wool"—wool with which to "weave" their spiritual garments— was not that easy to come by.

Furthermore, the color may have been chosen because of the type of individuals most likely to use the upscale products of the industry. The church was confident of its relative wealth (see next allusion) and "black wool garments," it has been argued, were the typical attire of "the wealthy Laodiceans."[130] The very color of the "garments" they took the most pride in reflected their lack of spiritual insight into the purity and truth of their Savior: They simply did not want to "buy" the right kind. This may be pressing John's point further than he intended, but it would still have been a natural thought to have occurred to well-to-do church members.

*Implications of Local Wealth (3:18)*

The church members had resources available on a spiritual plane just as they did on the temporal, for Jesus urges them "to buy from me gold refined in the fire, that you may be rich" (3:18).

Based upon the twin foundations of its banking and wool industries, the city took justifiable pride in its economic prosperity.[131] One individual alone provided two thousand talents' worth of monuments and improvements to the town—and then bequeathed it all his remaining wealth when he died.[132]

In A.D. 17 a huge earthquake leveled the town. Most cities would willingly have accepted Roman assistance—even lobbied for it. Not so wealthy, self-sufficient, and self-reliant Laodicea.[133] As Tacitus writes, "The same year, Laodicea, one of the famous cities of Asia, having been prostrated by an earthquake, recovered its pristine glory from its own resources, and without any relief from us."[134]

In A.D. 60 another mammoth earthquake leveled the city.[135] Again the city was rebuilt without outside assistance.[136] If John writes his mini-epistle after this event, he is surely making a double reference to both of these highlights of local history; if he writes *before,* he is alluding to the independent frame of mind that produced the decision to follow the same course in both cases.[137]

This wealth may also have led to Jesus' plea that they buy clothes from him. They were in the right socio-economic category to enjoy the pleasures of the gymnasium—where nudity during athletic endeavors was the norm and anything else an oddity.[138]

*Christ's Willingness to Dine with Them (3:20)*

Having rebuked them in several different ways, Jesus provides a word of reassurance, "Behold, I stand at the door and knock. If anyone hears my voice and opens the door, I will come in to him and dine with him, and he with me" (3:20). The whole emphasis here is on the hospitality being voluntary. In contrast the people were under legal obligation to provide lodging and provisions to Roman officials whenever requested by them.[139] In contrast, Jesus was not about to force himself upon anyone. He would dine only with those who wished it. Instead of being *required* to provide him with room and food, they would be marks of honor and respect that he *agreed* to accept.

# Notes

## INTRODUCTION

1. By "Asian" we refer to *Roman* Asia—western Turkey. "Asia Minor," when used, refers to the broader nearby regions, roughly equivalent to the entire country of contemporary Turkey.

2. Detailed in-depth study of various major deities is scattered through the various chapters, the location primarily being chosen upon the basis of the importance of the deity to that local community.

3. The factor called luck still plays a pivotal role in revealing what is known about ancient cities and what remains unknown. When Princeton University sent out an expedition in 1910, all it uncovered at Sardis were ruins from the Byzantine era—interesting in themselves but beyond the period we are interested in (Gonzalo Baez-Camargo, *Archaeological Commentary on the Bible*, trans. Eugene A. Nida [Garden City, N.Y.: Doubleday and Company, 1984], 263). When archaeologists returned decades later, they started uncovering an impressive body of ruins from the biblical period. Since financial and time limitations restrict the physical limits and duration of such "digs," the hit-and-miss nature of archaeological findings is inevitable.

4. Steven J. Friesen, "Revelation, Realia, and Religion: Archaeology in the Interpretation of the Apocalypse," *Harvard Theological Review* 88 (July 1996), 291–314, takes this approach. He negatively evaluates Sir William Ramsay's pioneering work on the seven churches in their local setting (291–301). Likewise note his negative interpretation of Colin Hemer's much more recent work (301–6). There seems to be a fundamental inconsistency in the critique of Ramsay in particular: while objecting to Ramsay's allegedly excessive historical allusions in the seven mini-epistles, Friesen sees nothing inconsistent in pointing out—at length—the predisposing factors that caused Ramsay to see such allusions. If external data can better help us understand the "why" and "wherefore" of one author's approach, where can the objection be for seeking out information to better understand those of a *different* author—John?

5. For a presentation receptive to this criticism see J. Ramsey Michaels, *Interpreting the Book of Revelation* (Grand Rapids, Mich.: Baker Book House, 1992), 36–39.

6. As claimed in ibid., 39, n. 20.

7. On utilizing, through creative intermixture, both Old Testament and local allusions, see Steve Moyise, *The Old Testament in the Book of Revelation* (Journal for the Study of the New Testament Supplement 115) (Sheffield, England: Sheffield Academic Press, 1995).

8. "Local References in the Letters to the Seven Churches," *New Testament Studies* 39 (October 1993):614–15.

## 1. GLORIOUS EPHESUS: THE CITY, THE HISTORY, THE CULTURE

1. Laurence Oliphant, *Haifa or Life in Modern Palestine*, ed. Charles A. Dane (New York: Harper & Brothers, 1886; 1887 printing), 1.

2. J. T. Wood, *Modern Discoveries on the Site of Ancient Ephesus* (Oxford: The Religious Tract Society, 1890), 24.

3. Robert Walsh, *Constantinople and the Scenery of the Seven Churches of Asia* (London: Fisher, Son & Company, 1838), 63.

4. Steven M. Baugh, "Paul and Ephesus: The Apostle Among His Contemporaries" (Ph.D. diss., University of California (Irvine), 1990), 20. Pliny was among those who believed that Ephesus had originally been "built by the Amazons" (*Natural History, Books III–VI* [Loeb Classical Library], trans. H. Rackam [Cambridge: Harvard University Press, 1942]).

5. Charles Seltman, *Riot in Ephesus: Writings on the Heritage of Greece* (London: Max Parrish, 1958), 75; Richard E. Oster, "Ephesus as a Religious Center Under the Principate: I. Paganism Before Constantine," in *Aufstieg und Niedergang der Romischen Welt* (Berlin: Walter de Gruyter, 1990), II, 18.3, 1720–21. This mythology originated in Asia Minor (Richard E. Oster, "Ephesus as a Religious Center," 1720). The Amazons were also credited with playing important roles in the early days of other religions of the region. In regard to Artemis in particular, the legends tell that after the amazons were finally defeated, some remained behind in Ephesus as servants of the goddess (Oster, "Ephesus as a Religious Center," 1721).

6. Since women have served in some twentieth century armies, Charles Seltman speculates there may have been a historical kernel in this ancient tale (*Riot in Ephesus*, 75).

7. Baugh, "Paul and Ephesus," 20.

8. Andrew E. Hill, "Ancient Art and Artemis: Toward Explaining the Polymastic Nature of the Figurine," *Journal of the Ancient Near*

*Eastern Society* 21 (1992):92. For ancient sources on the founding of Ephesus by Androkles (either son or grandson of a ruler of Athens) see Sjef van Tilborg, *Reading John in Ephesus* (Leiden: E. J. Brill, 1996), 33–35.

9. Ekrem Akurgal, *Ancient Civilizations and Ruins of Turkey: From Prehistoric Times until the End of the Roman Empire*, 3d ed. (Ankara [Turkey]: Turkish Historical Society Press/Haset Kitabevi, 1973), 142.

10. Akurgal, *Ancient Civilizations*, 142.

11. Baugh, "Paul and Ephesus," 21.

12. Ibid., 21; Akurgal, *Ancient Civilizations*, 142.

13. Musa Barra, *Ephesus and Its Surroundings*, trans. Hulya Terzioglu (Izmir [Turkey]: Molay Matbaacilik, 19–), 12.

14. U. Onen, *Ephesus: Ruins and Museum*, trans. by Nualla Yilmaz and Nanette T. Nelson (Izmir [Turkey]: Akademia, 1983), 4.

15. Akurgal, *Ancient Civilizations*, 143.

16. Onen, *Ephesus: Ruins and Museum*, 9.

17. Ibid., 9; Akurgal, *Ancient Civilizations*, 143.

18. William M. Ramsay, *The Letters to the Seven Churches of Asia* (New York: George H. Doran Company, 1905), 227. The actual number of Romans killed on Mithridates's instructions may well have been far smaller than claimed (as noted by Stephen Mitchell, *Anatolia: Land, Men, and Gods in Asia Minor*, vol. 1: *The Celts in Anatolia and the Impact of Roman Rule* [Oxford: Clarendon Press, 1993], 30), but it was still vast enough to startle and horrify the Roman government and people.

19. Ramsay, *Seven Churches*, 227; Merrill M. Parvis, "Archaeology and St. Paul's Journey in Greek Lands—Pare IV: Ephesus," *Biblical Archaeologist* 8 (1945), 66.

20. Baugh, "Paul and Ephesus," 23–24. On Ephesus's reversal of loyalties during Mithridates's attempt to expel the Romans from the region also see van Tilborg, *Ephesus*, 35–36.

21. Ibid., 25–26.

22. Ibid., 26–27.

23. Mitchell, *Celts*, implies a figure of about 180,000–200,000. Estimates expressed implicitly or explicitly as about 200,000 include George M. A. Hanfmann, *From Croesus to Constantine: The Cities of Western Asia Minor and Their Arts in the Greek and Roman Times*, Jerome Lectures: Tenth Series (Ann Arbor, Mich.: University of Michigan Press, 1975), 49 (as of second century at least); Bruce M. Metzger, *Breaking the Code: Understanding the Book of Revelation* (Nashville, Tenn.: Abingdon Press, 1993), 31; Richard Oster, "The Ephesian Artemis as an Opponent of Early Christianity," in *Jahrbuch fur Antike und Christendom* 19 (1976) (Munster [Germany]: Aschendorffsche Verlagsbuchlandlung, 1977), 24 note.

Estimates expressed explicitly as over 200,000 include Cemil Tok-soz, *Ephesus: Legends and Facts*, trans. Amhmet E. Uysal (Ankara [Turkey]: Ayvildiz Matbaasi, 1969), 15; Freys Stark, *Rome on the Euphrates: The Story of a Frontier* (London: John Murray, 1966), 221. Falling between 200,000 and 250,000: The German scholar Beloch estimated about 225,000 residents (cited by T. R. S. Broughton, "Roman Asia," in *An Economic Survey of Ancient Rome*, vol. 4, ed. Tenney Frank, 499–918 [Baltimore: Johns Hopkins Press, 1938], 813). Broughton first speaks in terms of a population exceeding 200,000 and then mentions that a "considerable increase" over Beloch's estimate could well be justified (813). Paul Trebilco, "Asia," in *The Book of Acts in Its First Century Setting*, vol. 2: *First Century*, ed. David W. J. Gill and Conrad Gempf, 291–362 (Grand Rapids, Mich.: Wm. B. Eerdmans Publishing Company, 1994), 307, places the number between 200,000 and 250,000.

24. Estimates expressed implicitly or explicitly in terms of "about" 250,000 include George E. Bean, *Aegean Turkey: An Archaeological Guide* (New York: Frederick A. Praeger, Publishers, 1966), 164; Dan P. Cole, "Corinth and Ephesus: Why Did Paul Spend Half His Journeys in These Cities?" *Bible Review* 4 (December 1988):26–27; Edwin M. Yamauchi, *The Archaeology of New Testament Cities in Western Asia Minor* (Grand Rapids, Mich.: Baker Book House, 1980), 79; Naci Keskin, *Ephesus*, trans. Ertugrul Uckun (Ankara [Turkey]: Keskin Color Ltd. Co. Printing House, 19–), 2 (this small volume contains over one-hundred color photographs of the ruins of Ephesus).

Estimates expressed explicitly in terms of at least 250,000 include M. H. H. Sitwell, *Roman Roads of Europe* (New York: St. Martin's Press, 1981), 192; G. Ernest Wright, *Biblical Archaeology* (Philadelphia: Westminster Press, 1957), 253. Estimates expressed implicitly or explicitly in terms of "more than" 250,000 include Robert H. Mounce, *New International Commentary on Revelation* (Grand Rapids, Mich.: Wm. B. Eerdmans Publishing Company, 1977), 85; Hans Lilje, *The Last Book of the Bible: The Meaning of the Revelation of St. John,* trans. Olive Wyon (from the fourth German edition) (Philadelphia: Muhlenberg Press, 1957), 67.

25. L. Selles, *The Book of Revelation*, vol. 1 (London, Ontario: Interleague Publication Board of Canadian Reformed Societies, 1965), 14.

26. F. E. Peters, *The Harvest of Hellenism: A History of the Near East from Alexander the Great to the Triumph of Christianity* (New York: Simon and Schuster, 1970), 517.

27. Paul MacKendrick, *The Greek Stones Speak: The Story of Archaeology in Greek Lands*, 2d ed. (New York: W. W. Norton & Company, 1981), 466; Alfons Wotxhitzky, "Ephesus: Past, Present, Future of an Ancient Metropolis," *Archaeology* 14 (1961), 212.

28.  J. C. Russell argues that within the city's 852 acres this was the most likely population (*Late Ancient and Medieval Population* [Philadelphia: American Philosophical Society, 1958], 80). Including the suburbs and nearby dependent areas would, of course, substantially increase this figure but presumably still only to a number far short of the modern consensus. S. M. Baugh's estimate of "about" 100,000 residents ("A Foreign World: Ephesus in the First Century," in *Women in the Church: A Fresh Analysis of 1 Timothy 2:9–15*, ed. Andreas J. Kostenberger, Thomas R. Schreiner, and H. Scott Baldwin, 13–52 [Grand Rapids, Mich.: Baker Books, 1995], 17) may represent either an independent estimate or be a typographical error (for the commonly found figure of 200,000).

29.  Thereby producing J. C. Russell's (*Population*, 80) surprisingly low estimate referred to above.

30.  Baugh, "A Foreign World," 17 n.20.

31.  Mitchell, *Celts*, 244 n.12 denies the validity of the evidence yet clearly implies in different contexts (see note 23 above) that it had a population in the range of 180,000–200,000. Paul Trebilco, "Asia," 307 n.68, concedes that the reading is erroneous but still holds to a 200,000-plus population for Ephesus since Pergamon had "between 180,000 and 200,000 in this period, and Ephesus was at least as large as Pergamum."

32.  Charles R. Giblin considers it one of the five largest cities (*The Book of Revelation: The Open Book of Prophecy* [Collegeville, Minn.: A Michael Glazier Book/The Liturgical Press, 1991], 53). Gerhard A. Kordel, however, lists it as the fourth largest—behind (in descending order) Rome, Alexandria, and Antioch (*Augsburg Commentary on the New Testament* [Minneapolis: Augsburg Publishing House, 1989], 104).

33.  Quoted by Toksoz, *Ephesus*, 15.

34.  William Barclay, *The Revelation of John*, vol. 1, rev. ed, {Philadelphia: Westminster Press, 1976), 59.

35.  Ibid.

36.  Cf. the town clerk's plea, "We are in danger of being called in question for today's uproar, there being no reason which we may give to account for this disorderly gathering" (Acts 19:40). One of the difficult questions in evaluating "democratic" institutions of the period lies in the question of the degree of genuine local choice being exercised versus traditional terminology being retained as a democratic veneer for greater centralized control. Terminology may remain consistent while the political realities (and who exercises the actual power) have shifted dramatically. On this problem see the remarks of Diana Delia, *Alexandrian Citizenship During the Roman Principate* (Atlanta, Ga.: Scholars Press, 1991). 5–6.

37.  For a discussion of local self-government, especially in Eph-

esus, see A. N. Sherwin-White, *Roman Society and Roman Law in the New Testament*, The Sarum Lectures, 1960–1961 (Oxford: Clarendon Press, 1963), 84–86.

38. See A. N. Sherwin-White (ibid., 86–87) for the evidence of regular meetings. He notes that Chrysostom in particular refers to three monthly meetings being held.

39. Baugh, "Paul and Ephesus," 55.

40. Ibid.

41. Sherwin-White, *Roman Law*, 83.

42. Ibid., 86.

43. Henry B. Sewete, *The Apocalypse of St. John" The Greek Text with Introduction, Notes, and Indices*, 3d ed. (London: Macmillan and Co., 1909; reprinted, 1911), lix.

44. For a discussion of the town clerk position, which is heavily documented in the early years of the second century, see Sherwin-White, *Roman Law*, 86–87.

45. As quoted by H. D. Saffrey, "The Piety and Prayers of Ordinary Men and Women in Late Antiquity," in *Classical Mediterranean Spirituality: Egyptian, Greek, Roman*, ed. H. A. Armstrong (New York: Crossroad, 1986), 198. He provides a commentary on this text on page 199.

46. Mounce, *Revelation*, 85; G. B. Caird, *Commentary on the Revelation of St. John the Divine*, in the Harper's New Testament Commentaries series (New York: Harper & Row, 1966), 29.

47. Caird, *Revelation*, 29.

48. E. M. Blaiklock writes: "Ephesus must have been a dying city....The ships went to Smyrna" (*Out of the Earth: The Witness of Archaeology to the New Testament* [Grand Rapids, Mich.: Wm. B. Eerdmans Publishing Company, 1957], 55). Likewise Robert T. Boyd writes that "in Paul's day this city was vibrant, but when John wrote to its members, Ephesus was a dying city. Business was lagging and the Ephesians seemed to have lost the fire and creativeness and hope that would have made it a metropolis where one of the seven wonders of the ancient world was located" (*Tells, Tombs, and Treasure: A Pictorial Guide to Biblical Archaeology* [Grand Rapids, Mich.: Baker Books, 1969; reprint, New York: Bonanza Books, 1975], 207).

49. Strabo, *The Geography of Strabo*, Greek text with English translation by Horace Leonard Jones [Loeb Classical Library] (London: William Heinemann, 1928), 12.8.15.

50. Ibid., 14.1.24.

51. Pliny, as quoted by Otto F. A. Meinardus, *St. John of Patmos and the Seven Churches of the Apocalypse* (New Rochelle, N. Y.: Caratzas Brothers, Publishers, 1979), 35.

52. Aristides, as quoted by Onen, *Ephesus: Ruins and Museum*, 9. David Magie (*Roman Rule in Asia Minor to the End of the Third Century After Christ*. 2 vols. [Princeton, N.J.: Princeton University Press, 1950; reprint Salem, N.H.: Ayer Company, Publishers, 1988], 583). (Volume 1 consists exclusively of text; volume 2 of notes and related materials. The page numbering is consecutive rather than beginning again in volume 2.) cited Philostratus's *Life of Apollonius* 8.7.28 as evidence that the overall economic situation remained favorable into the second century.

53. Akurgal, *Ancient Civilizations*, 143. Cf. Aristides's assertion of the pivotal role of banking in Ephesus in the previous paragraph.

54. Baugh, "Paul and Ephesus," 45.

55. Ibid.

56. Ibid., 42; cf. ibid., 45.

57. M. P. Charlesworth, *Trade Routes and Commerce of the Roman Empire*, 2d ed., rev. (Chicago: Ares Publishers, 1926; reprint, 1974), 94.

58. Ibid., 91.

59. F. I. Finley, *Economy and Society in Ancient Greece*, ed. Brent D. Shaw and Richard P. Satler (London: Chatto & Winus, 1981), 168.

60. Baugh, "Paul and Ephesus," 52–53.

61. Baugh cites other scholars who noted the lack of such estates but apparently missed this seemingly necessary inference (ibid., 53).

62. Ibid.

63. Clive Foss, *Ephesus After Antiquity: A Late Antique, Byzantine and Turkish City* (Cambridge: Cambridge University Press, 1979), 3.

64. Blaiklock, *Out of the Earth*, 55; Ramsay, *Seven Churches*, 233. Barry Cunliffe attributes the decision to "the tense political situation" existing in Ephesus, though he does not spell out what that situation was (*Rome and Her Empire* [New York: McGraw-Hill Book Company, 1978], 258). Later he makes reference to the ongoing silting problem that eventually "robbed" the city of its harbor (260).

65. Magie, *Asia Minor*, 564.

66. It is sometimes called the "Monumentum Ephesenum." For a discussion see G. H. R. Horsley, "The Inscriptions of Ephesus and the New Testament," *Novum Testaentum* 34 (April 1992), 134–35.

67. Christine Trevett, *Ignatius*, 78; E. M. Blaiklock, *Cities of the New Testament* (London: Pickering & Inglis, 1965), 64.

68. Trevett, *Ignatius*, 78.

69. Howard F. Vos, *Archaeology in Bible Lands*, (Chicago: Moody Press, 1977), 319.

70. William Barclay, *Revelation*, gives the six mile figure. Others refer to it as eight miles: Caird, *Revelation*, 29; Gerhard Krodel, *Augs-*

*burg Commentary on the New Testament: Revelation* (Minneapolis: Augsburg Publishing House, 1989), 105.

71. Caird, *Revelation*, 29. Robert Walsh's 1830 observations on the swamp conditions were quoted at the beginning of the chapter. Forty years later James S. Jewell wrote of how the swamp had expanded to cover not only the harbor but sections of the surrounding area that had once been dry land. "[The marshland] is thickly covered with tall reeds. By bending these down beneath the feet it was possible to walk out a short distance from the edge. Everywhere I did so I found great blocks of marble and fragments of marble columns rising above the mud, in many cases concealed by reeds" ("Topography of Ephesus," *Methodist Review* 53 [April 1871], 290–91).

72. Charles Ludwig, *Cities in New Testament Times* (Denver, Colo.: Accent Books, 1976), 71.

73. Clarence A. Wendel is skeptical of the widely embraced silting explanation for the degeneration of the harbor. In his opinion the river leading into the harbor was physically incapable of pouring out that much silt, although he concedes that a silting scenario may well explain the eventual destruction of Miletus's harbor ("Land-tilting or Silting? Which Ruined Ancient Harbors?" *Archaeology* 22 [1969], 322). As an alternative explanation for what happened to Ephesus, he speculates that the 17 A.D. earthquake involved massive changes in the physical underpinning of the coastal region and that from then on the seaport was living on borrowed time (323).

74. For the full text and a discussion of the background, see Fik Meijer and Onno van Nijf, *Trade, Transport and Society in the Ancient World: A Sourcebook* (London: Routledge, 1992), 189.

75. Saffrey, "Piety and Prayers," 197.

76. Exact measurements are not always easy to make, which presumably explains the differing figures as to the exact length of the street. For a discussion of the street see Barra, *Ephesus*, 64; Toksoz, *Ephesus*, 46; Ulgur Onen, *Ephesus: The Way It Was–The City Viewed in Reconstructions*, trans. Nualla Yilmaz and Nanette T. Nelson (Izmir [Turkey]: Akamedia, 1985), 61–62; Jack Finegan, *The Archaeology of the New Testament: The Mediterranean World of the Early Christian Apostles* (Boulder, Colo.: Westview Press, 1981), 162–63; Cemil Toksoz, *A Travel Guide to the Historic Treasures of Turkey* (Istanbul [Turkey]: Mobil Oil Turk A.S., 1977), 176.

77. For a discussion of the street see Onen, *Ephesus: Ruins and Museum*, 41; Onen, *Ephesus: The Way It Was*, 47–48; Toksoz, *Ephesus*, 61; Toksoz, *Travel Guide*, 176. The quotation from Dr. Onen comes from *Ephesus: The Way It Was*, 48.

78. For a discussion of the street see Barra, *Ephesus*, 43; U. Onen, *Ephesus: Ruins and Museum*, 23.

79. Toksoz, *Ephesus*, 61.

80. Toksoz, *Travel Guide*, 179.

81. Ibid., 178–79; Onen, *Ephesus: Ruins and Museum*, 29.

82. A. H. M. Jones, *The Greek City: From Alexander to Justinian* (Oxford: Clarendon Press, 1940; 1971 reprint), 220. The technical Greek terms for these various parts of the gymnasium complex have been eliminated from the quotation.

83. Onen, *Ephesus: The Way It Was*, 13–14.

84. P. J. J. Botha, "God, Emperor Worship and Society: Contemporary Experiences and the Book of Revelation," *Neotestamentica: Journal of the New Testament Society of South Africa* 22 (1988):92; Fikret K. Yegul, *The Bath-Gymnasium Complex at Sardis* (Cambridge, Mass.: Harvard University Press, 1986), xiii. Barra, *Ephesus*, 70, speaks of five.

85. Toksoz, *Ephesus*, 78–79.

86. Ibid., 48; Onen, *Ephesus: The Way It Was*, 61.

87. Onen, *Ephesus: The Way It Was*, 71; Toksoz, *Ephesus*, 39; Baugh, "Paul and Ephesus," 40. The Vedius Gymnasium is also called the Stadium Gymnasium (Toksoz, *Ephesus*, 75).

88. Finegan, *Archaeology*, 163; Alan W. Johnston and Malcolm A. R. Colledge, "The Classical World," in *Atlas of Archaeology*, ed. K. Branigan, 50–91 (New York: St. Martin's Press, 1982), 75. Mac-Kendrick, *Greek Stones Speak*, 468.

89. Steven J. Friesen, *Twice Neokoros: Ephesus, Asia and the Cult of the Flavian Imperial Family* (Leiden: E. J. Brill, 1993), 121–37, discusses the Olympiad explanation as well as providing a detailed discussion of the facility.

90. For information on the city's baths see Johnston and Colledge, "The Classical World," 75; Onen, *Ephesus: The Way It Was*, 13; Toksoz, *Ephesus*; Toksoz, *Travel Guide*, 178.

91. William H. Stephens, *The New Testament World in Pictures* (Nashville, Tenn.: Broadman Press, 1987), 101.

92. Ibid.

93. Ibid.

94. Ibid.

95. Ibid.

96. Ibid.

97. Citing a figure of twenty-four thousand: Barra, *Ephesus*, 58; Finegan, *Archaeology*, 162; Harry T. Frank, *An Archaeological Companion to the Bible* (London: SCM Press, 1972; Nashville, Tenn.: Abingdon Press, 1971), 312; Onen, *Ephesus: The Way It Was*, 59; Stewart Perowne,

*The Journeys of St. Paul* (London: Hamlyn, 1973), 79; Toksoz, *Travel Guide*, 174–75; Yamauchi, *New Testament Cities*, 95; Tim Cornell and John Matthews, *Atlas of the Roman Empire* (New York: Facts on File, 1982), 152; R. K. Harrison, *Archaeology of the New Testament* (New York: Association Press, 1964), 46; Hugh J. Schonfield, *The Bible Was Right: New Light on the New Testament* (London: Frederick Muller, 1958), 188; John D. Stambaugh and David L. Balsh, *The New Testament in Its Social Environment* (Philadelphia: Westminster Press, 1986), 151.

Citing a figure of twenty-five thousand: Boyd, *Tells, Tombs, and Treasure*, 197; Charles F. Pfeiffer and Howard F. Vos, *The Wycliffe Historical Geography of Bible Lands* (Chicago: Moody Press, 1967), 362; Toksoz, *Ephesus*, 49 (in *Travel Guide* he prefers twenty-four thousand), Edwin Yamauchi, *Harper's World of the New Testament* (San Francisco: Harper & Row, 1981), 118 (in *New Testament Cities* he prefers twenty-four thousand); Otto F. A. Meinardus, *St. Paul in Ephesus–and the Cities of Galatia and Cyprus* (New Rochelle, N.Y.: Caratzas Brothers, 1979), 96; Merrill C. Tenney, *New Testament Times* (Grand Rapids, Mich.: Wm. B. Eerdmans Publishing Company, 1965; 1984 reprint), 279.

Preferring a figure midway between these: 24,500, Ludwig, *Cities*, 74; J. A. Thompson, *The Bible and Archaeology* (Grand Rapids, Mich.: Wm. B. Eerdmans Publishing Company, 1972), 402; Major-General Sir Charles Wilson, *Handbook for Travellers in Asia Minor, Transcaucasia, Persia, etc.* (London: John Murray, 1895; 1911 reprint), 99; 24,550, Wright, *Biblical Archaeology*, 254.

Estimating a markedly smaller twenty thousand: Guy Pentreath, *Hellenic Traveller: A Guide to the Ancient Sites of Greece* (New York: Crowell Company, 1964), 232.

98. For descriptions of the facility see Barra, *Ephesus*, 58; Boyd, *Tells, Tombs, and Treasure*, 197; Frank, *Archaeological Companion*, 312.

99. MacKendrick, *Greek Stones Speak*, 466; Pfeiffer and Vos, *Historical Geography*, 362.

100. Bean, *Aegean Turkey*, 173.

101. Ibid., 172–73.

102. The plural is odd since only one proconsul served at a time. It could indicate that this was a transition period, with both the departing proconsul and the new one in residence. (The suggestion that one had died and had not yet been replaced [F. F. Bruce, *The Spreading Flame: The Rise and Progress of Christianity from Its First Beginnings to the Conversion of the English* {Grand Rapids, Mich.: Wm. B. Eerdmans Publishing Company, 1958}, 133] will not work, for in that case there would be *no* pronconsuls rather than two of them.)

Another explanation may establish the approximate chronological time for the event. Soon after Nero came to power in October of 54, Asia's government lost its official proconsul. Silanus occupied the position and, like Nero, was one of the great-grandsons of Emperor Augustus. Agrippina, Nero's mother, considered him a potential claimant to the throne and arranged for his assassination. Helius and his freedman Celer were the pivotal players in the murder and exercised de facto (proconsular) power until a replacement was sent. Bruce, *Spreading Flame*, 133–34, is moderately positive toward this reconstruction. E. M. Blaiklock is far more so in "The Acts of the Apostles as a Document of First Century History," in *Apostolic History and the Gospel*, ed. W. Ward Gasque and Ralph P. Martin ([Great Britain]: Paternoster Press, 1970), 50.

103.  The latter explanation is suggested by E. A. Judge, *The Social Pattern of Christian Groups in the First Century* (London: Tyndale Press, 1960), 69.

104.  Harrison, *Archaeology*, 129; Wright, *Biblical Archaeology*, 254; George S. Duncan, *St. Paul's Ephesian Ministry: A Reconstruction* (New York: Charles Scribner's Sons, 1930), 34; W. M. Ramsay, *The Church in the Roman Empire Before A.D. 170* (London: Hodder and Stoughton, 1895), 131.

105.  For descriptions of the facility see William R. Cannon, *Journeys After Paul: An Excursion into History* (New York: Macmillan Company, 1963), 82; MacKendrick, *Greek Stones Speak* 466–67; Onen, *Ephesus: Ruins and Museum*, 68–69; Onen, *Ephesus: The Way It Was*, 72; Toksoz, *Ephesus*, 41–42; Toksoz, *Travel Guide*, 173.

106.  For a description and history of the Halls see Onen, *Ephesus: Ruins and Museum*, 60–61.

107.  Toksoz, *Travel Guide*, 180. The remainder of the information concerning this cultural reading of the evidence and the facility's physical properties come from this source. Cf. Barra, *Ephesus*, 32; Onen, *Ephesus: Ruins and Museum*, 20; Onen, *Ephesus: The Way It Was*, 17.

108.  For the political reading of the site see Barra, *Ephesus*, 32; Onen, *Ephesus: Ruins and Museum*, 20.

109.  Barra, *Ephesus*, 59; Onen, *Ephesus: The Way It Was*, 53.

110.  Barra, *Ephesus*, 31; Onen, *Ephesus: The Way It Was*, 15.

111.  For a discussion of the overlap in personnel between the leaders of the two cults see R. A. Kearsley, "The Mysteries of Artemist at Ephesus," in *New Documents Illustrating Early Christianity*, vol. 6, ed. S. R. Llewelyn ([Marrickville, Australia]: Macquarie University/ Ancient History Documentary Research Center, 1992), 196–202. For a discussion of Hestia Boulaia in general see this source and Finegan, *Archaeology*, 160; Onen, *Ephesus: Ruins and Museum*, 18; Onen, *Ephesus: The Way It Was*, 19; Toksoz, *Travel Guide*, 180.

112. David R. Johnson, "The Library of Celsus, An Ephesian Phoenix," *Wilson Library Bulletin* 54 (1980), 651.

113. Ibid., 651; Cornell and Matthews, *Atlas*, 152; Johnston and Colledge, "The Classical World," 75.

114. Johnson, "Library of Celsus," 651.

115. Yamauchi, *New Testament Cities*, 98–99. In contrast to the 9,500 estimate of Johnson and Yamauchi, Johnston and Colledge place the figure at 12,000 scrolls ("The Classical World," 75). David R. Johnson estimates that 9,500 scrolls would translate into the equivalent of 730 printed books, each the length of Homer's *Iliad* ("Library of Celsus," 652).

116. Toksoz, *Ephesus*, 62. Yamauchi, *New Testament Cities*, 100–2, presents an effective summary of the arguments challenging the brothel identification of the site. As to the probability of various local brothels, see 102 n.71.

117. On the city water system see Barra, *Ephesus*, 73; Finegan, *Archaeology*, 159.

118. For a description of these "apartment buildings" (a somewhat misleading term for the reasons presented in the text), see Barra, *Ephesus*, 46; Hanfmann, *From Croesus to Constantine*, 50; Onen, *Ephesus: Ruins and Museum*, 36; J. B. Ward-Perkins, *Roman Imperial Architecture* (London: Penguin Books, 1981), 296.

119. Onen, *Ephesus: Ruins and Museum*, 36. Cf. George M. A. Hanfmann's description of the more luxurious homes in *From Croesus to Constantine*, 50.

120. Alfons Wotschitzky, "Ephesus: Past, Present, Future of an Ancient Metropolis," *Archaeology* 14 (1961):212.

121. John T. Townsend, "Ancient Education in the Time of the Early Roman Empire," in *The Catacombs and the Colosseum: The Roman Empire as the Setting of Primitive Christianity*, ed. Stephen Benko and John J. O'Rourke (Valley Forge, Pa: Judson Press, 1971), 150.

122. For an example see Baugh, "Paul and Ephesus," 84.

123. Ibid., 85.

124. Ibid., 85.

125. This appears to be the view of Steven M. Baugh (ibid., 85).

126. Ibid., 126.

127. Ibid.

128. Onen, *Ephesus: Ruins and Museum*, 4.

129. Philostratus, *The Life of Apollonius of Tyana* IV.2, trans. F. C. Coybeare [Loeb Classical Library] (London: William Heinemann, 1912).

130. Meinardus, *Patmos*, 43.

131. Ludwig, *Cities*, 73.

132. Magical incantations were a pervasive characteristic of all cultures in the ancient world. For a discussion see Edwin M. Yamauchi, "Magic Bowls: Cyrus H. Gordon and the Ubiquity of Magic in the Pre-Modern World," *Biblical Archaeologist: Perspectives on the Ancient World from Mesopotamia to the Mediterranean* 59 (March 1996):51–55.

133. Everett Ferguson, *Backgrounds of Early Christianity*, 2d ed. (Grand Rapids, Mich.: Wm. B. Eerdmans Publishing Company, 1993), 216; Pfeiffer and Vos, *Historical Geography*, 363; Leon Morris, *The Revelation of St. John*, Tyndale New Testament Commentary series (Grand Rapids, Mich.: Wm. B. Eerdmans Publishing Company, 1969), 59. The use of this expression as a catch-all phase for magical formulas continued for centuries. Henry J. Cadbury refers to this fact (*The Book of Acts in History* [London: Adam and Charles Black, 1955], 28) and observes (28, 31) that even Shakespeare was acquainted with the usage (*Comedy of Errors*, act I, scene ii, lines 97–102).

134. Barclay, *Revelation*, 59.

135. Ibid.

136. For a study of the professional magician/doctor Thessalos, who was born in Anatolia during the second century A.D., see Jonathan Z. Smith, *Map Is Not Territory: Studies in the History of Religions* (Leiden: E. J. Brill, 1978), 172–89.

137. Dieter Betz, "Introduction to the Greek Magical Papyri," in *The Greek Magical Papyri in Translation*, ed. Dieter Betz (Chicago: University of Chicago Press, 1986), xlvii. The volume is a major compilation of actual incantations and spells from the ancient world.

138. Smith, *Map Is Not Territory*, 192.

139. For the text of a late-second-century A.D. prohibition issued by the governor of Egypt see G. H. Horsley, "A Prefect's Circular Forbidding Magic," in *New Documents Illustrating Early Christianity*, vol. 1, ed. G. H. Horsley ([Marrickville, Australia]: Macquarie University/Ancient History Documentary Research Center, 1981), 47–51.

140. Broughton, "Roman Asia," 844; for a summary of the evidence from various cities see 841–44.

141. Baugh, "Paul and Ephesus," 112.

142. Ibid., 113. Baugh provides some educated guesses as to their possible locations within the city.

143. G. H. Horsley, "The Silversmiths at Ephesus," in *New Documents Illustrating Early Christianity*, vol. 4, ed. G. H. Horsley ([Marrickville, Australia]: Macquarie University/Ancient History Documentary Research Center, 1987), 7.

144. Baugh, "Paul and Ephesus," 82–84.

145. For a discussion of the *gerusia* in various Asian cities see

William M. Ramsay, *Cities and Bishoprics of Phrygia,* vol. 1: *The Lycos Valley and South-Western Phrygia* (Oxford: Clarendon Press, 1895), 110–14; James H. Oliver, *The Sacred Gerusia* ([Baltimore, Md.]: American School of Classical Studies at Athens, 1941), 28–38. Oliver's emphasis is on the *gerusia* in Ephesus.

146. Ramsay, *Phrygia,* 113–14.
147. Ibid., 113.
148. Ibid., 21.
149. For the Greek and English text of Hadrian's order see ibid., 89–90.
150. For Greek text and English translation see ibid., 55–85.
151. Ibid., 19–20.

### 2. GLORIOUS EPHESUS: ARTEMIS AND HER COMPETITORS

1. Francois de Polignac, "Mediation, Competition, and Sovereignty: The Evolution of Rural Sanctuaries in Geometric Greece," in *Placing the Gods: Sanctuaries and Sacred Space in Ancient Greece,* ed. Susan E. Alcock and Robin Osborne (Oxford: Clarendon Press, 1994), 15.
2. Quoted by Horsley, "Inscriptions of Ephesus," 154.
3. R. Oster, "Holy Days in Honour of Artemis," in Horsley, *New Documents Illustrating Early Christianity,* 4:79.
4. Horsley, "Inscriptions of Ephesus," 155; Oster, "Holy Days," 79–80. Oster lists twenty specific cities. For an example of how the cult could be consciously spread see Irad Malkin, *Religion and Colonization in Ancient Greece* (Leiden: E. J. Brill, 1987), 69–72, which discusses the spread of the religion from Phokaia in Asia Minor to Massalia about 600 B.C. and how Massalia, in turn, consciously took the Ephesian Artemis to the colonies it itself later formed.
5. Richard E. Oster, "Numismatic Windows in the World of Early Christianity: A Methodological Inquiry," *Journal of Biblical Literature* 101 (1982):215.
6. Ibid., 215–16. Although he appeals to other forms of evidence, Oster omits mention of the silversmiths' riot against Paul, which would seemingly be a manifestation (self-serving, admittedly) of that community attitude.
7. Anton Bammer, "Recent Excavations at the Altar of Artemis in Ephesus," *Archaeology* 27 (1974), 202.
8. Meinardus, *Patmos,* 33.
9. Ibid.
10. Quoted by Keskin, *Ephesus,* 5 (unnumbered page).

11. Catherine B. Avery, *The New Century Classical Handbook* (New York: Appleton-Century, Crofts, 1962), 441.

12. *The History of Herodotus*, 4 vols., trans. George Rawlinson (London: John Murray, 1858–60), 2.148.

13. Pausanias, *Description of Greece*, 3 vols., trans. Thomas Taylor (London: Richard Priestlly, High Holborn, 1824), 7.5.10. Also see the translation of Peter Levi, issued under the title of *Pausanias' Guide to Greece* ([Great Britain]: Penguin Books, 1979).

14. Antipater, from *Anth. Pal.*, trans. Tony Harrison, as quoted by Richard Stoneman, *Land of Lost Gods: The Search for Classical Greece* (Norman: University of Oklahoma Press, 1987), 225.

15. Hans Lietzman, *A History of the Early Church*, vol. 1: *The Beginnings of the Christian Church*, trans. Bertram L. Woof, 2d ed. (1949). Reprinted in one volume (London: Lutterworth Press, 1961), 159.

16. For inscriptional evidence covering Artemis and other cults, in both Ephesus and other Asian communities, see Sjef van Tilborg, *Ephesus*, 136–41, and for Artemis in Ephesus in particular, 94–95. On archaeological inscriptions referring to sacrifices in the temple of Artemis, see 71–73.

17. Barra, *Ephesus*, 22.

18. The 180 feet figure is given by Frank, *Bible Archaeology and Faith* (Nashville, Tenn.: Abingdon Press, 1971), 327; Boyd, *Tells, Tombs, and Treasure*, 97; Finegan, *Archaeology*, 156; Frank, *Archaeological Companion*, 311; Pfeiffer and Vos, *Historical Geography*, 361; Vos, *Archaeology*, 321. R. A. Tomlinson gives a figure of 180.5 feet (*Greek Sanctuaries* [New York: St. Martin's Press, 1976], 129).

Others provide a narrower width:

In excess of 160 feet—Everett F. Harrison, *The Apostolic Church* (Grand Rapids, Mich.: Wm. B. Eerdmans Publishing Company, 1985), 208; Wright, *Biblical Archaeology*, 253.

163 feet 9-1/2 inches—Wood, *Ancient Ephesus*, 73.

164 feet—Avery, *Classical Handbook*, 441; Thompson, *Archaeology*, 402.

A wider dimension is given by others:

220 feet—John A. Calkin, *Historical Geography of Bible Lands* (Philadelphia: Westminster Press, 1904), 106; Cannon, *Journeys After Paul*, 80.

225 feet—Meinardus, *Ephesus*, 53.

The 360-feet length figure is given by Frank, *Bible Archaeology*, 327; idem, *Archaeological Companion*, 311.

Others estimate the length as shorter:

340 feet—Everett F. Harrison, *Apostolic Church*, 208; Wright, *Biblical Archaeology*, 253.

342 feet—Avery, *Classical Handbook*, 441. Wood, *Ancient Ephesus*, 73.

343 feet—Thompson, *Archaeology*, 402.

Or longer:

375 feet—Finegan, *Archaeology*, 156.

377 feet—Boyd, *Tells, Tombs, and Treasure*, 97; Pfeiffer and Vos, *Historical Geography*, 361; Vos, *Archaeology*, 321.

377.5 feet—Tomlinson, *Greek Sanctuaries*, 29.

425 feet—Calkin, *Historical Geography*, 106; Meinardus, *Ephesus*, 53.

475 feet—Cannon, *Journeys After Paul*, 80.

Some of these figures are probably typographical errors that escaped the original writers' notice during the editing process; in other cases the writer rounds off (342 to 340 feet, for example). Some writer(s) may also, in part, be confusing temple size with the size of the platform beneath the temple, the latter being understandably larger.

19. The 239–feet figure is given by Frank, *Bible Archaeology*, 327; idem, *Archaeological Companion*, 311. J. T. Wood, who uncovered the temple in the nineteenth century, was even more precise: 239 feet 4-1/2 inches ("on the lowest step") (*Ancient Ephesus*, 70). The 418–feet figure is given by Frank, *Bible Archaeology*, 327; idem, *Archaeological Companion*, 311. J. T. Wood estimated the length as 418 feet 1-1/2 inches but noted that an exact figure was impossible (*Ancient Ephesus*, 70).

20. Cole, "Corinth and Ephesus," 27.

21. Stewart Perowne, *Archaeology of Greece and the Aegean* (New York: A. Studio Book/Viking Press, 1974), 121.

22. Akurgal, *Ancient Civilizations*. 152.

23. Ten steps are mentioned by Harry T. Frank (*Archaeological Companion*, 311) and R. A. Tomlinson (*Greek Sanctuaries*, 131); Ekrem Akurgal refers to thirteen (*Ancient Civilizations*, 152).

24. On the columns:

100 columns: Everett F. Harrison, *Apostolic Church*, 208; R. K. Harrison, *Archaeology*, 46; Wright, *Biblical Archaeology*, 253.

117 columns: Frank, *Bible Archaeology*, 327.

127 columns: Meinardus, *Ephesus*, 53.

25. Avery, *Classical Handbook*, 441; Frank, *Bible Archaeology*, 327.

26. On the height of the columns:

55 feet: Avery, *Classical Handbook*, 441; R. K. Harrison, *Archaeology*, 46; Wright, *Biblical Archaeology*, 253.

60 feet: Everett F. Harrison, *Apostolic Church*, 208.

27. Avery, *Classical Handbook*; Meinardus, *Ephesus*, 53; Pfeiffer and Vos, *Historical Geography*, 361.

28. Meinardus, *Ephesus*, 53; Tomlinson, *Greek Sanctuaries*, 131–32.

29. Thompson, *Archaeology*, 402; Vos, *Archaeology*, 321.

30. On the altar, see Thompson, *Archaeology*, 402; Vos, *Archaeology*, 321. The exact relationship of the statue to the altar is unknown, but this represents a likely reconstruction.

31. This is an estimate (Helen H. Miller, *Bridge to Asia: The Greeks in the Eastern Mediterranean* [New York: Charles Scribner's Sons, 1967], 129) and is taken by Guy Pentreath as a minimum one (*Hellenic Traveller*, 230).

32. In the sixth century B.C. the shepherd Pixodarus became a hero when he accidentally discovered an abundant source of marble near the city, thereby allowing the structure to be built far cheaper and quicker than if the product were purchased elsewhere. Not only did he receive repeated honors from the city during his lifetime, but as late as the fourth century A.D. he remained an object of cult worship at the quarry itself (Alison Burford, *Craftsmen in Greek and Roman Society* [Ithaca, N.Y.: Cornell University Press, 1972], 169; cf. 253 where, from the nature of where the cult remains have been found, she properly deduces that it was "presumably" a "quarrymen's cult" for "who else would be in the vicinity of a quarry long enough to take trouble with such a thing?").

33. Thompson, *Archaeology*, 402.

34. Bluma L. Trell, *The Temple of Artemis at Ephesus*, (New York: American Numismatic Society, 1945) discusses the known, probable, and speculative aspects of the temple and provides a reconstruction of its appearance based upon surviving coins. She also prints a number of coins illustrating various other ancient religious-cultic sites.

35. Barra, *Ephesus*, 22.

36. Seltman, *Riot in Ephesus*, 74.

37. Sharon Hodgin Gritz, *Paul, Women Teachers, and the Mother Goddess at Ephesus: A Study of 1 Timothy 2:9–15 in Light of the Religious and Cultural Milieu of the First Century* (Lanham, N.Y.: University Press of America, 1991), 38.

38. Thompson, *Archaeology*, 402; Vos, *Archaeology*, 321. J. T. Wood, who uncovered the temple site, accepted this approach as well (*Ancient Ephesus*, 77).

39. Seltman, *Riot in Ephesus*, 76, cf. 75–77. Seltman believes it was a kind of "hat" above the idol, but if the ancient claim of it being a heavenly image has a core of truth one would expect it to be an image of either the full person or at least a passable image of a significant part,

such as the head. Seltman believes the image was wooden and that all except the head, hands, and feet was covered with precious metal, "probably gold." The "goddess grew year by year blacker in the face from the constant use of rich olive-oil rubbed into the antique wood." He regards this as an aesthetic debasing of the original appearance, just as "brilliant old 'icons' and delicate medieval carved statues of the Virgin Mary and of Saints [have been] rendered aesthetically repellent by gold and silver plating sometimes encrusted with stones" (76).

40. Allen H. Jones, *Essenes: The Elect of Israel* (Lanham, Md.: University Press of America, 1985), 91; Boyd, *Tells, Tombs, and Treasure*, 196; Cornell and Matthews, *Atlas*, 153; Schonfield, *The Bible Was Right*, 166; Stephens, *Pictures*, 280; Tenney, *New Testament Times*, 280; Toksoz, *Ephesus*, 20. For large-size reproductions of the competing images of Artemis in the West and in Asia see Stephens, *Pictures*, 238–39, and (more numerous, but in smaller size), Lynn R. LiDonnici, "The Images of Artemis Ephesia and Greco-Roman Worship: A Reconsideration," *Harvard Theological Review* 85 (October 1992): 412–15.

41. Baugh, "A Foreign World," 30.

42. Ibid., 30–31.

43. For both arguments see ibid., 31.

44. Miller, *Bridge to Asia*, 129; Perowne, *Archaeology*, 116. George E. Bean calls this "the most recent opinion" and appears to embrace it (*Aegean Turkey*, 167). Also see the references in the following notes as to *specific* types of eggs.

45. "A familiar symbol of fertility" (Bean, *Aegean Turkey*, 167); "eggs, her symbol" (Finegan, *Archaeology*, 160).

46. John Ferguson refers to the belief of "some scholars" who adopt this interpretation, though he himself concedes that they "appear to be breasts" ("Divinities," in *Civilization of the Ancient Mediterranean*, vol. 2, ed. Michael Grant and Rachel Kitzinger [New York: Charles Scribner's Sons, 1988], 850).

47. Athens versus Ephesus imagery of a goddess: George W. Elderkin, "The Bee of Artemis," *American Journal of Philology* 60 (1939), 203. Ephesian Artemis as a bee: Jones, *Essenes*, 92.

48. Stated as fact: Elderkin, "Bee of Artemis," 203. Stated as probability: Jones, *Essenes*, 92. The probability is reinforced by the fact that Cybele, in addition to maintaining existence as a separate deity, was also merged into the popular conception of Artemis. Into the Christian era, the Phrygian Great-Mother, as she was known, was called the Queen-Bee and her chief priestesses were called "bees" (Jones, *Essenes*, 92).

49. Barra notes that "Ephesus was the only ancient city" utilizing

the bee as its symbol (*Ephesus*, 11). From prior to the sixth century to at the least third century B.C., the bee imagery appeared regularly on many of her coins (Jones, *Essenes*, 91–92). The city's name is derived from *aphasas*, a word meaning "home of bees" (Barra, *Ephesus*, 12).

50. "The egg-like objects just above her waist...are now correctly interpreted as ostrich eggs decorating her garment. Ostrich eggs, as a symbol of fertility may still be found today in nearly every Greek village church" (Wotschitzky, "Ephesus," 210).

51. Seltman, *Riot in Ephesus*, 77. Dan P. Cole refers to the interpretation but without adopting it ("Corinth and Ephesus," 28).

52. David W. J. Gill presents both the breast and the testicle interpretations as equally possible ("Acts and Roman Religion: A. Religion in a Local Setting," in *The Book of Acts in Its First Century Setting*, vol. 2: *The Book of Acts in Its Graeco-Roman Setting*, ed. David W. J. Gill and Conrad Gempf [Grand Rapids, Mich.: Wm. B. Eerdmans Publishing Company, 1994], 88),

53. Stambaugh and Balsh, *Social Environment*, 150, sum up the theory, appear receptive to it, but do not explicitly embrace it.

54. Hill, "Ancient Art and Artemis," 94.

55. Cf. ibid., 92.

56. Lynn R. LiDonnici implies that the non-breast interpretations of Artemis are usually the result of modern male bias ("The Images of Artemis Ephesia," 392–93). We will not speculate about alleged hidden agenda, since the accusation itself may just as well reflect those of the accuser rather than those actually held by the accused.

57. W. M. Ramsay, *Pauline and Other Studies in Early Christian History* (London: Hodder and Stoughton, 1916), 133–34.

58. Lewis R. Farnell, *The Cults of the Greek States*, vol. 2 (1895). Reprinted (Chicago: Aegean Press, 1971), 448.

59. Jones, *Essenes*, 95–96.

60. Esther Onstad, *Courage for Today–Hope for Tomorrow: A Study of the Revelation* (Minneapolis: Augsburg Publishing House, 1973, 1974), 16; Baugh, "Paul and Ephesus," 36.

61. Gritz, *Mother Goddess at Ephesus*, 40, makes the suggestion that it was an honorary title, while noting the minority of scholars who doubt that ritual prostitution continued to be practiced in the first century. If it *had* passed out of fashion, why would the title virgin necessarily be a courtesy title rather than a literal description? A courtesy-title scenario would be an appealing one if we could document that the priestesses underwent an annual rite parallel to Hera's, which "restored" their virginity. If one could, the description would make a

great deal of sense from the standpoint of the logic of the cult itself rather than from the standpoint of an outsider.

Of course if one viewed the priestess as a *surrogate for the goddess* one could also explain the usage: although the body being enjoyed would be that of a human female the "real" sexual partner was the goddess. The physical woman, therefore, was really not central to the scene at all and could retain the title virgin since her own sexual desires and passions were not involved. Here we seem to be verging on a kind of "pagan gnosticism" in which the body may be involved but since it is done in service for the goddess evil intent is missing and she remains pure and holy. The least complicated explanation—from the standpoint of what sticks closest to the known evidence and involves the least conjecture—is that there was more than one type of priestess in the cult, and each type served one aspect of the goddess's nature—the *parthenoi* for Artemis's virginity and those engaged in cultic prostitution in honor of her sexual nature, which bears fruit in childbearing.

62. Baugh, "Paul and Ephesus," 36.

63. Ibid., 36, citing Strabo 14.23; Gritz, *Mother Goddess at Ephesus*, 40–41.

64. Jones, *Essenes*, 94, speaks confidently of it being a group; George E. Bean is less certain whether the title went with a group or was restricted to one person (*Aegean Turkey*, 166).

65. Bean, *Aegean Turkey*, 166–67.

66. This has led some to suggest that Artemis herself had a lover who endured such a tragedy (Allen H. Jones, *Essenes*, 94, mentions the view but takes no position). The blending of the two goddesses seems to offer a better explanation.

67. John Ferguson, *The Religions of the Roman Empire*, (Ithaca, N.Y.: Cornell University Press, 1970), 27, favors the first interpretation and refers to problems in the logic of the second.

68. Strabo, *Geography* 14.1.23, as quoted by Baugh, "Foreign World," 28 n.59. In the text Baugh explicitly states that the group no longer existed (28).

69. Bean, *Aegean Turkey*, 167.

70. Jones, *Essenes*, 97. Jones deduces from the existence of this priesthood a movement toward greater sexual restraint after the days of excess, when the indulgences associated with the Earth-Mother concept tended to overwhelm the more temperate Greek-style traditional Artemis. "At any rate," he suggests, "it is clear that chastity and celibacy were of prime importance in the worship of the Ephesian Artemis during the Roman period" (97).

71. Bean, *Aegean Turkey*, 167–168. Allen H. Jones is more sceptical of pinning down specific functions for the group (*Essenes*, 97).

72. Bean, *Aegean Turkey*, 168.

73. Gritz, *Mother Goddess at Ephesus*, 40.

74. Ibid., 40.

75. Toksoz, *Ephesus*, 21.

76. Ramsay MacMullen, *Peasants in the Roman Empire* (New Haven, Conn.: Yale University Press, 1981), 21.

77. Ibid.

78. Ibid.

79. Ibid., 163.

80. Oster, "Ephesus as a Religious Center, 1720–21, includes a list of all twenty-three. Lily R. Taylor, "Artemis of Ephesus," in *The Beginnings of Christianity, Part I: The Acts of the Apostles* (volume five of the series), ed. Kirsopp Lake and Henry J. Cadbury (London: Macmillan and Company, 1933), 253–54.

81. Gritz, *Mother Goddess at Ephesus*, 40.

82. Toksoz, *Ephesus*, 21.

83. Magie, *Asia Minor*, 545, 1404.

84. Ibid., 1404.

85. Ibid.

86. For a discussion of the Ephesian scandal see Ibid., 544–546. The quotation from the proconsul comes from this source as well.

87. Ramsay MacMullen, *Paganism in the Roman Empire* (New Haven, Conn.: Yale University Press, 1981), 107.

88. For citations see Baugh, "Paul and Ephesus," 39. For ancient literary and inscriptional references to the Artemision functioning as a bank see van Tilborg, *Ephesus*, 73–74.

89. Dio Chrysostom, 31.54–55, as quoted by Wesley E. Thompson, "Insurance and Banking," in Grant and Kitzinger, *Civilization of the Ancient Mediterranean*, 2:832–33.

90. Richard Oster, "The Ephesian Artemis, 33, also notes that Chrysostom exaggerates the inviolability of the temple but is correct that it was *usually* as safe as humanly possible.

91. Floyd Filson, "Ephesus and the New Testament," *Biblical Archaeologist* 8 (1945): 73–80.

92. Oster, "Ephesian Artemis," 33–34.

93. Ibid., 33.

94. Oster, "Ephesus as a Religious Center," 1719.

95. Baugh, "Paul and Ephesus," 40.

96. Ibid.; Baugh, "A Foreign World," 22.

97. Oster, "Ephesian Artemis," 34, notes that ancient sources explicitly refer to this revenue source. He suggests the likelihood that the "sacred island" the temple owned provided a regular income from its resident deer herd (34).

98. Baugh, "Paul and Ephesus," 42.

99. Ibid., 41.

100. Ibid., 46. Explaining the labor utilization of the abundance of slaves in Asia in a nonagricultural context is a real problem: Could that many *really* have been used? And if not, which is wrong: the estimate of a high proportion of slaves in the province or the denial of major use in Asian agriculture? Asia was noted for its large supply of slaves to the remainder of the empire (46). Moreover Ephesus was the main wholesale market for obtaining slaves in the first century (45–46). Could it be that the province was more an exporter of slaves than an actual user of them? Yet if *that* were the case, how could there have been a sufficient number of local slaves to support continued massive sales to other regions?

101. F. Sokolowski, "A New Testimony to the Cult of Artemis of Ephesus," *Harvard Theological Review* 58 (1965):427–31.

102. Implied by ibid, 429, on the basis of the practice of other goddess cults. For examples of draping clothes over images of Artemis at temples located in Greece, see Mary B. B. Hollinshead, "Legend, Cult, and Architecture at Three Sanctuaries of Artemis" (Ph.D. diss., Bryn Mawr College, 1979), 46, 66–67.

103. Sokolowski, "New Testimony," 428.

104. Robert E. A. Palmer, *Roman Religion and Roman Empire: Five Essays* (Philadelphia: University of Pennsylvania Press, 1974), 72.

105. Bean, *Aegean Turkey*, 164.

106. Achilles Tatius, *Achilles Tatius [Clitophon and Leucippe]* [Loeb Classical Library], trans. S. Gaselee (London: William Heinemann, 1917), VIII.8. The hero refers to this in rebuking the effort of certain temple authorities to bestow temple protection to those who did not rightly deserve it. To what extent this may have been a problem in the first century is unknown.

107. Apollonius of Tyana, as quoted by Schonfield, *The Bible Was Right*, 186.

108. MacMullen, *Paganism*, 37; Terence Kelshaw, *Send This Message to My Church: Christ's Words to the Seven Churches of Revelation* (Nashville, Tenn.: Thomas Nelson Publishers, 1984), 50.

109. Cf. the remark of Ramsay MacMullen, "In Syria, even a little rural shrine might have five separate rooms for eating; even a remote center might boast a banquet hall with a portico around it" (*Paganism*,

37). From the size and number at various locations, it is clear that they were intended, unlike modern church social gatherings, for smaller groups of members and their friends, not the entire membership.

110. Van Tilborg, *Ephesus*, 139.

111. Ibid., 162; cf. 37.

112. Oster, "Ephesus as a Religious Center," 1720.

113. Filson, "Ephesus and the New Testament," 76.

114. Saffrey, "Piety and Prayers," 196–97.

115. Keskin, *Ephesus*, 2.

116. Achilles Tatius, *Clitophon and Leucippe*, VI.3.

117. Irene R. Arnold, "Festivals of Ephesus." *American Journal of Archaeology* 76 (1972):18.

118. Toksoz, *Ephesus*, 53; cf. Arnold, "Festivals of Ephesus," 18.

119. Saffrey, "Piety and Prayers," 197.

120. Toksoz, *Ephesus*, 21.

121. Arnold, "Festivals of Ephesus," 18.

122. Saffrey, "Piety and Prayers," 197.

123. Toksoz, *Travel Guide*, 175

124. Toksoz, *Ephesus*, 21.

125. Arnold, "Festivals of Ephesus," 18.

126. Oster, "Holy Days," 77.

127. Oster, "Ephesus as a Religious Center," 1709–10.

128. Strabo, 14.1.20, as quoted by Kearsley, "The Mysteries of Artemis," 197.

129. Quoted by ibid., 201.

130. Kearsley speculates that the two priestesses were sisters (ibid.).

131. Quoted by ibid.

132. Quoted by ibid., emphasis added.

133. Baugh, "Paul and Ephesus," 37. For a survey of the evidence see Oster, "Ephesus as a Religious Center," 1667–68.

134. Oster, "Ephesian Artemis," 26. Richard E. Oster, "Ephesus as a Religious Center," 1671, surveys the evidence.

135. Baugh, "Paul and Ephesus," 37; Oster, "Ephesian Artemis," 25. For a survey of the evidence see Richard E. Oster, "Ephesus as a Religious Center," 1671–73.

136. Oster, "Ephesus as a Religious Center," 1671.

137. Ibid., 1672.

138. Baugh, "Paul and Ephesus," 38.

139. Ibid.

140. Avery, *Classical Handbook*, 440.

141. Lietzman, *Early Church*, 158. In addition to this Ephesian

sanctuary, marble reliefs of the deity have been uncovered in other Asian sites, as well as a number of inscriptions mentioning her. For the locations where they were found and original language citations of the inscriptions see M. J. Vermaseren, *Corpus Cultus Cybelae Attidisque (CCCA) I. Asia Minor* (Leiden: E. J. Brill, 1987), 184–203 (numbered as entries 611–85). A building block from Sardis shows Cybele grasping a lion while Artemis holds a deer, which Edwin M. Yamauchi introduces as evidence of their continued existence as separate deities (*New Testament Cities*, 68–69).

142. Richard E. Oster surveys the evidence in "Ephesus as a Religious Center," 1669–70. Cf. Oster, "Ephesian Artemis," 25.

143. Baugh, "Paul and Ephesus," 38.

144. Richard E. Oster summarizes the evidence in "Ephesus as a Religious Center," 1668–69.

145. For a survey of the evidence concerning Dionysus worship at Ephesus see Ibid., 1673–76.

146. Lietzman, *Early Church*, 160.

147. Baugh, "Paul and Ephesus," 37.

148. A "strong presence," according to van Tilborg, *Ephesus*, 97.

149. For text citations and a different line of argumentation concerning the connection that could easily have been made see Ibid., 96–98.

150. Barra, *Ephesus*, 4–5, goes so far as to suggest that the owner may have been an antiquities dealer, but since antique *owners* are obviously more numerous than dealers, he is far more likely to have been a collector. This is certainly not incompatible with his having a religious or national-origin interest in the Egyptian deities as well.

151. Baugh, "Paul and Ephesus," 38.

152. Bean, *Aegean Turkey*, 176.

153. Musa Barra, *Ephesus*, 61; Onen, *Ephesus: The Way It Was*, 57. Richard E. Oster is highly skeptical whether the Serapis and Isis worship sites we will examine can be definitively established as such, though he carefully documents the presence of the cults in the city ("Ephesus as a Religious Center," 1677–81). At the Serapis site in particular a major support of that interpretation comes from a statue to the emperor Caracalla on which are the words, "For those who sacrifice to Sarapis in the presence of the Nile, my god." Some question whether the Greek text has been accurately read. Also, it has been challenged because the statue base, on which the text is found, may well have been originally erected in a different location. For a negative appraisal see Robert A. Wild, "The Known Isis-Sarapis Sanctuaries from the Roman Period," *Aufstieg und Niedergang der Romischen Welt* (Berlin: Walter de

Gruyter, 1984), II, 17.4, 1829–31. Wild's arguments should be contrasted with his argumentation concerning the possible Isis sanctuary at the State Agora. There he is tentatively willing to accept the identification even though the actual evidence seems more tenuous.

154. Bean, *Aegean Turkey*, 176.

155. Toksoz, *Ephesus*, 59.

156. Toksoz, *Travel Guide*, 176.

157. Ibid.

158. Robert A. Wild, "Isis-Sarapis Sanctuaries," 1775–76, discusses the pros and cons and is willing to accept the identification.

159. R. E. Sitt, "The Importance of Isis for the Fathers," *Studia Patristica* 8, part 2 (Berlin: Akademie-Verlag, 1966), 142.

160. Caird, *Revelation*, 29, and Donald L. Jones, "Christianity and the Roman Imperial Cult," *Aufstieg und Niedergang der Romischen Welt* (Berlin: Walter de Gruyter, 1980), II, 23.2, 1034. Cf. P. J. J. Botha, "God, Emperor Worship and Society: Contemporary Experiences and the Book of Revelation," *Neotestamentica: Journal of the New Testament Society of South Africa* 22 (1988):95; Oster, "Holy Days," 76.

161. Charles C. Whiting, *The Revelation of John* (Boston: Gorham Press, 1918), 69.

162. W. C. Friend, *Martyrdom and Persecution in the Early Church: A Study of a Conflict from the Maccabees to Donatus* (Oxford: Basil Blackwell, 1965), 194.

163. Oster, "Holy Days," 76.

164. R. A. Kearsley, "Ephesus: *Neokoros* of Artemis," in Llewelyn, *New Documents Illustrating Early Christianity*, 6:203–4.

165. Ibid., 204.

166. On the temple of the Sebastoi for emperor worship, see Steven Friesen, "Ephesus: Key to a Vision in Revelation." *Biblical Archaeology Review* 19 (May-June 1993):24–37.

167. Ibid., 205.

168. Thompson, *Archaeology*, 404. As to individuals in particular, see Kearsley, "Ephesus: *Neokoros* of Artemis," 206.

169. Josephus, *Wars*, V, ix.4, as quoted by Thompson.

170. Quoted by Kearsley, "Ephesus: *Neokoros* of Artemis," 203.

171. Whiting, *Revelation*, 69.

172. The view of David Magie, *Asia Minor*, 572; for a discussion of the pros and cons of who built the temple see the footnote section of Magie's work, 1432–34.

173. Onen, *Ephesus: Ruins and Museum*, 22.

174. Kenneth Scott, *The Imperial Cult Under the Flavians*

(Stuttgart [Germany]: W. Kohlhammer, 1936; reprinted, New York: Arno Press, 1975), 97.

175. Friesen, *Twice Neokoros*, 62.

176. Ibid., 62; cf. 60–61, where Friesen identifies the fragments as those of Titus.

### 3. MONOTHEISM IN EPHESUS

1. *Antiquities* 16.262–64. On the history of the Jewish presence in Ephesus see Irina Levinskaya, *The Book of Acts in Its First Century Setting*, vol. 5: *The Book of Acts in Its Diaspora Setting* (Grand Rapids, Mich.: Wm. B. Eerdmans Publishing Company, 1996), 143–48.

2. *Antiquities* 16.167, 172–73.

3. Irenaeus, Haer. 3.23, cited by A. Thomas Kraabel, "Judaism in Western Asia Minor Under the Roman Empire, with a Preliminary Study of the Jewish Community of Sardis, Lydia" (Ph.D. diss., Harvard University, 1968), 52, who is inclined to give extra credibility to the assertion on the grounds that Irenaeus was himself a resident of Asia Minor, apparently from Smyrna.

4. Ibid., 53.

5. Ibid.; Friend, *Martyrdom and Persecution*, 191; Bruce, *Spreading Flame*, 277.

6. Justin's account of the discussion is contained in his "Dialogue with Trypho," *The Ante-Nicene Fathers*; vol. 1: *Apostolic Fathers: Justin Martyr, Irenaeus*, ed. Alexander Roberts and James Donaldson (New York: Charles Scribner's Sons, 1899).

7. Eusebius, *Ecclesiastical History of Eusebius Pamphilus* (1833; reprint, London: G. Bell and Sons, Ltd., 1917), IV.18.

8. Bruce, *Spreading Flame*, 278.

9. Justin, "Dialogue with Trypho," chap. 92.

10. G. H. R. Horsley, "Jews at Ephesos," in Horsley, *New Documents Illustrating Early Christianity*, 4:231.

11. The ruins have not been uncovered but it is speculated by Otto A. Meinardus that it was close to the harbor in order to have easy access to the water used in various rituals (*Patmos*, 36–37).

12. For a discussion of the inconclusive nature of the data see Horsley, "Jews at Ephesos," 231–32.

13. Otto A. Meinardus, "The Christian Remains of the Seven Churches of Asia," in *Biblical Archaeologist Reader, IV*, ed. Edward F. Campbell Jr. and David Noel Freedman, 345–58 (Sheffield [England]: Almond Press, 1983), 348; Meinardus, *Patmos*, 37; Stambaugh and Balsh, *Social Environment*, 151.

14. Meinardus, "Christian Remains," 348. Cf. Meinardus, *Patmos*, 37.

15. Bruce, *Spreading Flame*, 130, speaks in terms of all being created in this period.

16. Ibid.

17. Everett F. Harrison, *The Apostolic Church*, 211.

18. Bruce, *Spreading Flame*, 132.

19. One student of the history of the city suggests that the animal imagery grows out of the fact that "the howling mob chanting" against him resembled "a pack of wolves" (Blaiklock, *Cities*, 65).

20. Arthur C. McGiffert, *A History of Christianity in the Apostolic Age* (Edinburgh: T. & T. Clark, 1897), 280. Cf. the discussion of these and other allegedly related texts in Robert E. Osborne, "Paul and the Wild Beasts," *Journal of Biblical Literature* 85 (1966):225–30.

21. Abraham H. Malherle, "The Beasts at Ephesus," *Journal of Biblical Literature* 87 (1968):71–72.

22. Adolph Schlatter, *The Church in the New Testament Period*, trans. Paul P. Levertoff (London: S.P.C.K., 1961), 164, introduces this as an argument. Arthur C. McGiffert, an advocate of a "literal" reading of the text, concedes that the omission "is surprising." He suggests that since Paul had mentioned it once there was no need to do so again. Furthermore, the near tragedy "was well known to his readers" and would come to their mind without any explicit inclusion of it (*Apostolic Age*, 281).

23. Malcolm O. Tolbert argues that there is no way to pinpoint the time of the rejection—past or present (*Layman's Bible Book Commentary*, vol. 22: *Colossians, Philippians, 1 and 2 Thessalonians, 1 and 2 Timothy, Titus, Philemon* (Nashville, Tenn.: Broadman Press, 1980), 133. But if it was in the past it was surely in the *near* past, for Paul's pain still cries out.

24. H. H. Harvey sees pro-Pauline witnesses as becoming "appalled by the danger in which they stood" ("First and Second Timothy," in *An American Commentary on the New Testament: Timothy to Peter* (Philadelphia: American Baptist Publication Society, 1890), 91. Thomas C. Oden carries this a step further and sees them as having returned to Asia from Rome and rebellious over reports that they had not been steadfast in Paul's behalf (*First and Second Timothy and Titus*, Interpretation commentary series [Louisville: John Knox Press, 1989], 160). Cf. Alfred Plummer's analysis of difficulties in this scenario (*The Pastoral Epistles* [New York: A. C. Armstrong & Son, 1893], 322–23). A. E. Hillard sees this as occurring during one of Paul's preaching tours rather than during an imprisonment, but with the same result of their returning to Asia (*The Pastoral Epistles of St. Paul* [London: Rivingtons, 1919], 86.

25. H. Armin Moellering summarizes the positive and negative arguments on the matter in "1 and 2 Timothy," in *Concordia Commentary: 1 Timothy-Philemon* (Saint Louis, Mo: Concordia Publishing House, 1970), 175–76.

26. "1 Timothy; 2 Timothy," in *The Expostior's Bible Commentary*, vol. 11: *Ephesians-Philemon* (Grand Rapids, Mich.: Zondervan Publishing House, 1978), 398; J. N. D. Kelly, *A Commentary on the Pastoral Epistles*, Harper's New Testament Commentary series (New York: Harper & Row, 1963), 217–18.

27. Roy S. Nicholson, "The Pastoral Epistles," in *The Wesleyan Bible Commentaries*, vol. 5: *Romans-Philemon*, ed. Charles W. Carter, et al. (Grand Rapids, Mich.: Wm. B. Eerdmans Publishing Company, 1965), 634. Ronald A. Ward sees this as a possibility, though he notes that the hostile action by Alexander might well have been the *cause* of the apostolic rejection (*Commentary on 1 and 2 Timothy and Titus* [Waco, Tex.: Word Books, 1974], 217–18.

28. Oden, *First and Second Timothy and Titus*, 179–80.

29. Ibid.; Harvey, "First and Second Timothy," 119.

30. Although they may hedge their answers, these commentators identify the two references as being to the same individual: Harvey, "First and Second Timothy," 119; Kelly, *Pastoral Epistles*, 58; Moellering, "1 and 2 Timothy," 173–74; Gordon D. Fee, *1 and 2 Timothy, Titus*, Good News Commentary series (San Francisco: Harper & Row, 1984), 245; Arland J. Hultgren, "1 and 2 Timothy," in Arland J. Gultgren and Roger Aus, *I-II Timothy, Titus, II Thessalonians*, Augusburg Commentary on the New Testament series (Minneapolis: Augsburg Publishing House, 1984), 62, cf. 143; E. F. Scott, *The Pastoral Epistles*, Moffatt New Testament Commentary series (London: Hodder and Stoughton, 1936; 1948 reprint), 138.

With various degrees of cautionary rhetoric other commentators deny the identification. The theory is labeled "rash" (E. K. Simpson, *The Pastoral Epistles* [London: Tyndale Press, 1954], 38) and "unlikely" (A. T. Hanson, *The Pastoral Epistles*, New Century Bible Commentary series [Grand Rapids, Mich.: Wm. B. Eerdmans Publishing Company, 1982], 66, 160). Donald Guthrie (*The Pastoral Epistles: An Introduction and Commentary*, Tyndale commentary series [Grand Rapids, Mich.: Wm. B. Eerdmans Publishing Company, 1957], 68) argues there is "insufficient" data, and Patrick Fairbairn ranks the identification as only a fifty-fifty proposition (*The Pastoral Epistles* [Edinburgh: T. & T. Clark, 1874], 397). Homer A. Kent argues that the very need of the additional phase "the coppersmith" indicates a distinction being made from the other Alexander (*The Pastoral Epistles: Studies in I and II Timothy and Titus* [Chicago: Moody Press, 1958], 98), as does A. E. Hillard (*Pastoral Epistles*, 16).

31. Some take it in both senses: Homer Hailey, *Revelation: An Introduction and Commentary* (Grand Rapids, Mich.: Baker Book House, 1979), 122; Alan F. Johnson, *Revelation* (Grand Rapids, Mich.: Zondervan Publishing House, 1983), 42; Hugh Martin, *The Seven Letters* (Philadelphia: Westminster Press, 1956), 49; Robert H. Mounce, *What Are We Waiting For? A Commentary on Revelation* (Grand Rapids, Mich.: Wm. B. Eerdmans Publishing Company, 1992), 7; Ray F. Robbins, *The Revelation of Jesus Christ* (Nashville, Tenn.: Press, 1975), 54.

32. Earl F. Palmer, *1, 2 and 3 John, Revelation,* in The Communicator's Commentary series (Waco, Tex.: Word Books, 1982), 128; Richard C. Trench, *Commentary on the Epistles to the Seven Churches in Asia* (New York: Charles Scribner & Co., 1872), 107; W. J. Limmer Sheppard, *The Revelation of St. John the Divine: I-XI* (London: Religious Tract Society, 1923), 27.

33. W. Boyd Carpenter implicitly deals with this objection when he writes that in spite of these accomplishments "the great Searcher of hearts detects the almost imperceptible symptoms of an incipient decay" (*The Revelation of St. John the Divine,* Ellicott Bible Commentary series [London: Cassell and Company, 1877; 1903 printing], 41). If the drift was virtually "imperceptible," wasn't it rather hasty to demand repentance—or else—in such severe terms? How does one recognize— much less repent of—something so "imperceptible" that we can barely recognize it? John, in the apostolic tradition, comes down heavy and hard on visible misconduct; such severe language against a fault that really wasn't even a fault yet would be unprecedented.

34. William Milligan, *The Book of Revelation,* Expositor's Bible (New York: Funk & Wagnalls Company, 1900), 45–46; Charles Brown, *Heavenly Visions: An Exposition of the Book of Revelation* (Boston: Pilgrim Press, 1910), 49; Raymond Calkins, *The Social Message of the Book of Revelation* (New York: Women's Press, 1920), 58. Donald Guthrie takes it this way but concedes that the double reference is possible (*The Relevance of John's Apocalypse* [Exeter, Devon (England): Paternoster Press, 1987], 74). Moses Stuart points to the *cure* for their weakened or lost love that is given in verse 5 ("repent and do the first *works*") as evidence that attitudes toward others—rather than Christ—are under consideration (*A Commentary on the Apocalypse,* vol. 2 [Andover: Allen, Morrill and Wardwell, 1845], 61).

Writing shortly after World War I, Isbon T. Beckwith observed that "most...recent commentators" take it in the sense that lack of inter-Christian love is under consideration. (*The Apocalypse of John* [New York: Macmillan Company, 1919], 450). Writing over sixty years later,

Alan F. Johnson observed that "most commentators" continued to prefer this interpretation, though he himself did not (*Revelation*, 42).

James T. Draper Jr., *The Unveiling* (Nashville, Tenn.: Broadman Press 1984), 38, provides an unusual twist to this approach that the search for orthodoxy had driven out love; he concedes that the quest for "sound doctrine" caused their lack of love but that it had also squeezed out their love for the Lord himself. They became more concerned with doctrine than with the Lord.

35.  David Chilton, *The Days of Vengeance: An Exposition of the Book of Revelation* (Fort Worth, Tex.: Dominion Press, 1987). "The question of 'doctrine *versus* love' is, Biblically speaking, a non-issue....Christians are required to be *both* orthodox *and* loving, and a lack of either will eventually result in the judgment of God" (95–96).

36.  About A.D. 107–8 has been the traditional date for Ignatius's visit but more recent scholarship has tended to date it in the following decade, between 110 and 117 (cf. Edgard J. Goodspeed, *The Apostolic Fathers: An American Translation* [New York: Harper & Brothers, 1950], 204). On Ignatius's letter to the Ephesians, see Anthony J. Blasi, "Office Charisma in Early Christian Ephesus." *Sociology of Religion* 56 (Fall 1995): 245–55.

37.  Ignatius, Epistle to the Ephesians, in "Epistles of Ignatius," *The Ante-Nicene Fathers*, vol. 1: *The Apostolic Fathers: Justin, Martyr, Irenaeus*, ed. Alexander Roberts and James Donaldson (New York: Charles Scribner's Sons, 1899), chap. 4.

38.  Ibid., chap. 20.

39.  Ibid., chap. 9.

40.  Ibid., chap. 13; cf. the admonition in Hebrews 10:25.

41.  Ibid., chap. 8.

42.  Sherman E. Johnson, "The Apostle Paul and the Riot in Ephesus," *Lexington Theological Quarterly* 14 (October 1979):82.

43.  *The Revelation of St. John,* Moffatt New Testament Commentary series (New York: Harper & Brothers, 1940), 23.

44.  Chilton, *Days of Vengeance,* 96–97.

45.  "Testament of Dan" and "Testament of Levi" are included as segments of "The Testaments of the Twelve Patriarchs." We have utilized the translation of M. de Jonge in *The Apocryphal Old Testament*, ed. H. F. D. Sparks (Oxford: Clarendon Press, 1984).

46.  *The Book of Enoch or I Enoch*, translated from the Ethiopian by R. H. Charles (Oxford: Clarendon Press, 1912).

47.  Ramsay, *Seven Churches,* 247–48.

48.  On the point in general, see Darice E. Birge, "Sacred Groves

in the Ancient Greek World (Ph.D. diss., University of California-Berkeley, 1982), 16.

49. Ibid., 215–16.

50. G. W. Bowersock, *Hellenism in Late Antiquity* (Ann Arbor, Mich.: University of Michigan Press, 1990), 3–4.

51. Cf. Martin R. Nilsson, *Greek Popular Religion* (New York: Columbia University Press, 1940), 16.

52. Birge, "Sacred Groves," 27; Bowersock, *Hellenism*, 3–4, 5. For a discussion of the rural/countryside orientation of the Artemis cult in Greece itself see Robert Parker, *Athenian Religion: A History* (Oxford: Clarendon Press, 1996), 25.

53. For a summary of the evidence see Colin J. Hemer, *The Letters to the Seven Churches of Asia in Their Local Setting*, Journal for the Study of the New Testament Supplement Series 11 (Sheffeld, England: University of Sheffield, 1986), 44–45. Cf. C. J. Hemer, "Seven Cities of Asia Minor," in *Major Cities of the Biblical World*, ed. R. K. Harrison, 234–48 (Nashville, Tenn.: Thomas Nelson Publishers, 1985), 238.

54. MacMullen, *Paganism*, 35.

55. Lietzman, *Early Church*, 1:159.

56. Blaiklock, *Cities*, 67.

57. For a summary of the coinage evidence see Hemer, *Local Setting*, 45–46. Cf. Palmer, *Revelation*, 130; J. Massyngberde Ford, *Revelation*, Anchor Bible series (Garden City, N.Y.: Doubleday and Company, 1975), 388.

Gerhard A. Krodel finds in the Artemis-tree connection not so much a parallel with the Biblical usage as an encouraging *contrast*: Just as accused criminals could find refuge in the temple of Artemis, Christians would ultimately find refuge *from* "the idolatry surrounding Artemis" in the heavenly paradise of refuge (*Revelation*, 109–10).

John W. Court argues that "both 'tree' and 'paradise' (2:7) are echoes of Genesis 2–3, but also parodies of the tree-shrine of Artemis (Diana) at Ephesus and of its sacred enclosure which offered asylum" (*Revelation*, 35). Of course, biblically, Paradise is depicted as a reward while Artemis's enclosure was not a reward but a place to avoid punishment. Even so, this contrast might be intended by John as a subtle reminder that while Artemis could afford a temporary hiding place, Jesus could offer an abiding place of permanent reward.

#### 4. RIVAL SMYRNA

1. Henry J. van Lennep, *Travels in Little-Known Parts of Asia Minor*, vol. 2 (London: John Murray, 1870), 285.

2. Ibid., 285–86.

3. W. M. Calder, "Smyrna as Described by the Orator Aelius Aristides," in *Studies in the History and Art of the Eastern Provinces of the Roman Empire*, ed. W. M. Ramsay (Aberdeen [Scotland]: Aberdeen University Press, 1906), 97. This was a common reaction to the site among both nineteenth- and twentieth-century visitors (see Cecil J. Cadoux, *Ancient Smyrna: A History from the Earliest Times to 324 A.D.* [Oxford: Basil Blackwell, 1938], 172–73, for citations and that author's own sentiments).

4. Alan Johnson, "Revelation," in *The Expositor's Bible Commentary*, vol. 12, ed. Frank E. Gaebelein (Grand Rapids, Mich.: Zondervan Publishing House, 1981), 437.

5. Lucian, *Imagines*, 2, quoted by Cadoux, *Smyrna*, 171.

6. Strabo, *Geography*, 646, as quoted by Calder, "Smyrna as Described," 114.

7. Quoted by Calder, "Smyrna as Described," 172.

8. Quoted by ibid.

9. Major-General Sir Charles Wilson, *Handbook for Travellers in Asia Minor, Transcaucasia, Persia, etc.* (London: John Murray, 1895; 1911 reprint), 71.

10. Toksoz, *Travel Guide*, 139.

11. Philostratus, *Lives of the Sophists*, in *Philostratus and Eunapius: The Lives of the Sophists*, trans. Wilmer C. Wright, rev. ed. [Loeb Classical Library] (London: William Heinemann, 1952), 582, cf. 583. The multiple nature of the quakes, dated by them as A.D. 178–80, are referred to by Pfeiffer and Vos, *Historical Geography*, 391, and LaMar C. Berrett, *Discovering the World of the Bible* (Provo, Utah: Young House, 1973), 623. Most writers confuse the reader by only referring to *one* massive tremor, presumably on the grounds that one was the crucial quake and the others simply made the bad situation even worse. Dating the quake A.D. 177 are Andrew Tait, *The Messages to the Seven Churches of Asia* (London: Hodder and Stoughton, 1884), 183; and Cornelius V. Vermuele, *Roman Imperial Art in Greece and Asia Minor* (Cambridge, Mass.: Belknap Press, 1968), 70. Dating the quake in A.D. 178 are Avery, *Classical Handbook*, 1018, and Finegan, *Archaeology*, 171.

12. Philostratus, *Lives of the Sophists*, 582. The authors in the previous footnote also mention the emperor's role in the rebuilding.

13. Marcus L. Loane, *They Overcame: An Exposition of the First Three Chapters of Revelation* ([n.p.]: Angus and Robertson, 1971; reprint, Grand Rapids, Mich.: Baker Book House, 1981), 47; Whiting, *Revelation*, 73. Rivka Gonen estimates the distance between the two cities as

forty-seven miles (*Biblical Holy Places–An Illustrated Guide* (Jerusalem: Palphot, 1987), 263).

14. Foss, *Ephesus After Antiquity*, 6.

15. Gonen, *Biblical Holy Places*, 271.

16. Cadoux, *Smyrna*, 186. Hanfmann, *From Croesus to Constantine*, 49. J. C. Russell, *Population*, 80, argues that since the city proper occupied only six hundred hectares that a figure of ninety thousand would be more probable

17. Alan Johnson, "Revelation," 436; Alan F. Johnson, *Revelation*, 44. Stark, *Rome on the Euphrates*, 221. T. R. S. Broughton accepts a population of 200,000 for Pergamon and believes that Smyrna had a larger population ("Roman Asia," 813). Stephen Mitchell, in *Celts* calls it one of "the three largest cities" (206) of Asia but does not provide an explicit population estimate. He uses the same language of Pergamon (ibid.) but later estimates its population to in the 180,000–200,000 range (243–44) and indicates no other city was likely larger (244). Hence a figure in this range would seem to represent his estimate of Smyrna's population as well.

18. Sitwell, *Roman Roads*, makes it "a close rival of Ephesus in the matter of size," which he puts at "at least" 250,000 (192).

19. Peters, *Harvest of Hellenism*, 517.

20. Dio Chrysostom cited Smyrna to the people of Prusa for its major geographic expansion, "A man must shape his shoe to suit his foot, and if he find it too large, cut it down. But a city must never be docked or stunted to one's individual standard or measured with reference to one's own soul, if that soul be puny or mean. You have examples of this principle in the case of Smyrna, Ephesus, Tarsus, Antioch" (xl. 11, as quoted by Calder, "Smyrna as Described," 107).

21. M. Terentius Varro, *On Agriculture* trans. William D. Hooper, rev. Harrison B. Ash [Loeb Classical Library] (Cambridge, Mass.: Harvard University Press, 1935; 1967 reprint), I.vii.6.

22. Charlesworth, *Commerce*, 91–92.

23. Pliny, *Natural History*, V.31.

24. Ford, *Revelation*, 394.

25. Caird, *Revelation*, 34.

26. Emil G. Kraeling, *Rand McNally Bible Atlas* (New York: Rand McNally & Company, 1956), 466–67; Whiting, *Revelation*, 73.

27. Ellen Clare Miller, *Eastern Sketches: Notes of Scenery, Schools, and Tent Life in Syria and Palestine* (Edinburgh [Scotland]: W. Oliphant, 1871; reprint, New York: Arno Press, 1977), 19.

28. William E. Curtis, *Today in Syria and Palestine* (Chicago: Fleming H. Revell Company, 1903), 21.

29. Laurence Oliphant, *Modern Palestine*, 1, wrote from Smyrna that all that had changed was visitor convenience: "In old days it was an easy two days' ride from Smyrna to Ephesus, the distance being about fifty miles, but the Smyrna and Aiden Railway speeds you to the ruins in about two hours now."

30. Kraeling, *Atlas*, 467; Toksoz, *Travel Guide*, 139; Wilson, *Handbook*, 73; Yamauchi, *New Testament Cities*, 58; Walter A. Hawley, *Asia Minor* (London: John Lane/Bodley Head, 1918), 95.

31. Toksoz, *Travel Guide*, 139.

32. Ibid.

33. Yamauchi, *New Testament Cities*, 58.

34. Ibid.

35. Wilson, *Handbook*, 73.

36. Toksoz, *Travel Guide*, 139 (citing Aristides).

37. Toksoz, *Travel Guide*, 143. Toksoz also provides evidence that the earliest possible date for the quake is A.D. 160. For a description of the agora, see 140–42.

38. Ibid., 142–43; Finegan, *Archaeology*, 171.

39. Kraeling, *Atlas*, 466–67.

40. Toksoz, *Travel Guide*, 139.

41. Strabo, *Geography* 14.1.37. Cf. Cadoux, *Smyrna*, 175.

42. Cadoux, *Smyrna*, 176.

43. Ibid.

44. Whiting, *Revelation*, 74. Whiting believes that the description is intended as a rebuke of Smyrna because it harbored the delusion of permanence that only deity can rightly enjoy (73).

45. Colin J. Hemer contends that William Ramsay overstated the certainty that the city disappeared (Ramsay, *Seven Churches*). Hemer surveys the evidence (*Local Setting*, 62–63). J. P. Sweet (*Revelation*, Westminster Pelican Commentaries series [Philadelphia: Westminster Press, 1979)], 84) is among those who speak as if an absolute destruction occurred. Charles H. H. Scobie, "Local References in the Letters to the Seven Churches," *New Testament Studies* 39 (October 1993), 613, notes that "many scholars" accept some form of the civic death/rebirth phenomena to be John's intended allusion.

46. As indicated by Hemer, *Local Setting*, 62–63. Cf. Ford, *Revelation*, 395.

47. Charles C. Whiting, *Revelation*, 74, in referring to the community's continued survival as a village, sees such a point behind John's allusion.

48. Pausanias, *Pausanias' Guide to Greece*, VII.1 (Levi translation).

49. Barclay, *Revelation*, 1:75–76.

50. Ibid., 81.

51. Giving several examples, Herman Hoeksema, *Behold, He Cometh! An Exposition of the Book of Revelation* (Grand Rapids, Mich.: Reformed Free Publishing Association, 1969), 72. Referring to the 10 plagues in particular: Eugenio Corsini, *Apocalypse: The Perennial Revelation of Jesus Christ*, trans. and ed. Francis J. Moloney (Wilmington, Del.: Michael Glazier), 105.

52. Hoeksema, *Behold, He Cometh!*, 72; Mounce, *Revelation*, 94; Adela Y. Collins, "Numerical Symbolism in Jewish and Early Christian Apocalyptic Literature, *Aufstieg und Niedergang der Romischen Welt* (Berlin: Walter de Gruyter, 1984), II, 21.2, 1243.

53. Fred D. Howard (*1, 2, and 3 John, Judge and Revelation*, in *Layman's Bible Book Commentary*, vol. 24 [Nashville, Tenn.: Broadman Press, 1982], 62) sees it growing out of a physical reality: "The Jews sometimes used the number ten to symbolize human completion, probably because normal people have ten fingers and ten toes." On the other hand, since normal people have both ten fingers and ten toes, wouldn't the moral natural numerical symbol of perfection be *twenty*?

54. Blaiklock, *Cities*, 100; Calkins, *Social Message*, 59; Ramsay, *Seven Churches*, 275; Martin F. Franzmann, *The Revelation to John* (St. Louis: Concordia, 1976), 42.

55. Barclay, *Revelation*, 79; Giblin, *Revelation*, 595; Krodel, *Revelation*, 113; Onstad, *Courage*, 18; Merrill F. Unger, *The New Unger's Bible Handbook*, rev. Gary N. Larson (Chicago: Moody Press, 1984), 652; Philip E. Hughes, *The Book of Revelation: A Commentary* (Grand Rapids, Mich.: Wm. B. Eerdmans Publishing Company, 1990), 42. One is hard-pressed to determine how to treat an interpretation that seems to go in contradictory directions at the same time: E. W. Hengstenberg takes the expression to mean "among short periods a long one" (*The Revelation of St. John*, trans. Patrick Fairbairn [New York: Robert Carter and Brothers, 1852], 174).

56. For example: Gn 24:55; Dn 1:12–14. For a fine introduction to the symbolism of numbers see John J. Davis, *Biblical Numerology: A Basic Study of the Use of Numbers in the Bible* (Grand Rapids, Mich.: Baker Book House, 1968). Davis indicates that ten is a number for which there is more consensus than in many other cases, most interpretations including some variant of the idea of "shortness" or "brevity" (122).

57. Cf. Hoeksema, *Behold, He Cometh!*, 71; Selles, *Revelation*, 1:18; John Tickle, *The Book of Revelation: A Catholic Interpretation of the Apocalypse* (Liguori, Mo.: Ligouri Publications, 1983), 35.

58. Stuart, *Apocalypse*, 2:70, presents the expression as alluding to either "a short time, a few days" or this longer alternative.

59. F. F. Bruce, "Revelation," in *A New Testament Commentary*, general editor G. C. D. Howley (Grand Rapids, Mich.: Zondervan Publishing House, 1969), 638. Leon Morris thinks in terms of a similar extended duration. Three and a half days "is John's usual expression for a trial of limited duration" (*Revelation*, 64).

60. This is based upon a year equaling a calendar year, as in Numbers 14:34 and Ezekiel 4:6. Hence ten years of persecution would be under consideration, a period said roughly to equal the duration of the imperial oppression under the Emperor Diocletian. What encouragement this promised to a generation yet unborn—indeed, a number of generations—seems marginal at the best. Andrew Tait, *Messages*, 204-5 discusses the rationale behind the theory and some of its difficulties.

61. Krodel, *Revelation*, 112.

62. Philostratus, *Lives of Sophists*, 613. The A.D. 230 date is that of the translator (xii).

63. Cicero, *Philippics,* trans. Walter C. A. Ker [Loeb Classical Library] (Cambridge, Mass.: Harvard University Press, 1926; 1969 reprint), XI.2.5.

64. Meinardus, *Patmos*, 62. William M. Ramsay (*Seven Churches*, 276) and J. Massyngberde Ford (*Revelation*, 395) render it as "the most faithful of our allies."

65. Ford, *Revelation*, 395.

66. Ramsay, *Seven Churches*, 275-76.

67. On Smyrna's record of loyalty in general and coming to the relief of the Roman army in particular, see Brown, *Heavenly Visions*, 63-64; Meinardus, *Patmos,* 62; Whiting, *Revelation*, 73.

68. Guthrie, *Apocalypse*, 73-74.

69. This is not to deny that political considerations played a major role—on both sides—in the development of the Smyrnaian-Roman alliance. Our point is that the alliance stood the test of time, even when Smyrna could have found it prudent to quietly backtrack from its commitment. The same temptation, of course, faced Smyrnaian Christians in the religious sphere. Just as their civic community had resisted the temptation, so should the believing community.

70. Hailey, *Revelation*, 128.

71. Loane, *They Overcame*, 53. Loane insists that "this Book is steeped in Hebrew imagery and does not draw even one of its word pictures from the world of heathen antiquity." To say that John did not exclusively (or, perhaps, even primarily) have in mind the beliefs and practices of the surrounding society is quite reasonable. To believe that he was

unaware of the obvious secular and religious pagan parallels would ascribe to him an incredible ignorance of the society in which he lived.

72. The best evidence for a regal crown comes from Revelation itself. In Revelation 20:4 we read of Christians sitting on "thrones" and "given authority to judge." The latter phrase suggests regal power being exercised, and the "thrones" suggest a regal position. Likewise, in Revelation 20:6 we read that they "shall reign with him a thousand years." When a this-world image is intended, athletic victories seem to be in mind (2 Tm 2:5; 1 Cor 9:24–27). The natural preference for an intra-Revelation textual explanation shifts the probability to royal crowns.

73. Jean-Pierre Prevost makes the "crown" refer to both the city's "fortifications" and "its games" in his *How to Read the Apocalypse*, trans. John Bowden and Margaret Lydamore (New York: Crossroad, 1993), 73. Bruce M. Metzger, *Code*, 33, suggests it refers to the garlands presented to winners of major athletic contests.

74. Sweet, *Revelation*, 86.

75. Henry B. Swete, *The Apocalypse of St. John: The Greek Text with Introduction, Notes, and Indices*, 3d ed. (London: Macmillan and Co., 1909; reprinted 1911), lxi.

76. Ibid.

77. Ibid., lxi-lxii.

78. Barclay, *Revelation*, 83.

79. G. R. Beasley-Murray, *The Book of Revelation*, New Century Bible series (Greenwood, S. C.: Attic Press, 1974), 83.

80. Ramsay, *Seven Churches*, 258.

81. George A. Barton, *Archaeology and the Bible*, 7th ed., rev. (Philadelphia: American Sunday-School Union, 1937), 272; Boyd, *Tells, Tombs, and Treasure*, 207; R. K. Harrison, *Archaeology*, 53; Alan F. Johnson, *Revelation*, 46; Thompson, *Archaeology*, 416.

82. Hemer, *Local Setting*, 73.

83. Accepted as fact by W. Boyd Carpenter, *Revelation*, 45. Colin J. Hemer, *Local Setting*, 72, notes that this has been challenged.

84. Sweet, *Revelation*, 86.

85. Cadoux, *Smyrna*, 195.

86. Ibid., 195–96. In footnote 8, page 319, Cadoux alludes to this civic-religious honor as the interpretation of the "crown" promised the triumphant believer but rejects it in the main text in favor of an allusion to "the victor's garland."

87. For a discussion of honorary crowns in Smyrna see Hemer, *Local Setting*, 73–74, 234 n. 58.

88. Alan F. Johnson, *Revelation*, sees this as the secondary reference.

## 5. MONOTHEISM AND POLYTHEISM IN SMYRNA

1. Ford, *Revelation*; Lilje, *Last Book*, 74.

2. As quoted by Bernadette J. Brooten, *Women Leaders in the Ancient Synagogue: Inscriptional Evidence and Background Issues* (Chico, Calif.: Scholars Press, 1982), 5.

3. Ibid., 11.

4. For a discussion of various interpretations see ibid., 6, 42. For another discussion of the nature of Rufina's synagogue leadership—and that of other women in Asia—see Paul R. Trebilco, *Jewish Communities in Asia Minor* (Cambridge: Cambridge University Press, 1991), 104–13.

5. For a discussion of such cases, see Trebilco, *Jewish Communities*, 113–16. During the reigns of Domitian and Hadrian, one Ephesian woman is described as of senatorial rank (van Tilborg, *Ephesus*, 162). Here, also, we find a terminological reference to a possible formal rank for women that defies normal usage of the age. It is at least partial evidence that one should be very cautious not to read not too much of a formal position into the allusions to women synagogue leaders.

6. Van Tilborg, 124.

7. Brooten, *Women Leaders*, 11.

8. Martin Hengel, *Judaism and Hellenism: Studies in Their Encounter in Palestine During the Early Hellenistic Period*, trans. John Bowden (Philadelphia: Fortress Press, 1974), 308, and W. W. Tarn, *Hellenistic Civilization*, 3d ed., rev. W. W. Tarn and G. T. Griffith (London: Edward Arnold & Co., 1952), 225, are inclined in this direction. Cuthbert H. Turner sees the possibility that the participants were involved in "some Judaeo-gnostic sect" that effectively destroyed their pretensions to still be Jews (commenting on "who say they are Jews and are not," Revelation 2:9) (*Studies in Early Church History* [Oxford: Clarendon Press, 1912], 202). Turner's preferred hypothesis is that these were Christian heretics: Christian Judaizers (207).

9. Tarn, *Helenistic Civilization*, 225.

10. Ibid., 226.

11. G. Campbell Morgan, *The Letters of Our Lord–A First Century Message to Twentieth Century Christians: Addresses Based upon the Letters to the Seven Churches of Asia* (New York: Fleming H. Revell Company, 1902), 61.

12. This is not to say that this was necessarily the only factor involved in Smyrnaian poverty. Paul implies in 1 Corinthians 1:26 that disciples came predominantly (but not exclusively) from the less well-established elements of society. In spite of the apparent tendency of Christianity to appeal to the lower classes of society (if not the outright

poor), the close textual connection between the reference to poverty and the presence of hostile Jews presses one to assume some additional action in either creating the poverty or at least magnifying its impact.

13. Scott G. Sinclair presents a variant of this when he argues that the persecution was a power play designed to destroy the viability of *Jewish* Christianity: "Apparently, the synagogues were gaining control over the Jewish community as a whole and, consequently, Jewish Christianity was withering" (*Revelation: A Book for the Rest of Us* [Berkeley, Calif.: Bibal Press, 1992], 52). Christianity might remain a viable option for Gentiles, but there was to be no toleration for it among ethnic Jews.

14. Schonfield, *The Bible Was Right*, 228, does not use these terms, but this appears to be the point of his argument.

15. A. Thomas Kraabel, "Impact of the Discovery of the Sardis Synagogue," in Andrew R. Seager and A. Thomas Kraabel, "The Synagogue and the Jewish Community," in *Sardis: From Prehistoric to Roman Times–Results of the Archaeological Exploration of Sardis, 1958–1975*, ed. George M. A. Hanfmann and William E. Mierse (Cambridge, Mass.: Harvard University Press, 1983), 180.

16. *Early Church History*, 207. Without a specific type of heresy in mind, John J. Pilch takes the reference to be a broad one to apostate Christians in general—considered as if a collectivity. ("Lying and Deceit in the Letters to the Seven Churches: Perspectives from Cultural Anthropology," *Biblical Theology Bulletin* 22 [Fall 1992]: 131).

17. "Martyrdom of Polycarp," also known as "The Encyclical Epistle of the Church at Smyrna concerning the Martyrdom of the Holy Polycarp," in *The Ante-Nicene Fathers*, vol. 1: *Apostolic Fathers: Justin Martyr, Irenaeus*, ed. Alexander Roberts and James Donaldson, 39–44 (New York: Charles Scribner's Sons, 1899).

18. Adela Y. Collins, "Vilification and Self-Definiton in the Book of Revelation," in *Christians Among Jews and Gentiles*, ed. George W. E. Nickelsburg and George W. MacRae (Philadelphia: Fortress Press, 1986), 313.

19. Herman Hoeksema, *Behold, He Cometh!*, 66–68, introduces the reference to "blasphemy" in 2:9 as evidence of such a character assault.

20. Ibid.

21. Cf. Hebrews 10:32–34: "But recall the former days in which, after you were illuminated, you endured a great struggle with sufferings: partly while you were made a spectacle both by reproaches and tribulations, and partly while you became companions of those who were so treated: for you had compassion on me in my chains, and joy-

fully accepted the *plundering of your goods,* knowing that you have a better and an enduring possession for yourself in heaven."

22.  W. J. Limmer Sheppard, *Revelation,* 32, suggests "the spoiling of their goods by hostile mobs" while Marcus L. Loane, *They Overcame,* 49, speaks more vaguely of persecution (though not excluding that at least a partial reference may be to the economic strata from which the church membership was drawn). Ray F. Robbins, *Revelation,* 58, considers unbeliever afflicted adversity as "probably" the reason for their lack of worldly status.

23.  Donald Guthrie, *Revelation,* 75, takes the Smyrnaians as representative of most early Christians in this regard. There are, of course, degrees of poverty. The members of the churches of Macedonia are described as living in "deep poverty," at least in comparison to their neighbors. We say in comparison because, in spite of their limited economic resources, they were still able to "abound" in their giving to support Paul in his missionary endeavors (2 Cor 8:2).

24.  A rare dissenter is Alan J. Beagley, *The "Sitz Im Leben" of the Apocalypse with Particular Reference to the Role of the Church's Enemies* (Berlin: Walter de Gruyter, 1987), 33, who contends that "only imprisonment [was] an imminent concrete danger facing the Christians in Smyrna." To him death is only a possible rather than a probable sequel to that imprisonment.

25.  Cf. J. Nelson Kraybill, "Cult and Commerce in Revelation 18" (Ph.D. diss., Union Theological Seminary, Richmond, Virginia, 1992), 24. Scholars first backed off from the idea of a major persecution by Nero outside the immediate area of Rome. In recent years there has been a trend to reconsider the degree of the later Domitian persecution, with some skeptical that Christians—as such—were targeted at all. (I retain the opinion that there was a moderate persecution that inevitably involved Christians, though they were only inadvertently or secondarily its targets.) In light of Revelation 2:10's terminological limitations and the evidence of the "Martyrdom of Polycarp," a reevaluation of the numerical amount of persecution demanded by the Revelation text is clearly demanded—both as to that which was imminent and that which John speaks of occurring in the future. Some have begun to deal with this by stressing the emotional or psychic impact of persecution on the believing community as being more important to the author than the empirical numbers actually involved. Assuming John to have been a true prophet—rather than apocalyptically deluded—an explanation above and beyond this would seem to be required.

26. This and the following chapter references are to "The Martyrdom of Polycarp," a contemporary account.

27. On the arrest of Polycarp—with the exception of the unusual courtesy extended him by the Roman governor—as illustrative of policing tactics in the region see Mitchell, *Celts*, 196–97.

28. The account claims that the fire did not kill Polycarp but merely darkened his body like "bread that is baked or as gold and silver glowing in a furnace"; instead of the stink of burning flesh, one could detect "a sweet odor...as if frankincense or some such precious spices" (chap. 15). Unable to destroy Polycarp by fire, "they commanded an executioner to go near and pierce him through with a dagger" (chap. 16). Assuming a historical root here, one expects some stratagem by the authorities, perhaps arranging the firewood in such a way as to suffocate him rather than to inflict the pain of death by burning. Certainly the restraint of the officials in their treatment of Polycarp—with its implied ambivalence or hostility toward the proceedings—makes some type of ameliorative action on their part quite credible.

After his death a Jewish clique convinced the father of Herod to demand that Polycarp's body not be buried lest the martyr become an object of worship in place of the One who had been crucified (chap. 17). This time the fire worked: "The centurion then, seeing the strife excited by the Jews, placed the body in the midst of the fire, and consumed it" (chap. 18). Since there seems no rationale for a miracle that would spare the same body in one case but not the other, some action by the executioners would more reasonably account for what happened the first time the body was exposed to fire.

29. Polycarp, "Epistle to the Philippians," in Roberts and Donaldson, *The Apostolic Fathers: Justin Martyr, Irenaeus*, 31–36.

30. Note that *deacon* has now evolved from its biblical-era idea of an officeholder who is a "servant" (the meaning of the word) to one who has some type of control or authority over others in the exercise of service to them. In doing this a clear step has been taken to "clericalize" the position.

31. Both letters are included in the "Epistles of Ignatius," in Roberts and Donaldson, *The Apostolic Fathers: Justin Martyr, Irenaeus*, 45–96. The following chapter references in the text are to these epistles.

32. As we read both scripture and history, bishops first exercised superior powers and minimized the opportunity to "rightly" remove them and then developed doctrines such as "apostolic succession" to "scripturalize" the new power structure. Certainly, if any doctrine of episcopate supremacy existed in the biblical period, one would expect Ignatius at least—if not Polycarp—to cite the precedents.

33. Material in brackets was inserted by the translator to complete the sense of the text.

34. Cf., in his personal letter to Polycarp, "My soul be for theirs that are submissive to the bishop, to the presbyters, and to the deacons, and may my portion be along with them in God!" (chap. 6)

35. Philostratus, *Lives of the Sophists*, 543.

36. Hawley, *Asia Minor*, 66.

37. J. Car Laney, *Baker's Concise Bible Atlas: A Geographical Survey of Biblical History* (Grand Rapids, Mich.: Baker Book House, 1988), 246.

38. Pausanias, *Pausanias' Guide to Greece*, II.7 (Levi translation).

39. Cadoux, *Smyrna*, 209.

40. Carpenter, *Revelation*, 43.

41. Cadoux, *Smyrna*, 208. Breseus is also rendered in English as Briseus or Breiseus.

42. Ibid.

43. Similar coins also have survived from the A.D. 211–17 period. Ibid., 208–9.

44. Finegan, *Archaeology*, 171.

45. Cadoux, *Smyrna*, 141.

46. Ibid., 211–12.

47. Strabo, 14.1.37, as quoted in ibid., 211.

48. For a collection of writings presenting the claim for Smyrna see Cadoux, *Smyrna*, 209–11.

49. Sweet, *Revelation*, 84.

50. For a discussion of how the temple location decision was made, see Magie, *Asia Minor*, 501.

51. Jones, "Roman Imperial Cult," 1037.

52. Luther H. Martin, *Hellenistic Religions: An Introduction* (New York: Oxford University Press, 1987), 83.

53. This is the traditional explanation for the Roman's embracing Cybele. E. O. James expresses it this way, "The situation was becoming desperate. The war had lasted for twelve years and its end was still nowhere in sight" (*The Cult of the Mother-Goddess: An Archaeolaogical and Documentary Study* [London: Thames and Hudson, 1959], 168–69).

54. This is the argument of Garth Thomas, "Magna Mater and Attis," in *Aufstieg und Niedergang der Romischen Welt* (Berlin: Walter de Gruyter, 1984), II, 17.3, 1503–1508. Of course in war there is a vast difference between success and continued success, and also between the retrospective certainty of victory and the contemporary jitteriness that can occur after a number of years in a (gradually) triumphing nation. Furthermore, major innovations in either religion or politics are rarely the result of one factor alone; even when one is dominant, other trends

or attitudes tend to reinforce and encourage that central reason. Hence, even if war nerves represent the *major* reason, that does not destroy the legitimacy of seeking additional factors that encouraged Rome in that direction.

55. Livy (Titus Livius), *The History of Rome (Books XXI-XXX)*, trans. D. Spillan and Cyrus Edmonds (New York: Harper & Brothers, Publishers, 1892), 29.11. For the enthusiastic reception in Rome see the description in 29.14.

56. Ferguson, *Backgrounds*, 264. Cf. Karl Baus, *Handbook of Church History*, vol. 1: *From the Apostolic Community to Constantine* (New York: Herder and Herder, 1965), 92, and Walter Burkert, *Ancient Mystery Cults* (Cambridge, Mass.: Harvard University Press, 1987), 6.

57. Lietzman, *Early Church*, 1:158.

58. Ibid.

59. Grant Showerman, "The Great Mother of the Gods" (Ph.D. diss., University of Wisconsin, 1900), reprinted in *Bulletin of the University of Wisconsin, Philology and Literature Series* 1, no. 3 (May 1901), 291.

60. Burkert, *Ancient Mystery Cults*, 5. In modern usage the Latin designation has been reversed to Magna Mater.

61. For example, see Joe B. McMinn, "Fusion of the Gods: A Religio-astrological Study of the Interpenetration of the East and the West in Asia Minor," *Journal of Near Eastern Studies* 15 (1956), 207.

62. Showerman, "Great Mother," 292.

63. Stephen Mitchell, *Anatolia: Land, Men, and Gods in Asia Minor*, vol. 2: *The Rise of the Church* (Oxford: Clarendon Press, 1993), 21–23.

64. Maaten J. Vermaseren, *Cybele and Attis–The Myth and the Cult* (London: Thames and Hudson, 1977), 27.

65. Ibid.

66. Ibid.

67. Ramsay, *Seven Churches*, 264; Bruce, "Revelation," 638.

68. Kraeling, *Atlas*, 467. The probable site was either on what is today called the hill Tepejik or nearby. Some have suggested a site to the south, in what was later known as the Valley of St. Anna. Cf. Vermaseren, *Corpus Cultus Cybelae*, 161.

69. Quoted by Anne Baring and Jules Cashford, *The Myth of the Goddess: Evolution of an Image* (New York: Viking Arkana, 1991), 394.

70. Quoted in ibid., 402–3.

71. In an effort to deny the originality of the New Testament picture of Jesus' resurrection some have cited the story of Attis as precedent for a resurrection doctrine. If one "spiritualizes" the concept of resurrection broadly and vaguely enough, one can erect a parallel, but

it is hard to see it as a meaningful one. How could an individual driven to madness and involuntary self-castration parallel a judicially murdered prophet who offended the religious authorities of his day? Furthermore, what in the New Testament parallels the crucial role played by a woman in bringing about the tragedy? For a discussion that denies the reading of the Attis myth as a precursor for Jesus' resurrection see Vermaseren, *Cybele and Attisu*, 110–12.

72. H. J. Rose, *A Handbook of Greek Mythology–Including Its Extension to Rome*, 6th ed. (London: Methuen and Company, 1958; 1965 reprint), 170. Will Roscoe cautions that this may not have been the only time when the self-castration was permitted. See his "Priests of the Goddess: Gender Transgression in Ancient Religion," *History of Religions* 35 (February 1996), 203. For an overview of the cult see 198–206.

Allen H. Jones suggests that self-castration not only reenacted the Attis myth but also alluded to Cybele's nickname: she was known as Queen Bee, and among bees, the male loses his sexual organ in the act of mating with the queen. By removing their own bodily parts they were reenacting among humans in a "bee" cult what happened among actual bees in the wild (*Essenes*, 93). Perhaps a similar purpose lay behind the castration of certain priests of Artemis, who was another "bee" goddess.

73. Stephen Benko, *The Virgin Goddess: Studies in the Pagan and Christian Roots of Mariology* (New York: E. J. Brill, 1993), refers specifically to Phrygia. If Rome's Cybele rituals were essential the same as those of Phrygia, one would naturally expect the similarity to be equal or more profound in Asia, which shares its borders.

74. The festival is described in detail in ibid., 71–74. For a more concise summary see Joscelyn Godwin, *Mystery Religions in the Ancient World* (San Francisco: Harper & Row, 1981), 112, which seems to end the festival on March 25 rather than March 27.

75. Censorinus, quoted by MacMullen, *Paganism*, 16.

76. Ibid.

77. Ibid., 21.

78. Ibid., 24.

79. Sharon K. Heybob, *The Cult of Isis Among Women in the Graeco-Roman World* (Leiden: E. J. Brill, 1975), 82.

80. There were exceptions, but few. Of the documentary evidence Heybob writes, "In all but one instance women were called priestesses of Isis, rather than priestesses of Sarapis or of Isis and Sarapis." She interprets this to mean, however, not sexual discrimination or limitation but the superior appeal of Isis to women of the ancient world (*Isis Among Women*, 89).

81. Wayne A. Meeks, *The First Urban Christians: The Social World of the Apostle Paul* (New Haven: Yale University Press, 1983), 25; Mary F. Thelen, *Historical Introduction to the Christian Religion*, part 1: *The Old Testament and the Hellenistic Background* ([n.p.]: [n.p.], 1956), 193. Thelen's book appears to have been self-published for use in her courses at Randolph-Macon's Woman's College.

82. This is reasonably deduced from inscriptions mentioning women found at various cultic sites. At Athens 48.6 percent of all inscriptions were from or concerning women in cultic positions. In Rome the percentage declines to 37.1 percent, and on the island of Rhodes none at all have been found. Of 1,099 surviving inscriptions only 18.2 percent mention women (see Heybob, *Isis Among Women*, 81–82, cf. 87.)

Although some would deduce from this evidence the need for a drastic downward revision of the role of women in the group (cf. ibid., 81), two factors argue against this interpretation. First, the surviving inscriptions indicate far more female participants in the A.D. centuries than in those prior to the birth of Christ. In Athens, for example, the number is more than double (ibid., 82). Second, there is the question of whether one would reasonably *expect* women to have inscriptions in proportion to their numbers. Their societal status and their general lack of independent wealth would seemingly result in an inevitable *under*-representation. Whatever their numerical status, it was sufficiently large (at least in proportion to other cultic groups) that ancient writers repeatedly stressed the appeal it had to women (ibid., 87).

83. Meeks, *Urban Christians*, 25.

84. Baus, *Handbook*, 91.

85. Barbara Watterson, *The Gods of Ancient Egypt* (London: B. T. Batsford, 1984), 89.

86. R. E. Witt, "The Importance of Isis for the Fathers," *Studia Patristica* 8, part 2, 135–45 (Berlin: Akademie-Verlag, 1966), 135–36.

87. Tran Tam Tinh, "Sarapis and Isis," in *Jewish and Christian Self-Definition*, vol. 3: *Self-Definition in the Greco-Roman World*, ed. Ben F. Meyer and E. P. Sanders (Philadelphia: Fortress Press, 1982), 103.

88. Quoted by R. E. Witt, *Isis in the Graeco-Roman World* (Ithaca, N.Y.: Cornell University Press, 1971), 149.

89. MacMullen, *Pagansim*, 161.

90. Tram tan Tinh, "Sarapis and Isis," 115. This author provides a useful discussion on the roots of the appeal of the two interlocked cults (111–16) and analyzes five in particular: (1) dreams and miracles; (2) asceticism; (3) mysticism; (4) religious ceremonies; and (5) divine inconography.

91. Gritz, *Mother Goddess at Ephesus*, 36.

92. Tram tan Tinh, "Sarapis and Isis," 115.

93. Quoted by Wayne A. Meeks, *Urban Christians*, 25, who is skeptical that the ancient followers of the goddess read such expressions as carrying the connotations assumed by twentieth century writers.

94. Quoted by Howard C. Kee, *Medicine, Miracle, and Magic in New Testament Times* (Cambridge: Cambridge University Press, 1986), 68.

95. The quotation and the generalization come from H. S. Versnel, *Inconsistencies in Greek and Roman Religion I: Ter Unus–Isis, Dionysos, Hermes: Three Studies in Henotheism* (Leiden: E. J. Brill, 1990), 46.

96. Quoted in ibid., 47. The exception was Apollo but even he normally had to accomplish this by trading another life for the one saved (see ibid., 48).

97. Ibid., 47.

98. Richard M. Krill, "Roman Paganism Under the Antonies and Severans," in *Aufstieg und Niedergang der Romischen Welt* (Berlin: Walter de Gruyter, 1978), 34.

99. We read in one document, "Thrason, you have in full the upshot of your Fate; not as Fate desired, but against the will of Fate: for I change the Fate" (quoted by Versnel, *Greek and Roman Religion*, 47).

100. Krill, "Roman Paganism," 34.

101. For a study of the subject see G. H. Horsley, "Invitations to the *Kline* of Sarapis," in Horsley, *New Documents Illustrating Early Christianity*, 1:5–9.

102. Ibid., 5–6.

103. Ibid., 7, for examples.

104. Horsley (ibid., 7) considers the meetings to have been exclusively for members, yet he also makes reference to this Pauline text (9), apparently missing the implication this passage carries against an exclusive members-only meal policy at the temples. Further complicating the situation is that we do not know the degree to which customary practice may have varied from one polytheistic sect to another and from community to community.

## 6. REGAL PERGAMON: THE CITY'S CIVIC MONUMENTS AND POLYTHEISTIC RELIGIONS

1. The history is treated briefly in many places, including Meinardus, *Patmos*, 77–79, and Ramsay, *Seven Churches*, 281–83.

2. On the circumstances leading to the ultimate shift, see Ramsay, *Seven Churches*, 296.

3. M. Rostovtzeff, *The Social and Economic History of the Roman Empire*, 2d ed., rev. P. M. Fraser (Oxford: Clarendon Press, 1957), 701.

4. Toksoz, *Travel Guide*, 95.

5. Magie, *Asia Minor*, 1422, discusses the evidence that the great fire simply provided a public relations excuse for an existing policy.

6. Ibid., 564.

7. Quoted by Meinardus, *Patmos*, 79.

8. Pausanias, *Pausanias' Guide to Greece*, 321 n.36 (Levi translation).

9. Geoffrey Rickman, *The Corn Supply of Ancient Rome* (Oxford: Clarendon Press, 1980), 119.

10. K. D. White, *Greek and Roman Technology* (Ithaca, N.Y.: Cornell University Press, 1984), 162.

11. Toksoz, *Pergamum: Its History and Archaeology*, trans. Ahmet E. Uysal (Ankara [Turkey]: Ayvildiz Matbaasi, 1960), 4.

12. Penreath, *Hellenic Traveller*, 235.

13. On its discovery and contents see J. M. Cook, *The Greeks–In Ionia and the East* (New York: Frederick A. Praeger, Publisher, 1963), 191–95.

14. Ibid., 191.

15. Cf. the observations of Jones, *Greek City*, 213, on the municipal role in road building in Greek cities.

16. Cook, *Greeks*, 191–92.

17. Ibid., 192–94, sums up these regulations.

18. Ibid., 194.

19. Ibid.

20. Ibid., 194–95.

21. On the history of the facility see Akurgal, *Ancient Civilizations*, 73.

22. Ibid., 83, Yamamuchi, *New Testament Cities*, 38, Stephens, *Pictures*, 84, all hold to the ten thousand figure; Cemil Toksoz accepts the larger one, *Travel Guide*, 103.

23. Yamauchi, *New Testament Cities*, 38. For a photograph, see page 37.

24. Toksoz, *Travel Guide*, 103.

25. Akurgal, Ancient *Civilizations*, 104, mentions both and their respective size. Helen H. Miller, *Bridge to Asia*, 234 refers to the thirty-thousand-person capacity theater and Cemil Toksoz, *Travel Guide*, 97, to the fifty-thousand-seat one.

26. On the origin of the amphitheater see Toksoz, *Travel Guide*, 95, 97. On its capacity see Miller, *Bridge to Asia*, 234; Toksoz, *Pergamum*, 11, 15; Toksoz, *Travel Guide*, 95; cf. 97

27. MacKendrick, *Greek Stones Speak*, 468.

28. See Humphrey's discussion in *Roman Circuses: Arenas for Chariot Racing* (Berkeley and Los Angeles: University of California Press, 1986), 526. Cemil Toksoz apparently has the same interpretation, for he refers to the existence of "a large circus" in both *Travel Guide*, 97, and *Pergamum* (15).

29. Martin Robertson, *A History of Greek Art*, vol. 1 (Cambridge: Cambridge University Press, 1975), 529; Robbins, *Revelation*, 62.

30. Toksoz, *Travel Guide*, 100. William H. Stephens, *Pictures*, 84, refers to it as a small scale copy of the Parthenon's statue of Athena.

31. Toksoz, *Travel Guide*, 100.

32. The 12,500 figure is adopted by Yamauchi, *New Testament Cities*, 36. The 17,000 estimate is from Zophia Archibald, *Discovering the World of the Ancient Greeks* (New York: Facts on File, 1991), 171. Akurgal prefers a figure of 15,000 (minimum) (*Ancient Civilizations*, 80).

33. Akurgal, *Ancient Civilizations*, 62; Robbins, *Revelation*, 62; Stephens, *Pictures*, 58; Yamauchi, *New Testament Cities*, 36.

34. Akurgal, *Ancient Civilizations*, 80. William H. Stephens, *Pictures*, 84, believes the transfer effort was carried out.

35. Parthian documents were maintained on parchment at least as far back as c. 195 B.C. Hence Pergamon's role was not so much *invention* as popularization. See Richard R. Johnson, "Ancient and Medieval Accounts of the 'Invention' of Parchment," *California Studies in Classical Antiquity*, 3:117–18.

36. On the traditional story and the repercussions of Egyptian hostility see George E. Bean, *Aegean Turkey*, 75. Johnson ("Ancient and Medieval Accounts of the 'Invention' of Parchment," 115–17) argues that the most likely time for the reported Egyptian prohibition of papyri exports was between 173 and 168 B.C. He argues that since this was a period of war, siege, and recuperation in Egypt, a dramatic decline of papyri shipments was inevitable. This does not rule out, however, a conscious intent to minimize exports of the limited amounts available. If someone must suffer, who better than one's perceived enemies?

37. Yamauchi, *New Testament Cities*, 38.

38. M. I. Finley, *Atlas of Classical Archaeology* (New York: McGraw-Hill Book Company, 1977), 206.

39. Akurgal, *Ancient Civilizations*, 95–96; cf Yamauchi, *New Testament Cities*, 39–40.

40. Toksoz, *Travel Guide*, 103–4.

41. As does Yamauchi, *New Testament Cities*, 38.

42. Ibid., 41, speaks of a population of 20,000 in the second century B.C. Hanfmann, *From Croesus to Constantine*, 49, uses the same number in a

context of second century A.D. or earlier. W. T. Arnold, *The Roman System of Provincial Administration*, 3d ed., rev. E. S. Bouchier (Oxford: Oxford University Press, 1914; reprint, Chicago: Ares Publishers, 1974), 166, uses it in regard to the third century A.D. The second century A.D. physician Galen is read as providing this size a population by Trevett, *Ignatius*, 37. Hanfmann does likewise, though he concedes that "this may [refer to] the entire *polis* territory, not just the urban area" (George M. A. Hanfmann, Fikret K. Yegul, and John S. Crawford, "The Roman and Late Antique Period," in Hanfmann and Mierse, *Sardis: From Prehistoric to Roman Times–Results of the Archaeological Exploration of Sardis, 1958–1975*, 146.

43. Clive Foss, "Byzantine Cities of Western Asia Minor" (Ph.D. diss., Harvard University, 1972), 239. Cemil Toksoz, *Travel Guide*, takes Galen's remarks to mean that "40,000 were natives and 120,000 foreigners." Ramsay MacMullen, "Late Roman Slavery," 362, implicitly accepts a population of 160,000, for he takes the reference to 40,000 by Galen as representing one-quarter of the total population.

44. Freys Stark, *Rome on the Euphrates*, 221, refers to the population being "over" 200,000. In three different ways T. R. S. Broughton ("Roman Asia") comes up with such a figure. In one place he implies that the population was near that figure by saying that it "rivalled" the 200,000 of Ephesus (816). In another (749), he speaks of it being "perhaps" this number. In a third context he again derives a similar figure. The root from which he works is Galen's own estimate: "If then our citizens amount to as many as 40,000, likewise if you add their wives and slaves, you will find yourself admitting that you are richer than 120,000 people" (quoted, 812). Compare how the writers above interpret this assertion by Galen. Assuming an average of two children in each family, Boughton then arrives at a population estimate of 200,000 people (813).

By working from Galen's numbers and adding in non-adult children of both genders, Stephen Mitchell, *Celts*, 243–44, arrives at a figure of 180,000–200,000. Without providing a specific explanation for the figure, Paul Trebilco also endorses the figure of 180,000–200,000 ("Asia," 2:307 n.68).

45. Richard Duncan-Jones, in *The Economy of the Roman Empire: Quantitative Studies*, 2d ed, (Cambridge: Cambridge University Press, 1982), 261, puts the second century A.D. figure as 180,000, including children.

46. J. C. Russell argues that the 160 hectares included within Pergamon had only twenty-four thousand people at the very most (*Population*, 80–81). Russell believes that Galen's much larger figure included "perhaps the total area dependent upon Pergamum" rather than the city in its strictest sense (81). Other alternatives are that Rus-

sell unduly underestimates the population concentration or that Pergamon as *popularly* defined included a broader geographic area than he concedes, though not necessarily as broad a region as all those areas he calls "dependent" upon the municipality.

47. Ramsay, *Seven Churches*, 284; John F. Walvoord, *The Revelation of Jesus Christ* (Chicago: Moody Press, 1966), 65. Alan F. Johnson considers the two most important ones to have been those of Dionysius and Asclepius (*Revelation*, 47).

48. Whiting, *Revelation*, 78.

49. Kraeling, *Atlas*, 468. In a similar vein, J. Massyngberde Ford (*Revelation*, 399), speaks of how her temple "crowned the acropolis." On her importance, cf. Stephens, *Pictures*, 84. For an in-depth study of the worship of Athena, from a "mainland" Greece perspective, see the essays in Jenifer Neils, ed., *Worshipping Athena: Panathenaia and Parthenon* (Madison, Wis.: University of Wisconsin Press, 1996).

50. John A. Hanson, *Roman Theater-Temples* (Princeton, N.J.: Princeton University Press, 1959), 36.

51. Toksoz, *Pergamum*, 24; idem, *Travel Guide*, 102.

52. Akurgal, *Ancient Civilizations*, 71. Akurgal believes that such social comforts came first and overt religion second. Although one can see some justice in this—the more elaborate the facility was—must one strip out *all* creature comforts to guarantee religion a dominant role?

53. Rostovtzeff, *Roman Empire*, 656.

54. Quoted by John Ferguson, *Greek and Roman Religion–A Source Book* (Park Ridge, N.J.: Noyes Press, 1980), 50. Cf. a different translation of the document found in Frederick C. Grant, *Hellenistic Religions: The Age of Syncretism* (Indianapolis, Ind.: Bobbs-Merrill Company, 1953), 6.

55. Ramsay, *Seven Churches*, 284–85; Whiting, *Revelation*, 77.

56. Ibid., 285.

57. Alan F. Johnson, *Revelation*, 47.

58. Lietzman, *Early Church*, 160; Ramsay, *Seven Churches*, 285; Whiting, *Revelation*, 77.

59. Lietzman, *Early Church*, 160.

60. MacMullen, *Paganism*, 151.

61. Archibald, *Ancient Greeks*, 170.

62. Akurgal, *Ancient Civilizations*, 71 (on its size) and 73 (on its rebuilding). On its destruction and reconstruction also see Toksoz, *Travel Guide*, 103.

63. Ekrem Arugał, *Ancient Civlizations*, 85.

64. Finegan, *Archaeology*, 173.

65. Yamauchi, *New Testament Cities*, 43.

66. Toksoz, *Travel Guide*, 97–98.

67. Akurgal, *Ancient Civilizations*, 104; Finegan, *Archaeology*, 173

68. Akurgal, *Ancient Civilizations*, 104.

69. Finegan, *Archaeology*, 173; Yamauchi, *New Testament Cities*, 43.

70. Ekrem Akurgal refers to it as a Sarapis worship site (*Ancient Civilizations*, 103) but then (104) implies that it is an inferential attribution rather than a certain one.

71. Robert A. Wild ("Isis-Sarapis Sanctuaries," 1805–7) argues that the type of finds that have been discovered have never previously been detected at a confirmable Sarapis temple; they are only found at sites dedicated to Isis. A drawing of the site and adjoining sites is included between pages 1806 and 1807.

72. Helmut Koester, "The Red Hall in Pergamon," in *The Social World of the First Christians: Essays in Honor of Wayne A. Meeks*, ed. L. Michael White and O. Larry Yarbrough, 265–74 (Minneapolis: Fortress Press, 1995), See his entire chapter for a detailed discussion of the hall and the adjoining complex.

73. An inscription dated between 260 and 245 B.C. refers to how the Pergamonese local governmental assembly desired to honor the five magistrates appointed by the emperor Eumenes:

> And in order that the demos may be clear in its support for Eumenes with regard to these men, be it resolved by the demos: to crown them at the Panathenaia with a gold crown on account of their virtue and their good-will toward Eumenes and the demos; and let the treasurers appointed for a year always give them a sheep at the Eumeneia, and *let them take it and sacrifice it to Eumenes Euergetes [the Benefactor]*, in order that the demos may be clear to all in its gratitude.

For the entire text and a discussion of what it implies for both local self-government and emperor worship, see Peter S. Bagnall and Peter Derow, *Greek Historical Documents: The Hellenistic Period*, SBL Sources for Biblical Study 16 (Chico, Calif.: Scholars Press for the Society of Biblical Literature, 1981), 115–16. This volume provides numerous extracts of ancient documents discussing then-contemporary events and problems, including a few concerning specific Asian cities such as Ephesus, Pergamon, and Smyrna.

74. Isager Signe, "Kings and Gods in the Seleucid Empire: A Question of Landed Property," in *Religion and Religious Practice in the Seleucid Kingdom*, ed. Per Bilde, et al. ([Denmark]: Aarhus University Press, 1990), 88.

75. Ford, *Revelation*, 399.

76. E. M. Blaiklock, *The Seven Churches: An Exposition of Revelation Chapters Two and Three* (London: Marshall, Morgan and Scott, 19–), 33.

77. Yamauchi, *New Testament Cities*, 42.

78. Ibid., 42; Toksoz, *Travel Guide*, 102.

79. Toksoz, *Travel Guide*, 102.

80. Yamauchi, *New Testament Cities*, 42.

81. Toksoz, *Travel Guide*, 102.

82. S. R. F. Price, *Rituals and Power: The Roman Imperial Cult in Asia Minor* (Cambridge: Cambridge University Press, 1984), 209.

83. Ibid., 90; cf. 209.

84. Quoted by Napthali Lewis, *Greek Historical Documents–The Roman Principate: 27 B.C.-285 A.D.* (Toronto: A. M. Hakkert Ltd., 1974), 125; for a lengthy translated extract sce 125–26.

85. MacMullen, *Paganism*, 150.

86. For these examples of dual duty, see ibid., 149, cf. 17.

87. On the Demeter site see Toksoz, *Pergamum*, 27; Yamauchi, *New Testament Cities*, 43. Cf. Susan Guettel Cole, "Demeter in the Ancient Greek City and Its Countryside," in *Placing the Gods: Sanctuaries and Sacred Space in Ancient Greece*, ed. Susan E. Alcock and Robin Osborne, 199–216 (Oxford: Clarendon Press, 1994), 214. On Demeter worship as it existed in Greece proper, see this entire essay.

88. On the Hera site see Toksoz, *Pergamum*, 27.

89. Ferguson, *Religions*, 29, notes that in the early Pergamon account the rite "implies not a sacrifice or baptism, but something more akin to a rodeo, and the lassoing of a wild buffalo, or something of the kind." In its fourth-century, fully developed form, a bull is slaughtered and the blood drips down to cover the celebrant.

90. Bean, *Aegean Turkey*, 83. For a detailed examination of contemporary claims of miraculous healing at the healing shrine at Epidauros, see Lynn R. LiDonnici, *The Epidaurian Miracle Inscriptions: Text, Translation, and Commentary* (Atlanta, Ga.: Scholars Press, 1995).

91. Plutarch, *Quaestiones Romane*, 94, as quoted by Walter A. Jayne, *The Healing Gods of Ancient Civilizations* (1925; reprint, New Hyde Park, N.Y.: University Books, 1962), 256.

92. Rose, *Greek Mythology*, 139. The latter appears to represent a better reading of the evidence.

93. The famous fifth-century Greek physician Hippocrates provides one of the occasional departures from this image. In a vision Asclepius appeared "with animated gesture, fearsome to behold." Huge snakes accompanied him and travel companies carried "very tightly bound boxes of drugs. Then the god stretched out his hand to me; I took it joyfully and besought him to join me and not to neglect my ministrations. But he said, 'At present you have no need of me, but this goddess [i.e., Truth], whom immortals and mortals share, will be your guide....'

And the divinity departed" (Hippocrates, *Letters*, 15, as quoted by David G. Rice and John E. Stambaugh, *Sources for the Study of Greek Religion* (Missoula, Mont.: Scholars Press, 1979), 72. For other source documents concerning the cult see pages 69–80 of the same work.

94. Michael Vickers, *Roman World*, 2nd ed. (New York: Peter Bedrick Books, 1989), 123.

95. Akurgal, *Ancient Civilizations*, 105.

96. Bluma L. Trell, *Temple of Artemis*, 39–40, discusses which building was represented.

97. Philostratus, *Life of Apollonius*, IV.11.

98. Kenneth Scott, *Imperial Cult*, 138, cites this act to show the pandering to imperial egos that occurred even among the most gifted: Martial wrote several poems in Earinus's honor. In one he confidently asserted that Pergamon would rather have the hair-locks of Earinus than those of the deity Ganymede! The praise, of course, was aimed at Domitian, who is pictured as being served by one greater than some of the gods. So how much greater must Domitian be than his godlike servant!

99. Berrett, *Discovering*, 615.

100. Yamauchi, *New Testament Cities*, 48. For a reconstruction of the layout of the facility after the changes in the mid-second century A.D., see Vickers, *Roman World*, 124. For another reconstruction/model see C. Kerenyi, *Asklepios: Archetypal Image of the Physician's Existence*, trans. Ralph Manheim (New York: Pantheon Books, 1959), 45.

101. Ekrem Akurgal, *Ancient Civilizations*, 105.

102. Ibid., 106–7; Toksoz, *Pergamum*, 12; Yamauchi, *New Testament Cities*, 48.

103. Akurgal, *Ancient Civilizations*, 107; Finegan, *Archaeology*, 174; MacMullen, *Paganism*, 20; Yamauchi, *New Testament Cities*, 48. Cemil Toksoz (*Pergamum*, 13, and *Travel Guide*, 97) estimates a seating capacity of five thousand.

104. Akurgal, *Ancient Civilizations*, 110.

105. Ibid., 110.

106. Berrett, *Discovering*, 615.

107. Akurgal, *Ancient Civilizations*, 107; Yamauchi, *New Testament Cities*, 48.

108. Ramsay MacMullen and Eugene N. Lane provide this dating and description in their *Paganism and Christianity, 100–425 C.E.–A Sourcebook* (Minneapolis: Fortress Press, 1992), 31–32.

109. Ibid., 32.

110. Vickers, *Roman World*, 123.

111. Sherman E. Johnson, "Asia Minor and Early Christianity," in

*Christianity, Judaism and Other Greco-Roman Cults: Studies for Morton Smith at Sixty*, vol. 2, ed. Jacob Neusner (Leiden: E. J. Brill, 1975), 81. Johnson bases this description on the fact that while ancient records refer to a multitude of miracles at the Epidaurus shrine, reference to such happenings at Pergamon "are quite infrequent."

112. Howard C. Kee, *Understanding the New Testament*, 4th ed. (Englewood Cliffs, N.J.: Prentice-Hall, 1983), 30.

113. Howard C. Kee, ("Self-Definition in the Asclepius Cult," in *Jewish and Christian Self-Definition*, vol. 3: *Self-Definition in the Greco-Roman World*, ed. Ben F. Meyer and E. P. Sanders [Philadelphia: Fortress Press, 1982]) cites Rhodes and Cyrene as places where apparent surgical tools have been uncovered at the god's shrines (212 provides a list of such sites). The total lack of such finds at Pergamon argues that reliance was strictly upon natural and miraculous methods rather than surgical ones (129).

114. Andre-Jean Festugiere, *Personal Religion Among the Greeks* (Berkeley and Los Angeles: University of California Press, 1954), 89–90. Festugiere provides lengthy translations from Aristides's *Hieroi Logoi (Sacred Discourses)*, 84–104. This is particularly useful since, as he notes, "there exists no modern translation" of the work (87).

115. Jayne, *Healing Gods*, 283.

116. Akurgal, *Ancient Civilizations;* Ferguson, *Religions*, 111.

117. Marcus Aurelius, V.8,1, quoted by Festugiere, *Personal Religion*, 91.

118. Galen, *de san. tuenda* I.8, 19–21, trans. and quoted by Festugiere, *Personal Religion*, 91–92.

119. For a collection of ancient texts related to the Asclepius cult (and their English translation), see Emma J. Edelstein and Ludwig Edelstein, *Asclepius: A Collection and Interpretation of the Testimonies*, vol. 1 (Baltimore: John Hopkins Press, 1945). These are collected from a variety of cites and cover various aspects of the cult including the purported miraculous and non-miraculous cures. References to the center at Pergamon are found scattered throughout, but especially on pages 405–17. For a collection of healing claims by those attending the Ascelpius shrine at Epidauros (and an analysis of them), see Lynn R. LiDonnici, "Epidaurian Miracles Cures," in *Society of Biblical Literature 1988 Seminar Papers*, ed. David J. Lull (Atlanta, Ga.: Scholars Press, 1988), 272–76.

120. MacMullen and Lane, *Paganism and Christianity*, 31.

121. Galenus, *Subfiguratio Empirica*, as cited in Edelstein and Edelstein, *Asclepius*, 250.

122. Rufus, a first century physician, as quoted by Oribasius, *col-*

*lectiones Medicae*, as cited in Greek and English translation by Emma J. Edelstein and Ludwig Edelstein, *Asclepius*, 239.

123. Kerenyi, *Asklepios*, 74.

124. For a discussion of the various aspects of the *Asklepieia* see Jayne, 297–98.

### 7. REGAL PERGAMON: DIVIDED CHRISTIANITY AND SOCIETAL ALLUSIONS IN JOHN'S MINI-EPISTLE

1. A. R. C. Leaney, *The Jewish and Christian World, 200 B.C. to A.D. 200* (Cambridge: Cambridge University Press, 1984), 35.

2. Adela Y. Collins, *Crisis and Catharsis: The Power of the Apocalypse* (Philadelphia: Westminster Press, 1984), 102.

3. Donald L. Jones, "Roman Imperial Cult," 1034.

4. E. W. Hengstenberg *(The Revelation of St. John)* argues that the name is used symbolically rather than as reference to an actual individual named Antipas: the name means "one who is against all" and since the name Timothy means "fear God" and one cannot truly do that without "standing forth against the world" (i.e., being an Antipas), *Timothy* is the individual actually martyred (179–80).

He backs up this once-popular assertion (179) with two basic arguments. First, he contends that "all other names in the Apocalypse are of a symbolical character" and as evidence he cites the examples of Jezebel and the Nicolatians (179). On the other hand, should we take John itself as a symbolic name? Furthermore, although it can serve both tactical purposes (to lower the status of an opponent by giving him a nasty epithet) and practical ones as well (not to elevate the prestige of a false teacher by applying his name to the movement), one finds it hard to see where any purpose would be solved by disguising the name of a valiant and orthodox hero of the faith.

Second, "in a period of general bloody persecution, only such a person could be specially noticed as occupied an important position in the church—one who enjoyed an apostolical, or almost apostolical dignity." No martyr of such a status is reliably known from the first century (179). This starts from a highly questionable assumption (a general violent persecution) and then reads into the text an explanation that will fit with that assumption. If we reverse the approach and *begin* with the text itself then the evidence is that there had been only *one* martyr in the city rather than a massive bloodletting. In such a case, the alleged insignificance and obscurity of the individual would be irrelevant: his name would be preserved simply because he was the sole person who suffered death. Hengstenberg's approach suffers from a severe ethical defect: it makes the importance of a marytrdom derive from one's church status rather than one's holy character and/or the particular circumstances under which one died.

5. A. N. Sherwin-White develops this theme in "The Early Persecutions and Roman Law Again," *Journal of Theological Studies* 3 (1952):199–213, especially 212–13.

6. I have not found this view actually advocated during the research for this book, but it would seem to be a logical reading of the text not heretofore carefully investigated.

7. For example, Mounce, *Waiting*, 9. Harry R. Boer notes that this "view has been generally accepted to the present day" but adds the caution, "but it does remain a supposition" (*The Book of Revelation* [Grand Rapids, Mich.: Wm. B. Eerdmans Publishing Company, 1979], 31). My own research in the commentaries did not seem to support the approach being this prevalent.

8. A further complication is that the existence of two groups does not necessarily mean that both were present in Pergamon. John's point could be that the strictly Pergamonese Balaamite movement held to the same immoral doctrine of the Nicolaitans. If so, the underlying argument would probably be that they recognized the Nicolaitan heresy to be just that but were blind to the same fundamental attitudes when they appeared under a different label in their own congregation.

9. Krodel, *Revelation*, 115.

10. Boring, *Revelation*, 92. Actually, the biblical text does not explicitly describe the doctrine of the Nicolaitans. The assumption that they are identical is derived from Revelation 2:16, but the presence of the word "also" in that verse seems to argue both for this *and* for their existence as two distinct heretical groupings.

11. Barclay, *Revelation*, 66.

12. Merrill F. Unger notes that "some take this symbolism, however, as indicating the origin of clericalism (*nikao*, 'conquer,' and *laos*, 'people'), making them a group that early favored a clerical system which later developed into the papal hierarchy" (*Handbook*, 652). John's accusations, however, concern moral conduct not church organizational structure.

13. Margaret N. Ralph discusses Paul's views and insists that "the author of the book of Revelation would have disagreed with Paul's reasoning" (*Discovering the First Century Church: The Acts of the Apostles, Letters of Paul and the Book of Revelation* [New York: Paulist Press, 1991], 238).

14. New Zealand scholar E. M. Blaiklock expresses this fact very well:

It is difficult for a modern Christian to grasp the pervasive nature of the paganism with which his spiritual forebears had to deal. Many pages in Tertullian reveal vividly the practical difficulties which at every turn confronted the Christian in the ancient world. "Why even the streets and the market-places," he writes (*De Spectaculis*, 8), "the baths and the taverns and our very dwelling-places, are not altogether free from idols. Satan and his angels have filled the whole world."

It was worse than this. The conscientious Christian had to absent himself from public festivals. They opened with pagan adoration and sacrifice. His membership of a trade guild, and in consequence his commercial standing and goodwill, involved the awkwardness of "sitting at meat in the idol's temple." His very shopping raised the problem of meat which had been sacrificed to idols [and which was sold in the marketplace]. (*The Christian in Pagan Society*, the Tyndale New Testament Lecture for 1951 [London: The Tyndale Press, n.d.], 19–20)

15. Blaiklock, ibid., sees these as trade-guild meetings, presumably on the basis of various guilds feeling that they had a special relation to certain deities, but it should be remembered that these facilities were also available on a wider basis to individuals who were connected with the cult.

16. The eating of meats offered to idols was but one aspect of the pagan customs a Christian had to come to terms with even on such seemingly innocent occasions. E. M. Blaiklock (*Seven Churches*, 19) reminds us that "the simplest rules of polite conduct had pagan associations. To dine with a neighbor meant to witness, condone, or share, his libation to the gods. It was a simple matter. One flicked the dregs of the wine cup on the floor with a brief and mechanical prayer. Was the Christian involved?"

17. Charles F. Pfeiffer and Howard F. Vos, *Historical Geography*, 396, limit the evil to "Christians marrying pagans and thus defiling their separation to God (Nm 31:15–16; 22:5; 23:8)." In a similar vein, John F. Walvoord, *Revelation*, 68, has the name utilized to describe the group because both encouraged intermarriage and the resulting idolatry. However, marriage is normally regarded in both testaments as the solution to sexual misbehavior rather than itself being sexual misbehavior. The temptation to fornication and adultery seems far more likely to be in John's mind; this was *always* regarded as wrong while marriage was *normally* always right. And Paul explicitly accepts the legitimacy of believer-unbeliever marriages (1 Cor 7:10–14); Peter has a similar attitude (1 Pt 3:1–2). Peter's epistle explicitly includes the Christians of Asia among its targeted recipients (1:1).

18. Homer Hailey considers "Satan's throne" to have been used because Pergamon was the provincial capital, it was the location of many "pagan deities," and the imperial cult was present (*Revelation*, 130). Harry R. Boer finds a reference to the Zeus altar, the Asclepius temple, and the imperial cult temple (*Revelation*, 32). George W. McDaniel combines the city's provincial capital status, with the presence of so many religions, with it being a major educational center (*The Churches of the New Testament* [New York: Richard R. Smith, 1921; 1930 printing], 272).

19. This is implicit in the remarks of Sherman E. Johnson, "Asia Minor," 93. George A. Barton, *Archaeology*, 268, grounds the label in the city's capital status and its rule as a cultic center of emperor worship. The same double reference is adopted by Charles C. Whiting, *Revelation*, 78–79. Charles Brown, *Heavenly Visions*, 70, makes the attribution while conceding the possibility that other reasons may be involved as well. George E. Bean, *Aegean Turkey*, 77, roots the image in the city's capital status but, in seemingly direct contradiction, also claims that "the most likely" explanation is to "the temple of Rome and Augustus."

20. Austin Farrer, *The Revelation of St. John the Divine* (Oxford: Clarendon Press, 1964), 73.

21. Collins, *Apocalypse*, 19. Cf. her remarks on the courtly interpretation below.

22. Adela Y. Collins, *Crisis and Catharsis*, 101. Bernhard Weis does not attempt to define the throne of Satan but describes its power as *manifested* through the "Gentile supreme court" located there (*Revelation*, 397). Colin J. Hemer, *Local Setting*, 37, sees the role of the government "as enforc[ing]" the imperial cult as the main reason for the reference. Since Antipas's death is mentioned in the same verse and since both that and John's exile were judicially decreed injustices, the rebuke of being Satan's throne would be a natural outgrowth of the internal psychology of the text. Shirley J. Case connects the expression to the repeated stress on persecution in Revelation. He implies that the imperial cult played a key role in stirring up such strife and thereby manifested "Satan's presence upon earth" (*The Revelation of John: A Historical Interpretation* [Chicago: University of Chicago Press, 1919], 220). Charles F. Pfeiffer and Howard F. Vos, *Historical Geography*, 395–96, allude to this linkage but ground the description in the broader generalization of the presence of the imperial cult.

Donald Guthrie finds "corroborative evidence supporting" the description as an outgrowth of persecution because of refusal to engage in emperor worship: This "may be present in the description of the Risen Christ as having a double-edged sword, since the proconsul would have had the right to such a word (*ius gladii*). In this way the

Christians were assured that the ultimate sovereignty did not rest with Rome" (*Apocalypse*, 77–78).

23. Kraeling, *Atlas*, 468. Kraeling implies that the secondary reason was the importance of the imperial cult to the city.

24. Stated without qualification as the explanation: James M. Efird, *Revelation for Today* (Nashville, Tenn.: Abingdon Press, 1989), 56; W. H. Boulton, *Archaeology Explains* (London: Epworth Press, 1952; 1953 reprint), 91; Boring, *Revelation*, 91; Krodel, *Revelation*, 115; Loane, *They Overcame*, 59; Turner, *Early Church History*, 203.

This scenario is described as "probably" the correct one by Morris Ashcroft, "Revelation," in *The Broadman Bible Commentary*, vol. 12: *Hebrews-Revelation* (Nashville, Tenn.: Broadman Press, 1972), 267 (and constitutes a "better explanation" than that of the Asclepius cult); Beckwith, *Apocalypse*, 458; Bruce, "Revelation," 638; Franzmann, *Revelation*, 43; Robbins, *Revelation*, 63; Thompson, *Archaeology*, 418.

The same conclusion is reached, using different terminology, by Fred D. Howard ("almost certainly," *Revelation*, 62); George Eldon Ladd ("most likely," *A Commentary on the Revelation of John* [Grand Rapids, Mich.: Wm. B. Eerdmans Publishing Company, 1972], 46); Mounce ("best understood," *Revelation*, 96). T. F. Glasson more moderately asserts only that this "may explain the description" (*The Revelation of John*, Cambridge Bible Commentary [Cambridge: Cambridge University Press, 1965], 27); since no other possibilities are presented this creates a de facto probable explanation. The same selection by sole mentioning is also the case in Gonzalo Baez-Camargo (*Archaeological Commentary*, 263) and G. Ernest Wright, *Biblical Archaeology*, 273.

25. Cited as the explanation by Donald L. Jones, "Roman Imperial Cult," 1034, and as a partial explanation by Hugh J. Schonfield, *The Bible Was Right*, 228. William Barclay goes so far as to assert that "undoubtedly [this] is why Pergamum was Satan's seat" (*Revelation*, 90).

26. Hugh J. Schonfield, *The Bible Was Right*, 228, cites terminological evidence for the propriety of Satan's throne as an epithet these archaeological findings, "The temple is depicted on coins issued by the Commune of Asia with the inscription ROMA. ET. AUG. Other inscriptions found at Pergamum refer to the cult of 'the god Augustus.' One on a marble pedestal reads, 'The Emperor, Caesar, Son of a God, the God Augustus, Overseer of every land and sea.'" Yet the imperial cult was pervasive. We would expect to find similar evidence in *any* major city. Again, what made Pergamon different, to be singled out for special condemnation?

27. Asserted but without mentioning either of the two supporting reasons following in this sentence: R. H. Charles, *Revelation*, vol. 1:

International Critical Commentary series (Edinburgh: T. & T. Clark, 1920; 1979 reprint); Meinardus, *Ephesus*, 73; C. Anderson Scott, *The Book of the Revelation* (New York: George H. Doran Company, n.d.), 85. Raymond Calkins seems to have this in mind as well in his vaguer remark that "this is an undoubted...reference to Pergamum as the seat of emperor-worship in Asia Minor" (*Social Message*, 60). Leon Morris, *Revelation*, 66, roots his argument in the "pre-eminence" of the cult in the city; other cities had major centers of Zeus and Asclepius worship, but Pergamon was a major center of imperial worship.

28. Citing the presence of an imperial temple in connection with the identification are Richard L. Jeske, *Revelation for Today: Images of Hope* (Philadelphia: Fortress Press, 1983), 46; Cady H. Allen, *The Message of the Book of Revelation* (Nashville, Tenn.: Cokesbury Press, 1939), 68; Wilson, *Handbook*, 87. Just as referring the expression to the imperial temple makes the allusion more specific than an allusion to the imperial cult (or emperor worship), Michael Grant makes the allusion even *more* specific by suggesting that "perhaps [it refer to] the altar of the imperial cult in that city" (*The Jews in the Roman World* [New York: Charles Scribner's Sons, 1973], 227). W. C. Friend refers the allusion to the presence of the "Temple of Augustus" and the Zeus altar (*Martyrdom and Persecution*, 194).

29. Lily Ross Taylor, *The Divinity of the Roman Emperor* (Middletown: American Philological Association, 1931; reprint, Philadelphia, Pa.: Porcupine Press, 1975), 244, notes that we lack details of the process of reasoning that led them to make such claims. (She does not discuss the meaning of the phrase in question.)

30. Evamaria Schmidt, *The Great Altar of Pergamon* (Boston: Boston Book and Art Shop, 1965), 5. This book contains a detailed description and many large illustrations of the altar and adjoining frieze.

31. Burford, *Craftsmen*, 96.

32. Cf. the remarks on this theme of Giovanni Becatti, *The Arts of Ancient Greece and Rome–From the Rise of Greece to the Fall of Rome*, trans. John Ross (Englewood Cliffs, N.J.: Prentice-Hall, 1967), 264. Ekrem Akurgal is even more cynical in that he considered the edifice as being primarily a war memorial "to a victory won by the Kingdom" (*Ancient Civilizations*, 71) of Pergamon over Galatia (73). The religious element is regarded as purely secondary.

33. J. T. Pollitt, *The Art of Ancient Greece: Sources and Documents* (Cambridge: Cambridge University Press, 1990), 114, refers to this fact and then proceeds to quote the short second-century reference by Ampelius, "At Pergamon there is a great marble altar, forty feet high,

and with extremely large sculptures; it [the sculptural decoration] consists of the battle of the giants" (*Liber Memorialis*, 8.14).

34. "So strongly original and expressive a language as that of the Pergamon altar could not fail to have a widespread influence on contemporary art," writes Giovanni Becatti, *Art of Ancient Greece*, 268. This reasonable deduction he then proceeds to document (268–71).

35. Vos, *Archaeology*, 330–31.

36. As in the case of the identification of the term with emperor worship and the imperial cult, hedging is common: Stephen Benko ("perhaps," *Pagan Rome and the Early Christians* [Bloomington: Indiana University Press, 1984], 140–41); R. K. Harrison ("may," *Archaeology*, 45, 115, reduced to the more modest "perhaps," 53); Wilfrid J. Harrington ("likely," *Revelation* [*Sacra Pagina*, volume 16] [Collegeville, Minn.:: Luturgical Press/A Michael Glazier Book, 1993], 61); Stambaugh and Balch, *Social Environment*, 153).

Those who speak without hedging include Blailkock, *Archaeology*, 58; Perowne, *Archaeology*, 124; Tarn, *Hellenistic Civilization*, 225.

37. Martin J. Price and Bluma L. Trell, *Coins and Their Cities: Architecture on the Ancient Coins of Greece, Rome, and Palestine* (Detroit: Wayne State University Press, 1977), 122. They concede that "there is no way of proving or disproving" the altar/Satan's throne identification (122). Also note their observations on possible errors in the German reconstruction of the altar that is on display in Berlin (122–23).

38. Giblin, *Revelation*, 57.

39. Robbins, *Revelation*, 62.

40. Conceded by Sweet, *Revelation*, 87, who does not believe Zeus or the altar to have been in John's mind.

41. E. M. Blailkock, *The Archaeology of the New Testament* (Grand Rapids, Mich.: Zondervan Publishing House, 1970), 126–28 seems to ground the identification on the throne argument, the use of the term *Savior*, and the use of the snake symbolism. Here he is quite firm on the linkage, going so far as to claim that "Satan's seat" "must" have represented a contemporary description of the altar. In contrast, in *Cities*, 105, he only suggests that "perhaps the altar" lies behind the terminology.

42. Cook, *Greeks*, 196.

43. This seems to be the underlying premise of Michael Avi-Yonah (*Views of the Biblical World*, vol. 5: *The New Testament* [Jerusalem: International Publishing Company, 1961], 271), who writes, "The frieze is one of the most magnificent works of Hellenistic sculpture, and the deep impression it made on even a hostile beholder is still evident from the appellation of 'Satan's seat' given it here."

Terence Kelshaw, *Message*, finds "strong support" in the overall

Revelation for the emperor/Satan identification and, hence, for the throne of Satan to mean emperor worship (90). Oddly enough, he then opts for the Zeus temple identification on grounds of its physical location higher than the other temples and the psychological impression that both its location and grandeur created (93–94).

44. Bean, *Aegean Turkey*, 77.

45. Barclay, *Revelation*, 89.

46. Ibid., 90.

47. Otto Pfleiderer, *Primitive Christianity: Its Writings and Teachings in Their Historical Connections*, vol. 3, trans W. Montgomery (London: Williams & Norgate, 1910), 415.

48. Asserted without supporting argumentation: Esther Onstad, *Courage*, 19, who considers the epithet aimed at a combination of the imperial cult and that of Asclepius.

49. Sweet, *Revelation*, 87. Sweet does not accept the Asclepius cult as being in John's mind, at least not being his "primary" frame of reference.

50. Ramsay, *Seven Churches*, 285–86. Ramsay prints a drawing of a Pergamonese coin to illustrate the snake usage: Emperor Caracalla is shown visiting the city and viewing with adoration the god Asclepius wrapped in snake form around a tree branch.

51. Sweet, *Revelation*, 87.

52. Pausanias, quoted by Blaiklock, *New Testament*, 126.

53. Swete, *Apocalypse*, 34.

54. Isbon T. Beckwith, *Apocalypse*, 458, argues that the cult was too highly developed in other Asian communities to justify describing it as a unique or special characteristic of Pergamon. He does note, however, that his view contradicts that of "a considerable number of scholars."

55. Sweet, *Revelation*, 87. Also see our discussion of the Asclepius cult in the preceding chapter.

56. Hemer, *Local Setting*, 85.

57. Guthrie, *Apocalypse*, 76.

58. Barclay, Revelation, 90.

59. Cf. Martin, *Seven Letters*, 69. Hans Lilje, *Last Book*, finds the term as "cover[ing] the whole space occupied by pagan cults" in the city (79) and "as the city of famous cults," especially the imperial one (80). Although Peter Wood's main interpretation concerns the appearance of the city to an arriving traveler, he also sees a secondary reference to the many pagan cults that functioned there ("Local Knowledge in the Letters of the Apocalypse," *Expository Times* 73 [1961–62], 264). For large color photographs of the remains of several cult sites see Eliot Porter, *The Greek World* (New York: E. P. Dutton, 1980), 85–88. G. B.

Caird, *Revelation*, 37, mentions first Asclepius and then Zeus Soter. Seeming to believe that neither alone does full justice to John's rhetoric, he seeks a more comprehensive interpretation by making it refer to "the religious monuments of Pergamum" in general.

60. Metzger, *Code*, 35.

61. Swete, *Apocalypse*, 34–35. Swete then finds drifts into more specific allusions: the "rampant paganism" becomes "symbolized by" the massive Zeus but also "chiefly perhaps...the new Caesar worship in which Pergamum was preeminent and which above all other impede the existence of the Church."

62. Frederick C. Grant, *Nelson's Bible Commentary*, vol. 7: *New Testament: Romans-Revelation* (New York: Thomas Nelson and Sons, 1962), 380, mentions both the imperial cult and Asclepius worship as important but stresses this broader phenomena.

63. Johnson, "Revelation," 440.

64. Cited and quoted by Henry Alford, *The New Testament for English Readers*, vol. 2, pt 2: *The Epistle to the Hebrews, the Catholic Epistles, and the Revelation*, new ed. (Boston: Lee and Shepard, 1880), 956.

65. W. E. Best, *Diminishing Spirituality in Local Churches: Studies in Revelation 2 and 3* (Houston, Tex.: South Belt Grace Church, 1986), 59.

66. E. W. Hengstenberg, *Revelation*, 178, cites the theory only to reject it on grounds of it being unprovable.

67. Unger, *Handbook*, 652.

68. Sweet, *Revelation*, 87 (note).

69. Beasley-Murray, *Revelation*, 84. His preferred interpretation is the Zeus altar, with this as a secondary alternative.

70. Tait, *Messages*, 225.

71. Ibid., 229.

72. Joseph A. Seiss, *Letters of Jesus* (1889; reprinted as *Letters to the Seven Churches* [Grand Rapids, Mich.: Baker Book House, 1956]), 100–101.

73. John T. Hinds, *A Commentary on the Book of Revelation* (Nashville, Tenn.: Gospel Advocate Company, 1937; 1974 reprint), 34.

74. Wood, "Local Knowledge," 264.

75. J. W. McGarvey, *Lands of the Bible* (Philadelphia: J. B. Lippincott & Company, 1881), 590–91.

76. Bean, *Aegean Turkey*, 68.

77. Ramsay, *Seven Churches*, 294.

78. Ibid., 295.

79. Ibid., 281–82.

80. Whiting, *Revelation*, 78.

81. Those making the connection between the city's capital sta-

tus and the right to exercise capital punishment are Mounce, *Waiting*, 9; and Ramsay, *Seven Churches*, 291–92. and Draper, *The Unveiling*, 54. Oddly, in discussing Satan's throne (see discussion above), Draper seems convinced that Satan was *literally* dwelling on earth and directing his operations from Pergamon! Polytheism can be accused of spiritual blindness, but such a literal reign would surely have been obvious even to the most callous minds of that age.

82. Ford, *Revelation*, 398. This applied only to capital cases, of course (Collins, *Crisis and Catharsis*, 101). He could not arbitrarily impose death for any offense that came his way. The Jesus/proconsul parallel implied relates only to the power to punish. In both John's Revelation and the remainder of the New Testament Jesus is pictured as having complete and total authority (Mt 28:18–20, for example) while a proconsul had only delegated authority. Cf. Charles W. Budden and Edward Hastings, *The Local Colour of the Bible*, vol. 3: *Matthew-Revelation* (Edinburgh: T. & T. Clark, 1925), 327.

83. Colin J. Hemer, *Local Setting*, 82–84, summarizes the evidence for both Ephesus and Pergamon and perceptively suggests that Rome may have intentionally left the situation ambiguous because of the tense civic rivalry between the two cities.

84. A reason suggested by Alan Johnson, "Revelation," 442.

85. Barclay, *Revelation*, 95.

86. Hughes, *Revelation*, 46.

87. The idea has sometimes been described as the "messianic banquet." Cf. Mounce, *Waiting*, 10.

88. Ladd, *Revelation*, 49.

89. Efird, *Revelation*, 57. He cites 2 Baruch 29:8 in particular.

90. Krodel, *Revelation*, 121.

91. John W. Court, *Myth and History in the Book of Revelation* (Atlanta, Ga.: John Knox Press, 1979), 33. Court sees a possible contrast "with food offerings in [the] imperial cult or other religious feasts" (32–33).

92. See "stone," in W. E. Vine's *Expository Dictionary of New Testament Words* (London: Oliphants, 1953).

93. Ramsay, *Seven Churches*, 302.

94. Avi-Yonah, *Views of the Biblical World*, 272.

95. As noted by Hengstenberg, *Revelation*, 189; Stuart, *Apocalypse*, 77. The following point is the author's own.

96. Lilje, *Last Book*, 82.

97. John Albert Bengel, *Gnomon of the New Testament*, vol. 5, trans. William Fletcher (Edinburgh: T. & T. Clark, 1859), 211.

98. Ford, *Revelation*, 400.

99. William M. Ramsay writes: "He was simply allowed to retire into private life after a proved and successful career, instead of being compelled to risk his reputation and life when his powers were failing" (*Seven Churches*, 303).

100. Ibid.

101. Barclay, *Revelation*, 96.

102. Colin J. Hemer, *Local Setting*, 99–100, surveys the evidence and concludes that the two letters probably did not stand for *spectatus* after all.

103. Efird, *Revelation*, 57.

104. Mounce, *Waiting*, 10. Cf. Wilfrid J. Harrington, *Revelation*, 62.

105. Johnson, "Revelation," 442.

106. Hemer, *Local Setting*, 98. Perhaps the best-known imperial precedent lay in the practice of the Emperor Titus issuing wooden admission tickets to those invited to his special entertainments. Although the specific means of admission are not documented for other emperors, a similar practice seems likely. (See Hemer, *Local Setting*, 98, for a consideration of imperial entertainment admission procedures.)

107. Giblin, *Revelation*, 57.

108. Howard, *Revelation*, 63.

109. Donald D. Guthrie, *The Apostles* (Grand Rapids, Mich.: Zondervan Publishing House, 1975), 390.

110. Loane, *They Overcame*, 63–64.

111. Chilton, *Days of Vengeance*, 110.

112. Although Ray F. Robbins, *Revelation*, 65, only says that this "may" be the explanation, it is likely the one he prefers or leans most toward as he places it first.

113. Carpenter, *Revelation*, 48.

114. William Barclay, *Revelation*, 96, argues a root in this relationship but emphasizes the resulting right to partake of "free gifts for life," which the patron would provide and which, in John's spiritual development of the theme, Christ can provide. Although that element would certainly be present, the public rationale would have been as a reward for loyalty and allegiance. Since John is discussing Christian *rewards*, this would have been the dominant idea he was trying to convey (though, as so often with John in chapters 2 and 3, quite possibly not the only idea).

115. Hemer, *Local Setting*, 98.

116. Ibid., 243, citing Suetonius, *Augustus* 40.2; 42:3.

117. Ibid., 243, citing Suetonius, *Augustus*, 41.

118. Ibid., 243.

119. For varying developments of this approach see: G. H. Lang, *The Revelation of Jesus Christ: Selected Studies* (self-published; distributed by London: Oliphants Ltd., 1945), 97–98; Harry R. Boer, *Revelation*, 32; William Ramsay, *Seven Churches*, 304.

Others find in the stone a symbolic indication of a Christian's faith in his own victory over death. John M. Court (*Revelation*, 68) argues that, "After recent archaeological excavations in London have revealed burials with white pebbles in the mouth, one might speculate that it was a concrete sign of a Christian in the rite of passage to the future life." Court, however, provides no indication of the dating of these finds nor whether those buried were Christians or pagans, all of which play a role in evaluating the relevance of his approach to the actual scriptural text.

120. Beasley-Murray, *Revelation*, 88. Examples are Isbon T. Beckwith, *Apocalypse*, 461; R. H. Charles, *Revelation*, 66–67; Gerhard A. Krodel, *Revelation*, 121; John Tickle, *The Book of Revelation*, 36.

121. Roy Kotansky, "Incantations and Prayers for Salvation on Inscribed Greek Amulets," in *Magika Hiera: Ancient Greek Magic and Religion*, ed. Christopher A. Faraone and Dirk Obbink (New York: Oxford University Press, 1991), 107. For a discussion of amulets within the Roman Empire at large see 107–37.

122. R. H. Charles, *Revelation*, 67, introduces a Talmudic tale of David "inscrib[ing] the Divine name on a potsherd" and casting it into a cistern to stop it from "overwhelm[ing] the world" with its water. In this example, though, the inscribed object (1) is a "potsherd," not a stone; (2) has the name of God, not the individual upon it; (3) is thrown away rather than kept, as implied in John's allusion; and (4) works a miracle, an attribute not claimed by John.

Johsua Trachtenberg, *Jewish Magic and Superstition: A Study in Folk Religion* (New York: Behrman's Jewish Book House, 1939), 132, 133–34 summarizes the Talmudic and later attitude concerning magical amulets:

> Their use was very extensive in the Talmudic period, and, accepted by the rabbinic authorities, impressed itself strongly upon the habits of later times. Jewish amulets were of two sorts: written, and objects such as herbs, foxes' tails, stones, etc. They were employed to heal or to protect men, animals, and even inanimate things....A Talmudic amulet which was widely employed in medieval times—it was well known to non-Jews also—was the so-called *even tekumah*, the "preserving stone," which was believed to prevent miscarriage. The Talmud does not tell us just what sort of stone this was. Several medieval writers were more informative, but unfortunately they employed one or perhaps several French equivalents whose mean-

ings in Hebrew transliteration are not altogether clear, but which show that these were in common use.

The inherent problem in establishing *first-century* attitudes and practice from the Talmud is that the bulk of it is from a later period and does not represent that earlier century. Separating later convictions from those of probable or possible first-century beliefs needs to be done.

123. For example, see David E. Aune, "Magic in Early Christianity," *Aufstieg und Niedergang der Romischen Welt* (Berlin: Walter de Gruyter, 1980), II, 23.2, 1556. Although he does not argue the case, he presents a clear rationale for the view: It grows out of his assumption that there are a number of parallels between John's rhetoric in the book of Revelation and that found in magic literature (1555–56).

Most of his evidence for that assumption is unpersuasive. "The imagery of the plagues of the Jewish exodus" certainly appears in magical literature—but why would John refer to a secondary source when his repeated quotations and allusions exhibit an intimate firsthand acquaintance with the root source, the Old Testament itself? "The frequent use of the numbers three and seven in the 'Apocalypse' has many magical parallels." Doubtless that is true, but by the same logic are we to say that the many occasions when at least the latter number is used in the *Old* Testament indicates that *those* are chosen because of the magical usage? The use of "the name of God" as a "protective...device" is yet another suggested parallel. Yet is not such common in the Old Testament? Even the repeated use by John of the adverb "quickly" is pointed to as parallel to magical usage. But what other word is John supposed to use, if he believed certain events were in the near future?

124. Isbon T. Beckwith, *Apocalypse*, 462, refers to this discrepancy but does not seem to regard it as an objection to his amulet interpretation.

125. Morris, *Revelation*, 68.

126. R. C. H. Lenski, *The Interpretation of St. John's Revelation* (Columbus, Ohio: Wartburg Press, 1943), 110.

127. In Isaiah 44:5 we read of individuals using names: only one is divine; the other two are nationalistic references (Jacob and Israel). None of the three represents a *new* name, at least not in the traditional sense of not being used before. Israel is pictured as, collectively, being given a new name by God in Isaiah 62:2, not every individual being given a unique name.

128. Ramsay, *Seven Churches*, 306.

129. Lilje, *Last Book*, 83.

130. Sheppard, *Revelation*, 41. F. F. Bruce, "Revelation," 639, also uses 3:12 to establish the name on the stone as that of Christ.

131. Krodel, *Revelation*, 121.

132. Ramsay, *Seven Churches*, 305.

133. Martin, *Seven Letters*, 77.

134. Ibid.

135. Cf. Colin J. Hemer's comments on this in *Local Setting*, 100.

136. Ibid., 100–101.

137. Blaiklock, *Seven Churches*, 40.

138. For a discussion of the premises behind granting (and seeking) the god's secret name see Ramsay, *Seven Churches*, 306–7.

139. L. van Hartinsveld, *Revelation: A Practical Commentary*, trans. John Vriend (Grand Rapids, Mich.: Wm. B. Eerdmans Publishing Company, 1985), 19.

140. Ford, *Revelation*, 399.

141. Ramsay, *Seven Churches*, 306. William Barclay, *Revelation*, 99, also refers to the custom but without details about when it came into existence.

142. Ramsay, *Seven Churches*, 310–11.

### 8. MERCANTILE THYATIRA

1. For the history of Thyatira see Meinardus, *Patmos*, 91–92.

2. Blaiklock, *Cities*, 108.

3. Ibid.

4. A. H. M. Jones, *The Cities of the Eastern Roman Provinces*, 2d ed., rev. Michael Avi-Yonah, et al. (Oxford: Clarendon Press, 1971), 83.

5. Mitchell, *Celts*, 244.

6. Ibid.

7. Ibid. In his *Roman Economy*, A. H. M. Jones also presents this deduction in regard to both Thyatira and Hierapolis but cautions "that this is a conjecture, and, even if true, the phenomen [of government by guild groups] is limited to a small group of towns" (*The Roman Economy: Studies in Ancient Economic and Administrative History*, ed. P. A. Brunt [Oxford: Basil Blackwell, 1974], 45). He notes that the evidence is stronger for Philadelphia. There one finds "inscriptions [that] record the 'sacred tribe of the woolworkers' and the 'sacred tribe of the leatherworkers.' 'Tribe' is normally the designation of the official political divisions of the people, and it may be that at Philadelphia the guilds held this position" (45).

8. Botha, "God, Emperor Worship and Society," 92; Jones, *Greek City*, 220; Yamauchi, *New Testament Cities*, 38.

9. Whiting, *Revelation*, 82. The same assertion is made by Blaiklock, *Pagan Society*, 25; R. K. Harrison, *Archaeology*, 54; Kraeling, *Atlas*, 469; and Ramsay, *Seven Churches*, 324–25.

10. For different parts of this list see Blaiklock, *Pagan Society*, 25; Ford, *Revelation*, 405; Jones, *Eastern Roman Provinces*, 83; Whiting, *Revelation*, 82.

11. Kraybill, "Cult and Commerce," 107; Selles, *Revelation*, 24.

12. Krodel, *Revelation*, 122.

13. Ibid.

14. Ibid.

15. Hemer, "Seven Cities," 243.

16. Ibid. For more detailed observations on how guild banquets, (and other social banquets for that matter) could translate into opportunities for sexual misconduct, see Kathleen E. Corley, "Were the Women Around Jesus Really Prostitutes? Women in the Context of Greco-Roman Meals," *Society of Biblical Literature 1989 Seminar Papers*, ed. David J. Lull (Atlanta Ga.: Scholars Press, 1989), 487–521.

17. S. Applebaum, "The Organization of the Jewish Communities in the Diaspora," in *The Jewish People in the First Century: Historical Geography, Political History, Social, Cultural and Religious Life and Institutions*, vol. 1, ed. S. Safari and M. Stern (Assen [Netherlands]: Van Gorcum & Company, 1974), 481.

18. Ibid.

19. Ibid.

20. Jones, *Roman Economy*, 45–46.

21. Rostovtzeff, *Roman Empire*, 619–20.

22. For the full text see Meijer and van Nijf, *Trade, Transport and Society*, 122.

23. W. H. Buckler, "Labour Disputes in Asia Minor," in *Anatolian Studies–Presented to Sir William Mitchell Ramsay*, ed. W. H. Buckler and W. M. Calder (Manchester: Manchester University Press, 1923).[28]

24. Ibid.

25. Ibid.

26. Barclay, *Revelation*, 101.

27. Whiting, *Revelation*, 83.

28. Vermaseren, *Corpus Cultus Cybelae*, 127. For inscriptions reprinted in the original languages, see 435–37.

29. Wilfrid J. Harrington, *Understand the Apocalypse* (Washington, D.C.: Corpus Books, 1969), 91; Barclay, *Revelation*, 105.

30. Hengel, *Judaism and Hellenism*, 308. Cf. Meinardus, *Patmos*, 95.

31. Ibid.

32. Kraeling, *Atlas*, 470; Mounce, *Revelation*, 101.

33. Finegan, *Archaeology*, 175; Whiting, *Revelation*, 83.

34. Kraeling, *Atlas*, 470. Cf. Mounce, *Revelation*, 101.

35. Charles C. Whiting, *Revelation*, 83.

36. Alan Kerkaslager, "Apollo, Greco-Roman Prophecy, and the Rider on the White Horse in Revelation 6:2," *Journal of Biblical Literature* 112 (Spring 1993):119.

37. Ibid., 119–21.

38. Elisabeth Schüssler Fiorenza, *Revelation: Vision of a Just World* (Minneapolis: Fortress Press, 1991), 54.

39. S. R. F. Price, "Between Man and God: Sacrifice in the Roman Imperial Cult," *Journal of Roman Studies* 70 (1980):32.

40. As does John F. Walvoord, *Revelation*, 72, for example.

41. For a discussion of Lydia's marital status see Bradley Blue, "Acts and the House Church," in Gill and Gempf, *The Book of Acts in Its Graeco-Roman Setting*, 184–86 and related notes.

42. On the art of purple dyeing in antiquity see J. Irving Zinderman, "Seashells and Ancient Purple Dyeing," *Biblical Archaeologist: Perspectives on the Ancient World from Mesopotamia to the Mediterranean* 53 (June 1990):98–101.

43. Kraeling, *Atlas*, 469. His insistence that this "must" have been the situation seems a little too positive.

44. G. H. Horsley, "The Purple Trade, and the Status of Lydia of Thyatira," *New Documents Illustrating Early Christianity*, vol. 2, ed. G. H. Horsley ([Marrickville, Australia]: Macquarie University/Ancient History Documentary Research Centre, 1982), 28. For a discussion of women having the right to act freely on their own see 28–32.

Horsley assumes that the purple is "royal" purple, over which the government had a monopoly. Most discussion concurs in this approach (C. J. Hemer, "The Cities of the Revelation" in *New Documents Illustrating Early Christianity*, vol. 3, ed. G. H. Horsley [{Marrickville, Australia}: Macquarie University/Ancient History Documentary Research Centre, 1983], 54). Hemer urges consideration for "the possibility that the purple in which Lydia dealt was not the Tyrian murex but a less expensive dye from the roots of the madder plant *(Rubia),* the so-called 'Turkey red,' whose use has a very long history in western Anatolia" (53). Its use continued in Turkey until the late nineteenth century and, interestingly enough in this context, a French writer observed in 1896 that it continued to be grown and used in the Thyatira area (53).

45. Meinardus, *Patmos*, 95–96.

46. Morris, *Revelation*, 74. Cf. Mounce, *Waiting*, 12.

47. Ford, *Revelation*, 407.

48. Ibid., 405. Cf. above's discussion of that god above.

49. Martin Kiddle, *The Revelation of St. John*, Moffatt New Testament Commentary series (New York: Harper & Brothers, 1940), 37.

50. For Tyrimnos references see ibid.; Mounce, *Revelation*, 101–2.

51. For a reference to the imperial cult see Kordel, *Revelation*, 122; Mounce, *Revelation*, 102.

52. Meinardus, *Patmos*, 94.

53. Blaiklock, *Pagan Society*, 109.

54. Ford, *Revelation*, 405.

55. Ibid.

56. Kiddle, *Revelation*, 37.

57. The comparison with Apollo is often far clearer than whether the authors have in mind the popular stereotype or a specific statue or statuary tradition: Boyd, *Tells, Tombs, and Treasure*, 208; R. K. Harrison, *Archaeology*, 54; Mounce, *Waiting*, 10.

58. R. K. Harrison, *Archaeology*, 54.

59. Except as a historical/theological curiosity, we can dismiss the ancient theory that Jezebel was the biblical convert Lydia. If Revelation was composed late in the century, it is quite likely that Lydia was dead (Loane, *They Overcame*, 68). Even assuming an early date, making Lydia the villain seems a bit of nasty character assassination growing not out of evidence—there is none—but out of the fact that hers is the *only* female name we know of from that congregation.

60. Austin Farrer, *Revelation*, 77, argues that John's condemnation would have been far more explicit if actual devil worship were intended. Alan F. Johnson, *Revelation*, 52, believes the prophetess herself would have called the evils Satanic but in a way that left her own teaching uncondemned by the admission: "The only effective way to confront Satan is to enter his strongholds; the real nature of sin can be learned only by experience, and therefore only those who have really experienced sin can truly appreciate grace. Thus by experiencing the depths of paganism ('the deep secrets of Satan'), one would be better equipped to serve Christ or to be an example of freedom to His brothers."

61. Caird, *Revelation*, 43.

62. Ford, *Revelation*, 403, provides citations of this approach.

63. Wilfrid J. Harrington, *Apocalypse*, 91.

64. We exclude the possibility that she was, openly at least, a never-converted polytheist. To gain substantial local Christian collaboration would surely have required at least the public veneer of Christian faith.

65. As George Eldon Ladd, *Revelation*, 52, observes, "The error of this Jezebel was the same as that of the Nicolaitans in Pergamum: full accommodation to pagan mores." David E. Aune, "The Social Matrix of the Apocalypse of John," *Biblical Research* 26 (1981), 27, goes so far

as to call these two and the Balaamite groups "identical" movements. On the other hand, John presents them as three different groups, so one would be on safer ground to retain that distinction while conceding that they shared a similar theological/moral view of the relationship of Christianity and the world.

66. For a discussion of this scenario see Blaiklock, *Cities*, 110.

67. Metzger, *Code*, 37.

68. For an analysis of the types of prostitution that existed in the ancient world and then-contemporary sources describing them see Ford, "Bookshelf on Prostitution," *Biblical Theology Bulletin* (Fall 1993): 128–34.

69. For example, Allen, *Message*, 70; Loane, *They Overcame*, 77.

70. To illustrate we might well examine the only three Old Testament "symbolic" usages cited (though not quoted) by Gerhard A. Krodel, *Revelation*, 117. Jeremiah 7:9 is provided as an example of spiritual transgression. However, when we examine the text it is thrown in with other literal, overt transgressions and *worshiping other gods* is listed as a distinct, separate evil. Jeremiah 23:10 is likewise cited, but here the "adultery" seems to be the outgrowth of (rather than identical with) the idol worship mentioned in the following verse. Isaiah 57:4 turns out to be even more removed from the question by branding Isaiah's listeners not as *committing* spiritual immorality but as "*sons* of the sorceress, you *offspring* of the adulterer and the harlot."

71. William Barclay, *Revelation*, 108, provides a blatant example of this misunderstanding when he cites as examples of the spiritual use of the term Jesus labeling his generation as "an evil and adulterous generation" (Mt 12:39; 16:4). On the other hand, if there is one universally agreed-upon point among the many contradictory schemes of interpretation of the ancient world, it is that the Jews of Israel in the first century were unbending *mono*theists. Hence, the literal act must have been under consideration. One can argue that they may have sold their souls to the noncanonical traditions that Jesus so vigorously rebuked [Mt 15], but these are still not *polytheistic* beliefs.

72. Martin, *Seven Letters*, 81.

73. Krodel, *Revelation*, 117. Without citing specific passages, Scott G. Sinclair, *Revelation*, 53, argues in a similar vein.

74. F. F. Bruce, "Revelation," 638, takes the sexual immorality in Revelation 3:14 to refer to "the contracting of marital unions prohibited by the law of Israel (Leviticus 18) but countenanced by pagan custom." A reading of that chapter, however, lists various sexual prohibitions that one would expect few pagans to quarrel with. What Bruce likely has in mind are the *marriage unions* between Israelite and Gentile that were

prohibited by the Torah. But marriage unions—except in those situations specifically prohibited—were accepted as inherently virtuous by the Old Testament. Would John have used a term normally applied to inherently illicit relationships to describe marriages? Perhaps, but if he did we could reasonably expect some clear indication in the context that he has this in mind. Cf. Jesus' startling use of the term adultery to apply to certain remarriages in Matthew 5:32 and 19:9.

75. J. P. W. Sweet, *Revelation*, 95, makes the adultery equivalent to "flirt with her teaching" and the reference to her children as "the totally converted." But how much more "converted" do they need to be than to "sleep" with her?

76. On this ambiguity element see Beckwith, *Apocalypse*, 467; Court, *Myth and History*, 35; Johnson, "Revelation," 444.

77. The distinction between Jezebel's partners in adultery and her "children," if any, has been a matter of disagreement. Homer Hailey, *Revelation*, 139, and J. P. W. Sweet, *Revelation*, 95, have the former refer to those on the fringe of the movement and the "children" the fully committed. Richard C. Trench, *Seven Churches*, 190, *reverses* this picture and sees the adulterers "as the chief furtherers and abettors of those evil things;" in contrast, the children are the "less forward members of the same wicked company, more the deceived, while the others were the deceivers."

78. This fact led Isbon T. Beckwith, *Apocalypse*, 467–68, to observe that the explicitly stated punishment of the children "is severer than that of" Jezebel herself. He argues that the deaths are not so much the punishment of the children but part of her punishment.

79. Martin, *Seven Churches*, 82. It should be remembered that *other* feasts were partaken of outside a guild context. Charles C. Whiting, *Revelation*, 87, takes it in this broader sense of "pagan feasts." Although Robert H. Mounce, *Waiting*, 11, speaks of guild membership being under rebuke by John, he believes that the writer has specifically in mind the elements of token polytheistic worship involved in their meetings.

80. Lilje, *Last Book*, 87.

81. Van Hartinsveld, *Revelation*, 21.

82. Beasley-Murray, *Revelation*, 94.

83. Otto F. A. Meinardus, *Patmos*, 95, suggests this contrast.

### 9. INVINCIBLE SARDIS

1. Johnson, "Asia Minor," 97, refers to this as a "general agreement." George M. A. Hanfmann, *Letters from Sardis* (Cambridge, Mass.:

Harvard University Press, 1972), 3, who investigated Sardis on site for many years, describes this as the view "of most scholars." Bryan Beyer, "Obadiah," in *Obadiah, Jonah: Bible Study Commentaries*, ed. Bryan Beyer and John Walton (Grand Rapids, Mich.: Lamplight Books/Zondervan Publishing House, 1988), 25, concedes that "many modern scholars" make the correlation of Sepharad and Sardis but cautions that "the identification must remain tentative."

Among those who accept the assumption are S. Applebaum, "The Legal Status of the Jewish Communities in the Diaspora," in Safari and Stern, *The Jewish People in the First Century*, 432; Ellen S. Saltman, "The Jews of Asia Minor in the Greco-Roman Period: A Religious and Social Study" (M.A. thesis, Smith College, 1971), 23.

A. Thomas Kraabel also accepts the identification in several of his published works: "Impact of the Discovery of the Sardis Synagogue," in *Diaspora Jews and Judaism: Essays in Honor of A. Thomas Kraabel*, South Florida Studies in the History of Judaism, no. 41, ed. A. Andrew Overman and Robert S. MacLennan (Atlanta, Ga.: Scholars Press, 1992), 270; "Religious Propaganda and Missionary Competition in the New Testament World," in *Immigrants, Exiles, Expatriates, and Missionary Competition in the New Testament World*, ed. Lukas Bormann, Kelly del Tredici, and Angela Standhartinger (Leiden: E. J. Brill, 1994), 73; "The Diaspora Synagogue: Archaeological and Epigraphic Evidence Since Sukenik," in *Aufstieg und Niedergang der Romischen Welt* (Berlin: Walter de Gruyter, 1979), II, 19.1, 484; "The Synagogue at Sardis: Jews and Christians," in *Sardis: Twenty-seven Years of Discovery*, ed. Eleanor Guralnick (Chicago: [n.p.], 1987), 66.

2. Hanfmann, *Letters*, 3–4.

3. Kraabel, "Sardis Synagogue," 178.

4. John D. W. Watts, *Books of Joel, Obadiah, Jonah, Nahum, Habakkuk and Zephaniah*, Cambridge Bible Commentary on the New English Bible (Cambridge: Cambridge University Press, 1975), 67.

5. Referred to by Douglas Stuart though he does not embrace it. See *Hosea-Jonah*, Word Biblical Commentary series (Waco, Tex.: Word Books, 1987), 421. So far as he is concerned, "the likely site, however, is Assyrian 'Saparda'/Persian 'Sparda,' a country south of Lake Urmia, north and west of Media."

6. John D. W. Watts, *Obadiah*, 67, though conceding that a location in "the lower Mesopotamian valley" is more likely, is tempted by the possibility that Obadiah refers to a "garrison of Hebrew mercenaries" that were stationed at "Hesperides near Benghazi on the North Africa coast." He concedes that their presence is only confirmed at a

later date than this but speculates that the garrison could date as far back as Obadiah's day. The Sardis interpretation is noticeably absent.

7. Blaiklock, *Cities*, 112.

8. Akurgal, *Ancient Civilizations*, 124; Perowne, *Archaeology*, 119. These were of both silver and gold (Blaiklock, *Cities*, 112; Mounce, *Revelation*, 109).

9. David Gordon Mitten, "A New Look at Ancient Sardis," *Biblical Archaeologist* 29 (1966), 56.

10. Hanfmann, *From Croessus to Constantine*, 5.

11. For a discussion of the site, discovered in 1968, see George M. A. Hanfmann and Jane C. Waldbaum, "New Excavations at Sardis and Some Problems of Western Anatolian Archaeology," in *Near Eastern Archaeology in the Twentieth Century: Essays in Honor of Nelson Glueck*, ed. James A. Sanders (Garden City, N.Y.: Doubleday and Company, 1970), 311–13.

12. For a good account of these events, see John G. Pedley, *Sardis in the Age of Croesus* (Norman: University of Oklahoma Press, 1968), 86–93.

13. Hanfmann, *Letters*, 15–16.

14. Ibid., 16; Avery, *Classical Handbook*, 983; Pfeiffer and Vos, *Historical Geography*, 398.

15. Akurgal, *Ancient Civilizations*, 124.

16. George M. A. Hanfmann and Jane C. Waldbaum, *A Survey of Sardis and the Major Monuments Outside the City Walls* (Cambridge, Mass.: Harvard University Press, 1975), 19.

17. Hanfmann, *Letters*, 134.

18. Ibid., 16.

19. Ibid., 17; Akurgal, *Ancient Civilizations*, 125.

20. George M. A. Hanfmann, *Letters*, 323, argues that the city was "continually alive and prosperous from the great earthquake of A.D. 17 to its destruction by Sassanian Persians in A.D. 616."

21. George M. A. Hanfmann, "Introduction," in Hanfmann, Yegul, and Crawford, "The Roman and Late Antique Period," 145. Although our interest is in Sardis, there were other nearby communities of which we know little. The reader interested in the study of one of these, Tmolus, located ten kilometers away, will find useful the study by Clive Foss, "A Neighbor of Sardis: The City of Tmolus and Its Successors," *California Studies in Classical Antiquity* 13, 178–201.

22. Kraeling, *Atlas*, 470–71.

23. Mounce, *Revelation*, 109.

24. This estimate is based upon excavation of about 5 percent of

the city area occupied in the period of his reign (Pedley, *Age of Croesus*, 122).

25. This is the minimum estimate for the fourth century A.D. of George M. A. Hanfmann, "Introduction," 146. Note, however, his own preference for a much higher figure in footnote 23.

26. George M. A. Hanfmann's maximum estimate of the fourth century, "Introduction," 146. Possibly exceeding 100,000 in the second century: Hanfmann and Waldbaum, *Survey*, chronological chart, 6. "May" have been "more than 100,000" in the first century (Finegan, *Archaeology*, 175). "Probably...around 100,000" in the second century (Trebilco, *Jewish Communities*, 37).

27. Of the second century in particular, Hanfmann, *From Croesus to Constantine*, 49.

28. Hanfmann and Waldbaum, *Survey*, 21.

29. Ibid., 20.

30. Ibid.

31. Jane C. Waldbaum, "Metalwork and Metalworking in Sardis," in Guralnick, *Sardis*, 42.

32. Foss, "Byzantine Cities," 43.

33. For the agricultural products of the area see Foss, "Byzantine Cities," 42–43, and Hanfmann and Waldbaum, *Survey*, 20.

34. In the third century A.D., however, it underwent a period of economic difficulty. See Marianne P. Bonz, "Differing Approaches to Religious Benefaction: The Late Third-Century Acquisition of the Sardis Synagogue," *Harvard Theological Review* 86 (April 1993): 146–48.

35. Yegul, *Bath-Gymnasium*, xiii. This volume provides a detailed study of the facility.

36. Akurgal, *Ancient Civilizations*, 126; Yamuchi, *New Testament Cities*, 68.

37. Humphrey, *Roman Circuses*, 526.

38. See the description in Hanfmann and Waldbaum, *Survey*, 6, 27. Also see Hanfmann, "Introduction," 142.

39. Yamuchi, *New Testament Cities*, 67.

40. Hanfmann, "Introduction," 141. For a picture of evacuated pipes that lay beneath the city see figure 593 in J. Stephens Crawford, *The Byzantine Shops at Sardis* (Cambridge, Mass.: Harvard University Press, 1990).

41. See Hanfmann and Waldbaum, *Survey*, 27.

42. *History of Herodotus* 1.93.

43. *Deipnosophistae* 12.515d-f, as quoted by John Griffiths Pedley, *Ancient Literary Sources on Sardis*, (Archaeological Exploration of Sardis, Monograph 2 (Cambridge, Mass.: Harvard University Press, 1972), 43.

44. Hanfmann, "Religious Life," in George M. A. Hanfmann, Louis Robert, and William Mierse, "The Hellenistic Period," in Hanfmann and Mierse, *Sardis: From Prehistoric to Rome Times–Results of the Archaeological Exploration of Sardis, 1958–1975*, 132; Hemer, *Local Setting*, 138; Whiting, *Revelation*, 92.

45. Hanfmann, "Religious Life," 132–33; Hemer, *Local Setting*, 138.

46. Hanfmann, "Religious Life," 133.

47. Hemer, *Local Setting*, 138.

48. Hanfmann, "Religious Life," 133; cf. Whiting, *Revelation*, 92.

49. Whiting, *Revelation*, 92.

50. Ibid. Edwin C. Yamauchi, *New Testament Cities*, 69, notes that though coins from Sardis have survived that bear her image, her actual temple site has not been recovered. Her worship was common throughout the empire. (Roman Garrison, *The Graeco-Roman Context of Early Christian Literature* [Journal for the Study of the New Testament Supplement 137] [Sheffield, England: Sheffield Academic Press, 1997], 29); for Christian criticisms of her worship in the early centuries see 29–30.

51. Hanfmann, "Religious Life," 131.

52. Blaiklock, *Seven Churches*, 60–61.

53. Fikret K. Yegul, "Roman Architecture at Sardis," in Guralnick, *Sardis*, 50.

54. Finegan, *Archaeology*, 175; William E. Mierse, "Artemis Sanctuary," in Hanfmann, Robert, and Mierse, "The Hellenistic Period," 120. There was a burst of building in the early third century B.C.: the temple to Artemis was built as well as a theater, stadium, and gymnasium (Susan Sherwin-White and Amelie Kuhrt, *From Samarkhand to Sardis: A New Approach to the Seleucid Empire* [London: Duckworth, 1993], 182). On the Sardis temple to Artmeis also see Horsley, "Inscriptions of Ephesus," 157.

55. Sometimes she is called Artemis Coloene, after the location of a shrine erected in her honor at nearby Lake Coloe. Cf. Hemer, *Local Setting*, 138.

56. Ibid., 265. Cf. Ashcroft, "Revelation," 270; Howard, *Revelation*, 65; Morris, *Revelation*, 75; Swete, *Apocalypse*, 48; Price and Trell, *Coins and Their Cities*, 137; Yamuchi, *New Testament Cities*, 69.

57. Pfeiffer and Vos, *Historical Geography*, 400; Vos, *Archaeology*, 333. Blaiklock, *Cities*, 118, has an apparent misprint when he calls it 160 by 100 feet. Kraeling, *Atlas*, 471, gives the measurement as 163 by 327 feet.

58. Pfeiffer and Vos, *Historical Geography*, 400.

59. Berrett, *Discovering*, 618. For a large color photograph of the surviving ruins see Porter, *Greek World*, 95.

60. Barton, *Archaeology*, 270–71. Cf. Fred H. Wight, *Highlights of Archaeology in Bible Lands* (Chicago: Moody Press, 1955), 188. Alan Johnson goes so far as to say that it was never completed in both his "Revelation," 447, and *Revelation*, 54.

61. Yegul, "Roman Architecture," 50.

62. Mierse, "Artemis Sanctuary," 120, 265.

63. Hanfmann, "Religious Life," 131; Mierse, "Artemis Sanctuary," 265

64. Hanfmann, "Religious Life," 129. In the second century A.D. we read of prominent citizens serving as priests of Zeus at the Artemis temple (ibid., 131).

65. Price and Trell, *Coins and Their Cities*, 137.

66. Mierse, "Artemis Sanctuary," 120.

67. That of Antonius Pius was placed in one *cella* while one of Faustina was added in the other. See Mierse, "Artemis Sanctuary," 265. Also on the subject of imperial religious statuary in the temple see Cornelius C. Vermeule, *Roman Imperial Art in Greece and Asia Minor* (Cambridge, Mass.: Belknap Press of Harvard University Press, 1968), 18–19.

68. Hanfmann, "Religious Life," 129, sees the two as representing separate rather than a shared religious tradition. In contrast, William E. Mierse is unwilling to assume a dramatic cleavage between the two (see his "Artemis Sanctuary," 265). G. H. R. Horsley asserts that there were "close links with the Ephesian cult" ("Inscriptions of Ephesus," 157).

This is not just a theoretical discussion. For example, if the Sardis temple was indeed an offshoot of the Ephesian one, we can answer the question of what the goddess looked like—almost certainly very similar to the image found at the "mother" site in Ephesus (cf. George M. A. Hanfmann and Jane C. Waldbaum, "Kybele and Artemis: Two Anatolian Goddesses at Sardis," *Archaeology* 22 [1969], 265).

Certain similarities were inevitable, not because of any actual relationship but because religions tended to function in a parallel manner regardless of their historic relationship. For example, just like the Artemis temple in Ephesus, the one in Sardis was involved in the loan business. For the text of a loan extension granted by the temple (c. 200 B.C.) see M. M. Austin, *The Hellenistic World from Alexander to the Roman Conquest: A Selection of Ancient Sources in Translation* (Cambridge: Cambridge University Press, 1981), 295–96.

69. See the discussion of the incident in the chapter on Ephesus. Also see the entire article of Sokolowski, "New Testimony," 427–31.

70. Price, *Rituals and Power*, 131–32.

71. Seton Lloyd, "Anatolia and Soviet Armenia," in *Atlas of*

*Ancient Archaeology*, ed. Jacquetta Hawkes (New York: McGraw-Hill Book Company, 1974), 144.

72. Hanfmann, *Letters*, 239, reproduces the relief and argues that it indicates the two deities remained separate beings. Others, of course, speak strongly for Artemis merely being the Sardisian form of Cybele. For example, Blaiklock, *Cities*, 118; Hemmer, *Local Setting*, 138, and Kraeling, *Atlas*, 471.

73. Sherman E. Johnson, "A Sabazios Inscription from Sardis," in *Religions in Antiquity: Essays in Memory of Erwin Ramsdell Goodenough*, ed. Jacob Neusner (Leiden: E. J. Brill, 1968), 543.

74. Ibid.

75. S. E. Johnson. "The Present State of Sabazios Research," in *Aufstieg und Niedergang der Romischen Welt* (Walter de Gruyter, 1984), II, 17.3, 1588. He could also be linked with several other gods, both male (Dionysus) and female (Cybele). Johnson lists nine such linkages but cautions (1600–1601) that the degree of linkage is sometimes exaggerated.

76. Johnson, "Sabazios Inscription," 544.

77. Johnson, "Sabazios Research," 1591. The "benedicto latina" refers to the second and third fingers of the right hand being held up as if to bless the people.

78. Ibid., 1599.

79. Quoted by A. Thomas Kraabel, "Paganism and Judaism: The Sardis Evidence," in Overman and MacLennan, *Diaspora Jews and Judaism*, 251. In contrast, Plutarch considered the Jews as engaged in a variety of Dionysus worship (ibid., 251).

80. Ibid., 250.

81. See citations in ibid., 251. Also see our remarks on this cult in the discussion of Thyatira.

82. Cf. the remarks in Kraabel, "paganism and Judaism," 251–52.

83. Ibid., 252.

84. Kraabel, "Judaism in Western Asia Minor," 192. Kraabel also points to the apparent lack of permanent worship facilities in the Sabazios cult, while in contrast everywhere Jews existed in any substantial number they built synagogues as fixed places of worship (192). There is also the matter of human nature when it rejects its past upbringing. As Martin Hengel, *Jews, Greeks and Barbarians: Aspects of the Hellenization of Judaism in the Pre-Christian Period*. trans. John Bowden (Philadelphia: Fortress Press, 1980), 107, astutely observes, "A Jew who broke with the Law is hardly likely to have turned to a semi-Jewish cult; he will have become completely assimilated to his Hellenistic environment."

85. Wayne A. Meeks, *Urban Christians*, 36; cf. H. Mary Smallwood, *The Jews Under Roman Rule: From Pompey to Diocletian*, vol. 20 of

*Studies in Judaism in Late Antiquity*, ed. Jacob Neusner (Leiden: E. J. Brill, 1978), 139.

86. Meeks, *Urban Christians*, 229, cf. 34.

87. Smallwood, *Jews Under Roman Rule*, 139.

88. Ibid., 142–43.

89. Ibid., 139–40.

90. Andrew Seager, "The Architecture of the Dura and Sardis Synagogues," in *The Dura-Europos Synagogue: A Re-evaluation (1932–1992)*, ed. Joseph Gutman (Atlanta, Ga.: Scholars Press, 1992), 84–85.

91. Kraabel, "Sardis Synagogue," 184.

92. Seager, "Architecture," 84.

93. Andrew R. Seager, "The Building," in Seager and Kraabel, "The Synagogue and the Jewish Community," 168. For a useful reconstruction of what this complex probably looked like, see the drawing in John S. Crawford, "Multiculturalism at Sardis: Jews and Christians Live, Work, and Worship Side by Side," *Biblical Archaeology Review* 22 (September-October 1996): 42–43.

94. Kraabel, "Sardis Synagogue," 179.

95. Kraabel, "Diaspora Synagogue," 487. Kraabel argues that this was probably the only synagogue in the city (483), and in light of its large size, he is likely correct.

96. Trebilco, *Jewish Communities*, 40.

97. Seager, "The Building," 172. For a concise analysis of physical changes to the Sardis synagogue through the centuries see Bonz, "Differing Approaches," 140–45.

98. For a description of the changes in the synagogue and the chronology found in this paragraph, see Trebilco, *Jewish Communities*, 40–43. Another description of the facility, with comparison to synagogues in other areas, is found in Hershel Shanks, *Judaism in Stone: The Archaeology of Ancient Synagogues* (New York: Harper & Row/Washington, D.C.: Biblical Archaeological Society, 1979), 169–75. For a comparison of the Sardis synagogue with that in Dura see Andrew Seager, "Architecture," 79–116.

99. A. Thomas Kraabel ("Religious Propaganda and Missionary Competition," 80–81) argues from an analogy with a Gentile (not Jewish) inscription from Aphrodisias the feasibility of this approach.

100. Ford, *Revelation*, 412.

101. This is the interpretation suggested by David Gordon Mitten, "Ancient Sardis," 61.

102. C. H. V. Sutherland, *Roman History and Coinage, 44*

*B.C.–A.D. 69: Fifty Points of Relation from Julius Caesar to Vespasian* (Oxford: Clarendon Press, 1987), 48.

103. Edward T. Salmon, *A History of the Roman World from 30 B.C. to A.D. 138* (London: Methuen, 1957), 43.

104. Ibid.

105. Barton, *Archaeology*, 270.

106. Hanfmann, "Historical Background," in Hanfmann, Robert, and Mierse, "The Hellenistic Period," 109.

107. George M. A. Hanfmann, "Previous Research and the Harvard-Cornell Excavation," in Hanfmann, Robert, and Mierse, "The Hellenistic Period," 114.

108. Sutherland, *Roman History*, 48.

109. Ibid., 48–49. on page 48 is a picture of the coin. Sutherland also discusses how this mint issue has been misdated to the year A.D. 30.

110. Yegul, "Roman Architecture," 47.

111. Ibid.

112. Strabo, *Geography* 13.4.8. He views the rebuilding, however, as having been completed by the time he wrote. As noted later in the text, though the bulk may well have been completed, the scope of the devastation probably required considerable additional construction beyond this initial period.

113. Ibid.

114. Ibid., 47–48.

115. Hanfmann, *Letters*, 145.

116. Hanfmann, "Introduction," 142.

117. Ibid.

118. Ibid.

119. Hanfmann, *Survey*, 31.

120. Among those interpreting the phrase in light of these double seizures are Caird, *Revelation*, 47, and Krodel, *Revelation*, 133.

121. Pfeiffer and Vos, *Historical Geography*, 398.

122. Xenophon, *Cyropaedia*, Greek text with English translation by Walter Miller [Loeb Classical Library] (London: William Heinemann, 1914), 7.2.2–3.

123. *History of Herodotus* 1.84,

124. *The Histories of Polybius*, vol. 1, trans. Evelyn S. Shuckburgh (1889; reprinted with a new introduction by F. W. Wilbank, Bloomington: Indiana University Press, 1962), 7.15.

125. Ibid., 7.15.

126. Ibid., 7.17.

127. Thucydides, "The Peloponnesian War," I.115.

128. We may find here a hint that the free-wheeling sexual "liber-

ties" of their society had become the lifestyle of a number of Christians. Gerhard A. Krodel, *Revelation*, 131, points out that, "The verb 'to soil' (Greek, *molynein*) is frequently used of cultic or sexual defilement (cf. Revelation 14:4; Jude 23)." His Revelation text, however, does not mention clothing. The Jude text refers to those so deep in sin that one approached them as if "hating even the garment defiled by the flesh." Perhaps a better place to vindicate a clothes/morality correlation would be Zechariah 3:3–5, where both dirty and clean garments are equated with one's inner character.

129.  Martin, *Seven Letters*, 90–91, cf. 93, 96. Adela Yarbor Collins also argues the same point in her *Apocalypse* in the New Testament Message: A Biblical-Theological Commentary series (Wilmington, Del.: Michael Glazier, 1979), 25. Oddly enough, she undermines her own case by conceding that in the earliest church "baptism was practiced by immersion" and that this was performed in the nude. Can one believe that the several thousand who were baptized in Acts 2 in the middle of Jerusalem were immersed in the nude? The scenario works no better in regard to individual conversions, since the timing and occasion of them would be unpredictable and preclude the presence of fresh garments.

130.  Guthrie, *Apocalypse*, 80. Guthrie writes: "This fits in well with the early Christian practice of giving people who had just been baptized a clean white robe." This is open to the same practical objections we just examined. Furthermore, in either case they had already worn/received the white garment; in contrast, John is discussing something to be given them as a reward at a future date. The chronology won't fit, though one might attempt to salvage the situation by arguing that John pictures them as permanently receiving the heavenly equivalent of what they had worn at/after baptism while on earth.

131.  Metzger, *Code*, 39–40.

132.  R. H. Charles, *Revelation*, 82, insists, "These garments are the spiritual bodies in which the faithful are to be clothed in the resurrection life." The various apocryphal and pseudeprighal sources he quotes (82–83), however, refer either to the individual *wearing* garments or *having* garments that are white in color. These fall considerably short of establishing the general rule he assumes.

What of biblical texts? He creatively introduces Matthew 13:43, which refers to how "the righteous will shine forth as the sun." Garments are not mentioned, and this would seem to more properly refer to their moral character shining outward to others. Charles insists that the idea is "clearly expressed" in 2 Corinthians 5:1, 4. Verse 1 implies the existence of a body under the image of having a "tent" to dwell in. At least verse 4 introduces the idea of being clothed in the resurrection, but the notion of color-free or white clothing as the reward is again absent. Charles ignores the basic difference between John's argument and Paul's. Paul (in context) is striving to prove that for a believer to enter heaven, the inner essence—the spirit, the soul—must be placed within a substitute for the physical body. Paul is discussing the nature of our existence in the resurrection. In contrast, John is discussing the *rewards* the righteous receive in the resurrection.

133. Ramsay, *Seven Churches*, 386.

134. Ford, *Revelation*, 409. Cf. Metzger, *Code*, 39.

135. M. Blaiklock, *Cities*, 117; Johnson, *Revelation*, 55.

136. Kelshaw, *Message*, 133–134.

137. Ford, *Revelation*, 410.

138. Ibid; Johnson, *Revelation*, 54; Mounce, *Revelation*, 112.

139. Blaiklock, *Cities*; Meinardus, *Patmos*, 106.

140. Ramsay, *Seven Churches*, 386.

141. Ibid., 387–88.

142. As quoted in ibid., 387.

143. Johnson, *Revelation*, 55.

144. Ibid., 54.

145. Wood, "Local Knowledge," 264.

146. Barclay, *Revelation*, 47; Kiddle, *Revelation*, 47.

147. Hemer, *Local Setting*, 148.

148. Quoted by ibid., 149.

149. Ibid.

150. Imagery found in other parts of the Revelation may also have been, partially, based upon that found in their pagan society. The image of a multi-headed creature finds an interesting parallel in Sardis. A carving of a multi-headed person was uncovered at "a Roman mausoleum found in Pactolus Cliff." It is the "head of a bearded man with [a] crown of twelve small diademed heads or busts, variously interpreted as emperors or the twelve Great Gods" (Hanfmann, *Letters*, 66; Hanfmann also includes a picture of the object). Although inappropriate for inclusion in the main text of a study of the historical and social allusions found in the mini-epistles, the existence of such phenomena should not be overlooked.

### 10. PHILADELPHIA: CITY OF OPPORTUNITY

1. Mounce, *Revelation*, 115.

2. J. C. Russell, *Population*, 80 provides the low figure. Since he concedes that the vast majority of scholars put the urban population of Asia Minor cities at much higher figures than he does, we speak in terms of the actual population being probably substantially higher.

3. Jones, *Greek City*, 162. Jones also reasons that since city citizenship was confined to tribe members, this resulted in only guild members being recognized as possessing city citizenship.

4. Jones, *Eastern Roman Provinces*, 80.

5. Johnson, "Revelation," 451.

6. Ibid.

7. Robbins, *Revelation*, 74.

8. Ibid.

9. E. M. Blaiklock, *Seven Churches*, 63, applies the expression to its religious aspect, while J. Massyngberde Ford, *Revelation*, 416, applies it to the broader area of Greek learning, culture, and ideals.

10. Yamauchi, *New Testament Cities*, 78.

11. Ashcroft, "Revelation," 272; Johnson, "Revelation," 451; Mounce, *Revelation*, 115; Robbins, *Revelation*, 74; Walvoord, *Revelation*, 83. Cf. Blaiklock, *Seven Churches*, 65; Laney, *Bible Atlas*, 248; Meinardus, *Ephesus*, 76.

12. Sherman E. Johnson, "Early Christianity in Asia Minor," *Journal of Biblical Literature* 77 (1958), 12.

13. Whiting, *Revelation*, 95.

14. Albert Henrichs, "Changing Dionysiac Identities," in Meyer and Sanders, *Self-Definition in the Greco-Roman World*, 147–49, attempts to limit the frequency with which such excesses occurred. The ease with which freely indulged alcohol removes sexual self-control in our own age argues strongly against going too far in that direction. In contrast, Stephen Benko, *Virgin Goddess*, 66, maintains that sexual license was a central tenet of certain of their celebrations.

15. Ross S. Kramer, "Ecstasy and Possession: The Attraction of Women to the Cult of Dionysos," *Harvard Theological Review* 72 (January 1979): 67.

16. Ibid., 55, 72. Perhaps the heavy female influence explains how the so-called demasculinization of the male gods (to soften their stern ruggedness) went so far in the cult. In contrast, Mithraists bent over backward to masculinize their cult, carrying it to the logical extreme of banning female participants. See Luther H. Martin, "The Pagan Religious Background," in *Early Christianity: Origins and Evolution to A.D. 600*, ed. Ian Hazlett (Nashville, Tenn.: Abingdon Press, 1991), 60–61.

17. Ferguson, *Backgrounds*, 245. In light of the tie-in between Dionysus and sexual and alcoholic excess, might this not be a legitimization of a lifestyle they would have lived regardless? Although one must be cautious in explaining religious choices on the basis of self-interest or self-rationalization, one would also be unwise in ignoring

their existence and the constant underlying pressure to create conformity between one's conduct and one's convictions.

18. Ibid., 246–48.

19. Godwin, *Mystery Religions*, 132.

20. Or, as Joscelyn Godwin prefers to word it, "[Dionysus] cannot be understood, only appreciated" (Ibid., 132).

21. For a presentation of Dionysus that develops this type of imagery, see Mario Vegetti, "The Greeks and Their Gods," in *The Greeks*, ed. Jean-Pierre Vernant, trans. Charles Lambert and Teresa Lavender Fagan (Chicago: University of Chicago Press, 1995), 266.

22. On this imagery see Charles Segal, "Spectator and Listener," in Revnant, *The Greeks*, 201.

23. Quoted in Grant, *Hellenistic Religions,* 29.

24. Onstad, *Courage*, 24.

25. Sweet, *Revelation*, 102.

26. Pfleiderer, *Primitive Christianity*, 102.

27. Ignatius, "Epistles of Ignatius," 93. The references in the text are to this volume.

28. The promise of a "crown" to faithful disciples (Rv 3:11) has also been taken as a reference to the ceremonial crowns received at Philadelphia festivals and athletic contests, for which the city is said to have had a special renown (Mounce, *Revelation*, 120). Such activities and games were exceedingly widespread and none of the sources utilized for this volume gave sufficient information to justify a separate section discussing this possible allusion. Indeed, Mounce, is the *only* writer to mention it, and his reference is a short one.

29. Among those who interpret the phrase within a missionary context are John M. Court, *Revelation*, 67; C. Anderson Scott, *Revelation*, 129; Bruce M. Metzger, *Code*, 41; Charles C. Whiting, *Revelation*, 98. William Ramsay, *Seven Churches*, 406, goes so far as to argue that Philadelphia was *already* noted for its missionary zeal and the reference to future opportunities is given for that very reason. Others prefer to make the spiritual point that of a guarantee that the believer would make it to heaven in spite of all the obstacles this earth might pose. Isbon T. Beckwith, *Apocalypse*, 480, cites several of the passages cited herein (Rv 3:20; 4:1; Acts 14:27; Jn 10:7, 9) to prove that "an admission into a place or state" is under consideration, and that it is heaven rather than providing missionary opportunities that is under consideration. Michael Wilcock, *I Saw Heaven Opened: The Message of Revelation* (London: Inter-Varsity Press, 1975), 55, takes a similar approach. Among certain of those holding to premillennialism in one of its various forms are those who take the place entered to be the (earthly/future/millennial)

kingdom rather than heaven itself. Alan Johnson, *Revelation*, 58, appears to favor this approach.

30. Brown, *Heavenly Visions*, 105–6; Ford, *Revelation*, 415; A. Meinardus, *Patmos*, 115.

31. Ford, *Revelation*, 416.

32. Ramsay, *Seven Churches*, 405.

33. Strabo, *Geography*, 12.8.18.

34. Ibid., 13.4.10. Cf. Pfeiffer and Vos, *Historical Geography*, 401.

35. Meinardus, *Ephesus*, 76; Toksoz, *Travel Guide*, 131. Several times before the A.D. 17 earthquake, earthquakes had inflicted major damage on the community. Cf. Walvoord, *Revelation*, 83.

36. Charles C. Whiting, *Revelation*, 98, stresses the ongoing, prolonged weakness of the city as the result of the quake. Charles C. Pfeiffer and Howard F. Vos, *Historical Geography*, 401, deny that there was any real loss of importance after the quake because "the city was quickly rebuilt." Even so, in the interim the city would have seemed weak and puny when compared to the scope of the task with them and a reference to that period would be appropriate. The theory of a *permanent* decline of the city is not required to erect a parallel with the church. Indeed, the fact that the city could "bounce back" would be an encouragement to a congregation acutely aware of its own present weakness.

37. Only Martin Kiddle, *Revelation*, 53, uses the reference to the pillar to make the point of stability in a city faced with a serious earthquake danger. In contrast, a number of commentarors use the reference "going out no more." For example, see Budden and Hastings, *Local Colour*, 329–30; Caird, *Revelation*, 55; Krodel, *Revelation*, 135; Wilfrid J. Harrington, *Revelation*, 71; Wilfrid J. Harrington, *Apocalypse*, 98; Wight, *Archaeology*, 188.

38. The high priest was to wear "a plate of pure gold" on which was the inscription "Holiness to the LORD" (Ex 28:36) while he offered sacrifices on behalf of the people (v. 38). Based on this text, Richard C. Trench argues that "in the 'kingdom of priests' this dignity shall not be any more the singular prerogative of one, but the common dignity of all" (*Seven Churches*, 244). On the other hand, the triple "imprinting" image of John is far more lengthy and seemingly far more profound in intention than mere ceremonial holiness while serving the Lord.

39. William Barclay, *Revelation*, 135, appeals to Numbers 6:27, where we read of the priests, "So they shall put my name on the children of Israel, and I will bless them." The right *words* are used, but the idea seems very different. In context, the Numbers text refers to receiving the *verbal* blessing God had decreed (vv. 24–26). Again, the triple

"imprinting" John refers to seems to require something far deeper and more profound.

40. Blaiklock, *Seven Churches*, 64.

41. Pfeiffer and Vos, *Historical Geography*, 401. Cf. Wight, *Archaeology*, 188–89.

42. Van Hartinsveld, *Revelation*, 23–24. Also holding this view are William Barclay, *Revelation*, 134–35, and J. Massyngberde Ford, *Revelation*, 417.

43. Hemer, *Local Setting*, 268.

44. Ibid., note.

45. Ibid.

46. Statue pedestals with names on them have been discovered in a number of places. See Avi-Yonah, *Views of the Biblical World*, 274.

47. Ford, *Revelation*, 417.

48. Avi-Yonah, *Views of the Biblical World*, 274. Avi-Yonah includes a picture of one such case, from Capernaum.

49. Quoted and discussed by Baez-Camargo, *Archaeological Commentary*, 264.

50. Court, *Revelation*, 68.

## 11. UNDECIDED LAODICEA

1. Ford, *Revelation*, 419.

2. Meinardus, *Patmos*, 125, and Cemil Toksoz, *Travel Guide*, 317, so date it. William M. Ramsay, *Phrygia*, 37, dates it 190 B.C.

3. M. Ramsay, *Phrygia*, 38.

4. Whiting, *Revelation*, 102.

5. Sherman E. Johnson, "Laodicea and Its Neighbors," *Biblical Archaeologist* 13 (February 1950): 12.

6. Ibid.

7. Hawley, *Asia Minor*, 187–88.

8. George E. Bean, *Turkey Beyond the Maeander*, rev. ed. (London: Ernest Benn, 1980), 216.

9. Johnson, "Laodicea and Its Neighbors," 12; Pfeiffer and Vos, *Historical Geography*, 379. George E. Bean, *Maeander*, 216, however, implies walls a kilometer in length and explicitly speaks in terms of a square kilometer being occupied by the city rather than a square mile.

10. Pfeiffer and Vos, *Historical Geography*, 379.

11. Bean, *Maeander*, 216; Toksoz, *Travel Guide*, 319.

12. Pfeiffer and V. Vos, *Historical Geography*, 379.

13. Loane, *They Overcame*, 101. For comparison, Philadelphia was forty miles away (ibid., 101) and Colossae ten miles (Ford, *Revelation*, 419).

14. Pfeiffer and Vos, *Historical Geography*, 379. Cf. Hawley, *Asia Minor*, 188.

15. Pfeiffer and Vos, *Historical Geography*, 379.

16. Bean, *Maeander*, 217.

17. Wendy Cotter, "Women's Authority Roles in Paul's Churches: Countercultural or Conventional?" *Novum Testamentum: An International Quarterly for New Testament and Related Studies* 36 (October 1994): 356.

18. As quoted in Meinardus, *Patmos*, 125.

19. Toksoz, *Travel Guide*, 317.

20. Ibid.; Bean, *Maeander*, 214–15.

21. Metzger, *Code*, 43; Pfeiffer and Voss, *Historical Geography*, 377; Ramsay, *Phrygia*, 39–40.

22. Cicero, *ad Fam.* iii. 5, as cited in Johnson, "Laodicea and Its Neighbors," 17, and Ramsay, *Phrygia*, 40.

23. Ramsay, *Phrygia*, 40.

24. Barclay, *Revelation*, 138.

25. Ramsay, *Phrygia*, 40.

26. Ibid., 40. It should be noted that wool was also exported after being manufactured into carpets (Ford, *Revelation*, 419).

27. For a description of the different types of garments that were manufactured see Ramsay, *Phrygia*, 40–42; see also idem, *Seven Churches*, 416.

28. Strabo, *Geography*, 12.8.16.

29. Saturnio Ximinez, *Asia Minor in Ruins*, trans. Arthur Chambers (London: Hutchinson & Co., 1925), 160.

30. Meeks, *Urban Christians*, 44.

31. Jones, *Eastern Roman Provinces*, 74. When William M. Ramsay, *Phrygia*, 60, wrote at a much earlier date, only the first three of these were documented.

32. Ramsay, *Phrygia*, 114.

33. Ibid., 71.

34. Bean, *Maeander*, 219.

35. Ximinez, *Asia Minor*, 160.

36. Yamauchi, *New Testament Cities*, 143.

37. Freya Stark, *Ionia: A Quest* (New York: Harcourt, Brace and Company, 1954), 224.

38. Hawley, *Asia Minor*, 188; Pfeiffer and Vos, *Historical Geography*, 379.

39. Toksoz, *Travel Guide*, 319.

40. Yamauchi, *New Testament Cities*, 140. Cf. Ramsay, *Phrygia*, 47–48.

41. In his description, Cemil Toksoz, *Travel Guide*, 319, is clearly skeptical.

42. Pfeiffer and Voss, *Historical Geography*, 379.

43. Cemil Toksoz, *Travel Guide*, 319, prefers this verbal formulation. William M. Ramsay preferred the term "amphitheatric stadium," *Phrygia*, 47. George E. Bean, *Maeander*, 217 prefers "amphitheatral stadium." We might, with justice, simply call it a combined amphitheater-stadium.

44. Bean, *Maeander*, 217.

45. Pfeiffer and Voss, *Historical Geography*, 379; Ramsay, *Phrygia*, 47.

46. Yamauchi, *Cities of New Testament*, 142.

47. George E. Bean, *Maeander*, 217, puts the figure at 380 yards, that is, 1,140 feet.

48. Stark, *Ionia*, 224.

49. Magie, *Asia Minor*, 572; Meinardus, "Christian Remains," 357. It may have been a reconstructed, rearranged, and expanded stadium. Saturnio Ximiniez, *Asia Minor*, 159, explicitly speaks in terms of the stadium being converted into an amphitheater, and it does seem more likely that a facility not matching the traditional form of either would result from an expansion of a preexisting facility.

50. Ximinez, *Asia Minor*, 159–160.

51. Quoted by Edwin M. Yamauchi, *New Testament Cities*, 142.

52. Bean, *Maeander*, 217; M. Yamauchi, *New Testament Cities*, 142.

53. Ramsay, *Phrygia*, 55–56.

54. Bean, *Maeander*, 217.

55. William M. Ramsay, *Phrygia*, 75–77, discusses the inscription and the two interpretations.

56. William J. Hamilton, *Researches in Asia Minor*, vol. 1 (London: John Murray, 1842; reprint: Hildescheim [Germany]: Georg Olms Verlag, 1984), 516.

57. Ibid., 515–16. These "stone barrel-pipes" are described by Freya Stark, *Ionia*, 224, as "mortar pipe laid through square joined blocks of chiselled stone." For a photograph of the pipe see the opposite page 224 in her work.

58. Bean, *Maeander*, 221.

59. Ibid., 220–21.

60. Ibid., 221.

61. Bean himself is inclined toward river based water supplies as adequate for the community up to the time this aqueduct system was erected (ibid.).

62. MacMullen, *Paganism*, 17.

63. Ibid., 16–17.

64. Ibid., 149.

65. Ibid., 16.

66. Yamauchi, *New Testament Cities*, 143–44.

67. Johnson, "Asia Minor," 84.

68. Yamauchi, *New Testament Cities*, 143.

69. Bean, *Maeander*, 215.

70. Yamauchi, *New Testament Cities*, 143.

71. Ibid., 145.

72. Ibid.

73. Cemil Toksoz, *Travel Guide*, 317, refers to both Zeus and Men as very popular in the city and makes no judgment between them. Both George E. Bean, *Maeander*, 215, and Edwin M. Yamauchi, *New Testament Cities*, 143, refer to Zeus as the most important.

74. Bean, *Maeander*, 215; Yamauchi, *New Testament Cities*, 143. William M. Ramsay notes speculation that Zeus Aseis was a Hellenized form of an original non-Greek "oriental" deity (*Phrygia*, 34). So far as Laodicea in particular goes (in possible contrast to other communities in the province), Ramsay identifies Zeus Aseis as specifically a Hellenized form of Men Karou (ibid., 52). On the problems involved in deciding whether similarly named deities are variants of the same god or genuinely distinct objects of worship see Mitchell, *Church*, 19.

75. Yamauchi, *New Testament Cities*, 143.

76. Ramsay, *Phrygia*, 53–54.

77. On his supposed preeminence as most important god of Laodicea see Robbins, *Revelation*, 78, and Whiting, *Revelation*, 102.

78. On his regional importance see Robbins, *Revelation*, 78; Whiting, *Revelation*, 102; Bean, *Maeander*, 215; Mitchell, *Church*, 24–25; and Toksoz, *Travel Guide*, 317.

79. Yamauchi, *New Testament Cities*, 145.

80. Whiting, *Revelation*, 103.

81. Charles C. Whiting, *Revelation*, 103, and Edwin M. Yamauchi, *New Testament Cities*, 145, indicate the lack of explicit mention. Others simply assume the school existed in Laodicea in their remarks: Richard L. Jeske, *Revelation*, 55; Sweet, *Revelation*, 118; and Wilfrid J. Harrington, *Revelation*, 75. M. J. S. Rudwick and E. M. Green, "The Laodicean Lukewarmness," *Expository Times* 69 (1957-58): 176, are among the few to assume that it was at the cult site outside the city. William Barclay, *Revelation*, 138, occupies a kind of mediating position; he believes the school *began* at the temple but was later *transferred* into Laodicea. J. Massyngberde Ford simply refers to the school as "near" the temple site (*Revelation*, 419).

82. Ramsay, *Seven Churches*, 418. The coins date as far back as the reign of Augustus (Blaiklock, *Cities*, 125).

83. Hemer, "Cities of the Revelation," 56.

84. Eugene N. Lane, "Men: A Neglected Cult of Roman Asia Minor," in *Aufstieg und Niedergang der Romischen Welt* (Berlin: Walter de Gruyter, 1990), II, 18.3, 2161–62.

85. See map 1 in ibid., 2161–62.

86. See map 2 in ibid.

87. Ibid., 2161.

88. G. H. Horsley, "Expiation and the Cult of Men," in Horsley, *New Documents Illustrating Early Christianity*, 21.

89. Lane, "Men," 2161.

90. Ibid.

91. Horsley, "Cult of Men," 30. Horsley points to the week or so that Paul ministered in Antioch in contrast with his multi-year labor in Ephesus and speculates that Paul's opposition to polytheism may have been more effectively turned against him in Antioch. He argues that the town officials were probably devotees of Men.

92. Toksoz, *Travel Guide*, 317.

93. Leaney, *Jewish and Christian World*, 35.

94. Cf. Ford, *Revelation*, 420; Ramsay, *Seven Churches*, 420.

95. Mounce, *Revelation*, 123–24.

96. P. R. Coleman-Norton, "The Apostle Paul and the Roman Law of Slavery," in *Studies in Roman Economic and Social History–in Honor of Allan Chester Johnson*, ed. P. R. Coleman-Norton with the assistance of F. C. Bourne and J. V. A. Fine (Princeton: Princeton University Press, 1951), 166. Coleman-Norton, 173–77, provides a useful and concise summary of Roman laws requiring the return of escaped slaves and surveying some of the punishments that Philemon's runaway slave, Onesimus, might have faced.

97. Meinardus, *Patmos*, 129.

98. For parallel-column Latin and English translation see John Rutherford, *St. Paul's Epistles to Colossae and Laodicea* (Edinburgh: T. & T. Clark, 1908), 45–47. For a critical introduction to this Latin document (no Greek text has yet been uncovered), as well as a more recent translation of the document itself, see Wilhelm Schneemelcher, "The Epistle to the Laodiceans," in *New Testament Apocrypha*, ed. Edgar Hennecke, rev. ed., ed. Wilhelm Schneemelcher, trans. R. McL. Wilson (Louisville, Ky: Westminster/John Knox Press, 1992), 42–46. On scholarly downplaying of the value of the pseudo-Laodicean epistle see Philip Sellew, "Laodiceans and the Philippians Fragments Hypothesis," *Harvard Theological Review* 87 (January 1994): 17–28, who cautions that

it might still provide useful information in regard to genuine Pauline works (21–22)

99.  Gary Demarest, *Colossians: The Mystery of Christ* (Waco, Tex.: Word Books, 1979), 189; Ralph R. Martin, *Ephesians, Colossians, and Philemon* (Atlanta, Ga.: John Knox Press, 1991), 131; Peter T. O'Brien, *Colossians, Philemon,* vol. 44 of the Word Biblical Commentary series (Waco, Tex.: Word Books, 1982), 258; Arthur G. Patzia, *Colossians, Philemon, Ephesians* (San Francisco: Harper & Row, 1984), 87; Petr Pokorny, *Colossians: A Commentary,* trans. Siegfried S. Schatzmann (Peabody, Mass.: Hendrickson Publishers, 1991), 194; Eduard Schweizer, *The Letter to the Colossians: A Commentary,* trans. Andrew Chester (Minneapolis: Augsburg Publishing House, 1976), 242; Tolbert, *Colossians...Philemon,* 63; Thoms L. Trevethan, *Our Joyful Confidence: The Lordship of Jesus in Colossians* (Downer's Grove, Ill.: InterVarsity Press, 1981), 161; George A. Turner, "Colossians," in Carter, et al., *Romans-Philemon,* 507; Meeks, *Urban Christians,* 210. Murray J. Harris, *Colossians and Philemon* (Grand Rapids, Mich.: Wm. B. Eerdmans Publishing Company, 1991), 214, implies its loss by accepting it as a genuine Pauline epistle and not suggesting that it may have survived under the name of one of his other epistles. Likewise, Charles B. Williams, *A Commentary on the Pauline Epistles* (Chicago: Moody Press, 1953), 426, implies its loss.

100.  Embracing the theory are G. B. Caird, *Paul's Letters from Prison: Ephesians, Philippians, Colossians, Philemon,* New Clarendon Bible Commentary series (Oxford: Oxford University Press, 1976), 212; Walter K. Firminger, *Colossians and Philemon,* Indian Church Commentaries (Madras [India]: S.P.C.K., 1921), 230; H. A. Ironside, *Lectures on the Epistle to the Colossians* (New York: Bible Truth Press, 1929), 184; Michael D. Goulder, "The Visionaries of Laodicea," *Journal for the Study of the New Testament* 43 (September 1991), 39; Maurice Jones, *The Epistle of St. Paul to the Colossians* (London: Society for Promotion of Christian Knowledge, 1923), 115; Archilbald T. Robertson, *Paul and the Intellectuals: The Epistle to the Colossians* (Garden City, N.Y.: Doubleday, Doran and Company, 1928), 209; W. H. Griffith Thomas, *Studies in Colossians and Ephesians* (Grand Rapids, Mich.: Kregel Publications, 1986), 134, and E. R. O. White, "Colossians," in *The Broadman Bible Commentary,* vol. 11: *2 Corinthians-Philemon,* ed. Clifton J. Allen (Nashville, Tenn.: Broadman Press, 1971), 255.

Those explicitly rejecting the theory include Eduard Lohse, *Colossians and Philemon,* ed. Helmut Koester, trans. William R. Poehlmann and Robert J. Harris (Philadelphia: Fortress Press, 1971), 175, and Petr Pokorny, *Colossians: A Commentary,* trans. Siegfried S. Schatzmann (Peabody, Mass.: Hendrickson Publishers, 1991), 194; Curtis Vaughn,

"Colossians," in *The Expositor's Bible Commentary*, vol. 11: *Ephesians-Philemon*, ed. Frank E. Gabelein (Grand Rapids, Mich.: Zondervan Publishing House, 1978), 226.

101. For a defense of this approach see C. P. Anderson, "Hebrews Among the Letters of Paul," *Studies in Religion/Sciences Religieuses* 5 (1975–76), 258–66. For a rejecting evaluation of this approach see J. B. Lightfoot, *Saint Paul's Epistles to the Colossians and to Philemon*, rev. ed. (London: Macmillan and Company, 1879), 280.

102. Mentioning the possibility but not explicitly embracing it are J. L. Houldon, *Paul's Letters from Prison: Philippians, Colossians, Philemon and Ephesians*, Westminster Pelican Commentaries series (Philadelphia: Westminster Press, 1977), and Schweizer, *Colossians*, 242. For negative evaluations see Ralph R. Martin, *Colossians and Philemon*, New Century Bible Commentary series (Greenwood, S.C.: Attic Press, 1974), 138; and Lightfoot, *Colossians*, 281.

103. For a defense of this approach see Charles P. Anderson, "Who Wrote 'the Epistle from Laodicea'?" *Journal of Biblical Literature* 85 (1966): 436–40. For arguments against see Martin, *Colossians*, 278.

104. The German commentator Baumgarten was attracted by this possibility. See Lightfoot, *Colossians*, 278.

105. Lightfoot, *Colossians*, 274–75.

106. For negative evaluations see Herbert W. Carson, *Colossians and Philemon*, Tyndale New Testament Commentary series (Grand Rapids, Mich.: Wm. B. Eerdmans Publishing Company, 1960), 101, and Jean Daille, *An Exposition of the Epistle of Saint Paul to the Colossians*, trans. F. S., rev. corrected by James Sherman (1648 original French printing; reprinted English translation, Philadelphia: Presbyterian Board of Publication, 18–), 683.

107. John Fellows, *Travels and Researches in Asia Minor* (London: John Murray, 1852), 212. C. H. Hemer sees the erection of the pipeline as an unsuccessful effort to overcome the foulness of the nearest water supplies: "The rings of lime deposit inside the pipes testify plainly after nineteen hundred years to the fact that this water too was warm and so impure that it must have made the traveler vomit" ("Seven Cities," 247–48). On the other hand, if the water through this region was *really* that bad, how did it support a human population at all?

108. Baez-Camargo, *Archaeological Commentary*, 264; Sweet, *Revelation*, 107.

109. Yamauchi, *New Testament Cities*, 141.

110. Johnson, "Laodicea and Its Neighbors," 11.

111. Selles, *Revelation*, 35. Similar direct linkage is found in Edwin Yamauchi, "Archaeology and the New Testament," in *Archaeology*

*and the Bible: An Introductory Study,* ed. Edwin Yamauchi (Grand Rapids, Mich.: Zondervan, 1979), 84. The linkage was accepted in ibid., 103, but rejected in his slightly later *New Testament Cities,* 141, in which he notes that the water pipes run in the wrong direction.

112. Usually only the southward direction is mentioned, along with the hot springs being in the area of the city of Denizli: M. J. S. Rudwick and E. M. Green, "The Laodicean Lukewarmness," *Expository Times* 69 (1957-58), 177; Bruce, "Revelation," 641; Finegan, *Archaeology,* 179; Court, *Myth and History,* 40; Mounce, *Revelation,* 123. Sherman E. Johnson, however, in "Laodicea and Its Neighbors," 10, explicitly points out that this excludes Hierapolis as a source of the city's water supply. Colin J. Hemer, *Local Setting,* 277, also does so in explicit terms. He cautions that pinpointing Denizli as the *specific* source of the water pushes the evidence beyond what it will clearly support. Freya Stark, *Ionia,* 224, believes that the water supply originated in the Denizli area, not from hot springs but from "the Lycus river."

113. Wilfrid J. Harrington, *Revelation,* 74. Cf. her similar remarks in *Apocalypse,* 100. A similar approach is taken by G. R. Beasley-Murray, *Revelation,* 105; Charles H. Giblin, *Revelation,* 65; Swete, *Apocalypse,* 60; and Whiting, *Revelation,* 104-5.

114. Sir John Fellows, *Travels and Reseaches,* 212, could clearly see it "six or seven miles" from Laodicea. However, he also writes, "My attention had been attracted at twenty miles' distance by the singular aspect of its hill, upon which there appeared to be perfectly white streams poured down its sides" (212).

115. Kelshaw, *Message,* 165.

116. Finegan, *Archaeology,* 182. Others who accept this tri-city interpretation include F. F. Bruce, "Colossian Problems, Part I: Jews and Christians in the Lycus Valley," *Bibliotheca Sacra* 141 (January-March 1984): 9; Court, *Revelation,* 36; Johnson in both "Revelation," 457, and *Revelation,* 63; Chilton, *Days of Vengeance,* 134; Jeske, *Revelation,* 55-56; and Rudwick and Green, "Laodicean Lukewarmness," 177.

117. Court, *Revelation,* 36.

118. Ramsay, *Phrygia,* 52.

119. Wilfrid J. Harrington, *Revelation,* 75; Jeske, *Revelation,* 55; Rudwick and Green, "Laodicean Lukewarmness, 176; Prevost, *Apocalypse,* 73; Sweet, *Revelation,* 118; Wight, *Archaeology,* 189; Wilcock, *Heaven Opened,* 56-57.

120. Hemer, "Cities of the Revelation," 56. In his "Seven Cities," 247, he simply speaks in terms of "eye ointments" available locally rather than this specific one. Edwin M. Yamauchi, *New Testament Cities,*

145–46, similarly speaks in broad terms of eye salves used for both cosmetic and curative purposes rather than of this one particular type.

121. Ramsay, *Phrygia*, 52.

122. Blaiklock, *Cities*, 125.

123. Harald Nielsen, a specialist on ancient eye medications, writes:

> The medicament was one of the miracle medicines of ancient times. It can also be seen that the juice from the balm (balsamodendron) is highly praised by the medical writers of antiquity.
>
> The tree opobalsamum (Burseraceae) originates in southern Arabia (Sheba), but was introduced into the valley of Jordan near Jericho (hence the nickname judaicum). The balsam was extracted from the tree through superficial cuts in its surface. The harvest however was not large. As a result, Alexander the Great, when he had conquered the areas in which the balsam tree grew, immediately gave orders for the collection of the precious balsam. After a whole day of collecting, the King had only obtained a basketful.
>
> "After a while the balsam tree was also cultivated in Egypt and Syria, but the Jewish balm continued to be considered the best. After Titus' campaign against the Israelites in 70 A.D., the rebellious population tried to wipe out the balsam trees in revenge. However the Romans succeeded in saving some of them, and one of the rescued trees was used as a trophy in Titus' triumph after the victory. Later the Romans tried to have the state pay for the reintroduction of the tree into the Engeddy valley near the Red Sea, to give work to the people of Palestine (Ancient Ophthalmological Agents, trans Lars McBride [Odense, Denmark: Odense University Press, 1974], 50-51).

124. Ibid., 100.

125. *Orah Hayim* cccxxviii. 21, as cited by Immanuel Jakobovits, *Jewish Medical Ethics*, 75, cf. 283.

126. John Guimond, *The Silencing of Babylon: A Spiritual Commentary on the Revelation of John* (New York: Paulist Press, 1991), 25.

127. Prevost, *Apocalypse*, 73.

128. Sitwell, *Roman Roads*, 193.

129. Bruce, "Revelation, 641; Hemer, "Seven Cities," 247; Ford,

*Revelation*, 419; Kraeling, *Atlas*, 472; Sweet, *Revelation*, 108; Sinclair, *Revelation*, 51.

130. Robbins, *Revelation*, 80. M. J. S. Rudwick and E. M. Green, "Laodicean Lukewarmness," 176, make the contrast not an economic one but a *fashion* one; to "the cloaks of black wool, called 'Laodicia,' for the manufacture of which the city was celebrated."

131. Colin J. Hemer, "Seven Cities," 247, sees John as alluding to Laodicea's status as "a great banking center." Jean-Pierre Prevost, *Apocalypse*, refers it to the city's "financial exploits." The importance of Laodicea's wool and garment industries should never be underestimated, however. Strabo certainly has them in mind when he refers to "the fertility of its territory and the prosperity of certain of its citizens" as combining to make the city "great" (*Geography*, 12.6.16).

132. The individual was Hiero. See Saturnio Ximinez, *Asia Minor*, 159.

133. Albert A. Bell Jr., "The Date of John's Apocalypse: Evidence of Some Roman Historians Reconsidered," *New Testament Studies* 25 (1978–79):101.

134. Tacitus, *The Works of Tacitus*, vol. 1: *The Annals*. Bohn's Classical Library: The Oxford Translation, rev. (London: Henry G. Bohn, 1854), xiv, 27.

135. Berrett, *Discovering*, 621; Blaiklock, *Cities*, 125; Hemer, "Seven Cities," 247; Kraeling, *Atlas*, 472; Ramsay, *Seven Churches*, 428; Walvoord, *Revelation*, 89. The earthquake did major damage to Hierapolis and Colossae as well. See Magie, *Asia Minor*, 1421; Emil Ilhan, "Earthquakes in Turkey," in *Geology and History of Turkey*, ed. Angus S. Campbell (Tripoli: Petroleum Exploration Society of Libya, 1971), 434.

136. Ramsay, *Seven Churches*, 428.

137. The A.D. 60 derives from Tacitus's dating of the quake, but both Orosius and Eusebius place it after the great fire in Rome during Nero's reign (Mounce, *Revelation*, 123). If the latter are correct, then John wrote after *two* major quakes, in both of which the city had shown its wealth and pride through independent rebuilding.

138. Ulrich B. Miller, "Apocalyptic Currents," in *Christian Beginnings: Word and Community from Jesus to Post-Apostolic Times*, ed. Jurgen Becker, 281-329 (Louisville, Ky.: Westminster/John Knox Press, 1993), 318, links the reference to their nakedness in 3:18 to the practice of the gymnasiums. If one accepts this, then a further link to the clothes-buying plea would be most natural.

139. Hemer, *Local Setting*, 204.

# Bibliography

In order to facilitate the use of this bibliography, the subject matter has been divided into several major sections. It should be noted, however, that a number of works might, just as appropriately, be listed under a different section.

Dashes as part of the date of a publication indicate that the publication date can only be determined to the degree of specificity indicated (century or decade).

Authors' names are as in the original books cited. Hence, the same individual may be listed under his or her initials *and* the full name because of a variance in procedure from one published work to another.

## Primary Sources: Ancient (Including Compendiums of Extracts from Ancient Sources)

Aristides, Aelius. "Roman Oration." In James H. Oliver, *The Ruling Power: A Study of the Roman Empire in the Second Century After Christ Through the Oration of Aelius Aristides*, 895–907 (English translation), 982–91 (Greek text). Philadelphia: American Philosophical Society, 1953.

*Apocalypse of Baurch*. Translated from the Syriac by R. H. Charles. London: Adam and Charles Black, 1896.

Austin, M. M. *The Hellenistic World from Alexander to the Roman Conquest: A Selection of Ancient Sources in Translation*. Cambridge: Cambridge University Press, 1981.

Bagnall, Roger S., and Peter Derow. *Greek Historical Documents: The Hellenistic Period*. SBL Sources for Biblical Study 16. Chico, Calif.: Scholars Press for the Society of Biblical Literature, 1981.

Bets, Hans Dieter. "Introduction to the Greek Magical Papyri." In *The Greek Magical Papyri in Translation*. Edited by Hans Dieter Beta, xli-liii. Chicago: University of Chicago Press, 1986.

Book of Enoch or 1 Enoch. Translated from the Ethiopian by R. H. Charles. Oxford: Clarendon Press, 1912.

Cicero. *Philippics*. Loeb Classical Library. Translated by Walter C. A. Ker. Cambridge, Mass.: Harvard University Press, 1926; 1969 reprint.

"Dialogue with Trypho." In *The Ante-Nicene Fathers*. Volume 1: *Apostolic Fathers: Justin Martyr, Irenaeus*. Edited by Alexander Roberts and James Donaldson. New York: Charles Scribner's Sons, 1899.

Dio. *Roman History* (Books LV-LX). Loeb Classical Library. London: William Heinemann, 19–.

Edelstein, Emma J., and Ludwig Edelstein. *Asclepius: A Collection and Interpretation of the Testimonies*. Volume 1. Baltimore: Johns Hopkins Press, 1945.

Eusebius. *Ecclesiastical History of Eusebius Pamphilus*. 1833; reprint, London: G. Bell and Sons, 1917.

Ferguson, John. *Greek and Roman Religion–A Source Book*. Park Ridge, N.J.: Noyes Press, 1980.

"First and Second Esdras" (New English Bible translation). In *The Cambridge Bible Commentary: First and Second Book of Esdras, with commentary* by R. J. Coggins and M. A. Knibb. Cambridge: Cambridge University Press, 1979.

Goodspeed, Edgar J. *The Apostolic Fathers: An American Translation*. New York: Harper & Brothers, 1950.

Grant, Frederick C. *Ancient Roman Religion*. New York: Liberal Arts Press, 1957.

———. *Hellenistic Religions: The Age of Syncretism*. Indianapolis, Ind.: Bobbs-Merrill Company, 1953.

Grant, Robert M. *The Apostolic Fathers: A New Translation and Commentary*. Volume 1: *An Introduction*. New York: Thomas Nelson and Sons, 1964. Volume 4: *Ignatius of Antioch*. New York: Thomas Nelson and Sons, 1966.

Gregg, Robert C., and Dan Urman. *Jews, Pagans, and Christians in the Golan Heights: Greek and Other Inscriptions of the Roman and Byzantine Eras*. South Florida Studies in the History of Judaism. Volume 140. Atlanta, Ga: Scholars Press, 1996.

Herodotus. *The History of Herodotus*. Translated by George Rawlinson. Four volumes. London: John Murray, 1858-60.

Ignatius. "Epistles of Ignatius." In *The Ante-Nicene Fathers*. Volume 1: *The Apostolic Fathers: Justin Martyr, Irenaeus*. Edited by Alexander Roberts and James Donaldson, 45–96. New York: Charles Scribner's Sons, 1899.

Josephus. *Josephus: Complete Works*. Translated by William Whiston

(1867). Reprint edition, Grand Rapids, Mich.: Kregel Publications, 1972.

Lefkowitz, Mary R., and Maureen B. Fant. *Women's Life in Greece and Rome: A Sourcebook in Translation.* Second edition. Baltimore: Johns Hopkins University Press, 1992.

Lewis, Naphtali. *Greek Historical Documents–The Roman Principate: 27 B.C.–285 A.D.* Toronto: A. M. Hakkert, 1974.

LiDonnica, Lynn R. *The Epidaurian Miracle Inscriptions: Text, Translation, and Commentary.* Atlanta, Ga.: Scholars Press, 1995.

Livy (Titus Livius). *The History of Rome (Books XXI-XXX).* Translated by D. Spillan and Cyrus Edmonds. New York: Harper & Brothers, Publishers, 1892.

MacMullen, Ramsay, and Eugene N. Lane. *Paganism and Christianity, 100–425 C.E.–A Sourcebook.* Minneapolis: Fortress Press, 1992.

"Martyrdom of Polycarp." ["The Encyclical Epistle of the Church at Smyrna Concerning the Martyrdom of the Holy Polycarp."] In *The Ante-Nicene Fathers,* Volume 1: *The Apostolic Fathers: Justin Martyr, Irenaeus.* Edited by Alexander Roberts and James Donaldson, 39–44. New York: Charles Scribner's Sons, 1899.

Meijer, Fik, and Onno van Nijf. *Trade, Transport, and Society in the Ancient World: A Sourcebook.* London: Routledge, 1992.

Pausanias. *Description of Greece.* Translated by Thomas Taylor. Three volumes. London: Richard Priestly, High Holborn, 1824.

Pausanias. *Pausanias' Guide to Greece.* Volume 1. Translated by Peter Levi. [Great Britain]: Penguin Books, 1979.

Pedley, John Griffiths. *Ancient Literary Sources on Sardis.* Archaeological Exploration of Sardis, Monograph 2. Cambridge, Mass.: Harvard University Press, 1972.

Philo. *The Embassy to Gaius.* Loeb Classical Library. *Philo,* volume 10. Translated by F. H. Colson. Cambridge, Mass.: Harvard University Press, 1962; reprint, 1971.

Philostratus. *The Life of Apollonius of Tyana.* Translated by F. C. Conybeare. Volume 1. Loeb Classical Library. London: William Heinemann, 1912.

Philostratus. *Lives of the Sophists.* In *Philostratus and Eunapius: The Lives of the Sophists.* Revised. Translated by Wilmer C. Wright. Loeb Classical Library. London: William Heinemann, 1952.

Pliny. *Natural History (Books III-VI).* Loeb Classical Library. Translated by H. Rackhan. Cambridge: Harvard University Press, 1942.

Pollitt, J. J. *The Art of Ancient Greece: Sources and Documents.* Cambridge: Cambridge University Press, 1990.

Polybius. *The Histories of Polybius.* Volume 1. Translated by Evelyn S.

Shuckburgh. 1889; reprinted with a new introduction by F. W. Wilbank, Bloomington: Indiana University Press, 1962.

Polycarp. "Epistle to the Philippians." In *The Ante-Nicene Fathers*. Volume 1: *The Apostolic Fathers: Justin Martyr, Irenaeus*. Edited by Alexander Roberts and James Donaldson, 31–36. New York: Charles Scribner's Sons, 1899.

Rice, David G., and John E. Stambaugh. *Sources for the Study of Greek Religion*. Missoula, Mont.: Scholars Press, 1979.

Schneemelcher, Wilhelm. "The Epistle to the Laodiceans." In *New Testament Apocrypha*. Edited by Edgar Hennecke. Revised edition edited by Wilhelm Schneemelcher, 42–46. Translated from the German by R. McL. Wilson. Louisville, Ky.: Westminster/John Knox Press, 1992.

Sherk, Robert K. *Roman Documents from the Greek East: "Senatus Consulta" and "Epistulae" to the Age of Augustus*. Baltimore: Johns Hopkins Press, 1969.

Stern, Menahem. *Greek and Latin Authors on Jews and Judaism*. Volume 1: *From Herodotus to Plutarch*. Jerusalem: Israel Academy of Sciences and Humanities, 1974. Volume 2: *From Tacitus to Simplicius*. Jerusalem: Israel Academy of Sciences and Humanities, 1980.

Strabo. *The Geography of Strabo*. Greek text with English translation by Horace Leonard Jones. Loeb Classical Library. Books 10–12: London: William Heinemann, 1928. Books 13–14: London: William Heinemann, 1929.

Suetonius. *The Lives of the Twelve Caesars*. Translated by Alexander Thomson. Revised by T. Forester. London: George Bell & Sons, 1896 reprint.

Sweet, Waldo. *Sport and Recreation in Ancient Greece: A Sourcebook with Translations*. New York: Oxford University Press, 1987.

"Syriac Apocalypse of Baruch." Translated by R. H. Charles. Revised by L. H. Brockington. In *The Apocryphal Old Testament*. Edited by H. F. D. Sparks. Oxford: Clarendon Press, 1984.

Tacitus. *The Works of Tacitus*. Volume 1: *The Annals*. Bohn's Classical Library: The Oxford Translation, Revised. London: Henry G. Bohn, 1854.

[Tatius, Achilles.] *Achilles Tatius [Clitophon and Leucippe]*. Loeb Classical Library. Translated by S. Gaselee. London: William Heinemann, 1917.

"Testament of Dan" and "Testament of Levi." In "The Testaments of the Twelve Patriarchs." Translated by M. de Jonge. In *The Apocryphal Old Testament*. Edited by H. F. D. Sparks. Oxford: Clarendon Press, 1984.

Thucydides, "The Peloponnesian War." Translated by Benjamin Jowett. In *The Greek Historians: The Complete and Unabridged Historical Works of Herodotus, Thucydides, Xenophon, Arrian*. Edited by Francis R. B. Godolphin. New York: Random House, 1942.

Varro, M. Terentius. *On Agriculture*. Loeb Classical Library. Translated by William D. Hooper. Revised by Harrison B. Ash. Cambridge, Mass.: Harvard University Press, 1935; 1967 reprint.

Vermaseren, M. J.. *Corpus Cultus Cybelae Attidisque (CCCA) I. Asia Minor*. Leiden: E. J. Brill, 1987.

Victronius. "Commentary on the Apocalypse of the Blessed John." Translated by Robert E. Wallis. In *The Ante-Nicene Fathers*. Volume 7: *Lactantius, Venantius, Asterius, Victroninus, Dionysius, Apostolic Teaching and Constitutions, Homily, and Liturgies*. Edited by Alexander Roberts and James Donaldson. Buffalo, N.Y.: Christian Literature Company, 1886.

Whittaker, Molly. *Jews and Christians: Graeco-Roman Views*. Cambridge [England]: Cambridge University Press, 1984.

Workman, B. K. *They Saw It Happen in Classical Times: An Anthology of Eyewitnesses' Accounts of Events in the Histories of Greece and Rome, 1400 B.C.–A.D. 540*. Oxford: Basil Blackwell, 1964.

Xenophon. *Cyropaedia*. Greek text with English translation by Walter Miller. Loeb Classical Library. London: William Heinemann, 1914.

## Primary Sources: Modern

Curtis, William E. *Today in Syria and Palestine*. Chicago: Fleming H. Revell Company, 1903.

Durbin, John P. *Observations in the East: Chiefly in Egypt, Palestine, Syria, and Asia Minor*. Volume 2. New York: Harper & Brothers, Publishers, 1845.

Fellows, [Sir] Charles. *Travels and Researches in Asia Minor*. London: John Murray, 1852.

Hamilton, William J. *Researches in Asia Minor*. Volume 1. London: John Murray, 1842. Reprint: Hildesheim [Germany]: Georg Olms Verlag, 1984.

Hawley, Walter A. *Asia Minor*. London: John Lane/Bodley Head, 1918.

McGarvey, J. W. *Lands of the Bible*. Philadelphia: Lippincott, 1881.

Miller, Ellen Clare. *Eastern Sketches: Notes of Scenery, Schools, and Tent Life in Syria and Palestine*. Edinburgh [Scotland]: W. Oliphant, 1871; reprint, New York: Arno Press, 1977.

Oliphant, Laurence. *Haifa or Life in Modern Palestine*. Edited by Charles A. Dane. New York: Harper & Brothers, 1886; 1887 printing.

Pentreath, Guy. *Hellenic Traveller: A Guide to the Ancient Sites of Greece*. New York: Crowell Company, 1964.

Stark, Freya. *Ionia: A Quest*. New York: Harcourt, Brace and Company, 1954.

Tozer, Henry F. *The Islands of the Aegean*. Oxford: Oxford University Press, 1889; reprinted, Chicago: Obol International, 1976.

Van Lennep, Henry J. *Travels in Little-Known Parts of Asia Minor*. Volume 2. London: John Murray, 1870.

Walsh, Robert. *Constantinople and the Scenery of the Seven Churches of Asia*. London: Fisher, Son, and Co., 1838.

Wilson, Charles Major-General Sir. *Handbook for Travellers in Asia Minor, Trans-caucasia, Persia, etc.* London: John Murray, 1895; 1911 reprint.

Wood, J. T. *Modern Discoveries on the Site of Ancient Ephesus*. Oxford: The Religious Tract Society, 1890.

Ximinez, Saturnio. *Asia Minor in Ruins*. Translated from the Spanish by Arthur Chambers. London: Hutchinson & Co., 1925.

## Commentaries and Related Literature: Revelation

Alford, Henry. *The New Testament for English Readers*. Volume 2, Part 2: *The Epistle to the Hebrews, the Catholic Epistles, and the Revelation*. New edition. Boston: Lee and Shepard, 1880.

Allen, Cady H. *The Message of the Book of Revelation*. Nashville, Tenn.: Cokesbury Press, 1939.

Ashcroft, Morris, "Revelation." In *The Broadman Bible Commentary*. Volume 12: *Hebrews-Revelation*. Nashville, Tenn.: Broadman Press, 1972.

Barclay, William. *The Revelation of John*. Volume 1. Revised edition. Chapters 1–5. Philadelphia: Westminster Press, 1976.

Baucham, Richard. *The Theology of the Book of Revelation*. Cambridge: Cambridge University Press, 1993.

Beagley, Alan J. *The "Sitz Im Leben" of the Apocalypse with Particular Reference to the Role of the Church's Enemies*. Berlin: Walter de Gruyter, 1987.

Beasley-Murray, G. R. *The Book of Revelation*. New Century Bible series. Greenwood, S.C.: Attic Press, 1974.

Beckwith, Isbon T. *The Apocalypse of John*. New York: Macmillan Company, 1919.

Best, W. E. *Diminishing Spirituality in Local Churches: Studies in Revelation 2 & 3*. Houston, Tex.: South Belt Grace Church, 1986.

Blaiklock, E. M. *The Seven Churches: An Exposition of Revelation Chapters Two and Three*. London: Marshall, Morgan and Scott, 19–.

Boer, Harry R. *The Book of Revelation*. Grand Rapids, Mich.: William B. Eerdmans Publishing Company, 1979.

Boring, M. Eugene. *Revelation*. Interpretation Commentary series. Louisville, Ky.: John Knox Press, 1989.

Brown, Charles. *Heavenly Visions: An Exposition of the Book of Revelation*. Boston: Pilgrim Press, 1910.

Bruce, F. F. "Revelation." In *A New Testament Commentary*. General editor G. C. D. Howley. Grand Rapids, Mich.: Zondervan Publishing House, 1969.

Caird, G. B. A *Commentary on the Revelation of St. John the Divine*. Harper's New Testament Commentaries series. New York: Harper & Row, Publishers, 1966.

Calkins, Raymond. *The Social Message of the Book of Revelation*. New York City: Women's Press, 1920.

Carpenter, W. Boyd. *The Revelation of St. John the Divine*. Ellicott Bible Commentary series. London: Cassell and Company, 1877. 1903 printing.

Case, Shirley J. *The Revelation of John: A Historical Interpretation*. Chicago: University of Chicago Press, 1919.

Charles, R. H. *Revelation*. Volume 1: International Critical Commentary series. Edinburgh: T. & T. Clark, 1920; 1979 reprint.

Chilton, David. *The Days of Vengeance: An Exposition of the Book of Revelation*. Fort Worth, Tex.: Dominion Press, 1987.

Collins, Adela Yarbro. *Apocalypse*. New Testament Message: A Biblical-Theological Commentary series. Wilmington, Del.: Michael Glazier, 1979.

―――. *Crisis and Catharsis: The Power of the Apocalypse*. Philadelphia: Westminster Press, 1984.

Corsini, Eugenio. *The Apocalypse: The Perennial Revelation of Jesus Christ*. Translated and edited by Francis J. Moloney. Wilmington, Del.: Michael Glazier.

Court, John W. *Myth and History in the Book of Revelation*. Atlanta, Ga.: John Knox Press, 1979.

―――. *Revelation*. New Testament Guides series. Huddersfield [Great Britain]: Scheffield Academic Press, 1994.

Draper, James T., Jr. *The Unveiling*. Nashville, Tenn.: Broadman Press 1984.

Efird, James M. *Revelation for Today*. Nashville, Tenn.: Abingdon Press, 1989.

Farrer, Austin. *The Revelation of St. John the Divine*. Oxford: Clarendon Press, 1964.

Fiorenza, Elisabeth Schüssler. *Revelation: Vision of a Just World*. Minneapolis: Fortress Press, 1991.

Ford, J. Massyngberde. *Revelation*. Anchor Bible series. Garden City, N.Y.: Doubleday and Company, 1975.

Franzmann, Martin F. *The Revelation to John*. St. Louis: Concordia, 1976.

Gentry, Kenneth L., Jr. *Before Jerusalem Fell: Dating the Book of Revelation*. Tyler, Tex.: Institute for Christian Economics, 1989.

Giblin, Charles H. *The Book of Revelation: The Open Book of Prophecy*. Collegeville, Minn.: A Michael Glazier Book/The Liturgical Press, 1991.

Glasson, T. F. *The Revelation of John*. Cambridge Bible Commentary. Cambridge: Cambridge University Press, 1965.

Grant, Frederick C. *Nelson's Bible Commentary*. Volume 7: *New Testament: Romans-Revelation*. New York: Thomas Nelson and Sons, 1962.

Guimond, John. *The Silencing of Babylon: A Spiritual Commentary on the Revelation of John*. New York: Paulist Press, 1991.

Guthrie, Donald. *The Relevance of John's Apocalypse*. Exeter, Devon [England]: Paternoster Press, 1987.

Hailey, Homer. *Revelation: An Introduction and Commentary*. Grand Rapids, Mich.: Baker Book House, 1979.

Harrington, Wilfrid J. *Revelation* (*Sacra Pagina*, volume 16). Collegeville, Minn:: Luturgical Press/A Michael Glazier Book, 1993.

———. *Understanding the Apocalypse*. Washington, D.C.: Corpus Books, 1969.

Hengstenberg, E. W. *The Revelation of St. John*. Translated from the German by Patrick Fairbairn. New York: Robert Carter and Brothers, 1852.

Hinds, John T. *A Commentary on the Book of Revelation*. Nashville, Tenn.: Gospel Advocate Company, 1937; 1974 reprint.

Hoeksema, Herman. *Behold, He Cometh! An Exposition of the Book of Revelation*. Grand Rapids, Mich.: Reformed Free Publishing Association, 1969.

Howard, Fred D. *1, 2, & 3 John, Jude & Revelation*. Volume 24 in the Layman's Bible Book Commentary. Nashville, Tenn.: Broadman Press, 1982.

Hughes, Philip E. *The Book of the Revelation: A Commentary*. Grand Rapids, Mich.: William B. Eerdmans Publishing Company, 1990.

Jeske, Richard L. *Revelation for Today: Images of Hope*. Philadelphia: Fortress Press, 1983.

Johnson, Alan. "Revelation." Volume 12 in *The Expositor's Bible Commentary*. Edited by Frank E. Gaebelein. Grand Rapids, Mich.: Zondervan Publishing House, 1981.

———. *Revelation*. Grand Rapids, Mich.: Zondervan Publishing House, 1983.

Kee, Howard C. *Understanding the New Testament*. Fourth edition. Englewood Cliffs, N.J.: Prentice-Hall, Inc., 1983.

Kelshaw, Terence. *Send This Message to My Church: Christ's Words To The Seven Churches of Revelation*. Nashville, Tenn.: Thomas Nelson Publishers, 1984.

Kent, Charles Foster. *The Work and Teachings of the Apostles* ("The Historical Bible"). New York: Charles Scribner's Sons, 1916.

Kiddle, Martin. *The Revelation of St. John*. Moffatt New Testament Commentary series. New York: Harper and Brothers Publishers, 1940.

Krodel, Gerhard A. *Revelation*. Augsburg Commentary on the New Testament series. Minneapolis: Augsburg Publishing House, 1989.

Ladd, George Eldon. *A Commentary on the Revelation of John*. Grand Rapids, Mich.: William B. Eerdmans Publishing Company, 1972.

Lang, G. H. *The Revelation of Jesus Christ: Select Studies*. Self-published. Distributed by London: Oliphants, 1945.

Lenski, R. C. H. *The Interpretation of St. John's Revelation*. Columbus, Ohio: Warburg Press, 1943.

Lilje, Hans. *The Last Book of the Bible: The Meaning of the Revelation of St. John*. Translated from the fourth German edition by Olive Wyon. Philadelphia: Muhlenberg Press, 1957.

Loane, Marcus L. *They Overcame: An Exposition of the First Three Chapters of Revelation*. [N.p.]: Angus and Robertson, 1971; reprint, Grand Rapids, Mich.: Baker Book House, 1981.

Martin, Hugh. *The Seven Letters*. Philadelphia: Westminster Press, 1956.

McDaniel, George W. *The Churches of the New Testament*. New York: Richard R. Smith, 1921; 1930 printing.

Meinardus, Otto F. A. *St. John of Patmos and the Seven Churches of the Apocalypse*. New Rochelle, N.Y.: Caratzas Brothers, 1979.

———. *St. Paul in Ephesus–and the Cities of Galatia and Cyprus*. New Rochelle, N.Y.: Caratzas Brothers, 1979.

Milligan, William. *The Book of Revelation (Expositor's Bible)*. New York: Funk & Wagnalls Company, 1900.

Morgan, G. Campbell. *The Letters of Our Lord–A First Century Message to*

*Twentieth Century Christians: Addresses based upon the Letters to the Seven Churches of Asia.* New York: Fleming H. Revell Company, 1902.

Morris, Leon. *The Revelation of St. John,* Tyndale New Testament Commentary series. Grand Rapids, Mich.: William B. Eerdmans Publishing Company, 1969.

Mounce, Robert H. *New International Commentary on Revelation.* Grand Rapids, Mich.: William B. Eerdmans Publishing Company, 1977.

————. *What Are We Waiting For? A Commentary on Revelation.* Grand Rapids, Mich.: Wm. B. Eerdmans Publishing Co., 1992.

Moyise, Steve. *The Old Testament in the Book of Revelation.* Journal for the Study of the New Testament Supplement 115. Sheffield, England: Sheffield Academic Press, 1995.

Onstad, Esther. *Courage for Today–Hope for Tomorrow: A Study of the Revelation.* Minneapolis: Augsburg Publishing House, 1973, 1974.

Palmer, Earl F. *1, 2 and 3 John, Revelation.* The Communicator's Commentary series. Waco, Tex.: Word Books, 1982.

Pieters, Albertus. *The Lamb, the Woman, and the Dragon: An Exposition of the Revelation of St. John.* Grand Rapids, Michigan, 1937. Reprinted as *Studies in the Revelation of St. John.* Grand Rapids, Mich.: Wm. B. Eerdmans Publishing Company, 1943, 1950.

Prevost, Jean-Pierre. *How to Read the Apocalypse.* Translated from the French by John Bowden and Margaret Lydamore. New York: Crossroad, 1993.

Ramsay, William M. *The Letters to the Seven Churches of Asia.* New York: George H. Doran Company, 1905.

Robbins, Ray F. *The Revelation of Jesus Christ.* Nashville, Tenn.: Broadman Press, 1975.

Scott, C. Anderson. *The Book of the Revelation.* New York: George H. Doran Company, (n.d.).

Seiss, Joseph A. *Letters to the Seven Churches.* Grand Rapids, Mich.: Baker Book House, 1956. Reprint of *Letters of Jesus,* 1889.

Selles, L. *The Book of Revelation.* Volume 1. London, Ontario: Interleague Publication Board of Canadian Reformed Societies, 1965.

Sheppard, W. J. Limmer. *The Revelation of St. John the Divine: I-XI.* London: Religious Tract Society, 1923.

Sinclair, Scott G. *Revelation: A Book for the Rest of Us.* Berkeley, Calif.: Bibal Press, 1992.

Stuart, Moses. *A Commentary on the Apocalypse.* Volume 2. Andover: Allen, Morrill and Wardwell, 1845.

Sweet, J. P. W. *Revelation.* Westminster Pelican Commentaries series. Philadelphia: Westminster Press, 1979.

Swete, Henry B. *The Apocalypse of St. John: The Greek Text with Introduction, Notes, and Indices*. Third edition. London: Macmillan and Co., 1909; reprinted, 1911.

Tait, Andrew. *The Messages to the Seven Churches of Asia*. London: Hodder and Stoughton, 1884.

Thompson, Steven. *The Apocalypse and Semitic Syntax*. Cambridge: Cambridge University Press, 1985.

Tickle, John. *The Book of Revelation: A Catholic Interpretation of the Apocalypse*. Liguori, Mo.: Liguori Publications, 1983.

Tremmel, Willliam C. *The Twenty-Seven Books that Changed the World: A Guide to Reading the New Testament*. New York: Holt, Rinehart and Winston, 1981.

Trench, Richard C. *Commentary on the Epistles to the Seven Churches in Asia*. New York: Charles Scribner & Co., 1872.

Van Hartingsveld, L. *Revelation: A Practical Commentary*. Translated from the Dutch by John Vriend, Grand Rapids, Mich.: Wm. B. Eerdmans Publishing Co., 1985.

Walvoord, John F. *The Revelation of Jesus Christ*. Chicago: Moody Press, 1966.

Weiss, Bernhard. *A Commentary on the New Testament*. Volume 4: *Thessalonians-Revelation*. Translated by George H. Schodde and Epiphanius Wilson. New York: Funk & Wagnalls Company, 1906.

Whiting, Charles C. *The Revelation of John*. Boston: Gorham Press, 1918.

Wilcock, Michael. *I Saw Heaven Opened: The Message of Revelation*. London: Inter-Varsity Press, 1975.

## Commentaries and Related Literature: Other Bible Books

Aune, David E. "Magic in Early Christianity." *Aufstieg and Niedergang der Romischen Welt*, II,23.2, 1507–57. Berlin: Walter de Gruyter, 1980.

Avi-Yonah, Michael. *Views of the Biblical World*. Volume 5: *The New Testament*. Jerusalem: International Publishing Company, 1961.

Bacon, Charles Foster. *The Work and Teachings of the Apostles*. Volume 6 of *The Historical Bible*. New York: Charles Scribner's Sons, 1916.

Baez-Camargo, Gonzalo. *Archaeological Commentary on the Bible*. Translated by Eugene A. Nida. Garden City, N.Y.: Doubleday and Company, 1984.

Barclay, William. *The Letters to the Philippians, Colossians and Thessalonians*. Revised edition. Daily Study Bible series. Philadelphia: Westminster Press, 1975.

Bengel, John Albert. *Gnomon of the New Testament.* Volume 5. Translated by William Fletcher. Edinburgh: T. & T. Clark, 1859.

Beyer, Bryan. "Obadiah." In Bryan Beyer and John Walton, *Obadiah, Jonah: Bible Study Commentaries.* Grand Rapids, Mich.: Lamplight Books/Zondervan Publishing House, 1988.

Blaiklock, E. M. "The Acts of the Apostle as a Document of First Century History." In *Apostolic History and the Gospel.* Edited by W. Ward Gasque and Ralph P. Martin, 41–54. [Great Britain]: Paternoster Press, 1970.

Bruce. F. F. *New International Commentary on the New Teatament: The Epistles to the Colossians, to Philemon, and to the Ephesians.* Grand Rapids, Mich.: William B. Eerdmans Publishing Company, 1984.

Cadbury, Henry J. *The Book of Acts in History.* London: Adam and Charles Black, 1955.

Caird, G. B. *Paul's Letters from Prison: Ephesians, Philippians, Colossians, Philemon.* New Clarendon Bible Commentary series. Oxford: Oxford University Press, 1976.

Carson, Herbert M. *Colossians and Philemon.* Tyndale New Testament Commentary series. Grand Rapids, Mich.: Wm. B. Eerdmans Publishing Company, 1960.

Cassidy, Richard J. *Society and Politics in the Acts of the Apostles.* Maryknoll, N.Y.: Orbis Books, 1987.

Daille, Jean. *An Exposition of the Epistle of Saint Paul to the Colossians.* Translated from the French by F. S. Revised and corrected by James Sherman. 1648 original French edition. Reprinted English translation, Philadelphia: Presbyterian Board of Publication, 18–.

Dargen, Edwin C. "Colossians." In *An American Commentary on the New Testament: Corinthians to Thessalonians.* Philadelphia: American Baptist Publication Society, 1890.

Demarest, Gary. *Colossians: The Mystery of Christ.* Waco, Tex.: Word Books, 1979.

Duncan, George S. *St. Paul's Ephesian Ministry: A Reconstruction.* New York: Charles Scribner's Sons, 1930.

Earle, Ralph. "1 Timothy; 2 Timothy." In *Ephesians-Philemon.* Volume 11 in *The Expositor's Bible Commentary.* Grand Rapids, Mich.: Zondervan Publishing House, 1978.

Fairbairn, Patrick. *The Pastoral Epistles.* Edinburgh: T. & T. Clark, 1874.

Fee, Gordon D. *1 and 2 Timothy, Titus.* Good News Commentary series. San Francisco: Harper & Row, Publishers, 1984.

Festugiere, Andre-Jean. *Personal Religion Among the Greeks.* Berkeley and Los Angeles: University of California Press, 1954.

Firminger Walter, K. *Colossians and Philemon* ("Indian Church Commentaries"). Madras [India]: S.P.C.K., 1921.

Fornberg, Tord. *An Early Church in a Pluralistic Society: A Study of 2 Peter.* Translated by Jean Gray. [Sweden]: CWK Gleerup, 1977.

Goodspeed, Edgar J. *Introduction to the New Testament.* Chicago: University of Chicago Press, 1937.

Gritz, Sharon Hodgin. *Paul, Women Teachers, and the Mother Goddess at Ephesus: A Study of 1 Timothy 2:9–15 in Light of the Religious and Cultural Milieu of the First Century.* Lanham, N.Y.: University Press of America, 1991.

Guthrie, Donald. *The Pastoral Epistles: An Introduction and Commentary.* Tyndale New Testament Commentary series. Grand Rapids, Mich.: Wm. B. Eerdmans Publishing Company, 1957.

Guthrie, Donald. *The Apostles.* Grand Rapids, Mich.: Zondervan Publishing House, 1975.

Hanson, A. T. *The Pastoral Epistles.* New Century Bible Commentary series. Grand Rapids, Mich.: Wm. B. Eerdmans Publishing Company, 1982. [British edition: London: Marshall, Morgan & Scott, Publishers.]

Harris, Murray J. *Colossians and Philemon.* Grand Rapids, Mich.: William B. Eerdmans Publishing Company, 1991.

Harvey, H. H. "First and Second Timothy." In *An American Commentary on the New Testament: Timothy to Peter.* Philadelphia: American Baptist Publication Society, 1890.

Hillard, A. E. *The Pastoral Epistles of St. Paul.* London: Rivingons, 1919.

Houlden, J. L. *Paul's Letters from Prison: Philippians, Colossians, Philemon, and Ephesians.* Westminster Pelican Commentaries series. Philadelphia: Westminster Press, 1977.

Hultgren, Arland J. "1 & 2 Timothy." In Arland J. Hultgren and Roger Aus, *I-II Timothy, Titus, II Thessalonians.* Augsburg Commentary on the New Testament series. Minneapolis: Augsburg Publishing House, 1984.

Ironside, H. A. *Lectures on the Epistle to the Colossians.* New York: Bible Truth Press, 1929.

Jones, Maurisc. *The Epistle of St. Paul to the Colossians.* London: Society for Promotion of Christian Knowledge, 1923.

Kelly, J. N. D. *A Commentary on the Pastoral Epistles.* Harper's New Testament Commentary series. New York: Harper & Row, Publishers, 1963.

Kent, Homer A. *The Pastoral Epistles: Studies in I and II Timothy and Titus.* Chicago: Moody Press, 1958.

Lightfoot, J. B. *Saint Paul's Epistles to the Colossians and to Philemon.* Revised edition. London: Macmillan and Company, 1879.

Lohse, Eduard. *Colossians and Philemon.* Edited by Helmut Koester. Translated from the German by William R. Poehlmann and Robert J. Harris. Philadelphia: Fortress Press, 1971.

Lyall, Francis. *Slaves, Citizens, Sons: Legal Metaphors in the Epistles.* Grand Rapids, Mich.: Academie Books: Zondervan Publishing House, 1984.

Martin, Ralph R. *Colossians and Philemon.* New Century Bible series. Greenwood, S.C.: Attic Press, 1974.

Martin, Ralph R. *Ephesians, Colossians, and Philemon.* Atlanta, Ga.: John Knox Press, 1991.

Metzger, Bruce M. *Breaking the Code: Understanding the Book of Revelation.* Nashville, Tenn.: Abingdon Press, 1993.

Michaels, J. Ramsey. *Interpreting the Book of Revelation.* Grand Rapids, Mich.: Baker Book House, 1992.

Moellering, H. Armin. "I and 2 Timothy." In *1 Timothy-Philemon.* Concordia Commentary series. St. Louis: Concordia Publishing House, 1970.

Nicholson, Roy S. "The Pastoral Epistles." In *Romans-Philemon.* Volume 50 in the Wesleyan Bible Commentaries. Grand Rapids, Mich.: William B. Eerdmans Publishing Company, 1965.

O'Brien, Peter T. *Colossians, Philemon.* Volume 44 in the Word Biblical Commentary series. Waco, Tex.: Word Books, Publishers, 1982.

Oden, Thomas C. *First and Second Timothy and Titus.* Interpretation Commentary series. Louisville, Ky.: John Knox Press, 1989.

Patzia, Arthur G. *Colossians, Philemon, Ephesians.* San Francisco: Harper & Row, Publishers, 1984.

Perowne, Stewart. *The Journeys of St. Paul.* London: Hamlyn, 1973.

Pfleiderer, Otto. *Primitive Christianity: Its Writings and Teachings in Their Historical Connections.* Volume 3. Translated from the German by W. Montgomery. London: Williams and Norgate, 1910.

Plummer, Alfred. *The Pastoral Epistles.* New York: A. C. Armstrong and Son, 1893.

Pokorny, Petr. *Colossians: A Commentary.* Translated from the German by Siegfried S. Schatzmann. Peabody, Mass.: Hendrickson Publishers, 1991.

Ralph, Margaret N. *Discovering the First Century Church: The Acts of the Apostles, Letters of Paul and the Book of Revelation.* New York: Paulist Press, 1991.

Robertson, Archibald T. *Paul and the Intellectuals: The Epistle to the Colossians.* Garden City, N.Y.: Doubleday, Doran and Company, 1928.

Rutherford, John. *St. Paul's Epistles to Colossae and Laodicea*. Edinburg: T. & T. Clark, 1908.

Schweizer, Eduard. *The Letter to the Colossians: A Commentary*. Translated from the German by Andrew Chester. Minneapolis: Augsburg Publishing House, 1976.

Scott, E. F. *The Pastoral Epistles*. Moffatt New Testament Commentary series. London: Hodder and Stoughton, 1936; 1948 reprint.

Simpson, E. K. *The Pastoral Epistles*. London: Tyndale Press, 1954.

Stuart, Douglas. *Hosea-Jonah*. Word Biblical Commentary series. Waco, Tex.: Word Books, 1987.

Thomas, W. H. Griffith. *Studies in Colossians and Ephesians*. Grand Rapids, Mich.: Kregel Publications, 1986.

Tolbert, Malcolm O. *Layman's Bible Book Commentary*. Volume 22: *Colossians, Philiplppians, 1 & 2 Thessalonians, 1 & 2 Timothy, Titus, Philemon*. Nashville, Tenn.: Broadman Press, 1980.

Trevethan, Thomas L. *Our Joyful Confidence: The Lordship of Jesus in Colossians*. Downer's Grove, Ill.: InterVarsity Press, 1981.

Turner, George A. "Colossians." In *Romans-Philemon*. Volume 5 in the Wesleyan Bible Commentary. Edited by Charles W. Carter, et al. Grand Rapids, Mich.: William B. Eerdmans Publishing Company, 1965.

Unger, Merrill F. *The New Unger's Bible Handbook*. Revised by Gary N. Larson. Chicago: Moody Press, 1984.

Vaughn, Curtis. "Colossians." In *Ephesians-Philemon*. Volume 11 in *The Expositor's Bible Commentary*. Edited by Frank E. Gaebelein. Grand Rapids, Mich.: Zondervan Publishing House, 1978.

Ward, Ronald A. *Commentary on 1 and 2 Timothy and Titus*. Waco, Tex.: Word Books, Publishers, 1974.

Watts, John D. W. *Books of Joel, Obadiah, Jonah, Nahum, Habakkuk and Zephaniah* in the *Cambridge Bible Commentary on the New English Bible*. Cambridge: Cambridge University Press, 1975.

White, E. R. O. "Colossians." In *2 Corinthians-Philemon*. Volume 11 of *The Broadman Bible Commentary*. Edited by Clifton J. Allen. Nashville, Tenn.: Broadman Press, 1971.

Williams, Charles B. *A Commentary on the Pauline Epistles*. Chicago: Moody Press, 1953.

## Histories and Related Works

Adams, J. Mckee. *Biblical Backgrounds*. Revised by Joseph A. Callaway. Nashville, Tenn.: Broadman Press, 1965.

Akurgal, Ekrem. *Ancient Civilizations and Ruins of Turkey: From Prehis-*

*toric Times Until the End of the Roman Empire.* Third edition. Ankara [Turkey]: Turkish Historical Society Press/Haset Kitabevi, 1973.

Applebaum, S. "The Legal Status of the Jewish Communities in the Diaspora." In *The Jewish People in the First Century: Historical Geography, Political History, Social, Cultural and Religious Life and Institutions.* Edited by S. Safari and M. Stern, 420–63. Volume 1. Assen [Netherlands]: Van Gorcum & Company, B.V., 1974.

———. "The Organization of the Jewish Communities in the Diaspora." In *The Jewish People in the First Century: Historical Geography, Political History, Social, Cultural and Religious Life and Institutions.* Edited by S. Safari and M. Stern, 464–503. Volume 1. Assen [Netherlands]: Van Gorcum & Company, B. V., 1974.

Applebaum, Shimon. *Jews and Greeks in Ancient Cryene.* Leiden: E. J. Brill, 1979.

Archibald, Zophia. *Discovering the World of the Ancient Greeks.* New York: Facts on File, 1991.

Arnold, W. T. *The Roman System of Provincial Administration.* Third edition. Revised by E. S. Bouchier. Oxford: Oxford University Press, 1914; reprint, Chicago: Ares Publishers, 1974.

Aune, David E. "Magic in Early Christianity." In *Aufstieg und Niedergang der Romischen Welt,* II,23.2, 1507–57. Berlin: Walter de Gruyter, 1980.

Aurenhammer, Maria. "Sculptures of Gods and Heroes from Ephesos." In *Ephesos: Metroplis of Asia–An Interdisciplinary Approach to Its Archaeology, Religion, and Culture.* Edited by Helmut Koester, 251–80. Harvard Theological Studies 41. Valley Forge, Pa.: Trinity Press International, 1995.

Avery, Catherine B. *The New Century Classical Handbook.* New York: Appleton-Century, Crofts, 1962.

Badian, E. *Publicans and Sinners: Private Enterprise in the Service of the Roman Republic.* Oxford: Basil Blackwell, 1972.

Ballance, Michael H., and Olwen Brogan, "Roman Marble: A Link Between Asia Minor and Libya." In *Geology and History of Turkey.* Edited by Angus S. Campbell, 33–38. Tripoli [Libya]: Petroleum Exploration Society of Libya, 1971.

Balsdon, J. P. V. D. *Romans and Aliens.* Chapel Hill, N.C.: University of North Carolina Press, 1979.

———. *Rome: The Story of an Empire.* New York: McGraw-Hill Book Company, 1970.

Bara, Musa. *Ephesus and Its Surroundings.* Translated by Hulya Terzioglu. Izmir [Turkey]: Molay Matbaacilik, 19–.

Baring Anne and Jules Cashford. *The Myth of the Goddess: Evolution of an Image*. New York: Viking Arkana, 1991.

Barnes, Timothy. "Pagan Perceptions of Christianity." In *Early Christianity: Origins and Evolution to A.D. 600*. Edited by Ian Hazlett, 231–43. Nashville, Tenn.: Abingdon Press, 1991.

Barr, David L. "Elephants and Holograms: From Metaphor to Methodology in the Study of John's Apocalypse." In *Society of Biblical Literature Seminar Papers Series: 1986*. Edited by Kent H. Richards, 400–411. Atlanta, Ga.: Scholars Press, 1986.

Barton, Geroge A. *Archaeology and the Bible*. Seventh edition. Revised. Philadelphia: American Sunday-School Union, 1937.

Bauer, Walter. *Orthodoxy and Heresy in Earliest Christianity*. Second German edition translated by Robert A. Kraft, David Hay, et al. Edited by Robert A Kraft and Gerhard Krodel. Philadelphia: Fortress Press, 1971.

Baugh, S. M. "A Foreign World: Ephesus in the First Century." In *Women in the Church: A Fresh Analysis of 1 Timothy 2:9–15*. Edited by Andreas J. Kostenberger, Thomas R. Schreiner, and H. Scott Baldwin, 13–52. Grand Rapids, Mich.: Baker Books, 1995.

Baus, Karl. *Handbook of Church History*. Volume 1: *From the Apostolic Community to Constantine*. Translated from the German. New York: Herder and Herder, 1965.

Bean, George E. *Aegean Turkey: An Archaeological Guide*. New York: Frederick A. Praeger, Publishers, 1966.

———. *Turkey Beyond the Maeander*. Revised edition. London: Ernest Benn, 1980.

Beagley, Alan J. *The "Sitz Im Leben" of the Apocalypse with Particular Reference to the Role of the Church's Enemies*. Berlin: Walter de Gruyer, 1987.

Becatti, Giovanni. *The Art of Ancient Greece and Rome–From the Rise of Greece to the Fall of Rome*. Translated by John Ross. Englewood Cliffs, N.J.: Prentice-Hall, 1967.

Bengston, Hermann. *History of Greece–From the Beginning to the Byzantine Era*. Translated from the German and updated by Edmund F. Bloedow. Ottawa: University of Ottawa Press, 1988.

Benko, Stephen. "Pagan Criticism of Christianity During the First Two Centuries A.D." *Aufstieg und Niedergang der Romischen Welt*, II,23.2, 1055–1118. Berlin: Walter de Gruyter, 1980.

———. *Pagan Rome and the Early Christians*. Bloomington: Indiana University Press, 1984.

———. *The Virgin Goddess: Studies in the Pagan and Christian Roots of Mariology*. New York: E. J. Brill, 1933.

Berrett, LaMar C. *Discovering the World of the Bible*. Provo, Utah: Young House, 1973.

Blaiklock, E. M. *The Archaeology of the New Testament*. Grand Rapids, Michigan, Zondervan Publishing House, 1970.

———. *The Christian in Pagan Society*. The Tyndale New Testament Lecture for 1951. London: The Tyndale Press, 19–.

———. *Cities of the New Testament*. London: Pickering & Inglis, 1965.

———. *Out of the Earth: The Witness of Archaeology to the New Testament*. Grand Rapids, Mich.: Wm. B. Eerdmans Publishing Co., 1957.

Blue, Bradley. "Acts and the House Church." In *The Book of Acts in Its Graeco-Roman Setting*. Edited by David W. J. Gill and Conrad Gempf, 119–222. Volume 2 of *The Book of Acts in Its First Century Setting*. Grand Rapids, Mich.: William B. Eerdmans Publishing Company, 1994.

Boulton, W. H. *Archaeology Explains*. London: Epworth Press, 1952; 1953 reprint.

Bowersock, G. W. *Augustus and the Greek World*. Oxford: Clarendon Press, 1965.

———. *Hellenism in Late Antiquity*. Ann Arbor: University of Michigan Press, 1990.

———. "The Imperial Cult: Perceptions and Persistence." In *Jewish and Christian Self-Definition*. Volume 3: *Self-Definition in the Greco-Roman World*. Edited by Ben F. Meyer and E. P. Sanders, 183–241. Philadelphia: Fortress Press, 1982.

Boyd, Robert T. *Tells, Tombs and Treasure: A Pictorial Guide to Biblical Archaeology*. 1969: Baker Books; reprint, New York: Bonanza Books, 1975.

Brooten, Bernadette J. *Women Leaders in the Ancient Synagogue: Inscriptional Evidence and Background Issues*. Chico, Calif.: Scholars Press, 1982.

Broughton, T. Robert. "New Evidence on Temple-Estates in Asia Minor." In *Studies in Roman Economic and Social History–in Honor of Allan Chester Johnson*. Edited by P. R. Coleman-Norton with the assistance of F. C. Bourne and J. V. A. Fine, 236–50. Princeton: Princeton University Press, 1951.

Broughton, T. R. S. "Roman Asia." In *An Economic Survey of Ancient Rome*. Volume 4. Edited by Tenney Frank, 499–918. Baltimore: Johns Hopkins Press, 1938.

Bruce, F. F. *The Spreading Flame: The Rise and Progress of Christianity from Its First Beginnings to the Conversion of the English*. Grand Rapids, Mich.: Wm. B. Eerdmans Publishing Company, 1958.

Buchan, John. *Augustus*. Boston: Houghton Mifflin Company, 1937.

Buckler, W. H. "Labour Disputes in Asia Minor." In *Anatolian Studies–Presented to Sir William Mitchell Ramsay*. Edited by W. H. Buckler and W. M. Calder. Manchester: Manchester University Press, 1923.

Budden, Charles W., and Edward Hastings. *The Local Colour of the Bible*. Volume 3: *Matthew-Revelation*. Edinburgh: T. & T. Clark, 1925.

Burford, Allison. *Craftsmen in Greek and Roman Society*. Ithaca, N.Y.: Cornell University Press, 1972.

Burkert, Walter. *Ancient Mystery Cults*. Cambridge, Mass.: Harvard University Press, 1972.

Cadoux, Cecil J. *Ancient Smyrna: A History from the Earliest Times to 324 A.D.* Oxford: Basil Blackwell, 1938.

Calder, W. M. "Smyrna as Described by the Orator Aelius Aristide." In *Studies in the History and Art of the Eastern Provinces of the Roman Empire*. Edited by W. M. Ramsay, 95–116. Aberdeen, Scotland: Aberdeen University Press, 1906.

Calkin, John A. *Historical Geography of Bible Lands*. Philadelphia: Westminster Press, 1904.

Cannon, William R. *Journeys After Paul: An Excursion into History*. New York: Macmillan, 1963.

Carson, R. A. G. *Coins of the Roman Empire*. London: Routledge, 1990.

Cassidy, Richard J. *John's Gospel in New Perspective: Christology and the Realities of Roman Power*. Maryknoll, N.Y.: Orbis Books, 1992.

Cerfaux, Lucien. "The Church in the Book of Revelation." In *The Birth of the Church: A Biblical Study*. Translated by Charles Underhill Quinn. Staten Island, NY: Alba House, 1969.

Charlesworth, M. P. *Trade Routes and Commerce of the Roman Empire*. Second edition, Revised. Chicago: Ares Publishers, 1926. Reprint, 197–.

Cole, Susan Guettel. "Demeter in the Ancient Greek City and Its Countryside." In *Placing the Gods: Sanctuaries and Sacred Space in Ancient Greece*. Edited by Susan E. Alcock and Robin Osborne, 199–216. Oxford: Clarendon Press, 1994.

Coleman-Norton, P. R. "The Apostle Paul and the Roman Law of Slavery." In *Studies in Roman Economic and Social History–in Honor of Allan Chester Johnson*. Edited by P. R. Coleman-Norton, with the assistance of F. C. Bourne and J. V. A. Fine, 155–77. Princeton: Princeton University Press, 1951.

Collins, Adela Y. "Numerical Symbolism in Jewish and Early Christian Apocalyptic Literature." In *Aufstieg und Niedergang der Romischen Welt*, II,21.2, 1221–87. Berlin: Walter de Gruyter, 1984.

———. "Vilification and Self-Definition in the Book of Revelation." In

*Christians Among Jews and Gentiles*. Edited by George W. E. Nickelsburg and George W. MacRae, 308–20. Philadelphia: Fortress Press, 1986.

Cook, J. M. *The Greeks–In Ionia and the East*. New York: Frederick A. Praeger, Publisher, 1963.

Corley, Kathleen E. "Were the Women Around Jesus Really Prostitutes? Women in the Context of Greco-Roman Meals." In *Society of Biblical Literature 1989 Seminary Papers*. Edited by David J. Lull, 1989, 487–521. Atlanta Ga.: Scholars Press, 1989.

Cornell, Tim, and John Matthews. *Atlas of the Roman Empire*. New York: Facts on Files, 1982.

Countryman, L. William. "Welfare in the Churches of Asia Minor under the Early Roman Empire." *Society of Biblical Literature 1979 Seminar Papers*. Volume 1. Edited by Paul J. Achtemeier, 131–46. Atlanta, Ga.: Scholars Press, 1979.

Crawford, Stephen J. *The Byzantine Shops at Sardis*. Cambridge, Mass.: Harvard University Press, 1990.

Cunliffe, Barry. *Rome and Her Empire*. New York: McGraw-Hill Book Company, 1978.

Davies, Roy W. "The Daily Life of the Roman Soldier Under the Principate." In *Aufstieg und Niedergang der Romischen Welt*, II,1, 299–338. Berlin: Walter de Gruyter, 1974.

Davis, John J. *Biblical Numerology: A Basic Study of the Use of Numbers in the Bible*. Grand Rapids, Mich.: Baker Book House, 1968.

Delia, Diana. *Alexandrian Citizenship During the Roman Principate*. Atlanta, Ga.: Scholars Press, 1991.

Duff, A. M. *Freedmen in the Early Roman Empire*. Oxford University Press, 1928; reprint, Cambridge: W. Heffer & Sons, 1958.

Duncan-Jones, Richard. *The Economy of the Roman Empire: Quantitative Studies*. Second edition. Cambridge: Cambridge University Press, 1982.

Enslin, Morton S. "Rome in the East." In *Religions in Antiquity: Essays in Memory of Erwin Ramsdell Goodenough*. Edited by Jacob Neusner. Leiden: E. J. Brill, 1968.

Farnell, Lewis R. *The Cults of the Greek States*. Volume 2. 1895. Reprinted, Chicago: Aegean Press, 1971.

Ferguson, Everett. *Backgrounds of Early Christianity*. Second edition. Grand Rapids, Mich.: William B. Eerdmans Publishing Company, 1993.

Ferguson, John. "China and Rome." In *Aufstieg und Niedergang der Romischen Welt*, II,9.2, 581–603. Berlin: Walter de Gruyter, 1978.

―――. "Divinities." In *Civilization of the Ancient Mediterranean* Volume

2. Edited by Michael Grand and Rachel Kitzinger, 847–60. New York: Charles Scribner's Sons, 1988.

————. *The Religions of the Roman Empire.* Ithaca, N.Y.: Cornell University Press, 1970.

Festugiere, Andre-Jean. *Personal Religion Among the Greeks.* Berkeley and Los Angeles: University of California Press, 1954.

Finegan, Jack. *The Archaeology of the New Testament: The Mediterranean World of the Early Christian Apostles.* Boulder, Colo.: Westview Press, 1981.

Finley, M. I. *The Ancient Economy.* Berkeley and Los Angeles: University of California Press, 1973.

————. *Atlas of Classical Archaeology.* New York: McGraw-Hill Book Company, 1977.

————. *Economy and Society in Ancient Greece.* Edited by Brent D. Shaw and Richard P. Satler. London: Chatto & Winus, 1981.

Finn, T. M. "Social Mobility, Imperial Civil Service and the Spread of Early Christianity." *Studia Patristica* 17, part 1, 31–37. Ocfore: Pergamon Press, 1982.

Foss, Clive. *Ephesus After Antiquity: A Late Antique, Byzantine and Turkish City.* Cambridge: Cambridge University Press, 1979.

Francois, de. *Cults, Territory, and the Origins of the Greek City-State.* Translated by Janet Lloyd. Chicago: University of Chicago Press, 1995.

Frank, Harry T. *An Archaeological Companion to the Bible.* London: SCM Press, 1972; Nashville, Tenn.: Abingdon Press, 1971.

————. *Bible Archaeology and Faith.* Nashville, Tenn.: Abingdon Press, 1971.

French, David. "Acts and the Roman Roads of Asia Minor." In *The Book of Acts in Its Graeco-Roman Setting.* Edited by David W. J. Gill and Conrad Gempf, 49–58. Volume 2 of *The Book of Acts in Its First Century Setting.* Grand Rapids, Mich.: William B. Eerdmans Publishing Company, 1994.

Friend, W. C. *Martyrdom and Persecution in the Early Church: A Study of a Conflict from the Maccabees to Donatus.* Oxford: Basil Blackwell, 1965.

Friesen, Steven. "The Cult of the Roman Emperors in Ephesos: Temple Wardens, City Titles, and the Interpretation of the Revelation of John." In *Ephesos: Metroplis of Asia–An Interdisciplinary Approach to its Archaeology, Religion, and Culture.* Edited by Helmut Koester, 229–50. Harvard Theological Studies 41. Valley Forge, Pa.: Trinity Press International, 1995.

Friesen, Steven J. *Twice Neokoros: Ephesus, Asia, and the Cult of the Flavian Imperial Family.* Leiden: E. J. Brill, 1993.

Gager, John G. *Kingdom and Community: The Social World of Early Christianity*. Englewood Cliffs, N.J.: Prentice-Hall, 1975.

————. "Religion and Social Class in the Early Roman Empire." In *The Catacombs and the Colosseum: The Roman Empire as the Setting of Primitive Christianity*. Edited by Stephen Benko and John J. O'Rourke, 99–120. Valley Forge, Pa.: Judson Press, 1971.

Garlan, Yvon. *War in the Ancient World–A Social History*. Translated from the French by Janet Lloyd. New York: W. W. Norton & Co., 1975.

Garnsey, Peter. *Famine and Food Supply in the Graeco-Roman World: Responses to Risk and Crisis*. Cambridge: Cambridge University Press, 1988.

————. "Grain for Rome." In *Trade in the Ancient Economy*. Edited by Peter Garnsey, Neither Hopkins, and C. R. Whittaker. Berkeley and Los Angeles: University of California Press, 1983.

————. "Religious Toleration in Classical Antiquity." In *Persecution and Toleration*. Volume 21 of *Studies in Church History*. Edited by W. J. Sheils, 1–28. [Great Britain]: Basil Blackwell, 1984.

————. *Social Status and Legal Privilege in the Roman Empire*. Oxford: Clarendon Press, 1970.

Garnsey, Peter, and Richard Saller. *The Roman Empire: Economy, Society and Culture*. Berkeley and Los Angeles: University of California Press, 1987.

Garrison, Roman. *The Graeco-Roman Context of Early Christian Literature*. Journal for the Study of the New Testament Supplement 137. Sheffield, England: Sheffield Academic Press, 1997.

Gill, David W. J. "Acts and Roman Religion: A. Religion in a Local Setting." In *The Book of Acts in Its Graeco-Roman Setting*. Edited by David W. J. Gill and Conrad Gempf, 79–92. Volume 2 of *The Book of Acts in Its First Century Setting*. Grand Rapids, Mich.: William B. Eerdmans Publishing Company, 1994.

Gill, David W. J. "Acts and the Urban Elites.." In *The Book of Acts in Its Graeco-Roman Setting*. Edited by David W. J. Gill and Conrad Gempf, 93–103. Volume 2 of *The Book of Acts in Its First Century Setting*. Grand Rapids, Mich.: William B. Eerdmans Publishing Company, 1994.

Godwin, Joscelyn. *Mystery Religions in the Ancient World*. San Francisco: Harper & Row, Publishers, 1981.

Goldenberg, Robert. "The Jewish Sabbath in the Roman World up to the Time of Constantine the Great." In *Aufstieg und Niedergang der Romischen Welt*, II,19.1, 414–47. Berlin: Walter de Gruyter, 1979.

Gonen, Rivka. *Biblical Holy Places–An Illustrated Guide*. Israel: Palphot, 1987.

Goodspeed, Edgar J. *Introduction to New Testament*. Chicago: University of Chicago Press, 1937.

Grant, Michael. *Gladiators*. New York: Delacorte Press, 1967.

———. *The Jews in the Roman World*. New York: Charles Scribner's Sons, 1973.

Grant, Robert M. *Augustus to Constantine: The Thrust of the Christian Movement into the Roman World*. New York: Harper & Row, Publishers, 1970.

———. "The Social Setting of Second Century Christianity." In *Jewish and Christian Self-Definition*. Volume 1: *The Shaping of Christianity in the Second and Third Centuries*. Edited by E. P. Sanders, 16–29. Philadelphia: Fortress Press, 1980.

Greene, Kevin. *The Archaeology of the Roman Economy*. Berkeley and Los Angeles: University of California Press, 1986.

Gruen, Erich S. *The Hellenistic World and the Coming of Rome*. Volume 2. Berkeley and Los Angeles: University of California Press, 1984.

Guthrie, Donald. *The Apostles*. Grand Rapids, Mich.: Zondervan Publishing House, 1975.

Halsberghe, Gaston H. *The Cult of Sol Invictus*. Leiden: E. J. Brill, 1972.

Hanfmann, George M. A. *From Croesus to Constantine: The Cities of Western Asia Minor and Their Arts in the Greek and Roman Times*. Jerome Lectures: Tenth Series. Ann Arbor: University of Michigan Press, 1975.

———. "Historical Background." Chapter subsection in George M. A. Hanfmann, Louis Robert, and William Mierse, "The Hellenistic Period." In *Sardis: From Prehistoric to Roman Times–Results of the Archaeological Exploration of Sardis, 1958–1975*. Edited by George M. A. Hanfmann and William E. Mierse, 112–14. Cambridge, Mass.: Harvard University Press, 1983.

———. "Introduction." Chapter subsection in George M. A. Hanfmann, Fikret K. Yegul, and John S. Crawford, "The Roman and Late Antique Period." In *Sardis: From Prehistoric to Roman Times–Results of the Archaeological Exploration of Sardis, 1958–1975*. Edited by George M. A. Hanfmann and William E. Mierse, 139–48. Cambridge, Mass.: Harvard University Press, 1983.

———. *Letters from Sardis*. Cambridge, Mass.: Harvard University Press, 1972.

———. "Previous Research and the Harvard-Cornell Excavation." Chapter subsection in George M. A. Hanfmann, Louis Robert, and Willliam E. Mierse, "The Hellenistic Period." In *Sardis: From Prehistoric to Roman Times–Results of the Archaeological Exploration of Sardis, 1958–1975*. Edited by George M. A. Hanfmann and

William E. Mierse, 109–11. Cambridge, Mass.: Harvard University Press, 1983.

―――. "Religious Life." Chapter subsection in George M. A. Hanfmann, Louis Robert, and William Mierse, "The Hellenistic Period." In *Sardis: From Prehistoric to Roman Times–Results of the Archaeological Exploration of Sardis, 1958–1975*. Edited by George M. A. Hanfmann and William E. Mierse, 128–36 (text), 264–65 (footnotes). Cambridge, Mass.: Harvard University Press, 1983.

Hanfmann, George M. A., and Jane C. Waldbaum. "New Excavations at Sardis and Some Problems of Western Anatolian Archaeology." In *Near Eastern Archaeology in the Twentieth Century: Essays in Honor of Nelson Glueck*. Edited by James A. Sanders, 307–26. Garden City, N.Y.: Doubleday & Company, 1970.

―――. *A Survey of Sardis and the Major Monuments Outside the City Walls*. Cambridge, Mass.: Harvard University Press, 1975.

Hansen, Esther V. *The Attalids of Pergamon*. Second edition. Revised and expanded. Ithaca, N.Y.: Cornell University Press, 1971.

Hanson, John A. *Roman Theater-Temples*. Princeton, N.J.: Princeton University Press, 1959.

Harris, William V. *Ancient Literacy*. Cambridge, Mass.: Harvard University Press, 1989

―――. "Towards a Study of the Roman Slave Trade." In *The Seaborne Commerce of Ancient Rome: Studies in Archaeology and History*. Volume 36 of the Memoirs of the American Academy in Rome. Edited by J. H. D'Arms and E. C. Kopff, 117–40. Rome: American Academy in Rome, 1980.

Harrison, Everett F. *The Apostolic Church*. Grand Rapids, Mich.: William B. Eerdmans Publishing Company, 1985.

Harrison, R. K. *Archaeology of the New Testament*. New York: Association Press, 1964.

Heichelheim, Fritz M. *An Ancient Economic History*. Volume 3. Translated by Mrs. Joyce Stevens. Leyden [Netherlands]: A. W. Sijthoff, 1970.

Helgeland, John. "Roman Army Religion." In *Aufstieg und Niedergang der Romischen Welt*, 16.2, 1470–1550. Berlin: Walter de Gruyter, 1978.

Hemer, C. J. "The Cities of the Revelation." In *New Documents Illustrating Early Christianity*. Edited by G. H. Horsley. Volume 3, 51–58. [Marrickville, Australia]: Macquarie University/Ancient History Documentary Research Center, 1983.

―――. "Seven Cities of Asia Minor." In *Major Cities of the Biblical World*. Edited by R. K. Harrison, 234–48. Nashville, Tenn.:

Thomas Nelson Publishers, 1985.

Hengel, Martin. *Jews, Greeks and Barbarians: Aspects of the Hellenization of Judaism in the Pre-Christian Period.* Translated from the German by John Bowden. Philadelphia: Fortress Press, 1980.

————. *Judaism and Hellenism: Studies in Their Encounter in Palestine During the Early Hellenistic Period.* Translated from the German by John Bowden. Philadelphia: Fortress Press, 1974.

Henrichs, Albert. "Changing Dionysiac Indentities." In *Jewish and Christian Self-Definition.* Volume 3: *Self-Definition in the Graeco-Roman World.* Edited by Ben F. Meyer and E. P. Sanders, 137–60. Philadelphia: Fortress Press, 1982.

Heybob, Sharon K. *The Cult of Iris Among Women in the Graeco-Roman World.* Leiden: E. J. Brill, 1975.

Hopkins, Keith. *Conquerors and Slaves: Sociological Studies in Roman History.* Volume 1. Cambridge: Cambridge University Press, 1978.

Horbury, William. "The Jewish Dimension." In *Early Christianity: Origins and Evolution to A.D. 600.* Edited by Ian Hazlett, 40–51. Nashville, Tenn.: Abingdon Press, 1991.

Horsley, G. H. "Doctors in the Graeco-Roman World." *New Documents Illustrating Early Christianity*, Volume 2. Edited by G. H. Horsley, 7–25 [Marrickville, Australia]: Macquarie University: Ancient History Documentary Research Centre, 1982.

————. "Expiation and the Cult of Men." In *New Documents Illustrating Early Christianity.* Volume 3. Edited by G. H. Horsley, 20–31 [Marrickville, Australia]: Macquarie University: Ancient History Documentary Research Centre, 1983.

————. "Inscriptions of Ephesus and the New Testament." In *New Documents Illustrating Early Christianity.* Volume 3. Edited by G. H. Horsley [Marrickville, Australia]: Macquarie University: Ancient History Documentary Research Centre, 1983.

————. "Invitations to the *Kline* of Sarapis." In *New Documents Illustrating Early Christianity.* Volume 1. Edited by G. H. Horsley, 5–9 [Marrickville, Australia]: Macquarie University: Ancient History Docmentary Research Centre, 1981.

————. "A Prefect's Circular Forbidding Magic." In *New Documents Illustrating Early Christianity.* Volume 1. Edited by G. H. Horsley, 47–51 [Marrickville, Australia]: Macquarie University: Ancient History Documentary Research Centre, 1982.

————. "The Purple Trade, and the Status of Lydia of Thyatira." In *New Documents Illustrating Early Christianity.* Volume 2. Edited by G. H. Horsley, 25–32 [Marrickville, Australia]: Macquarie University: Ancient History Documentary Research Centre, 1982.

Horsley, G. H. R. "Jews at Ephesos." In *New Documents Illustrating Early Christianity*. Volume 4. Edited by G. H. R. Horsley, 231–32 [Marrickville, Australia]: Macquarie University: Ancient History Documentary Research Centre, 1987.

———. "The Silversmiths at Ephesos." In *New Documents Illustrating Early Christianity*. Volume 4. Edited by G. H. R. Horsley, 7–10 [Marrickville, Australia]: Macquarie University: Ancient History Documentary Research Centre, 1987.

Humphrey, John H. *Roman Circuses: Arenas for Chariot Racing*. Berkeley and Los Angeles: University of California Press, 1986.

———. "Roman Games." In *Civilization of the Ancient Mediterranean* Volume 2. Edited by Michael Grant and Rachel Kitzinger, 1153–66 New York: Charles Scribner's, 1988.

Ilhan, Emil. "Earthquakes in Turkey." In *Geology and History of Turkey*. Edited by Angus S. Campbell, 432–42. Tripoli: Petroleum Exploration Society of Libya, 1971.

Inan, Jale, and Elisabeth Rosenbaum. *Roman and Early Bysantine Portrait Sculpture in Asia Minor*. London: Published for the British Academy by the Oxford University Press, 1966.

Jakobovits, Immanuel. *Jewish Medical Ethics: A Comparative and Historical Study of the Jewish Religious Attitude to Medicine and Its Practice*. New York: Bloch Publishing Company, 1959.

James, E. O. *The Cult of the Mother-Goddess: An Archaeologican and Documentary Study*. London: Thames and Hudson, 1959.

Jayne, Walter A. *The Healing Gods of Ancient Civlizations*. 1925; reprint, New Hyde Park, N.Y.: University Books, 1962.

Johnson, Allan C. *Egypt and the Roman Empire*. Jerome Lectures: Second Series. Ann Arbor: University of Michigan Press, 1951.

Johnson, S. E. "The Present State of Sabazios Research." In *Aufsteig und Niedergang der Romischen Welt*, 17.3, 1583–1613. Berlin: Walter de Gruyter, 1984.

Johnson, Sherman E. "Asia Minor and Early Christianity." In *Christianity, Judaism and Other Greco-Roman Cults: Studies for Morton Smith at Sixty*, Volume 2. Edited by Jacob Neusner, 77–145. Leiden: E. J. Brill, 1975.

———. "A Sabazios Inscription from Sardis." In *Religions in Antiquity: Essays in Memory of Erwin Ramsdell Goodenough*. Edited by Jacob Neusner, 542–50. Leiden: E. J. Brill, 1968.

Johnston, Alan W., and Malcolm A. R. Colledge. "The Classical World." In *Atlas of Archaeology*. Edited by K. Branigan, 50–91. New York: St. Martin's Press, 1982.

Jolowicz, H. F., and Barry Nicholas. *Historical Introduction to the Study of*

*Roman Law*. Third edition. Cambridge: Cambridge University Press, 1972.

Jones, A. H. M. *The Cities of the Eastern Roman Provinces*. Second edition. Revised by Michael Avi-Yonah, et al. Oxford: Clarendon Press, 1971.

———. *The Decline of the Ancient World*. London: Longman, 1966.

———. *The Greek City: From Alexander to Justinian*. Oxford: Clarendon Press, 1940; 1971 reprint.

———. *A History of Rome Through the Fifth Century*. Volume 2: *The Empire*. London: Macmillan, 1970.

———. *The Roman Economy: Studies in Ancient Economic and Administrative History*. Edited by P. A. Brunt. Oxford: Basil Blackwell, 1974.

Jones, Allen H. *Essenes: The Elect of Israel*. Lanham, Md.: University Press of America, 1985.

Jones, Donald L. "Christianity and the Roman Imperial Cult." In *Aufstieg und Niedergang der Romischen Welt*, II,23.2, 1023–54. Berlin: Walter de Gruyter, 1980.

Judge, E. A. *The Social Pattern of Christian Groups in the First Century*. London: Tyndale Press, 1960.

Kearsley, R. A. "The Asiarchs." In *The Book of Acts in Its Graeco-Roman Setting*. Edited by David W. J. Gill and Conrad Gempf, 363–76. Volume 2 of *The Book of Acts in Its First Century Setting*. Grand Rapids, Mich.: William B. Eerdmans Publishing Company, 1994.

———. "Ephesus: *Neokoros* of Artemis." In *New Documents Illustrating Early Christianity*, Volume 6. Edited by S. R. Llewleyn, 203–6. [Marrickville, Australlia]: Macquarie University: Ancient History Documentary Research Centre, 1992.

———. "The Mysteries of Artemis at Ephesus." In *New Documents Illustrating Early Christianity*, Volume 6. Edited by S. R. Llewelyn, 196–202. [Marrickville, Australia]: Macquarie University: Ancient History Documentary Research Centre, 1992.

———. "Some Asiarchs of Ephesos." In *New Documents Illustrating Early Christianity*, Volume 4. Edited by G. H. R. Horsley, 46–55. [Marrickville, Australia]: Macquarie University: Ancient History Documentary Research Centre, 1987.

Kee, Howard, C. *Medicine, Miracle, and Magic in New Testament Times*. Cambridge: Cambridge University Press, 1986.

———. "Self-Definition in the Asclepius Cult." In *Jewish and Christian Self-Definition*. Volume 3: *Self-Definition in the Graeco-Roman World*. Edited by Ben F. Meyer and E. P. Sanders, 118–36. Philadelphia: Fortress Press, 1982.

Kerenyi, C. *Asklepios: Archetypal Image of the Physician's Existence*. Translated from the German by Ralph Manheim. New York: Pantheon Books, 1959.

Keresytes, Paul. "The Imperial Government and the Christian Church. I. From Nero to the Severi." In *Aufstieg und Niedergang der Romischen Welt*, II,23.1, 247–315. Berlin: Walter de Gruyter, 1979.

Keskin, Naci. *Ephesus*. Translated by Ertugrul Uckun. Ankara [Turkey]: Keskin Color Ltd. Co. Printing House, 19–.

Kidd, B. J. *A History of the Church to A.D. 461*. Volume 1. Oxford: Clarendon Press, 1922. Reprint, [n.p.]: AMS, 1976.

Knibbe, Dieter. "*Via Sacra Ephesiaca:* New Aspects of the Cult of Artemis Ephesia." In *Ephesos: Metroplis of Asia–An Interdisciplinary Approach to Its Archaeology, Religion, and Culture*. Edited by Helmut Koester, 141–55. Harvard Theological Studies 41. Valley Forge, Pa.: Trinity Press International, 1995.

Koester, Helmut. "Ephesos in Early Christian Literature." In *Ephesos: Metroplis of Asia–An Interdisciplinary Approach to Its Archaeology, Religion, and Culture*. Edited by Helmut Koester, 119–40. Harvard Theological Studies 41. Valley Forge, Pa.: Trinity Press International, 1995.

———. *History, Culture, and Religion of the Hellenistic Age*. Volume 1. Translated from the German. Philadelphia: Fortress Press, 1982.

———. "The Red Hall in Pergamon." In *The Social World of the First Christians: Essays in Honor of Wayne A. Meeks*. Edited by L. Michael White and O. Larry Yarbrough, 265–74. Minneapolis: Fortress Press, 1995.

Kotansky, Roy. "Incantations and Prayers for Salvation on Inscribed Greek Amulets." In *Magika Hiera: Ancient Greek Magic and Religion*. Edited by Christopher A. Faraone and Dick Obbink, 107–37. New York: Oxford University Press, 1991.

Kottek, Samuel. "Medicinal Drugs in the Works of Flavius Josephus." In *The Healing Past: Pharmaceuticals in the Biblical and Rabbinic World*. Edited by Irene and Walter Jacob, 95–105. Leiden: E. J. Brill, 1993.

Kraabel, A. Thomas. "The Diaspora Synagogue: Archaeological and Epigraphic Evidence Since Sukenik." In *Aufstieg und Niedergang der Romischen Welt*, II,19.1, 477–510. Berlin: Walter de Gruyter, 1979.

———. "Impact of the Discovery of the Sardis Synagogue." In *Diaspora Jews and Judaism: Essays in Honor of A. Thomas Kraabel*. South Florida Studies in the History of Judaism. Number 41. Edited by J. Andrew Overman and Robert S. MacLennan, 269–92. Atlanta, Ga.: Scholars Press, 1992.

————. "Impact of the Discovery of the Sardis Synagogue." Chapter subsection in Andrew R. Seager and A. Thomas Kraabel, "The Synagogue and the Jewish Community." In *Sardis: From Prehistoric to Roman Times–Results of the Archaelolgical Exploration of Sardis, 1958–1975.* Edited by George M. A. Hanfmann and William E. Mierse, 178–90. Cambridge, Mass.: Harvard University Press, 1983.

————. "Paganism and Judaism: The Sardis Evidence." In *Diaspora Jews and Judaism: Essays in Honor of A. Thomas Kraabel.* South Florida Studies in the History of Judaism, Number 41. Edited by J. Andrew Overman and Robert S. MacLennan, 237–56. Atlanta, Ga.: Scholars Press, 1992.

————. "Religious Propaganda and Missionary Competition in the New Testament World." In *Immigrants, Exiles, Expatriates, and Missionary Competition in the New Testament World.* Edited by Lukas Bormann, Kelly del Tredici, and Angela Standhartinger, 71–88. Leiden: E. J. Brill, 1994.

————. "The Synagogue at Sardis: Jews and Christians." In *Sardis: Twenty-seven Years of Discovery.* Edited by Eleanor Gurainick, 62–73. Chicago: [n.p.], 1987.

Kraeling, Emil G. *Rand McNally Bible Atlas.* New York: Rand McNally & Company, 1956.

Kraemer, Ross, S. "Hellenistic Jewish Women: The Epigraphical Evidence." In *Society of Biblical Literature Seminar Papers Series: 1986.* Edited by Kent H. Richards, 183–200. Atlanta Ga.: Scholars Press, 1986.

Kraft, Robert A. "Judaism on the World Scene." In *The Catacombs and the Colosseum: The Roman Empire as the Setting of Primitive Christianity.* Edited by Stephen Benko and John J. O'Rourke, 81–98. Valley Forge, Pa.: Judson Press, 1971.

Krill, Richard M. "Roman Paganism Under the Antonies and Severans." In *Aufstieg und Niedergang der Romischen Welt,* 16.1, 27–44. Berlin: Walter de Gruyter, 1978.

Krodel, Gerhard. "Persecution and Toleration of Christianity Under Hadrian." In *The Catacombs and the Colosseum: The Roman Empire as the Setting of Primitive Christianity.* Edited by Stephen Benko and John J. O'Rourke, 255–67. Valley Forge, Pa.: Judson Press, 1971.

Kunke, Wolfgang. *An Introduction to Roman Legal and Constitutional History.* Second edition, based on the sixth German edition. Translated by J. M. Kelly. Oxford: Clarendon Press, 1973.

Lambert, Royston. *Beloved and God: The Story of Hadrian and Antinous.* New York: Viking, 1984.

Lampe, Peter, and Ulrich Luz. "Post-Pauline Christianity and Pagan Society." Chapter translated by Annemarie S. Kidder. In *Christian Beginnings: Word and Community from Jesus to Post-Apostollic Times.* Edited by Jergen Becker, 242–80. Louisville, Ky.: Westminster/John Knox Press, 1993.

Lane, Eugene N. "Men: A Neglected Cult of Roman Asia Minor." In *Aufsteig und Niedergang der Romischen Welt,* II,18.3, 2161–74. Berlin: Walter de Gruyter, 1990.

Laney, J. Car. *Baker's Concise Bible Atlas: A Geographical Survey of Bible History.* Grand Rapids, Mich.: Baker Book House, 1988.

Leaney, A. R. C. *The Jewish and Christian World, 200 B.C. to A.D. 200.* Cambridge: Cambridge University Press, 1984.

Lease, Gary. "Mithraism and Christianity: Borrowings and Transformations." In *Aufstieg und Niedergang der Romischen Welt,* II,23.2, 1306–32. Berlin: Walter de Gruyter, 1980.

Levick, Barbara. *Roman Colonies in Southern Asia Minor.* Oxford: Clarendon Press, 1967.

Levinskaya, Irina. *The Book of Acts in Its Diaspora Setting.* Volume 5 of *The Book of Acts in Its First Century Setting.* Grand Rapids, Mich.: William B. Eerdmans Publishing Company, 1996.

LiDonnici, Lynn R. "Epidaurian Miracle Cures." In *Society of Biblical Literature 1988 Seminar Papers.* Edited by David J. Lull, 272–76. Atlanta, Ga.: Scholars Press, 1988.

Liebeschuetz, J. H. W. G. *Continuity and Change in Roman Religion.* Oxford: Clarendon Press, 1979.

Lietzman, Hans. *A History of the Early Church.* Volume 1: *The Beginnings of the Christian Church.* Translated by Bertram L. Woolf. Second edition, 1949; reprinted in one volume, London: Lutterworth Press, 1961.

Lloyd, Seton. "Anatolia and Soviet Armenia." In *Atlas of Ancient Archaeology.* Edited by Jacquetta Hawkes, 131–45. New York: McGraw-Hill Book Company, 1974.

Ludwig, Charles. *Cities in New Testament Times.* Denver, Colo.: Accent Books, 1976.

MacKendrick, Paul. *The Greek Stones Speak: The Story of Archaeology in Greek Lands.* Second edition. New York: W. W. Norton & Co., 1981.

MacMullen, Ramsay. *Corruption and the Decline of Rome.* New Haven: Yale University Press, 1988.

———. *Paganism in the Roman Empire.* New Haven: Yale University Press, 1981.

————. "Peasants During the Principate." In *Aufstieg und Niedergang der Romischen Welt*, II,1, 253–61. Berlin: Walter de Gruyter, 1974.

————. *Roman Social Relations: 508 B.C. to A.D. 284*. New Haven: Yale University Press, 1974.

Magie, David. *Roman Rule in Asia Minor to the End of the Third Century After Christ*. 2 volumes. Princeton, N.J.: Princeton University Press, 1950. Reprint edition, Salem, N.H.: Ayer Company, Publishers, 1988. (Volume 1 consists exclusively of text; volume 2 of notes and related materials. The page numbering is consecutive rather than beginning again in volume 2.)

Malina, Bruce J. *On the Genre and Message of Revelation: Star Visions and Sky Journeys*. Peabody, Mass.: Hendrickson Publishers, 1995.

Malkin, Irad. *Religion and Colonization in Ancient Greece*. Leiden: E. J. Brill, 1987.

Marco, Anthony D. "The Cities of Asia Minor Under the Roman Imperium." In *Aufstieg und Niedergang der Romischen Welt*, II.7.2, 698–729. Berlin: Walter de Gruyter, 1980.

Marsh, Frank B. *The Reign of Tiberius*. [Oxford]: Oxford University Press, 1931.

Marti-Ibanez, Felix. *A Prelude to Medical History*. New York: MD Publications, 1961.

Martin, Luther H. *Hellenistic Religions: An Introduction*. New York: Oxford University Press, 1987.

————. "The Pagan Religious Background." In *Early Christianity: Origins and Evolution to A.D. 600*. Edited by Ian Hazlett, 52–64. Nashville, Tenn.: Abingdon Press, 1991.

Maxnes, Halvor. "Patron-Client Relations and the New Community in Luke-Acts." In *The Social World of Luke-Acts: Models for Intepretation*. Edited by Jerome H. Neyrey, 241–68. Peabody, Mass.: Hendrickson Publishers, 1991.

Mayerson, Philip. "What in the Roman World: An Addendum." *Classical Quarterly* 34 (1984), 243–45, as reprinted in Philip Mayerson, *Monks, Martyrs, Soldiers, and Saracens: Papers on the Near East in Late Antiquity (1962–1993)*, 222–24. Jerusalem: Israel Exploration Society, in association with New York University, 1994.

McGiffert, Arthur C. *A History of Christianity in the Apostolic Age*. Edinburgh: T. & T. Clark, 1897.

Meeks, Wayne A. *The First Urban Christians: The Social World of the Apostle Paul*. New Haven: Yale University Press, 1983.

Meinardus, Otto F. A. "The Christian Remains of the Seven Churches of Asia." In *Biblical Archaeologist Reader, IV*. Edited by Edward F.

Campbell Jr. and David Noel Freedman, 345–58. Sheffield [England]: Almond Press, 1983.

Mellor, R. "The Goddess Roma." In *Aufstieg und Niedergang der Romischen Welt*, II,17.2, 950–1030. Berlin: Walter de Gruyter, 1981.

Mierse, William E. "Artemis Sanctuary." Chapter subsection in George M. A. Hanfmann, Louis Robert, and William Mierse, "The Hellenistic Period." In *Sardis: From Prehistoric to Roman Times–Results of the Archaeological Exploration of Sardis, 1958–1975*. Edited by George M. A. Hanfmann and William E. Mierse, 119–21. Cambridge, Mass.: Harvard University Press, 1983.

Miles, M. F. "Ignatius and the Church." *Studia Patristica*, 17, Part 2, 750–55. Oxford: Pergamon Press, 1982.

Miller, Helen H. *Bridge to Asia: The Greeks in the Eastern Mediterranean*. New York: Charles Scribner's Sons, 1967.

Miller, Ulrich B. "Apocalyptic Currents." Chapter translated by Annemarie S. Kidder. In *Christian Beginnings: Word and Community from Jesus to Post-Apostolic Times*. Edited by Jurgen Becker, 281–329. Louisville, Ky.: Westminster/John Knox Press, 1993.

Mitchell, Stephen. *Anatolia: Land, Men, and Gods in Asia Minor*. Volume 1: *The Celts in Anatolia and the Impact of Roman Rule*. Oxford: Clarendon Press, 1993.

———. *Anatolia: Land, Men, and Gods in Asia Minor*. Volume 2: *The Rise of the Church*. Oxford: Clarendon Press, 1993.

———. "The Roman Empire in the East." In *The Cambridge Encyclopedia of Archaeology*. Edited by Andrew Sherratt, 239–44. New York: Crown Publishers/Cambridge University Press, 1980.

Momigliano, Arnaldo. *On Pagans, Jews, and Christians*. Middletown, Conn.: Wesleyan University Press, 1987.

Mommsen, Theodor. *The Provinces of the Roman Empire*. Volume 1. Translated by William P. Dickson. London: 1909; reprint, Chicago: Ares Publishers, 1974.

Mosse, Claude. "The Economist." In *The Greeks*. Edited by Jean-Pierre Vernant, 23–52. Translated by Charles Lambert and Teresa Lavender Fagan. Chicago: University of Chicago Press, 1995.

Muckelroy, Keith, General Editor. *Archaeology Under Water: An Atlas of the World's Submerged Sites*. New York: McGraw-Hill Book Company, 1980.

Neils, Jenifer, ed. *Worshipping Athena: Panathenaia and Parthenon*. Madison: University of Wisconsin Press, 1996.

Neusner, Jacob. *A History of the Jews in Babylon*. Volume 1: *The Parthlian Period*. Leiden: E. J. Brill, 1965.

Newmyer, Stephen. "Aspah the Jew and Greco-Roman Pharmaceutics."

In *The Healing Past: Pharmaceuticals in the Biblical and Rabbinic World*. Edited by Irene and Walter Jacob, 107–20. Leiden: E. J. Brill, 1993.

Nielsen, Harald. *Ancient Ophthalmological Agents: A Pharmaco-historical Study of the Collyria and Seals for Collyria Used During Roman Antiquity, as Well as of the Most Frequent Components of the Collyria*. Translated from the Danish by Lars McBride. Odense, Denmark: Odense University Press, 1974.

Nilsson, Martin R. *Greek Popular Religion*. New York: Columbia University Press, 1940.

———. *Imperial Rome*. London: G. Bell & Sons, 1962; reprint, New York: Schocken Books, 1967.

North, Robert. "Medical Discoveries of Biblical Times." In *Scripture and Other Artifacts: Essays on the Bible and Archaeology in Honor of Philip J. King*. Edited by Michael D. Coogan, J. Cheryl Exum, and Lawrence E. Stager, 311–32. Louisville, Ky.: Westminster John Knox Press, 1994.

Oakman, Douglas E. "The Countryside in Luke-Acts." In *The Social World of Luke-Acts: Models for Intepretation*. Edited by Jerome H. Neyrey, 151–79. Peabody, Mass.: Hendrickson Publishers, 1991.

Oliver, James H. *The Sacred Gerusia*. [Baltimore]: American School of Classical Studies at Athens, 1941.

Onen, U. *Ephesus: Ruins and Museum*. Translated by Nualla Yilmaz and Nanette T. Nelson. Izmir [Turkey]: Akademia, 1983.

Onen, Ulgur. *Ephesus: The Way It Was–The City Viewed in Reconstructions*. Translated by Nualla Yilmaz and Nanette T. Nelson. Izmir: Akademia, 1985.

O'Rouke, John J. "Roman Law and the Early Church." In *The Catacombs and the Colosseum: The Roman Empire as the Setting of Primitive Christianity*. Edited by Stephen Benko and John J. O'Rourke, 165–86. Valley Forge, Pa.: Judson Press, 1971.

Oster, R. "Holy Days in Honour of Artemis." In *New Documents Illustrating Early Christianity*, Volume 4. Edited by G. H. R. Horsley, 74–82. [Marrickville, Australia]: Macquarie University: Ancient History Decomentary Research Centre, 1987.

Oster, Richard E. "The Ephesian Artemis as an Opponent of Early Christianity." In *Jahrbuch fur Antike und Christentum*. Volume 19 (1976), 24–44. Munster [Germany]: Aschendorffsche Verlagsbechhandlung, 1977.

———. "Ephesus as a Religious Center Under the Principate: I. Paganism Before Constantine." In *Aufstieg und Niedergang der Romischen Welt*, II,18.3, 1661–1728. Berlin: Walter de Gruyter, 1990.

Palmer, Robert E. A. *Roman Religion and Roman Empire: Five Essays.* Philadelphia: University of Pennsylvania Press, 1974.

Parker, H. M. D. *The Roman Legions,* 1928. Reprint (with minor corrections of factual errors). Chicago, Ill.: Ares Publishers, 1954, 1980.

Parker, Robert. *Athenian Religion: A History.* Oxford: Clarendon Press, 1996.

Paul-Louis [no other name]. *Ancient Rome at Work: An Economic History of Rome from the Origins to the Empire.* Translated by E. B. F. Wareing, 1927; reprint, New York: Barnes & Nobles, 1965.

Pedley, John G. *Sardis in the Age of Croesus.* Norman [Oklahoma]: University of Oklahoma Press, 1968.

Pentreath, Guy. "Early Christianity in 'Asia.'" In *Geology and History of Turkey.* Edited by Angus S. Campbell, 39–48. Tripoli: Petroleum Exploration Society of Libya, 1971.

Perowne, Stewart. *Archaeology of Greece and the Aegean.* New York: A. Studio Book/Viking Press, 1974.

Peters, F. E. *The Harvest of Hellenism: A History of the Near East from Alexander the Great to the Triumph of Christianity.* New York: Simon and Schuster, 1970.

Petit, Paul. *Pax Romana.* Translated by James Willis. London: B. T. Batsford, 1976.

Pfeiffer, Charles F., and Howard F. Vos. *The Wycliffe Historical Geography of Bible Lands.* Chicago: Moody Press, 1967.

Polignac, Francois, de. "Mediation, Competition, and Sovereignty: The Evolution of Rural Sanctuaries in Geometric Greece." In *Placing the Gods: Sanctuaries and Sacred Space in Ancient Greece.* Edited by Susan E. Alcock and Robin Osborne, 5–18. Oxford: Clarendon Press, 1994.

Porter, Eliot. *The Greek World.* New York: E. P. Dutton, 1980.

Price, Martin J., and Bluma L. Trell. *Coins and Their Cities: Architecture on the Ancient Coins of Greece, Rome, and Palestine.* Detroit: Wayne State University Press, 1977.

Price, S. G. R. F. *Rituals and Power: The Roman Imperial Cult in Asia Minor.* Cambridge: Cambridge University Press, 1984.

Ramage, Nancy H., and Andrew Ramage. *Roman Art–Romulus to Constantine.* New York: Harry N. Abrams, 1991.

Ramsay, W. M. *The Church in the Roman Empire Before A.D. 170.* London: Hodder and Stoughton, 1895.

―――. *The Historical Geography of Asia Minor.* Volume 4 of Royal Geographical Society: Supplementary Papers. London: John Murray, 1890.

————. *Pauline and Other Studies in Early Christian History*. London: Hodder and Stoughton, 1916.

————. *St. Paul the Traveller and the Roman Citizen*. New York: G. P. Putnam's Sons, 1896; 1905 reprint.

Ramsay, William, M. *Cities and Bishoprics of Phrygia*. Volume 1: *The Lycos Valley and South-Western Phrygia*. Oxford: Clarendon Press, 1895.

————. *The Social Basis of Roman Power in Asia Minor*. Aberdeen [Scotland]: Aberdeen University Press, 1941; reprinted, Amsterdam: Adolf M. Hakkert, Publisher, 1967.

Raschke, Manfred G. "New Studies in Roman Commerce with the East." In *Aufstieg und Niedergang der Romiachen Welt*, II,9.2, 604–1378. Berlin: Walter de Gruyter, 1978.

Rickmann, Geoffrey. *The Corn Supply of Ancient Rome*. Oxford: Clarendon Press, 1980.

Robertson, Martin. *A History of Greek Art*. Volume 1. Cambridge: Cambridge University Press, 1975.

Rogers, Robert S. *Studies in the Reign of Tiberius*. Baltimore: Johns Hopkins Press, 1943.

Rohrbaugh, Richard L. "The Pre-industrial City in Luke-Acts: Urban Social Relations." In *The Social World of Luke-Acts: Models for Intepretation*. Edited by Jerome H. Neyrey, 125–49. Peabody, Mass.: Hendrickson Publishers, 1991.

Rose, H. J. *A Handbook of Greek Mythology–Including Its Extension to Rome*. Sixth edition. London: Methuen and Company, 1958, 1965 reprint.

Rostovtzeff, M. *The Social and Economic History of the Roman Empire*. Second edition. Revised by P. M. Fraser. Two volumes with consecutive page numbering throughout. Oxford: Clarendon Press, 1957.

Rowland, C. "Moses and Patmos: Reflections on the Jewish Background of Early Christianity." In *Words Remembered, Texts Renewed: Essays in Honour of John F. A. Sawyer*. Edited by Jon Davies, Graham Harvey and Wilfred G. E. Watson, 280–99. Journal for the Study of the Old Testament, Supplement 195. Sheffield, England: Sheffield Academic Press, 1995.

Russell, J. C. *Late Ancient and Medieval Population*. Philadelphia: American Philosophical Society, 1958.

Saffrey, H. D. "The Piety and Prayers of Ordinary Men and Women in Late Antiquity." In *Classical Mediterranean Spirituality: Egyptian, Greek, Roman*. Edited by A. H. Armstrong. New York: Crossroad, 1986.

Salmon, Edward T. *A History of the Roman World from 30 B.C. to A.D. 138*. London: Metheun, 1957.

Scarborough, John. "Roman Medicine to Galen." In *Aufstieg und Niedergang der Romischen Welt,* II,27.1, 3–48. Berlin: Walter de Gruyter, 1993.

Scherrer, Peter. "The City of Ephesos from the Roman Period to Late Antiquity." In *Ephesos: Metropolis of Asia–An Interdisciplinary Approach to Its Archaeology, Religion, and Culture.* Edited by Helmut Koester, 1–25. Harvard Theological Studies 41. Valley Forge, Pa.: Trinity Press International, 1995.

Schlatter, Adolph. *The Church in the New Testament Period.* Translated from the German by Paul P. Levertoff. London: S.P.C.K., 1961.

Schmidt, Evamaria. *The Great Altar of Pergamon.* Boston: Boston Book and Art Shop, 1965.

Schoedel, William R. "Theological Norms and Social Perspectives in Ignatius of Antioch." In *Jewish and Christian Self-Definition.* Volume 1: *The Shaping of Christianity in the Second and Third Centuries.* Edited by E. P. Sanders, 30–56. Philadelphia: Fortress Press, 1980.

Schonfield, Hugh J. *The Bible Was Right: New Light on the New Testament.* London: Frederick Muller Ltd., 1958.

Scott, Kenneth. *The Imperial Cult Under the Flavians.* Stuttgart [Germany]: W. Kohlhammer, 1936; reprinted, New York: Arno Press, 1975.

Seager, Andrew. "The Architecture of the Dura and Sardis Synagogues." In *The Dura-Europos Synagogue: A Re-evaluation (1932–1992).* Edited by Joseph Gutmann, 79–116. Atlanta, Ga.: Scholars Press, 1992.

———. "The Buildling." Chapter subsection in Andrew R. Seager and A. Thomas Kraabel, "The Synagogue and the Jewish Community." In *Sardis: From Prehistoric to Roman Times–Results of the Archaeological Exploration of Sardis, 1958–1975.* Edited by George M. A. Hanfmann and William E. Mierse, 168–78. Cambridge, Mass.: Harvard University Press, 1983.

Segal, Charles. "Spectator and Listener." In *The Greeks.* Edited by Jean-Pierre Revnant, 184–217. Translated by Charles Lambert and Teresa Lavender Fagan. Chicago: University of Chicago Press, 1995.

Seltman, Charles. *Riot in Ephesus: Writings on the Heritage of Greece.* London: Max Parrish, 1958.

Shanks, Hershel. *Judaism in Stone: The Archaeology of Ancient Synagogues.* New York: Harper & Row, Publishers/Washington, D. C.: Biblical Archaeological Society, 1979.

Sherwin-White, A. N. "The Roman Citizenship: A Survey of Its Development into a World Franchise." In *Aufstieg und Niedergang der Romischen Welt,* I,2, 23–58. Berlin: Walter de Gruyter, 1972.

————. *Roman Society and Roman Law in the New Testament.* The Sarum Lectures, 1960–61. Oxford: Clarendon Press, 1963.

Sherwin-White, Susan, and Amelie Kuhrt. *From Samarkhand to Sardis: A New Approach to the Seleucid Empire.* London: Duckworth, 1993.

Signe, Isager. "Kings and Gods in the Seleucid Empire: A Question of Landed Property." In *Religion and Religious Practice in the Seleucid Kingdom.* Edited by Per Bilde, Troels Engberg-Pedersen, Lise Hannestad, and Jan Zahle. [Denmark]: Aarhus University Press, 1990.

Simon, Marcel. *Verus Israel: A Study of the Relations Between Christians and Jews in the Roman Empire (135–425).* Translated from the French by H. McKeating. Oxford: Oxford University Press, 1986.

Sitwell, M. H. H. *Roman Roads of Europe.* New York: St. Martin's Press, 1981.

Smallwood, H. Mary. *The Jews Under Roman Rule: From Pompey to Diocletian.* Volume 20 of *Studies in Judaism in Late Antiquity.* Edited by Jacob Neusner. Leiden: E. J. Brill, 1978.

Smith, Charles E. *Tiberius and the Roman Empire.* Baton Rouge: Louisiana State University Press, 1942.

Smith, Jonathan Z. *Map Is Not Territory: Studies in the History of Religions.* Leiden: E. J. Brill, 1978.

Speidel, Michael P. "Legionaries from Asia Minor." In *Aufstieg und Niedergang der Romischen Welt,* II,7.2, 730–46. Berlin: Walter de Gruyter, 1980.

Stambaugh, John D., and David L. Balsh. *The New Testament in Its Social Environment.* Philadelphia: Westminster Press, 1986.

Stark, Freys. *Rome on the Euphrates: The Story of a Frontier.* London: John Murray, 1966.

Ste Croix, G. E. M., de. *The Class Struggle in the Ancient Greek World–from the Archaic Age to the Arab Conquests.* Ithaca, N.Y.: Cornell University Press, 1981.

Stephens, William H. *The New Testament World in Pictures.* Nashville, Tenn.: Broadman Press, 1987.

Stoneman, Richard. *Land of Lost Gods: The Search for Classical Greece.* Norman: University of Oklahoma Press, 1987.

Strong, Donald. *Roman Art.* Prepared for press by J. M. C. Toynbee. Revised and annotated by Roger Ling. Middlesex [England]: Penguin Books, 1988.

Strubbe, J. H. M. "Cursed Be He That Moves My Bones." In *Magika Hiera: Ancient Greek Magic and Religion.* Edited by Christopher A. Faraone and Dirk Obbink, 33–59. New York: Oxford University Press, 1991.

Sutherland, C. H. V. *Roman History and Coinage, 44 B.C.–A.D. 69: Fifty Points of Relation from Julius Caesar to Vespasian.* Oxford: Clarendon Press, 1987.

Tam Tinh, Tran. "Sarapis and Isis." In *Jewish and Christian Self-Definition. Volume 3: Self-Definition in the Greco-Roman World.* Edited by Ben F. Meyer and E. P. Sanders, 101–17. Philadelphia: Fortress Press, 1982.

Tarn, W. W. *Hellenistic Civilization.* Third edition. Revised by W. W. Tarn and G. T. Griffith. London: Edward Arnold & Co., 1952.

Taylor, Lily R. "Artemis of Ephesus." In *The Beginnings of Christianity, Part 1: The Acts of the Apostles.* Volume 5. Edited by Kirsopp Lake and Henry J. Cadbury, 251–55. London: Macmillan and Company, 1933.

————. "Asiarchs." In *The Beginnings of Christianity, Part 1: The Acts of the Apostles.* Volume 5. Edited by Kirsopp Lake and Henry J. Cadbury, 256–61. London: Macmillan and Company, 1933.

Taylor, Lily Ross. *The Divinity of the Roman Emperor.* Middletown: American Philological Association, 1931; reprint, Philadelphia, Pa.: Porcupine Press, 1975.

Tenney, Merrill C. *New Testament Times.* Grand Rapids, Mich.: William B. Eerdmans Publishing Company, 1965; 1984 reprint.

Thelen, Mary F. *Historical Introduction to the Christian Religion.* Part 1: *The Old Testament and the Hellenistic Background.* [n.p.], 1956.

Thomas, Christine. "At Home in the City of Artemis: Religion in Ephesos in the Literary Imagination of the Roman Period." In *Ephesos: Metroplis of Asia–An Interdisciplinary Approach to Its Archaeology, Religion, and Culture.* Edited by Helmut Koester, 81–117. Harvard Theological Studies 41. Valley Forge, Pa.: Trinity Press International, 1995.

Thomas, Garth. "Magna Mater and Attis." In *Aufstieg und Niedergangder Romischen Welt,* II,17.3, 1500–35. Berlin: Walter de Gruyter, 1984.

Thompson, J. A. *The Bible and Archaeology.* Grand Rapids, Mich.: Wm. B. Eerdmans Publishing Co., 1972.

Thompson, Wesley E. "Insurance and Banking." In *Civilization of the Ancient Mediterranean.* Volume 2. Edited by Michael Grant and Rachel Kitzinger, 829–36. New York: Charles Scribner's Sons, 1988.

Throckmorton, Peter. "Romans on the Sea." In *A History of Seafaring–Based on Underwater Archaeology.* Edited by George F. Bass, 65–86. New York: Walker and Company, 1972.

Throckmorton, Peter, and A. J. Parker. "A Million Tons of Marble." In

*The Sea Remembers: Shipwrecks and Archaeology*. Edited by Peter Throckmorton, 72–77. New York: Weidenfeld & Nicolson, 1987.

Toksoz, Cemil. *Ephesus: Legends and Facts*. Translated by Amhmet E. Uysal. Ankara [Turkey]: Ayvildiz Matbaasi, 1969.

———. *Pergamum: Its History and Archaeology*. Translated by Ahmet E. Uysal. Ankara [Turkey]: Ayvildiz Matbaasi, 1969.

———. *A Travel Guide to the Historic Treasures of Turkey*. Istanbul [Turkey]: Mobil Oil Turk A.S., 1977.

Tomlinson, R. A. *Greek Sanctuaries*. New York: St. Martin's Press, 1976.

Toutain, Jules. *The Economic Life of the Ancient World*. Translated by M. R. Dobie. London: Kegan Paul, Trench, Trubner & Co., 1930.

Townsend, John T. "Ancient Education in the Time of the Early Roman Empire." In *The Catacombs and the Colosseum: The Roman Empire as the Setting of Primitive Christianity*. Edited by Stephen Benko and John J. O'Rourke, 139–64. Valley Forge, Pa.: Judson Press, 1971.

Trachtenberg, Joshua. *Jewish Magic and Superstitution: A Study in Folk Religion*. New York: Behrman's Jewish Book House, 1939.

Trebilco, Paul. "Asia." In *The Book of Acts in Its Graeco-Roman Setting*. Edited by David W. J. Gill and Conrad Gempf, 291–362. Volume 2 of *The Book of Acts in Its First Century Setting*. Grand Rapids, Mich.: William B. Eerdmans Publishing Company, 1994.

Trebilco, Paul R. *Jewish Communities in Asia Minor*. Cambridge: Cambridge University Press, 1991.

Trell, Bluma L. *The Temple of Artemis at Ephesos*. New York: American Numismatic Society, 1945.

Trevett, Christine. *The Study of Ignatius of Antioch in Syria and Asia*. Lewiston, N.Y.: Edwin Mellen Press, 1992.

Turner, Cuthbert H. *Studies in Early Church History*. Oxford: Clarendon Press, 1912.

Van Der Heyden, A. A. M., and H. H. Scullard. *Atlas of the Classical World*. London: Thomas Nelson and Sons, 1959.

Van Der Horst, Peter W. *Essays on the Jewish World of Early Christianity*. Gottingen [Germany]: Vandenhoech & Ruprecht, 1990.

van Tilborg, Sjef. *Reading John in Ephesus*. Leiden: E. J. Brill, 1996.

Vegetti, Mario. "The Greeks and Their Gods." In *The Greeks*. Edited by Jean-Pierre Vernant, 254–84. Translated by Charles Lambert and Teresa Lavender Fagan. Chicago: University of Chicago Press, 1995.

Vermaseren, Maaten, J. *Cybele and Attis–The Myth and the Cult*. London: Thames and Hudson, 1977.

Vermeule, Cornelius C. *Roman Imperial Art in Greece and Asia Minor*. Cambridge, Mass.: Belknap Press of Harvard University Press, 1968.

Vernant, Jean-Pierre. "Introduction." In *The Greeks*. Edited by Jean-Pierre Vernant, 1–22. Translated by Charles Lambert and Teresa Lavender Fagan. Chicago: University of Chicago Press, 1995.

Versnel, H. S. *Inconsistencies in Greek and Roman Religin 1: Ter Unus–Isis, Dionyson, Hermes; Three Studies in Henotheism*. Leiden: E. J. Brill, 1990.

Vickers, Michael. *The Roman World*. Second edition. New York: Peter Bedrick Books, 1989.

Vine, W. E. *Expository Dictionary of New Testament Words*. London: Oliphant, 1953.

Vos, Howard F. *Archaeology in Bible Lands*. Chicago: Moody Press, 1977.

Waldbaum, Jane C. "Metalwork and Metalworking in Sardis." In *Sardis: Twenty-Seven Years of Discovery*. Edited by Eleanor Guralnick, 36–45. Chicago: [n.p.], 1987.

Walden, John W. H. *The Universities of Ancient Greece*. New York: Charles Scribner's Sons, 1909; 1910 printing.

Walters, James. "Egyptian Religions in Ephesos." In *Ephesos: Metroplis of Asia–An Interdisciplinary Approach to Its Archaeology, Religion, and Culture*. Edited by Helmut Koester, 281–310. Harvard Theological Studies 41. Valley Forge, Pa.: Trinity Press International, 1995.

Ward-Perkins, J. B. *Roman Imperial Architecture*. London: Penguin Books, 1981.

Watterson, Barbara. *The Gods of Ancient Egypt*. London: B. T. Batsford, 1984.

Webber, Randal C. "Group Solidarity in the Revelation of John." In *Society of Biblical Literature 1988 Seminar Papers*. Edited by David I. Lull, 132–40. Atlanta, Ga.: Scholars Press, 1988.

Webster, Graham. *The Roman Imperial Army of the First and Second Centuries A.D.* Third edition. Totowa, N.J.: Barnes & Noble Books, 1985.

Wengst, Klaus. *Pax Romana and the Peace of Jesus Christ*. Translated from the German by John Bowden. Philadelphia: Fortress Press, 1987.

Westermann, William L. *The Slave Systems of Greek and Roman Antiquity*. Philadelphia: American Philosophical Society, 1955.

White, K. D. *Greek and Roman Technology*. Ithaca, N.Y.: Cornell University Press, 1984.

White, L. Michael. "Urban Development and Social Change in Imperial Ephesos." In *Ephesos: Metroplis of Asia–An Interdisciplinary Approach to Its Archaeology, Religion, and Culture*. Edited by Helmut Koester, 27–79. Harvard Theological Studies 41. Valley Forge, Pa.: Trinity Press International, 1995.

Wiedermann, Thomas. *Emperors and Gladiators*. London: Routledge, 1992.

———. *Greek and Roman Slavery*. London: Routledge, 1981.

Wight, Fred H. *Highlights of Archaelolgy in Bible Lands*. Chicago: Moody Press, 1955.

Wild, Robert A. "The Known Isis-Sarapis Sanctuaries from the Roman Period." In *Aufstieg und Niedergang der Romischen Welt*, II,17.4, 1739–1851. Berlin: Walter de Gruyter, 1984.

Winter, Bruce W. "Acts and Food Shortages." In *The Book of Acts in Its Graeco-Roman Setting*. Edited by David W. J. Gill and Conrad Gempf, 59–78. Volume 2 of *The Book of Acts in Its First Century Setting*. Grand Rapids, Mich.: William B. Eerdmans Publishing Company, 1994.

———. "Acts and Roman Religion:...B. The Imperial Cult." In *The Book of Acts in Its Graeco-Roman Setting*. Edited by David W. J. Gill and Conrad Gempf, 93–103. Volume 2 of *The Book of Acts in Its First Century Setting*. Grand Rapids, Mich.: William B. Eerdmans Publishing Company, 1994.

Witt, R. E. "The Importance of Isis for the Fathers." *Studia Patristica* 8, part 2, 135–45. Berlin: Akademie-Verlag, 1966.

Wright, G. Ernest. *Biblical Archaeology*. Philadelphia: Westminster Press, 1957.

Yamauchi, Edwin. "Archaeology and the New Testament." In *Archaeology and the Bible: An Introductory Study*. Edited by Donald J. Wiseman and Edwin Yamauchi, 63–109. Grand Rapids, Mich.: Zondervan, 1979.

———. *The Archaeology of New Testament Cities in Western Asia Minor*. Grand Rapids, Mich.: Baker Book House, 1980.

———. *Harper's World of the New Testament*. San Francisco: Harper & Row, Publishers, 1981.

Zabehlicky, Heinrich. "Preliminary Views of the Ephesian Harbor." In *Ephesos: Metropolis of Asia–An Interdisciplinary Approach to Its Archaeology, Religion, and Culture*. Edited by Helmut Koester, 201–15. Harvard Theological Studies 41. Valley Forge, Pa.: Trinity Press International, 1995.

## Articles

Amitai, Pinchas. "Scorpion Ash Saves Woman's Eyesight." *Bible Review* 11 (April 1995): 36–37.

Anderson, C. P. "Hebrews Among the Letters of Paul." *Studies in Religion/Sciences Religieuses* 5 (1975–76): 258–66.

Anderson, Charles P. "Who Wrote 'the Epistle from Laodicea'?" *Journal of Biblical Literature* 85 (1966): 436–40.

Arnold, Irene R. "Festivals of Ephesus." *American Journal of Archaeology* 76 (1972): 17–22.

Atkinson, K. M. T. "The Governors of the Province of Asia in the Reign of Augustus." *Historia* 7 (1958): 300–330.

Aune, David E. "The Influence of the Roman Imperial Court Ceremonial on the Apocalypse of John." *Biblical Research* 28 (1983): 5–26.

———. "The Social Matrix of the Apocalypse of John." *Biblical Research* 26 (1981): 16–32.

Bammer, Anton. "Recent Excavations at the Altar of Artemis in Ephesus." *Archaeology* 27 (1974): 202–5.

Barnett, Paul W. "Revelation in Its Roman Setting." *Reformed Theological Review* 50 (May-August 1991): 59–68.

Bell, Albert A., Jr. "The Date of John's Apocalypse: Evidence of Some Roman Historians Reconsidered." *New Testament Studies* 25 (1978–79): 93–102.

Bent, J. Theodore. "What St. John Saw on Patmos." *Nineteenth Century* 24 (1888): 813–21.

Blasi, Anthony J. "Office Charisma in Early Christian Ephesus." *Sociology of Religion* 56 (Fall 1995): 245–55.

Bonz, Marianne P. "Differing Approaches to Religious Benefaction: The Late Third-Century Acquisition of the Sardis Synagogue." *Harvard Theological Review* 86 (April 1993): 139–50.

Borgen, Peder. "Moses, Jesus, and the Roman Emperor: Observations in Philo's Writings and the Revelation of John." *Novum Testamentum: An International Quarterly for New Testament and Related Studies*. 38 (April 1996): 145–59.

Boring, M. Eugene. "The Voice of Jesus in the Apocalypse of John." *Novum Testamentum: An International Quarterly for New Testament and Related Studies* 34 (October 1992): 334–59.

Botha, P. J. J. "God, Emperor Worship and Society: Contemporary Experiences and the Book of Revelation." *Neotestamentica: Journal of the New Testament Society of South Africa* 22 (1988): 87–102.

———. "The Historical Domitian—Illustrating Some Problems of Historiography." *Neotestamentica: Journal of the New Testament Society of South Africa* 23 (1989): 45–59.

Brettler, Marc Z., and Michael B. Poliakoff. "Rabbi Simeon ben Lakish at the Gladiator's Banquet: Rabbinic Observations on the Roman Arena." *Harvard Theological Review* 83 (January 1990): 93–98.

Bruce, F. F. "Colossian Problems, Part I: Jews and Christians in the Lycus Valley." *Bibliotheca Sacra* 141 (January-March 1984): 3–15.

Burton, G. P. "Proconsuls, Assizes and the Administration of Justice Under the Empire." *Journal of Roman Studies* 65 (1975): 92–106.

Charles, J. Daryl. "Imperial Pretensions and the Throne-Vision of the Lamb: Observations on the Function of Revelation 5." *Criswell Theological Review* 7 (Fall 1993): 85–97.

Cole, Dan P. "Corinth and Ephesus: Why Did Paul Spend Half His Journeys in These Cities?" *Bible Review* 4 (December 1988): 20–30.

Cotter, Wendy. "Women's Authority Roles in Paul's Churches: Counter-cultural or Conventional?" *Novum Testamentum: An International Quarterly for New Testament and Related Studies* 36 (October 1994): 350–72.

Crawford, John S. "Multiculturalism at Sardis: Jews and Christians Live, Work, and Worship Side by Side." *Biblical Archaeology Review* 22 (September-October 1996): 38–47, 70.

Daniel, Jerry L. "Anti-Semitism in the Hellenistic-Roman Period." *Journal of Biblical Literature* 98 (1979): 46–65.

D'Angelo, Mary Rose. "'Abba and father'; Imperial Theology and the Jesus Traditions." *Journal of Biblical Literature* 111 (Winter 1992): 611–30.

DeSilva, David A. "Exchanging Favor for Wrath." *Journal of Biblical Literature* 115 (Spring 1996): 91–116.

———. "The 'Image of the Beast' and the Christians in Asia Minor: Escalation of Sectarian Tension in Revelation 13." *Trinity Journal* 12 (Fall 1991): 185–208.

Elderkin, George W. "The Bee of Artemis." *American Journal of Philology* 60 (1939): 202–13.

Filson, Floyd. "Ephesus and the New Testament." *Biblical Archaeologist* 8 (1945): 73–80.

Fitzgerald, Michael. "The Ship of Saint Paul, Part 2: Comparative Archaeology." *Biblical Archaeologist: Perspectives on the Ancient World from Mesopotamia to the Mediterranean* 53 (March 1990): 31–39.

Ford, J. Massynbaerde. "Bookshelf on Prostitution." *Biblical Theology Bulletin* (Fall 1993): 128–34.

Foss, Clive. "A Neighbor of Sardis: The City of Tmolus and Its Successors." *Studies in Classical Antiquity* 1 (*California Studies in Classical Antiquity*, 13), 178–201.

Friesen, Steven. "Ephesus: Key to a Vision in Revelation." *Biblical Archaeology Review* 19 (May-June 1993): 24–37.

———. "Revelation, Reality, and Religion: Archaeology in the Interpretation of the Apocalypse." *Harvard Theological Review* 88 (July 1996): 291–314.

Ginsburg, Michael J. "Fiscus Judaicus." *Jewish Quarterly Review* 21 (1930–1931): 281–91.

Goldsmith, Raymond W. "An Estimate of the Size and Structure of the National Product in the Early Roman Empire." *Review of Income and Wealth* 30 (1984): 263–88.

Gordon, Mary. "The Freedman's Son in Municipal Life." *Journal of Roman Studies* 21 (1931): 65–77.

Goulder, Michael D. "The Visionaries of Laodicea." *Journal for the Study of the New Testament* 43 (September 1991): 15–39.

Habicht, Christian. "New Evidence on the Province of Asia." *Journal of Roman Studies* 65 (1975): 64–91.

Hanfmann, George M. A., and Jane C. Waldbaum. "Cybele and Artemis: Two Anatolian Goddesses at Sardis." *Archaeology* 22 (1969): 264–69.

Hardy, E. R. "The Priestess in the Greco-Roman World." *Churchman: A Quarterly Journal of Anglican Theology* 84 (1970): 264–70.

Hill, Andrew E. "Ancient Art and Artemis: Toward Explaining the Poly-mastic Nature of the Figurine." *Journal of the Ancient Near Eastern Society* 21 (1992): 91–94.

Hirschfeld, Nicolle. "The Ship of Saint Paul, Part 1: Historical Back-ground." *Biblical Archaeologist: Perspectives on the Ancient World from Mesopotamia to the Mediterranean* 53 (March 1990): 25–30.

Hopkins, Keith. "Taxes and Trade in the Roman Empire (200 B.C.–A.D. 400)." *Journal of Roman Studies* 70 (1980): 102–25.

Horsley, G. H. R. "The Inscriptions of Ephesus and the New Testa-ment." *Novum Testamentum* 34 (April 1992): 105–68.

Jewell, James Stewart. "Topography of Ephesus." *Methodist Review* 53 (April 1871): 279–96.

Johnson, David R. "The Library of Celsus, an Ephesian Phoenix." *Wilson Library Bulletin* 54 (1980): 651–53.

Johnson, Richard R. "Ancient and Medieval Accounts of the 'Invention' of Parchment." *California Studies in Classical Antiquity* 3: 115–22.

Johnson, Sherman E. "Early Christianity in Asia Minor." *Journal of Biblical Literature* 77 (1958): 1–17.

———. "Laodicea and Its Neighbors." *Biblical Archaeologist* 13 (February 1950): 1–18.

———. "The Apostle Paul and the Riot in Ephesus." *Lexington Theological Quarterly* 14 (October 1979): 79–88.

Kee, Alistair. "The Imperial Cult: The Unmasking of an Ideology." *Scottish Journal of Religious Studies* 8 (Autumn 1985): 112–28.

Kerkaslager, Alan. "Apollo, Greco-Roman Prophecy, and the Rider on the White Horse in Revelation 6:2." *Journal of Biblical Literature* 112 (Spring 1993): 116–21.

Koester, Helmut. "A Political Christmas Story." *Bible Review* 10 (October 1994): 23, 58.

Kraemer, Rose S.. "On the Meaning of the Term 'Jew' in Greco-Roman Inscriptions." *Harvard Theological Review* 82 (January 1989): 36–53.

Kramer, Ross S. "Ecstasy and Possession: The Attraction of Women to the Cult of Dionysos." *Harvard Theological Review* 72 (January 1979): 55–80.

Kreitzer, Larry. "Apotheosis of the Roman Emperor." *Biblical Archaeologist: Perspectives on the Ancient World from Mesopotamia to the Mediterranean* 53 (December 1990): 210–17.

Kreitzer, Larry J. "A Numismatic Clue to Acts 19:23–41: The Ephesian Cistophori of Claudius and Agrippina." *Journal for the Study of the New Testament* 30 (1987): 59–70.

Laeuchli, Samuel. "Urban Mithraism." *Biblical Archaeologist* 31 (1968): 73–99.

Levick, Barbara. "Domitian and the Provinces." *Latomus* 41 (1982): 50–73.

Lewis, Kevin. "John on Patmos and the Painters." *ARTS: The Arts in Religious and Theological Studies* 5 (Summer 1993): 18–23.

LiDonnici, Lynn R. "The Images of Artemis Ephesia and Greco-Roman Worship: A Reconsideration," *Harvard Theological Review* 85 (October 1992): 389–415.

MacMullen, Ramsay. "Imperial Bureaucrats in the Roman Provinces." *Harvard Studies in Classical Philology* 68 (1964): 305–16.

———. "Late Roman Slavery." *Historia* 36 (1987): 359–82.

———. "Women in Public in the Roman Empire." *Historia* 29 (1980): 208–18.

Malherle, Abraham H. "The Beasts at Ephesus." *Journal of Biblical Literature* 87 (1968): 71–80.

Malina, Bruce J. "Mediterranean Sacrifice: Dimensions of Domestic and Political Religion." *Biblical Theology Bulletin* 26 (Spring 1996): 26–44.

Marshall, A. J. "Flaccus and the Jews of Asia (Cicero Pro Flacco 28.67–69)." *Phoenix* 29 (1975): 139–54.

Mellink, Machteld J. "Archaeology in Asia Minor." *American Journal of Archaeology* 81 (1977): 289–321.

McMinn, Joe B. "Fusion of the Gods: A Religio-astrological Study of the Interpenetration of the East and the West in Asia Minor." *Journal of Near Eastern Studies* 15 (1956): 201–13.

Mitchell, Stephen. "The Plancii in Asia Minor." *Journal of Roman Studies* 64 (1974): 27–39.

Mitten, David Gordon. "A New Look at Ancient Sardis." *Biblical Archaeologist* 29 (1966): 38–68.

Moore, Stephen D. "The Beatific Vision as a Posing Exhibition: Revelation's Hypomasculine Deity," *Journal for the Study of the New Testament* 60 (December 1995): 27–55.

Osborne, Robert E. "Paul and the Wild Beasts." *Journal of Biblical Literature* 85 (1966): 225–30.

Oster, Richard E. "Numismatic Windows in the World of Early Christianity: A Methodological Inquiry." *Journal of Biblical Literature* 101 (1982): 195–223.

Parvis, Merrill M. "Archaeology and St. Paul's Journey in Greek Lands—Part IV: Ephesus." *Biblical Archaeologist* 8 (1945): 62–73.

Pilch, John J. "Lying and Deceit in the Letters to the Seven Churches: Perspectives from Cultural Anthropology." *Biblical Theology Bulletin* 22 (Fall 1992): 126–35.

Price, S. R. F. "Between Man and God: Sacrifice in the Roman Imperial Cult." *Journal of Roman Studies* 70 (1980): 28–43.

Provan, Iaian. "Foul Spirits, Fornication and Finance: Revelation 18 from an Old Testament Perspective." *Journal for the Study of the New Testament* 64 (December 1996): 81–100.

Ramsay, William. "Ephesus." *Biblical World* 17 (1901): 167–77.

———. "A Sketch of the History of Asia Minor." *National Geographic* 42 (November 1922): 553–70.

Roscoe, Will. "Priests of the Goddess: Gender Transgression in Ancient Religion." *History of Religions* 35 (February 1996).

Rudwick, M. J. S., and E. M. Green, "The Laodicean Lukewarmness." *Expository Times* 69 (1957–58): 176–78.

Scherer, Steven J. "Signs and Wonders in the Imperial Cult—Revelation 13:13–15." *Journal of Biblical Literature* 103 (1984): 599–610.

Scobie, Charles H. H. "Local References in the Letters to the Seven Churches." *New Testament Studies* 39 (October 1993): 606–24.

Sellew, Philip. "Laodiceans and the Philippians Fragments Hypothesis." *Harvard Theological Review* 87 (January 1994): 17–28.

Sherwin-White, A. N. "The Early Persecutions and Roman Law Again." *Journal of Theological Studies* 3 (1952): 199–213.

Silberschlag, E. "The Earliest Record of Jews in Asia Minor." *Journal of Biblical Literature* 52 (1933): 66–77.

Sokolowski, F. "A New Testimony to the Cult of Artemis of Ephesus." *Harvard Theological Review* 58 (1965): 427–31.

Smith, Philip K. "The Apocalypse of St. John and the Early Church." *Journal of Bible and Religion* 25 (1957): 187–96.

Stanley, Christopher D. "'Neither Jew Nor Greek': Ethnic Conflict in Graeco-Roman Society." *Journal for the Study of the New Testament* 64 (December 1996): 101–24.

Stoops, Robert F., Jr. "Riot and Assembly: The Social Context of Acts 19:23–41." *Journal of Biblical Literature* 108 (Spring 1989): 73–91.

Thompson, A. "Domitian and the Jewish Tax." *Historia* 31 (1982): 329–42.

Thompson, Leonard. "A Sociological Analysis of Tribulation in the Apocalypse of John." *Semeia* no. 36 (1986): 147–74.

Trudinger, Paul. "The Ephesus Milieu." *Downside Review* 105 (October 1988): 286–98.

Tyree, E. Loeta, and Evangelia Stefanoudaki. "The Olive Pit and Roman Oil Making." *Biblical Archaeologist: Perspectives on the Ancient World from Mesopotamia to the Mediterranean* 59 (September 1996): 171–78.

Ulansey, David. "Solving the Mithraic Mysteries." *Biblical Archaeology Review* 20 (September/October 1994): 41–53.

Vinson, Steve. "Ships in the Ancient Mediterranean." *Biblical Archaeologist: Perspectives on the Ancient World from Mesopotamia to the Mediterranean* 53 (March 1990): 13–18.

Ward, Roy B. "Women in Roman Baths." *Harvard Theological Review* 85 (April 1992): 125–47.

Wendel, Clarence A. "Land-tilting or Silting? Which Ruined Ancient Harbors?" *Archaeology* 22 (1969): 322–24.

Wilson, J. Christian. "The Problem of the Domitianic Date of Revelation." *New Testament Studies: An International Journal* 39 (October 1993): 587–605.

Wood, Peter. "Local Knowledge in the Letters of the Apocalypse." *Expository Times* 73 (1961–62): 263–64.

Wotschitzky, Alfons. "Ephesus: Past, Present, Future of an Ancient Metropolis." *Archaeology* 14 (1961): 205–12.

Yamauchi, Edwin M. "Magic Bowls: Cyrus H. Gordon and the Ubiquity of Magic in the Pre-Modern World." *Biblical Archaeologist: Perspectives on the Ancient World from Mesopotamia to the Mediterranean* 59 (March 1996): 51–55.

Zinderman, J. Irving. "Seashells and Ancient Purple Dyeing." *Biblical Archaeologist: Perspectives on the Ancient World from Mesopotamia to the Mediterranean* 53 (June 1990): 98–101.

## Dissertations and Theses

*Italized titles are published dissertations; titles in quotation marks are unpublished.*

Bartchy, S. Scott. *First-Century Slavery and the Interpretation of I Corinth 7:21*. Dissertation Series, 11. Missoula, Mont.: Society of Biblical Literature, 1973.

Baugh, Steven M. "Paul and Ephesus: The Apostle Among His Contemporaries." Ph.D. dissertation, University of California (Irvine), 1990.

Birge, Darice E. "Sacred Groves in the Ancient Greek World." Ph.D. dissertation, University of California-Berkeley, 1982.

Foss, Clive. "Byzantine Cities of Western Asia Minor." Ph.D. dissertation. Harvard University, 1972.

Hemer, Collin J. *The Letters to the Seven Churches of Asia in Their Local Setting*. Sheffield, England: University of Sheffield, 1986. Journal for the Study of the New Testament Supplement Series 11.

Hollinshead, Mary B. B. "Legend, Cult, and Architecture at Three Sanctuaries of Artemis," Ph.D. dissertation, Bryn Mawr College, 1979.

Kraabel, A. Thomas. "Judaism in Western Asia Minor Under the Roman Empire, with a Preliminary Study of the Jewish Community of Sardis, Lydia." Ph.D. dissertation, Harvard University, 1968.

Kraybill, J. Nelson. "Cult and Commerce in Revelation 18." Ph.D. dissertation, Union Theological Seminary (Richmond, Virginia), 1992.

Saltman, Ellen S. "The Jews of Asia Minor in the Greco-Roman Period: A Religious and Social Study." M.A. thesis, Smith College, 1971.

Saunders, Fuller B. "The Seven Churches of the Apocalypse." Ph.D. dissertation, Southern Baptist Theological Seminary, 1949.

Showerman, Grant. "The Great Mother of the Gods." Ph.D. dissertation, University of Wisconsin, 1900. Reprinted in *Bulletin of the University of Wisconsin, Philology and Literature Series*, vol. 1, no. 3 (Madison, Wisconsin, May 1901): 221–329.

# Index

Aegean Sea, 16
Alyattes (king) of Lydia, 74
Alexander (of Ephesus),
57–58
Alexander the Great, 11, 32,
44, 106, 171; second
founder of Smyrna, 75
Alexandria (Egypt): library of,
24, 110
Amazons: traditional founders
of Ephesus, 10
Amulets, 28, 84, 148–49; in
Jewish tradition, 285–86
n. 122
Antioch: housing in, 25
Antiochus the Great, 11, 186
Antiochus III, 154
Antonius Pius (emperor), 12
Antipater of Sidon, 33
Antipater of Thessalonica:
praise of Artemis temple,
33
Aphrodite: in Ephesus, 48; in
Philadelphia, 194; in
Sardis, 175
Apollo (god), 117; in Miletus,
99; in Sardis, 175; in
Smyrna, 98; in Thyatira,
157–58; "prophets" of in
Laodicea, 211; worshiped
under varied names in
Ephesus, 48
Apollonius of Tyana, 23, 63;
on abuse of right of
sanctuary, 44–45; rebuke
of Ephesian lack of
respect for philosophy,
27–28; visit to
Asklepieion, 117
Appian, 11
Apples, 173
Arcadius (emperor), 18
Archaeology: limitations of
date, 220 n. 3
Architects, 29
Aristides, Aelius: on
importance of Ephesus,
15; seeks physical healing
at Asclepeion, 119–20;
vivid description of
earthquake in Smyrna, 70
Arsenic, 172
Artemis of Ephesus (goddess
and cult), 10, 32, 73, 118,
157, 173; as protector of
women, 44; blessing of
Ephesus's port by priests,
17; choirs, 115; Curete
priesthood, 40; defense
of against Christian

critics, 35; differing image of in east and west, 35; dominant religious cult in Ephesus, 31; "Essene" priesthood in, 40; government decree praising her, 31; impact of beliefs concerning on evolving church doctrine of the virgin Mary, 61–62; male eunuchs in, 39–40; music in, 40; mystical rites, 47–48; origin of cult, 32; patron goddess of Ephesus, 24; period of decline in support and popularity, 33–34; relationship to burial society, 30; ritual bathing of image, 37–38; ritual dancing as worship, 40–41; selling of priesthood positions, 41; sexual prostitution in, 37, 238–39 n. 61; symbolically pictured as a bee, 36; virgin priesthood in, 38–39

Artemis of Ephesus (temple of): ancient praise for, 33; appearance of cult statue, 35–36, 236–37 n. 39; appearance of temple, 236 n. 34; burning of temple, 32–33; expenses and repair of facility, 42; facilities for social functions of worshipers, 45, 241–42, n. 109; gifts to, 43; land ownership, 16, 43; originally had no temple, 67; place for public display of art, 45; right of sanctuary, 44–45; right of sanctuary violated, 11; scandals involving administration, 41–42; size and layout of temple, 34; slaves owned by, 43–44; social welfare activities, 45; ultimate destruction, 34

Artemis of Sardis: temple of, 175–76; dependence and independence of Cybele with this Artemis, 176–77; relationship to Artemis of Ephesus cult, 176, 297 n. 68

Artemisia (Ephesus's month-long festival in honor of Artemis): activities at Great Theater, 46–47; athletic contests, 47; cultural activities, 47; formal sacrifices and processions, 47; modern calendar date, 45–46; observances at other times, 47; popularity of, 46; separate observances linked into one, 46

Asclepeion (Asclepius's healing shrine at Pergamon): Apollonius's visit, 117; coins depicting, 117;

description of visit of Aelius Aristides, 119; healing regimen sought through dreams, 118–19; lack of surgical options, 273 n. 113; patterned after similar shrine on Epidaurus, 116; physical exercise used in healing, 119–21; size of facility, 117; visit of emperor to, 109–10

Asclepius (healing deity): choirs, 115; festival in honor of, 122; group hymn singing as worship, 211; in Ephesus, 26, 48; in Pergamon, 134–36; in Smyrna, 98; possibly a folk hero before becoming a deity, 116; turning a disease into one easier to heal, 121–22

Asia (Roman): religious institutions' ownership of property in, 16; Roman taxes in, 11; usefulness of cultural and historical background, 1, 5–6

Athena (goddess), 110, 122; in Ephesus, 48; in Laodicea, 211; in Pergamon, 108, 112; in Sardis, 175; rituals of, 113; symbolically pictured as an owl, 36; temple in Pergamon, 113; temple in Smyrna, 98

Athens/Athenians, 10

Attalus II (king), 194

Attalus III (king), 106

Attis (god), 39, 101, 102; as alleged precursor of resurrection doctrine, 262–63, n. 71

Augustus (emperor), 50, 52, 100, 165; new name adopted, 152–53; temple to, 114

Aurelius, Marcus (emperor), 70; on physical exercise being recommended by the gods, 121

Bakers, 29

Bankers, 29; temple of Artemis as banker, 42

Baptism, 151, 188

Barley, 173

Bithynia, 83

Black Sea, 15, 32

Caesar, Julius, 110

Cappadocia, 83, 170

Caracalla (emperor), 50, 70; rebuilt temple of Athena in Pergamon, 113; temple of in Pergamon, 108; visit to Asian cities, 171; visit to Pergamon healing shrine, 109–10, 117

Carthage, 78

Cayster River, 17, 43, 63

Chariot racing, 110

Christians and Christianity (Ephesus): how the faith brought to city, 53–54;

John's picture of internal
church conditions,
58–59; possible impact of
environment on
evolution of faith, 61–62;
shifting organizational
pattern of church, 59–61;
societal allusions in
John's mini-epistle, 62–69
Christians and Christianity
(Laodicea): congregation
in second century, 213;
founding of
congregation, 213;
identifying epistle from
Laodicea, 213–14;
societal allusions in
John's mini-epistle,
214–19
Christians and Christianity
(Pergamon): danger of
persecution, 124–25;
establishment of
congregation, 124;
internal divisions of
church, 125–26; only
known martyr, 124,
274–75 n. 4; problem of
eating food sacrificed to
idols, 127–29; problem of
sexual license, 129–30;
societal allusions in
John's mini-epistle,
130–53; theories of
origin of Balaamite and
Nicolaitan movements,
126–27, 275 n. 8
Christians and Christianity
(Philadelphia): insights
into from John's
mini-epistle, 197; martyrs
in, 77; societal allusions
in John's mini-epistle,
198–204
Christians and Christianity
(Sardis): minimal
knowledge concerning,
182; letter of Ignatius to,
197–98; societal allusions
in John's mini-epistle,
182–93
Christians and Christianity
(Smyrna): economic and
social status of church
members, 88–89, 257–58
n. 12; founding of local
church, 88; Ignatius's
epistle to church, 94–96;
local persecution against,
88–89; martyrdom of
Polycarp, 91–93;
methods of executing
believers, 90–91; number
of martyrs, 90; societal
allusions in John's
mini-epistle, 74–81;
theory that "synagogue of
Satan" describes splinter
Christian groups, 87–88
Christians and Christianity
(Thyatira): conjectural
founding of
congregation, 158;
identity of "Jezebel,"
158–59, 162–67, 290 n.
59; societal allusions in
John's mini-epistle to,
159–68

Cicero, 16, 207, 209; on loyalty of Smyrna to Rome, 77
Cimmerians, 10
Claros, 9
Claudius (emperor), 22, 41, 70, 154; coins, 13; financed Sardis's aqueduct, 173
Cleopatra, 110
Coins: invention of by Sardis, 169; of Ephesus, 68; of Thyatira, 154
Colophon, 9
Colossae (city), 15, 206, 208; water of, 216
Colossus of Rhodes, 33
Cos (city), 41
Cosmetics, 172
Courts: in Ephesus, 12
Croesus (king), 10; gifts to Artemis temple, 32; origin of his connection to gold, 169–70
Crowns: differing types and purposes, 79–81
Cybele (mother goddess of Asia): annual festival, 101; burning of Sardis shrine, 171; castrated priests, 40, 101; dancing as worship for the deity, 102; decline of popularity, 100; honorary crowns for ritual use, 80; in Pergamon, 116; in Thyatira, 157; instrumental music in her worship, 102; introduction of cult into Rome, 100; other names for, 100; physical appearance, 36; priests, 80; praise by emperor for her cult, 101; relationship to evolution of Artemis of Ephesus, 32, 48; relationship to evolution of Artemis of Sardis, 176–77; sample hymn in her honor, 100–101; self–castration of priests, 263 n. 72; spread of cult from Phrygia to Greece, 100; temple locations, 100
Cyrus (king), 170

Delphi, 107
Demeter (goddess): in Ephesus, 48; in Pergamon, 116; in Smyrna, 73
Demosthenes, 212
Dio Chrysostom: on ancient trust in inviolability of money stored at Artemis temple in Ephesus, 42–43
Diodorus: on healing power of Isis, 104
Dionysus (god), 122, 138, 211; appeal of, 195, 196; cult dancers, 113; "new Dionysus," 113; in Ephesus, 48–49; in Philadelphia, 194–95; in Sardis, 175; in Smyrna,

80, 98; possession of worshiper by the god, 195; rites, 113, 195; symbolic crowns in worship, 80; titular ruler of Pergamon, 113; youthful versus mature images of, 98

Domitian (emperor), 51, 60, 117; as persecutor, 259 n. 25; destruction of statue of in Ephesus, 23

Earinus, 117
Earthquakes, 72, 107, 173, 176, 180, 183–84, 200–201, 202, 204, 218–19
Elaia: nearest port to Pergamon, 107
Ephesus, 140; acceptance and rejection of Mithridates, 11; annual blessing of port, 17; assize city, 12; banking center, 15; bee as symbol of city, 237–38 n. 49; Bouleuterion (Council Hall), 23; brothels, 18, 24; burials inside city prohibited, 24; burial society, 30; capital of province, 107; cargo dumping in harbor, 17; Celsus Library, 18; civic calendar for honoring gods, 14; coinage, 13; Commercial Agora (marketplace), 23; council, 12–13;

description of by nineteenth-century travelers, 9–10; degree of political independence, 224 n. 36; description of by Aristides, 15; description of by Pliny, 15; description of by Strabo, 15; "Ephesian letters" (magical amulets and charms), 28; fishing customs office, 16; Fountain of Trajan, 19; "free city" status, 12; gates, 18; Government Agora, 23–24; Great Theater, 18, 20, 22, 46–47, 49; guilds, 20, 29; gymnasiums, 19–21, 22; Halls of Verulanus (athletic facility), 23; harbor improvements, 16; Harbor Street, 18; historical founding of by Greek colonists, 10, 32; housing in, 25–26; idol manufacture in, 22; legendary founding by Amazons, 10; Library of Celsus, 24; manure collection, 21; Marble Street, 18; medicine in, 26–27; Odeion (concert hall), 23; Olympic games at, 20–21; population estimates, 11–12; power structure in city, 12–14; Prytaneion (town hall), 24; public baths, 21;

public toilets, 20; religious responsibilities of city leader, 14; respected educational center, 27; riots, 22; sea food products, 16; sea trade of, 15–16; sewage system, 18, 19; silting of harbor, 9, 10, 16–17, 227 n. 71, n. 73; slave trade, 16; stadium, 22–23; statues for prominent citizens, 18–19; societal faults, 62–63; streets, 18; Street of Curetes, 18–19; tariffs for sea trade, 16; town clerk, 13; visit of Alexander the Great, 33; water supply, 25, 236 n. 32; wine production, 71

Epidaurus (Peloponese island), 116; Asclepius shrine at, 116

Epiphanius of Cyprus, 159

Eumenes (king), 106

Euphrates (river and valley), 15, 169

Eutropios, 18

France: and Artemis worship, 32

Galatia: exports of, 14–15; prominence of women in, 83

Galen: on mental and physical exercise as curative, 121

Gallus River, 101

Gingrich, Newt, 5–6

Gladiators, 22, 110, 144; tombs, 209

Guilds: in Ephesus, 20, 29; in Philadelphia; in Thyatira, 155–56

Gymnasiums: attire in, 189–90; in Ephesus, 20–22; layout of typical facility, 19–21

Hadrian (emperor), 13, 18, 23, 47, 114, 171, 208; diverted River Cayster, 17; imperial temples honoring, 99; intervention of requested, 30; temple of in Ephesus, 21; temple of in Pergamon, 115

Harpocrates (god), 114

Helios (god), 194, 211

Hera (goddess): in Laodicea, 211; in Pergamon, 116; restorable virginity of, 37–38

Heracles (god), 175

Heraclitus "the Dark," 27

Herakleides, 80

Hermes (god), 175

Herodotus, 33; on fall of Sardis, 185–86; on superiority of even deities to fate, 104

Hestia Boulaia (goddess), in Ephesus, 24, 48

Hierapolis, 206, 208; burial society, 30; guilds, 155; water of, 215

Homer: claims of Smyrna concerning, 98–99; statues of, 110

Hygieia (goddess), 117

Ignatius, and Ephesus, 59–61, 249 n. 36; and Philadelphia, 197–98; and Smyrna, 94–96; on rights of bishops, 96–98, 198

Imperial cult: athletic competitions in honor of, 79; choirs, 115–16; Ephesians temples for, 50–51; high priest, 203; huge image in Ephesian temple, 51; in Laodicea, 211; in Philadelphia, 194; in Sardis, 175; in Smyrna, 99; official center at Pergamon, 114; sponsored gladiator fights, 209; temples to in Pergamon, 114–15

Irenaeus, 52

Isis (Egyptian goddess): female priests, 103; geographic variations in women's role, 264 n. 82; healing powers, 104; in Laodicea, 211; popularity of, 49, 103; possible temple in Ephesus, 50; "Red Hall" in Pergamon, 113–14; roots of widespread appeal, 103–4; superior even to fate, 104; worshiped either with

Sarapis or separate from, 103

Italy: and Artemis cult, 32

Jerome, on Artemis, 35

Jews and Judaism (Ephesus), 30, 52–53; archaeological evidences of presence, 53; prominent Jewish Ephesians, 26, 52; reconciling personal monotheism with government's public polytheism, 26–27; synagogue in Ephesus, 53

Jews and Judaism (Laodicea): censure of by rabbis, 213; possible "tribe" for government purposes, 208; seizure of temple tax by local authorities, 212–13

Jews and Judaism (Pergamon): minimal knowledge concerning, 123–24

Jews and Judaism (Philadelphia): little knowledge of has survived, 197

Jews and Judaism (Sardis): likelihood of Old Testament–era colony there, 169, 179; "orthodoxy" of congregation, 181; rights of Jewish community, 179; success of individual Jews, 179–80; synagogue of city, 180–81

Jews and Judaism (Smyrna):
synagogue remnants, 82;
known members of
synagogue, 83–84;
meaning of "synagogue
of Satan," 84–87;
women's leadership in,
82–83
Jews and Judaism (Thyatira):
little known of
community, 158;
possibility of ethnically
Jewish guilds, 155–56
Josephus, 52
Julian (emperor), 101

Kore (goddess), 175, 176

Laodicea, 177; agriculture in
region, 207; appearance
of site, 206; city walls,
206; clothes-making
industry, 207, 217–18;
earthquakes, 218–19;
economic conditions,
206–7; eye medication
available, 216–17, 314 n.
123; founding of, 205;
Greek cultural outlet for
surrounding region, 205;
gymnasium, 208;
population, 206; stadium,
208, 209; "tribes" in, 208;
theaters, 208; water
supply, 209–10, 214–16;
wealth of citizens, 218–19
Lead, 16
Libraries, 24, 110

Livy, 107
Lsimachos (king), 11
Lucian: on beauty of Smyrna
and its women, 69–70
Lucius: on worship of Isis, 103
Lycus (river and valley), 15,
205
Lysimachus (king), 106

Macedonia, 119
Marble, 172
Maeander (river and valley),
15, 208
Magic, 28–29, 286 n. 123
Magnesia (city), 15
Marnas River, 25
Men (god), 211–12
Menander of Laodicea,
210–11
Miletus, 16, 17; gods in, 99;
sale of pagan priesthoods
in, 41
Mithras (god): in Laodicea,
211
Mithridates, 11, 78, 205
Montanism, 159
Mount Pagos, 72, 73, 75
Mount Solmissus, 47
Mount Tmolus, 172

Nero (emperor), 18, 22, 57,
59; and Asian tariffs, 16;
and Pergamon art works,
107
Nile River, 114

Occult, 28–29
Olives, 173
Olympia: art works of, 107

Olympic games, 20–21
Onesimus (bishop), 59
Osiris (god), 103
Oysters, 16

Panionic Wars, 10
Parthenon, 34
Paul: alienation from Asian
    Christians, 56–57; and
    "school of Tyrannus," 55;
    in Ephesus, 54–56
Pausanias, description of
    Asian temples, 33; on
    priests of Artemis, 40; on
    refounding of Smyrna, 75
Peaches, 16
Pella, 33
Peloponnesian War, 10, 187
Pergamon, 75, 154, 177, 200,
    212; amphitheater, 110;
    chariot racing, 110; city-
    owned slaves, 109;
    development of
    parchment, 111, 267, n.
    36; early history, 106;
    earthquake damage, 107;
    food supply, 107–8;
    gymnasiums, 111; library,
    24, 110; literally passed
    by will to Rome, 106;
    local laws, 109; local
    ordinances for road and
    street upkeep, 108–9;
    location, 107; medicine
    in, 26; moral level of
    community, 137–38;
    original capital of Roman
    Asia, 106, 140; physical
    appearance, 108;

polytheism in, 136–37;
    population, 111, 267–69
    nn. 42, 43, 44, 45, 46;
    rejected for second
    imperial temple, 99;
    seizure of art works by
    Roman emperor, 107;
    similarity of setting of
    city to a giant throne,
    138–40; temples, 108;
    theater, 108, 109–10;
    water supply, 108
Persia, 131, 170
Phasis River, 15
Philadelphia, 177; city name
    changed, 202;
    earthquakes, 200–201,
    204; economy, 194;
    founding of, 194; spread
    Greek culture in region,
    200; tribal–guild political
    organization of city, 194;
    wine production, 71, 194
Phillipi: second century
    church in, 93–94
Philetaerus (king), 106
Philosophy, 27–28
Philostratus, on Smyrna, 77,
    98
Phoenicia, 32
Plague, 107
Plato, 111
Pliny, 15; on contest for Asian
    leadership between
    Smyrna and Ephesus, 71
Plutarch, 11, 40; 178; on site
    of Asclepius worship, 116
Polycarp, 53, 77, 88, 90; epistle
    to the Philippians, 93–94;

martyrdom described, 91–93, 260 n. 28
Pontus, 83
Poseidon (Neptune) (god), in Smyrna, 73
Ptolemy I, 49, 103, 110
Pyramids, 33

Riots, 22
Rivers, 9
Romans: attitude of upper class toward business involvement, 16
Rome: civil wars of, 11; housing in, 25; imports of, 16; receives Cybele cult into city, 100

Sabazios cult, 157; dominant motif, 177–78; geographic spread of sect, 177; identification with God of Israel, 178–79
Samos (island), 9
Sarapis (Egyptian god): creation of cult, 49; cultic meals, 105; healing power of, 104; in Laodicea, 211; judge of the dead, 104; power over fate, 104; priesthood, 103; possible temple in Pergamon, 114; temple in Ephesus, 49–50
Sardis, 15, 177, 200, 212; burial site, 191–92; competition for leading city of Asia, 75; Croesus

as ruler, 169–70; coins, 169, 175; earthquakes, 173, 176, 180, 183–84; economy, 172; food supply, 173; gymnasium, 173, 189–90; military conquest of, 184–88; Old Testament reference to, 169; siege of by Persians, 170–71; military strength of location, 171; population, 171; race track, 173; reputation for moral laxity, 174; theater, 173; visited by emperors, 171; water supply, 173; wine production, 71; wool trade, 190
Seleucids, 11, 78
Selinus River, 114
Seven churches of Asia: communication between, 8; limits of usefulness of historical background data, 7
Severus (emperor), 70; temple to, 114
Sidyma (city): burial society, 30
Silversmiths, 22, 29
Slave dealers, 29, 155, 157
Slaves and slavery, 82; agricultural use, 241 n. 100; city owned, 109; ownership by religious institutions, 43–44; potential for guild membership, 155
Smyrna, 119, 212; acropolis as

a visual "crown" on the city, 81; agricultural produce, 71; appearance to nineteenth-century travelers, 69; athletic competitions, 79; civic loyalty, 77–78; climate, 70; coins, 70; competition for leading city of province, 75; expansion of city, 252 n. 20; honorary crown for service to community, 80; Cybele worship, 80; drainage system, 73; earthquakes, 70; Government Agora, 72–73; gymnasium, 70; harbor, 70, 72; history of, 74–75; location, 71; main trade rival to Ephesus, 71–72; medicine in, 26; population, 71, 252 n. 27; reputation of Smyra's for beauty, 69, 70; respected educational center, 27; reputation for civic moderation, 76–77; sea trade, 71; stadium, 69; theater, 69, 72; water supply, 73; wine production, 71

Socrates, 111

Soothsayers, 29

Spain, 169; and cult of Artemis, 32

Sparta/Spartans, 10

Strabo, 15; on Artemis priesthood, 39; on beauty of city of Smyrna, 70; on earthquakes, 184, 200, 201; on festival in honor of Artemis's birth, 47–48; on layout of city streets, 73; on population of Laodicea, 206

Straits of Gibraltar, 15

Superstition, 28

Susa, 171

Tacitus, 107, 183, 218–19

Talmud, 217, 285–86, n. 122

Telesphoros, 117

Theodotion, 52

Thrace, 119, 121

Thyatira: bronze metal and statues, 161–62; geographic size, 154; government as honest broker between guilds and employers, 156–57; Macedonian colony, 154; military weakness of city's location, 160; official god of local guilds, 157–58; possible governance by guilds, 154–55; types of guilds, 155–56

Tiberius (emperor), 176, 202

Titus (emperor), 51

Trajan, 13, 22, 155; monument in Ephesus to his victory over Parthians, 19; temple to in Pergamon, 108, 114

Tree of life: in biblical sources, 64–65, in noncanonical

sources, 65–67; positive tree imagery in polytheistic myths and thought, 67–68

Troas, 200

Tyrimnos (god), 157, 160–61

Urim and Thummin, 145–46

Valerius I (emperor), 107

Varro (ancient agricultural author): on productivity of region of Smyrna, 71

Vespasian (emperor), 51, 202, 209

Vestal Virgins, 40

Virginity: in goddesses, 37–38

Wheat, 173

Wolves, 10

Wood, 172

Xenophon, 106, 171; account of fall of Sardis, 185

Xerxes: war with Greece, 32

Zeus (god), 118, 122; altar and cult in Pergamon, 108, 112, 117, 132–34; in Laodicea, 211, 309 n. 74; in Philadelphia, 194; in Sardis, 175, 176; hymn singing in honor of, 211; linkage with Sabazios, 177; popular in Smyrna, 98; priesthood in, 40; worship of in Ephesus, 48

Zodiac, 36